New Technology and Human Error

:

WILEY SERIES

NEW TECHNOLOGIES AND WORK

Series Editor: **Bernhard Wilpert**
Technische Universitat Berlin

NEW TECHNOLOGY AND HUMAN ERROR

Edited by Jens Rasmussen, Keith Duncan and Jacques Leplat

Further titles in preparation

New Technology
And
Human Error

Edited
by
Jens Rasmussen, **Keith Duncan** and **Jacques Leplat**

JOHN WILEY & SONS

Chichester · New York · Brisbane · Toronto · Singapore

Reprinted May 1988
Reprinted December 1988

Library of Congress Cataloging-in-Publication Data:
New technology and human error.
  Includes index.
: 1. Industrial safety. 2. Accidents—Prevention. 3. Man–Machine systems. I. Rasmussen,
Jens, 1926–   II. Duncan, Keith.   III. Leplat, Jacques.
T55.N463 1987   620.8'6   86-5607
ISBN 0 471 91044 9

British Library Cataloguing in Publication Data:

New technology and human error.
  1. Man–machine systems
  I. Rasmussen, Jens II. Duncan, Keith
  III. Leplat, Jacques
  620.8'2   TA167

  ISBN 0 471 91044 9

Printed in Great Britain by St Edmundsbury Press Ltd.
Bury St Edmunds, Suffolk

Contents

Part 4: Human Error and Safety at Work

Part 5: Industrial Studies of Human Error — I

Part 6: Industrial Studies of Human Error — II

Part 7: Error Sources, Reasons or Causes

List of Contributors

Lisanne Bainbridge — Department of Psychology, University College London, Gower Street, London WC1E 6BT, UK.

Berndt Brehmer — Department of Psychology, Uppsala University, Box 227, S-751 04 Uppsala, Sweden.

Dietrich Dörner — Universität Bamberg, Lehrstuhl Psychologie II, Postfach 1549, D-8600 Bamberg, F. R. Germany.

Keith Duncan — UWIST, Department of Applied Psychology, Llwyn-y-Grant, Penylan, Cardiff CF3 7UX, UK.

Martine Griffon-Fouco — Service de la Production Thermique, Département Exploitation Sûreté Nucleaire, EDF, 3, rue de Messine, F-75008 Paris, France.

Nadine Herry — CEN-FAR, BP No 6, F-92265 Fontenay-aux-Roses, France.

Veronique de Keyser — Université de Liege, Institut de Psychologie et des Sciences de l'Éducation, Bâtiment B-32, 4000 Liege 1, Belgium.

Urban Kjellén — Norsk Hydro A/S, Safety Section, P.O. Box 200, N-1321 Stabekk, Sweden.

Jacques Leplat — École Pratique des Hautes Études, Laboratoire de Psychologie du Travail, 41, rue Gay-Lussac, F-75005 Paris, France.

Deborah Lucas — University of Lancaster, Department of Psychology, Fylde College, Bailrigg, Lancaster LA1 4YF, UK.

John Patrick   UWIST, Department of Applied Psychology, Llwyn-y-Grant, Penylan, Cardiff CF3 7UX, UK.

S. A. Ruiz Quintanilla   Technische Universität Berlin, Sekr. DO 303, Institut für Psychologie, Dovestrasse 1-5, D-1000 Berlin 10, F. R. Germany.

Jens Rasmussen   Risø National Laboratory, PO Box 49, DK-4000 Roskilde, Denmark.

James Reason   Department of Psychology, University of Manchester, Manchester M13 9PL, UK.

Donald Taylor   Donald Taylor & Associates Ltd, Old Manor House, Chilworth Science Park, Chilworth, Southampton SO9 1XB, UK.

Gilbert de Terssac   Chargé de Recherche CNRS, Laboratoire d'Automatique et d'Analyse des Systèmes, 7 avenue du Colonel Roche, F-31400 Toulouse, France.

Foreword

Major trends in technological development increase the demand for systematic consideration of the effects of human errors. Centralization leads to large units in industrial installations bringing with it the potential for large-scale economic losses, damage to equipment, and danger to the environment. Consequently, designers have to consider accidental events of very low probability. Furthermore, there may now be a very short time span from conceptualization of new products and processes to large-scale production, and the design of industrial installations can no longer be based on empirical data from accidents during small-scale prototype operation. The 'pilot plant' which can verify safety targets is becoming a thing of the past.

It follows that any responsible design must then rely on an *ab initio* analytical assessment of the ultimate risk involved in operation. Such an analysis will inevitably include models of human functions, models which will almost certainly be flawed and incomplete, but arguably better than none at all. Even the most rudimentary analysis demands a minimal understanding of function. Just how feasible the whole enterprise may be, including as it must the notorious human factor, is one of the major issues addressed in this book.

It will be essential to understand the error characteristics of all the components of a system which, of course, includes the human beings involved. Information on human error must be expressed with regard to human characteristics, ideally in task-independent terms, not in terms of task failure statistics. Moreover, unlike the assembly-line situation of the 1930s, the design of large-scale, centralized systems must often contend with the potentially drastic consequences of maloperation following a slip or mistake by just one person and, increasingly, legal and economic considerations come to predominate at the design stage.

A related issue which is not always recognized, but which is especially stark in some advanced technologies, is the ethical component of systems design. For example, people should not be caught by irreversible consequences of errors which in their normal life would be accepted as typical features of everyday human behaviour — 'to err is human'. System design techniques are required which, if not 'divine' in their forgivingness, at least increase error tolerance to match their increasing demands. Again the feasibility question looms large — how far off are such system design techniques and, to the extent that they exist, what is entailed in enabling or persuading system designers to use them?

Microcomputers are now extremely cheap and powerful and give designers virtually unlimited freedom in the selection and pre-processing of the data to represent the conditions of the system confronting the user. This introduces great potential for matching tasks to human abilities and preferences, but also brings with it the risk of the user loosing control when unforeseen situations arise, if the design is based on a misconception of human cognitive functioning. In particular, when information is selected and pre-processed, it is important to take account of the different modes of human failure and the kind of information needed in order to recover from slips and mistakes.

Against this background, the study of human cognitive processes and the related error mechanisms has gained rapidly increasing interest over the last decade. Risk analysts have been asking for human error data to be used in the analyses necessary to verify the acceptability of nuclear power and chemical plants. These requests have become more pressing after the accidents at Flixborough, Seveso, and Three Mile Island, for which post-accident analyses have revealed the important role of human beings in precipitating as well as in preventing accidents. On the one hand, engineers collecting plant component failure statistics have started to develop taxonomies of human error data to include in their data banks. On the other hand, control system designers have been asking for data on human cognitive processes and error mechanisms for the design of better control rooms and computer-based support of diagnosis and decision making.

Essentially these are requests for information on human 'mental' processes which, after the early days of *denkpsychologie*, were typically neglected or treated as suspect subject matter for psychology, at least in academic circles. The ascendancy of radical behaviourism, coupled with the burgeoning psychological tests of ability and personality, directed many psychologists either to infra-human species or to sophisticated statistical analyses of correlations. Nevertheless the interest in human cognition persisted. In Europe, it was kept alive notably by Piaget and his associates and by the Cambridge group led by Bartlett. A renaissance of the interest in cognition followed developments in linguistics, and recognition of the potential of computers for information processing. The 'computer metaphor' and similar expressions became common coin, and the distinction between 'hard-wired' and software programs was a beguiling one to the student of human development.

More recently a new 'cognitive science' has emerged, closely linked with the techniques of artificial intelligence. Cognitive science, however, has until very recently been preoccupied with well-specified 'micro-worlds' like games and cryptograms and has not yet proved a fruitful source of ideas for the design of real-life work situations. Some would say that a purely computational cognitive science has still to prove its viability and will only contribute to models of human intelligence or performance by smuggling in psychological data in one guise or another. Nevertheless cognitive science continues to be influential and has the salutary effect of obliging psychologists to take more seriously the intricate problems of human cognition.

The situation is now changing rapidly. Mental mechanisms are acceptable topics for Ph.D. theses, analyses of verbal reports are again being used in fundamental and applied research, and the study of human errors is prominent in university programmes. Moreover the phenomenon of human error is not exclusively accounted for by cognitive mechanisms, but is determined by or related to other proximal and distal factors which may be affective, motivational, or embedded in organizational and social conditions. The field of study is thus truly cross-disciplinary.

It therefore seems timely to bring together representatives from the various professions, with their different approaches to human error analysis, to exchange ideas and to compare methods. With the ever-increasing rate of technological change, it is extremely important to coordinate the resources available to research on human error mechanisms if, indeed, it is to stand a chance of influencing the design of systems still to come.

This book is the product of a workshop with that specific aim in view. To make a start it seemed a good idea to bring together people from Europe working within engineering, psychology, sociology, and systems design, who were all actively engaged in the problem of human error and who shared a common interest in the effects of human error on the use of new technologies and vice versa.

The content of the book reflects its beginnings in a forum of intense cross-disciplinary debate. Each part includes pre-circulated papers of participants, grouped by topic, but inevitably papers in different parts sometimes cross-refer in important ways. Hopefully the introductions to parts have identified at least some of these. Also included are several position papers, some of which were circulated before the workshop and re-written afterwards in response to the discussions, while others were contributed after the meeting.

By organizing the book in this way, it was hoped to go beyond the familiar collection of formally presented conference papers and to get to grips in a modest way with the interplay of ideas in an active group of enthusiastic specialists. The reader may judge whether this was too ambitious.

Acknowledgements

The book is based on papers and discussions from a workshop on 'New Technology and Human Error' and subsequent interaction in the group of scientists representing psychology, social science, and system design. The workshop was the first in a series of meetings of an international, interdisciplinary study group on 'New Technology and Work' (NeTWork) sponsored by Maison de Sciences de l'Homme, Paris, and Werner Reimers Foundation, Bad Homburg.

To facilitate the interaction at the workshop, participants were in advance asked to circulate papers which demonstrated their research approach and findings. Some of these papers have been published previously, and the courtesy of the publishers in permitting the inclusion of revised versions in the present collection is acknowledged.

PART 1

Jens Rasmussen: 'The definition of human error and a taxonomy for technical system design'. Figures 5 and 6 are reproduced from: Human errors. A taxonomy for describing human malfunction in industrial installations. In: *Journal of Occupational Accidents*, 4, nos 2–4, September 1982. Elsevier Scientific Publishing Company. Figure 1 is reproduced from: Outlines of a hybrid model of the process plant operator. In: *Monitoring Behavior and Supervisory Control*, T. B. Sheridan and G. Johannsen (Eds). Plenum Publishing Corp.

Donald H. Taylor: 'The hermeneutics of accidents and safety'. Reprinted from *Ergonomics* (1981), 24, no. 6. Taylor & Francis.

PART 2

Jens Rasmussen: 'Cognitive control and human error mechanisms'. Figure 1 is reproduced from: What Can Be Learned from Human Error Reports? In: *Changes in Working Life*, K. D. Duncan, M. M. Gruneberg, and D. Wallis (Eds). John Wiley.

PART 3

Berndt Brehmer: 'Models of diagnostic judgements'. Reprinted from: *Human Detection and Diagnosis of System Failures*, J. Rasmussen and W. B. Rouse (Eds). Plenum Publishing Corp.

Dietrich Dörner: 'On the difficulties people have in dealing with complexity'. Revised version from: *Simulation and Games*, Vol. 11. Sage Publications, Inc.

PART 4

Jacques Leplat: 'Accidents and incidents production — Methods of analysis'. Reprinted from: *Journal of Occupational Accidents*, (1982), **4**. Elsevier Science Publishers.

Urban Kjellen: 'Deviations and the feedback control of accidents'. Revised version of: The deviation concept in occupational accident control — I. Definition and classification. II. Data collection and assessment of significance. In: *Accident Analysis and Prevention*, **16**, no. 4. Pergamon Press.

Jacques Leplat and Jens Rasmussen: 'Analysis of human errors in industrial incidents and accidents for improvement of work safety'. Revised version of: Analysis of human errors in industrial incidents and accidents for improvement of work safety. In: *Accident Analysis and Prevention*, **16**, no. 2. Pergamon Press.

PART 5

Jacques Leplat: 'Occupational accident research and systems approach'. Reprinted from: *Journal of Occupational Accidents* (1984), **6**, nos 1–3. Elsevier Science Publishers.

M. Griffon-Fouco and F. Ghertman: 'Data collection on human factors'. Reprinted from *Operational Safety of Nuclear Power Plants*, **1**. International Atomic Energy Agency.

PART 6

Lisanne Bainbridge: 'Ironies of automation'. Reprinted from: *Automatica*, **19**, no 6. Pergamon Press.

New Technology and Human Error
Edited by J. Rasmussen, K. Duncan and J. Leplat
© 1987 John Wiley & Sons Ltd

Part 1: Definition and Taxonomies of Human Error

INTRODUCTION

When the nature and origin of the events called human errors are discussed from different professional points of view, it immediately becomes apparent that the concept of human error is elusive, and that a discussion of the definitions adopted in the various studies is essential, together with a review of the categories used for description and analysis of errors.

To illustrate the relative nature of the concepts involved, contributions have been chosen from an academic psychologist, who focuses on the relationships between categories of behaviour called human errors and features of the underlying cognitive control; a systems engineer, whose concern is with the role of human errors in control of complex installations and their potential for unacceptable effects upon the environment; and, finally, a social psychologist, who looks at the meaning of actions, including human errors, as construed by the individual agent in a context of personal morality and shared social values.

These three authors clearly illustrate the different starting points with their differences in definitions and taxonomies. They were the subject of sustained arguments at the workshop but, with hindsight, the viewpoints are complementary rather than conflicting. Indeed, the differences are such that the approaches scarcely could conflict unless one of them were to claim exclusive validity which, in the light of later contributions, particularly the position papers in Part 7, they do not. Following the interactions during and after the workshop, the different approaches, taken together, constitute a sound basis for matching new technology to the characteristics of human users.

In the course of his descriptions and classifications, Reason makes a distinction between slips and mistakes. Slips occur when a person's actions are not in accordance with the actions actually intended, whereas mistakes are actions performed as intended but with effects which turn out, immediately or at a

1

later stage, not to be in accordance with the person's intended goal. Since Reason's point of view is that of the individual actor, there are no problems, in principle, in incorporating the notion of goal into a definition of human error. A human error is simply an act which is counter-productive with respect to the person's private or subjective intentions or goals.

This route to definition of human error is not so straightforward, in the context of process control, discussed by Rasmussen. Here human errors are typically revealed by analysis after an industrial incident or accident. In this case, the identification of the initial event in the accidental chain of events, including both component faults and human errors, is undertaken from a systems point of view, in order to identify the appropriate counter-measures, be they technical changes or training of personnel. Error is still defined as counter-productive to the goal. But at the systems engineering level there may be several goals, e.g., a production goal, a safety goal, or goals prescribed by regulation or law. Moreover several different people may pronounce on whether goals have been satisfactorily achieved. Consequently, the question of an appropriate definition of human error is necessarily discussed in some detail by Rasmussen. He points out that, in situations where several goals may be articulated, the definition of human errors is equivocal or even fraught with contradiction, and is closely related to questions of operator responsibility and guilt.

In his paper (Chapter 4), Taylor moves this discussion still further in the direction of the question: Are not human errors, as seen from the outside of a person, very likely to be misinterpreted or misunderstood? At best they are only partly understood, unless it is possible to elucidate the meaning of the acts in question to the person concerned. If actions are labelled as error without reference to individual value systems and experience of responsibility, serious problems of safety or error prevention will arise. For prevention of some errors, persuasion in some form is essential, but not likely to be effective without more insights into how users and operators value their transactions with the physical environment and with other humans in the error situation. Even then, Taylor argues, there may be serious limits to the success of measures taken in the hope of preventing human errors. The implications of this view for the design of large centralized systems demand very careful consideration.

Turning now from questions of definition, to the question of classification or taxonomy, it will be clear from the papers that some systematic categorization of the great variety of human errors reported is essential for their proper consideration in systems design, as well as for their scientific study. In the last resort, the taxonomy adopted for classification will often depend on the application.

Thus Rasmussen's paper (Chapter 3) describes how taxonomies generated in industrial systems are often aiming at a classification scheme suited to the analysis and organization of existing human error data from analysis of operations during previous system failures. This is to provide a basis for improvement of system reliability and for predicting human reliability during operation of new systems. Such an approach may succeed when the rate of change in technological development is slow and the elements of operator tasks and interface designs therefore rather stable. In these circumstances, the taxonomy used by system designers may be rather simple, even simplistic, consisting of questionable types of 'task elements'. The model implicit in such taxonomies is a model of the task rather than the person. However, Rasmussen argues that the present rapid technological change in industry makes such simple taxonomies inadequate. Human errors must be classified in terms of human characteristics.

Existing human error data banks are seen to be of little help to those who have tried to use them. The emphasis must shift from tasks to the man–task mismatch as a basis for analysis and classification of human errors. The development of taxonomies for engineering use must encompass the analysis, not only of manual task elements, but also of internal cognitive task components, and the psychological mechanisms associated with both. Rasmussen has in mind the as yet unknown human errors which may arise with the adoption of interface designs made possible by the new information technologies. He also cites the severe need in systems design for data on error modes and probabilities during more complex decision tasks involved in emergencies, which cannot be obtained from error reports, partly because reports from such situations are few, but mainly because the cognitive activities involved cannot easily be included in them. These requirements for developments in human error taxonomy are a formidable interdisciplinary challenge. However, recent efforts within psychological research and systems engineering seem to make the necessary interaction both feasible and fruitful.

The question of taxonomy is treated in some detail by Reason. In Chapter 1 Reason argues that 'basic error tendencies', for example resource limitations, heuristics, interact with information processing domains, such as recognition, action control, to produce 'primary error groupings', e.g., various misperceptions, unintended words or actions. He identifies and describes eight such error groupings, from the interaction of five error tendencies with eight information processing domains. It is important to note that he is arguing, not for these particular tendencies, domains, and their interactions, but rather that this is a sensible taxonomic principle. He goes on to urge the importance of recognizing that, although human errors can be correctly placed into rather few classes, the number and variety of contextual determinants remains large.

His approach to rationality in the second paper (Chapter 2) is similar, deriving three broad classes from a continuum between the powerful, analytic, innovative 'attentional' mode, and the less effortful, swift, stereotypic 'schematic' mode. In both papers (Chapters 1 and 2) Reason emphasizes an important point underlying a lot of subsequent discussion — that it is necessary to understand the formal properties of human error, while acknowledging its manifold origins in specific conditions of particular environments and indeed of the human actor. To look ahead, the latter will include transitory influences, such as moods, and more enduring ones, such as beliefs, values, and temperaments. We can no more ignore these influences than we can ignore temporary states of the weather or the persisting trends of climates.

An important feature common to the taxonomies described in this section is that they do not produce hierarchical, generic classification schemes. Instead, they lead to multifaceted descriptive systems which make it possible to obtain rather fine discrimination between the descriptions of particular error situations by means of only a limited number of categories on each dimension of the taxonomy. This is consistent with the idea that the seemingly immense variety of human errors observed may reflect complexity of the environment, rather than complexity in the psychological mechanisms involved.

The categories used in any scheme for the description of human errors should explicitly refer to a model, indeed, as noted above, even the simplest attempts to classify human error data subscribe by default to an implicit model. Ideally the model should relate error categories to the mental processes and mechanisms involved. The discussion of taxonomies is therefore closely linked to the discussion of cognitive control mechanisms in Part 2, and to the control structures inferred which are explicitly compared in the position papers in Part 7.

New Technology and Human Error
Edited by J. Rasmussen, K. Duncan and J. Leplat
© 1987 John Wiley & Sons Ltd

1. A Framework for Classifying Errors

James Reason
University of Manchester

SUMMARY

A classificatory framework is outlined which locates eight primary error groupings in a matrix defined by five basic error tendencies, and eight information-processing domains. Within each grouping, predictable error forms are identified by situational factors.

INTRODUCTION

A central problem in error classification is the difficulty of reconciling the often highly specific contextual triggers of a particular error form with the fact that it may also manifest the influence of some very general adaptive process, or basic error tendency. A classification that emphasizes the former at the expense of the latter is likely to overlook the broad regularities in the predictable varieties of human error. Yet one that neglects the local contextual factors (e.g., task and situational considerations) will not only be of limited use to the practitioner, it will also fail to accommodate the theoretically important causal interactions between basic error tendencies and immediate task features.

The present paper outlines not a classification as such, but a set of principles by which it is possible to build a flexible taxonomic framework that encompasses both the psychological roots of systematic error forms and the local environmental factors which elicit them. Since no one error taxonomy will satisfy all possible needs, it is more profitable to define the important dimensions of a taxonomic structure than to strive for a universally acceptable classificatory scheme.

AN OUTLINE OF THE ORGANIZING DIMENSIONS

The first step is to identify the eight primary error groupings (PEGs). These emerge as clusters of interactive 'nodes' in a matrix defined by five basic error tendencies (BETs) and eight information-processing domains (IPDs). Within each grouping, the predictable error forms (PEFs) are further distinguished according to the situational factors (SFs) that are known to

5

promote their occurrence. Age-related and pathological dispositions to commit certain kinds of error are only introduced once the PEFs have been located in this fashion. It is assumed that these individual factors do not produce unique error forms, only an exaggerated liability to forms already delineated within the previously defined framework. The framework can thus be summarized as follows:

1. $BETs \times IPDs \rightarrow PEGs$
2. $PEGs \times SFs \rightarrow PEFs$

A predictable error form is one for which it is possible to specify (in a probabilistic rather than a deterministic fashion) both the circumstances that will promote its occurrence and the likely form it will take. The formal characteristics of a particular error are described largely by the first interaction, and its local triggers by the second interaction. The first stage acknowledges that the pervasive BETs can manifest themselves somewhat differently in different cognitive domains (see Figure 1). The second stage indicates that a further important source of variation is introduced by the kind of situation involved and the type of activity being carried out. Each major dimension of this classificatory framework is considered further below.

THE BASIC ERROR TENDENCIES

Examination of a wide variety of error forms suggests that they manifest the influence of one or more of the following basic error tendencies: ecological constraints, change-enhancing biases, resource limitations, schema properties and the use of particular strategies or heuristics. These tendencies, it is argued, constitute the fundamental roots of most, if not all, of the systematic varieties of human error. Each of these error tendencies is necessary for normal psychological functioning. It is from this necessity that they derive their great power to induce systematic error.

Ecological constraints

Despite the apparent naturalness of the lifestyle created by the accelerating rate of technological achievement, the ecological constraints remain unchanged. They are the product of countless generations of evolutionary adjustment to a particular kind of environment, and continue to hold sway even though our present way of living, in which passive has largely superseded active locomotion, may render them obsolete and even dangerous. No matter how far or fast we are capable of travelling, or how esoteric the environments that can now sustain human life, our senses as well as our capacity for processing information remain those of a self-propelled terrestrial creature designed to move at around three to four miles per hour under conditions of normal gravity and above ground.

Change-enhancing biases

Measuring instruments such as thermometers, speedometers, ammeters, and the like, are designed to give consistent readings. Within narrow and usually known error limits, we can reasonably expect that they will indicate the same scale values for identical physical quantities measured on different occasions. Psychological scaling mechanisms, however, operate on quite different principles. Their calibration is not fixed, but changes systematically from one occasion to the next so as to exaggerate their responses to changing quantities, and to attenuate the values assigned to steady states. In short, the nervous system is essentially a change-detector, and this general principle appears to hold throughout the animal kingdom in all modalities and for all types of psychophysical judgement.

Resource limitations

A very large number of predictable error forms stem either directly or indirectly from the fact that human beings, like other information-handling systems, possess only finite processing resources. Useful definitions of what is meant by the terms 'resource' and 'process' have been given by Bobrow and Norman (1975): 'Any information-processing device has programs and some mechanisms for executing these programs. When a program is executed, it requires input data and it consumes resources. A set of programs that is being executed for a common purpose and for which resources are allocated as a unit is called a process. Resources are such things as processing effort, the various forms of memory capacity, and communication channels' (p. 45). Where and how these resources are limited has been a primary concern of cognitive psychologists for the past twenty years.

It is not difficult to see how overloading this limited resource can lead to error; but what are its adaptive advantages? The short answer is selection. The possession of a limited processing resource ensures that only a restricted number of cognitive structures will be maximally active at any one time. Without this facility, it would be impossible to derive meaning from sensory data, or to arrange our thoughts, speech and actions into coherent, goal-directed sequences. To understand this more fully, however, we need to consider the nature of the knowledge structures which ultimately govern and preserve this order.

Schema properties

The very rapid handling of information characteristic of human cognition is possible because the regularities of the world, as well as our routine dealings with it, are represented internally as schemata. The price we pay for this largely automatic processing of information is that perceptions, memories, thoughts and actions have a tendency to err in the direction of the familiar and the expected. In short, errors take the form of 'default assignments'.

As Taylor and Crocker (1981) pointed out, '. . . virtually any of the properties of schematic function that are useful under some circumstances will be liabilities under others. Like all gamblers, cognitive gamblers sometimes lose.' Systematic errors can arise: (a) from fitting the data to the wrong schema; (b) from employing the correct schema too enthusiastically so that gaps in a stimulus configuration are filled with best guesses rather than available sensory data; and (c) from relying too heavily upon active or salient schemata. Such errors are most likely to occur at times of change when existing routines are no longer appropriate for new circumstances or revised goals.

Strategies and heuristics

Strategies are both governed by and carried out in relation to the schematic knowledge base. If one were to imagine all the schemata possessed by a given person as being laid out on a vast two-dimensional space, rather like the squares on a chess board, then strategies could be represented as the rules which govern the movements of the limited processing resource over this 'mind-scape'.

Success in searching for a particular target in a visual array, or in solving a problem, or in retrieving an item from memory, or in putting together a plan of action will largely depend upon the manner in which the component operations are selected and ordered. An inadequate strategy will lead to particular kinds of error, as will an excessive reliance on a few well-tried rules of thumb (heuristics). A major development in contemporary cognitive psychology has been the discovery of both inadequate and over-used strategies.

THE COGNITIVE DOMAINS

This section is concerned with identifying the eight cognitive domains which form the second principal axis of the classificatory framework. These domains represent various stages or operations in human information processing. They are: sensory registration, input selection, temporary memory (including prospective memory), long-term memory, recognition processes, judgemental processes, inferential processes, and action control. This selection was largely guided by the way the error data were clustered in the psychological literature. In classifying errors, as in dividing an orange, it is much easier to go with the existing segmentation than against it.

Only in a few cases is it reasonable to regard a domain as being structurally and/or functionally distinct from some or all of the remainder. In this respect, sensory registration stands apart as being dependent upon the general and specific characteristics of the senses. It is also reasonable to make a distinction between temporary or 'volatile' memory and long-term memory since they have been shown to display markedly different operating characteristics. Less obvious, though, are the grounds for distinguishing input selection from temporary memory (both are intimately bound up with the limits of consciousness), and judgemental from inferential processes. These distinctions will be discussed further in the next section.

GENERATING THE PRIMARY ERROR GROUPINGS

As indicated at the outset, the primary error groupings are generated from the points of interaction — or 'nodes' — between the basic error tendencies and the cognitive domains. Eight such primary error groupings are identified in this manner: false sensations, attentional failures, memory lapses, inaccurate recall, misperceptions, errors of judgement, inferential errors, and unintended actions. A matrix displaying these interactions and their associated error clusters is shown in Figure 1.

Two kinds of nodes are represented in Figure 1: primary and secondary. Primary nodes represent points within the information-processing sequence (i.e., cognitive domains) at which the basic error tendencies are known to exercise a strong influence. Secondary nodes are of two kinds. They indicate either less certain points of interaction (e.g., the effects of resource limitations upon long-term memory), or points at which the basic error tendencies exert an influence that is consequent upon some primary effect at an earlier stage of information processing (e.g., the effects of ecological constraints upon the recognition processes).

From Figure 1, it is evident that the basic error tendencies alone make poor discriminators of error clusters. With the exception of the rather specialized sensory registration nodes associated with ecological constraints and change enhancement, the remaining error tendencies are remarkably pervasive in their influence, acting in concert upon all other sensory domains.

So far, eight primary error groupings have been distinguished. The next stage of the classificatory process is to sub-divide them further according to contextual or task considerations. The major sub-divisions for each grouping are outlined below.

False sensations

A large proportion of human errors are due either directly or indirectly to a lack of correspondence between our subjective experience of the world and the objective reality. Stated very simply, these discrepancies may arise

for one of two possible reasons: either because aspects of the physical world
have been distorted or misrepresented by the sensory apparatus; or because
the higher brain centres have placed a wrong interpretation upon otherwise
veridical sense data. This grouping is concerned only with the former error
type.

False sensations can be elicited in the following circumstances: (a) during
and immediately after exposure to steady-state inputs in any modality; (b)
in conditions of simultaneous and successive contrast; (c) when viewing two-
dimensional representations of three-dimensional objects; (d) in atypical
force environments involving periods of constant velocity rotation, or variations in the strength or direction of the gravito-inertial vector; (e) during
and immediately following exposure to visual or intertial rearrangement; (f)
when viewing large-scale moving visual scenes; (g) in high-speed flight; (h)
under water.

| | Basic Error Tendencies | | | | |
	ECOLOGICAL CONSTRAINTS	CHANGE EN-HANCEMENT	RESOURCE LIMITATIONS	SCHEMA PROPERTIES	STRATEGIES HEURISTICS
SENSORY REGISTRATION	_____ False sensations* _____				
	X	X			
INPUT SELECTION			Attentional failures*		
			X	X	O
VOLATILE MEMORY			Memory lapses*		
			X	X	O
LONG-TERM MEMORY			Inaccurate recall*		
			O	X	X
RECOGNITION PROCESSES		Misperceptions*			
	O	O	X	X	X
JUDGEMENTAL PROCESSES		Errors of judgement*			
		X	X	X	X
INFERENTIAL PROCESSES			Reasoning errors*		
			X	X	X
ACTION CONTROL			Unintended words/actions*		
			X	X	O

X = Primary node   O = Secondary node

*Primary error groupings

Figure 1. Matrix for classifying primary error groupings

Attentional failures

Although much of the laboratory-based evidence relating to attentional failures is concerned with the selection of items for further processing, the naturalistic study of errors, as they occur across a wide variety of cognitive domains, strongly suggests that attention can be more broadly defined as a universal though limited control resource which plays a fundamental role in the initiation and guidance of all mental activities.

The major contextual sub-divisions of this group are as follows: (a) coping with distraction; (b) processing simultaneous inputs; (c) focusing attention upon one of two concurrent messages; (d) dividing attention between the performance of two concurrent tasks; (e) tasks providing limited opportunity for the appropriate combination of object features (illusory conjunction); and (f) monitoring, custodial and verification tasks.

Memory lapses

The cognitive domain associated with this error grouping has been labelled temporary or 'volatile' memory so that it might embrace not only the now classical view of short-term memory (Atkinson and Shiffrin, 1968), and more recent variants such as working memory (Baddeley and Hitch, 1974; Baddeley, 1976; Hitch, 1980), but also the much less well-understood processes involved in remembering to do things (Harris and Wilkins, 1982). Failures of prospective memory constitute the commonest form of everyday memory lapse (Reason, 1984).

The main task-related sub-divisions of this error group are as follows: (a) forgetting list items (under this heading falls the bulk of the very large experimental literature on memory); (b) forgetting intentions; and (c) losing track of previous actions.

Unintended words and actions

This error group comprises all the absent-minded deviations of words, signs and actions from their intended path. They are the quintessential slips: potentially observable, and arising from failures of execution rather than from inadequate plans. The principal sub-divisions are: (a) slips of the tongue; (b) slips of the pen; (c) slips of the hand — in sign language; (d) slips of action; and (e) Freudian slips.

Recognition failures

These are the misperceptions, alluded to earlier, in which an erroneous cognitive interpretation is placed upon sensory data. Most typically, they occur when the sensory evidence is either incomplete or impoverished, and when there is a strong schema-based expectation to perceive either the presence or the absence of a particular stimulus configuration. In one case, the error can consist of wrongly identifying something which is not actually present; in the other, it can involve not recognizing something which is in fact there. The patterns exhibited by these errors show a close resemblance to those found in inaccurate recall.

The principal sub-divisions are: (a) experimental manipulations — as with the memory lapses, it is convenient to treat the psychological laboratory as a specific task area; (b) mishearing speech; (c) misreading text; (d) misreading signals and instruments; (e) misperceptions in routine action; and (f) misperceptions of people.

Inaccurate and blocked recall

All the errors in this group share a common process, that of recollection, and, as with previous groupings, the major sub-divisions are mainly defined by the objects of that process: (a) misremembering sentences; (b) misremembering stories; (c) misremembering places; (d) misremembering faces; (e) misremembering events; and (vi) blocked recall. It should be noted that blocked recall is a phenomenon which has much in common with memory lapses, but which also displays evidence of schematic bias (Reason and Lucas, 1984), and thus more properly belongs with the long-term memory failures.

Errors of judgement

The term 'thinking' is often taken to embrace both reasoning and judgement. Clearly, these two processes are intimately interlinked, and some recent authors do not even attempt to distinguish them (e.g., Nisbett and Ross, 1980). The justification for doing so here is twofold. In the first place, despite several points of overlap (see Johnson-Laird and Wason, 1977; Johnson-Laird, 1983; Pollard, 1982), the literature relating to judgemental and reasoning errors derives from somewhat different research traditions, and hence tends to be organized separately. Secondly, it is convenient to follow the distinction made by Johnson (1955) between 'thought as problem-solving' and 'thought as judgement'.

In keeping with most other error groupings, the major sub-divisions here relate to what is being judged, that is to the nature of the task. These divisions are: (a) psychophysical misjudgements; (b) temporal misjudgements; (c) misconceptions of chance; (d) misconceptions of covariation; (e) misjudgements of risk; (f) misdiagnoses; (g) fallacies in probability judgements; and (h) erroneous social assessments.

Reasoning errors

Most of the error data relating to this group is derived from laboratory studies in which there was a deliberate attempt to make explicit the normally covert operations involved in reasoning. This research tradition has a very long history in both philosophy and psychology. Interest has centred around two issues. To what extent can most individuals be considered as naturally rational thinkers? How and why do intelligent people make systematic errors when required to draw inferences from evidence? As Wason and Johnson-Laird (1972) pointed out: 'In at least one respect, research on reasoning is like research on perception: it is often most revealing when "error" occurs' (p. 6).

The sub-divisions of this grouping largely reflect the kinds of reasoning task that have been employed in the psychological laboratory. They include: (a) errors in deductive reasoning; (b) errors in propositional reasoning; (c) reasoning with positive and negative instances; (d) reasoning with abstract and concrete instances; (e) errors in concept formation; and (f) errors in hypothesis testing.

A POSTSCRIPT ON LEVELS

Notwithstanding the number and diversity of existing error taxonomies, it is possible to penetrate beyond their surface idiosyncracies to distinguish at least three levels in the classificatory process. These are the behavioural, the contextual and conceptual levels of classification, and correspond approximately to the 'What?', 'How?', and 'Why?' questions about human error (see Reason, 1984).

On the face of it, the business of assembling and categorizing a corpus of errors bears some resemblance to that of collecting and classifying butterflies. There is, however, a fundamental difference between these two enterprises. Although butterflies display an enormous variety in their surface characteristics and habitats, they can nevertheless be allocated to a limited number of meaningful classes. But in the case of errors, the pattern is almost the reverse. Here the complexity lies not in their observable features, but in the largely hidden causal realms beneath. At a surface level, human error divides readily into a very limited number of behavioural categories. Unfortunately, membership of most of these categories tells us little or nothing about their origins. Rather, the evidence suggests that members of the same behavioural error class can arise from quite different causal factors, and that members of different behavioural categories can share common aetiologies (see Norman, 1981; Reason and Mycielska, 1982; Reason, 1984).

The present paper has been concerned with presenting a classificatory framework which primarily seeks to integrate the contextual and conceptual levels of analysis. The emphasis throughout has been not upon identifying specific categories, but upon devising a set of flexible taxonomic principles. It does not require detailed agreement with either the basic error tendencies, listed above, or with the cognitive domains identified, to produce a classificatory scheme which embodies the same general taxonomic principles as those espoused here. Both error tendencies and cognitive domains could be added to or deleted from this classificatory framework without altering its underlying structure.

To be of value in either a theoretical or a practical context, a classificatory framework must both simplify the available error data and acknowledge the multiplicity of possible causal interactions. Most importantly, however, it must recognize that predictable error and correct performance are two sides of the same coin, and hence demand common explanatory principles.

REFERENCES

Atkinson, R. C., and Shiffrin, R. M. (1968) Human memory: A proposed system and its control processes. In: K. W. Spence and J. T. Spence (Eds), *The Psychology of Learning and Motivation*, vol. 2. New York: Academic Press.

Baddeley, A. D. (1976) *The Psychology of Memory*. London: Harper.

Baddeley, A. D., and Hitch, G. (1974) Working memory. In: G. H. Bower (Ed.), *The Psychology of Learning and Motivation*, Vol. 8. New York: Academic Press.

Bobrow, D. G., and Norman, D. A. (1975) Some principles of memory schemata. In: D. Bobrow and A. Collins (Eds), *Representation and Understanding: Studies in Cognitive Science*. New York: Academic Press.

Harris, J. E., and Wilkins, A. J. (1982) Remembering to do things: A theoretical framework and illustrative experiment. *Human Learning*, **1**, 123–36.

Hitch, G. (1980) Developing the concept of working memory. In: G. Claxton (Ed.), *Cognitive Psychology: New Directions*. London: Routledge & Kegan Paul.

Johnson, D. M. (1955) *The Psychology of Thought and Judgement*. New York: Harper.

Johnson-Laird, P. N. (1983) *Mental Models*. New York: Cambridge University Press.

Johnson-Laird, P. N., and Wason, P. C. (Eds) (1977) *Thinking*. Cambridge: Cambridge University Press.

Nisbett, R., and Ross, L. (1980) *Human Influence: Strategies and Shortcomings of Social Judgment*. Englewood Cliffs, NJ: Prentice-Hall.

Norman, D. A. (1981) Categorization of action slips. *Psychological Review*, **88**, 1–15.

Pollard, P. (1982) Human reasoning: Some possible effects of availability. *Cognition*, **10**, 65–96.

Reason, J. T. (1984) Lapses of attention. In: R. Parasuraman and D. Davies (Eds), *Varieties of Attention*. New York: Academic Press.

Reason, J. T., and Lucas, D. (1984) Absent-mindedness in shops: Its incidence, correlates and consequences. *British Journal of Clinical Psychology*, **23**, 121–31.

Reason, J. T., and Mycielska, K. (1982) *Absent-Minded? The Psychology of Mental Lapses and Everyday Errors*. Englewood Cliffs, NJ: Prentice-Hall.

Taylor, S. E., and Crocker, J. (1981) Schematic bases of social information processing. In: E. Higgins, C. Herman, and M. Zanna (Eds), *Social Cognition The Ontario Symposium*, Vol. 1. Hillsdale, NJ: Erlbaum.

Wason, P. C., and Johnson-Laird, P. B. (1972) *The Psychology of Reasoning: Structure and Content*. London: Batsford.

New Technology and Human Error
Edited by J. Rasmussen, K. Duncan and J. Leplat
© 1987 John Wiley & Sons Ltd

2. A Preliminary Classification of Mistakes

James Reason
University of Manchester

SUMMARY

Mistakes (planning failures) are classified into three classes according to shortcomings and limitations within the underlying rational processes: (a) bounded rationality; (b) imperfect rationality; (c) reluctant rationality. Irrational mistakes are also discussed.

INTRODUCTION

Like slips (see Norman, 1981; Reason and Mycielska, 1982), mistakes* can be classified at different levels, either according to theoretical assumptions about their origins within the cognitive apparatus, or by their observable surface characteristics. At a global level of analysis, it is clear that Bacon's dictum still applies, namely that '. . . the human understanding is like a false mirror, which, receiving rays irregularly, distorts and discolours the nature of things by mingling its own nature with it' (Anderson, 1960, p. 48). But, as with Bacon's 'Idols of the Tribe', it is necessary to specify the various forms taken by these distortions. One approach that would be compatible with Bacon's observations on human fallibility and also with much of the contemporary research literature is to classify mistakes according to the failures or limitations of rationality that seem to underlie them. However, we first need to be clear about what is meant by the term 'rationality'.

A useful starting point is Simon's (1957) definition of rationality as being '. . . concerned with the selection of preferred behaviour alternatives in terms of some system of values whereby the consequences of behaviour can be evaluated' (p. 75). In this sense, a rational plan is simply one that involves choosing a course of action that, on the available evidence, will result in some psychological or material benefit to the planner. To be rational, therefore, a plan does not necessarily have to be based upon an elaborate consideration of all the available alternatives and their likely outcomes. This may be prudent, but the skimping of these extended deliberations does not, of itself, deny rationality. As Harrison (1975) pointed out: 'All that is necessary to

15

make the choice a rational one is the existence of an objective and the selection of some alternative that promises to meet the objective as seen by the decision maker' (p. 61).

Initially, we will examine how well planning mistakes can be categorized according to three principles of less-than-perfect rationality: bounded, imperfect and reluctant rationality. Having assessed these three principles of flawed rationality, we will then be in a position to see to what extent it is necessary to invoke the principle of irrationality in order to accommodate any residual and unclassified error tendencies.

This preliminary classification of mistakes is guided by a theoretical framework that assumes all human actions, whether internal or external, to be governed by the complex interplay between two modes of control: attentional and schematic. The former has powerful, feedback-driven, information-processing capabilities, and is essential for coping with novel situations; but is limited, slow, laborious, sequential and difficult to sustain. The schematic or 'default' mode has no known limits on its capacity, and can process familiar information rapidly and in parallel without conscious involvement or effort; but is relatively ineffective in the face of unforeseen circumstances. Both modes, therefore, have their particular strengths and weaknesses. Although presented in dichotomous form, they are perhaps better regarded as the extremes of a graded dimension along which the current focus of control continually shifts.

MISTAKES OF BOUNDED RATIONALITY

In general terms, bounded rationality means that only a small aspect of the total problem space will be 'displayed' in the working database. (*See* Ch.5) These restrictions derive from the inherent limitations of the attentional mode of control. In particular, they stem from the narrowness of effective attentional focus, our inability to maintain the direction of that focus, and the small amount of remembered information that can be presented to its scrutiny. These limitations are further exacerbated by the fact that we possess only partial control over the contents of the working database. This will be invaded both by irrelevent environmental information and by fragments from activated schemata that may or may not bear upon the problem.

It seems reasonable to assume that the mistakes due to bounded rationality will be characterized by over-simplification. The search for objectives will be restricted, and those chosen will be short term rather than long term, and merely adequate rather than ideal. Similarly, fewer ways of attaining these objectives are likely to be considered than are potentially available. Categorizations of plan-related factors will be based on global rather than subtle discriminations, and the possibility of complex interactions between them will either be overlooked or underestimated. Attempts at 'thinking through' the consequences of the planned actions will be partial rather than complete, since this activity is extremely demanding of attentional effort and is further restricted by memory considerations and by 'mind-wandering' (see 'reluctant rationality', below).

MISTAKES OF IMPERFECT RATIONALITY

Watkins (1970) distinguished between a strong and a weak form of the rationality principle. The former identifies rational decision making with optimality: '. . . to decide rationally is to make a decision that could not be bettered, given one's present situational information (which may, however, be more or less incomplete or incorrect)' (p. 179). The weaker form accepts that people's decisions are, in reality, usually sub-optimal; but continues to maintain that theories of optimal decision making play a useful normative role. But, Watkins argued, they break down even as normative theories; so that we are driven to adopt some still weaker principle — that of imperfect rationality.

Watkins's view of imperfect rationality also embraced the features of bounded rationality described above. But psychological — as distinct from philosophical — considerations are better served by keeping them at least notionally separate. Accordingly, it is suggested that whereas the mistakes of bounded rationality derive mainly from the limitations of the attentional mode of control, those of imperfect rationality are primarily due to the characteristics of the schematic mode.

The schematic knowledge-base comprises an apparently limitless number of experts, or specialized theories, each one dealing with a particular aspect of the world through one or a variety of cognitive domains (e.g., perception, action, memory retrieval, thought, judgement, etc.). Together they constitute a richly interconnected, immensely powerful, labour-saving apparatus for governing the largely predictable and routine activities of life. But they do not come 'hard-wired'. In their beginnings, they make heavy demands upon the limited attentional resource; but then they gradually acquire a large measure of autonomy — to such an extent, in fact, that we are only aware of their outputs (as actions, perceptions, or conscious thought processes), and not of the operations that produced them (see Dennett, 1979).

Nor are they to be regarded as passive entities that lie dormant until called into action by some higher authority. Each schema has, as it were, a 'mind' of its own, albeit a very narrow one. Although, as stated earlier, they can be triggered by some intentional process (and usually are, since for the most part our actions do go as planned), they can also be activated by a variety of non-intentional factors that include the recency and frequency of their employment, influences from related schemata, environmental triggers, and their current emotional significance. It is to these features that we owe their uncalled-for appearance in the working database, and also the fact that vivid or emotionally charged material claims privileged access.

Given these general characteristics of schema function, what are the principal ways in which mistakes of imperfect rationality can manifest themselves? Clearly, we are not in a position to list them all; but some of them are highly predictable. If they share anything in common, it is likely to that they will cause us to err in the direction of being too much in tune with past circumstances than is demanded by present or future states. In other words, the schematic mode will yield procedures that are too rule-bound, too rigid, and too conservative. Solutions to previous problems will continue to be applied, and too little account will be taken of actual or potential change.

A close similarity is evident between these mistakes and the strong habit intrusions that constitute the largest proportion of the slips of action, investigated previously (see Reason and Mycielska, 1982). And this is hardly surprising since both owe their origins to the schematic mode of control. However, whereas these slips reflect the unintentional activation of relatively low order control structures, the corresponding kinds of mistake appear to arise from the often intended but contextually inappropriate application of judgemental and inferential heuristics. These represent in some shorthand form the abstracted wisdom acquired over many years of superficially comparable experiences.

Clearly, the over-utilization of these intuitive rules of thumb is not, of itself, an indication of non-rationality. Given the nature of our lives and of our cognitive control mechanisms, we have little choice in the matter. Nevertheless, it is equally true that this over-routinization of judgement and reasoning can lead to imperfect rationality, since it allows us to formulate plans that have little hope of achieving their desired ends. The heart of the problem seems to lie somewhere between our remarkable ability to model the regularities of the past and our conspicuous inability to predict the irregularities of the future.

MISTAKES OF RELUCTANT RATIONALITY

Whereas the mistakes of bounded rationality arise primarily from the limitations of the working database, and those of imperfect rationality from the conservative forces within the schematic knowledge base, the mistakes of reluctant rationality stem from the interplay between the attentional and schematic modes of control.

One way of regarding this interaction is to imagine the working database — the focus of rational thought — as a small boat attempting to steer a course across the waters of the schematic knowledge base. But this boat is powered by a weak and intermittently functioning motor. Moreover, the waters over which it moves are subject to strong tides and currents. In psychological terms, these tides and currents always run in the direction of the boat's previous routes. If the intended voyage conforms to these established routes, then no effort is required to achieve the objective; the boat simply drifts with the current. Difficulties arise when new directions must be taken across or against the prevailing forces. Although the charted route may be suitable, the boat lacks sufficient power to hold this bearing. Whenever the motor cuts out or loses propulsive force, the boat will be driven off course in a direction dictated by the current.

The principle of reluctant rationality relates very closely to what Bruner et al. (1956) called 'cognitive strain'. Within the terms of the boat analogy, this arises whenever a mental course must be steered across rather than with the prevailing schematic currents. It is the cost of the attentional effort (James, 1890; Kahneman, 1973) necessary to pursue a novel line of thought. This effort cannot be sustained for very long. As a consequence, the attentional 'vessel' either drifts off course along habitual routes, or, more actively, is pulled towards emotionally or contextually charged schemata in the semantic vicinity.

William James (1908) discussed this phenomenon in regard to the difficulties of maintaining concentration on a boring topic; but these intermittencies also occur in the laborious pursuit of novel lines of thought:

> When we are studying an uninteresting subject, if our mind tends to wander, we have to bring back our attention every now and then by using distinct pulses of effort . . . Voluntary attention, in short, is only a momentary affair. (James, 1908, pp. 101–2)

The pioneering studies of Bruner and his colleagues (Bruner et al., 1956) demonstrated that people adopt strategies designed to minimize cognitive strain in problem-solving and concept-attainment tasks. These strategies may be either efficient or inefficient, depending upon the particular circumstances. For example, subjects were found to resort to a criterion of verisimilitude when using and evaluating cues in a categorization task. That is, when attempting to distinguish exemplars from non-exemplars of a category, they tended to fall back on cues that had proved useful in the past, and thus had the 'look of truth' about them, regardless of their present utility. This strategy, termed 'persistence forecasting', costs little effort and has value in regular or familiar environments; but it can prevent the adoption of informationally efficient strategies in unconventional or unusual situations. In one study, the use of such a strategy predisposed problem solvers to carry out successive testing of 'reasonable' hypotheses, when a focused search would have been more effective.

In summary, reluctant rationality, the need to avoid cognitive strain, is likely to lead to an excessive reliance on what appear to be familiar cues, and to the over-ready application of well-tried problem solutions. It therefore operates, as does imperfect rationality, to direct out thoughts along well-trodden as opposed to novel pathways. And, like bounded rationality, it will act to restrict potentially profitable explorations of the problem space.

IRRATIONAL MISTAKES

What remains to be assigned to this category? Some theorists, notably Nisbett and Ross (1980), would answer that there are fewer truly irrational mistakes than were ever dreamt of in most laypersons' psychology. Under the heading of 'psychodynamics versus psychologic', they considered the claims of both motivational and cognitive interpretations of erroneous behaviour, in particular those associated with self-serving biases and with racial prejudice. They concluded their analysis with the following comments:

> Examination of these topics suggests that motivational interpretations, despite their intuitive appeal, are hardly demanded by the evidence. In both cases nonmotivational factors seem sufficient to account for most of the phenomena . . . To us, the real phenomenon to be explained is the widespread and generally uncritical acceptance of motivational explanations for erroneous and damaging beliefs. People's use of the representativeness heuristic in general, and their susceptibility to the fundamental attribution error in particular, seem to be reflected in their tendency to embrace motivational explanations. (Nisbett and Ross, 1980, pp. 247–8)

Accepting the argument that people's cognitive biases will cause them to impute more irrational tendencies to others than are actually there, have we any grounds for abandoning this category of irrational mistakes altogether? It is suggested we do not, and for the following reasons.

In the first place, there can be little doubt from Janis's (See Ch.11) description of the 'groupthink' syndrome that group dynamics can introduce genuine irrationality into the planning process. How else could one label the conspiracy to repress adverse signs, or the excessive confidence shown by these group members? One definition of irrational behaviour could be the wilful suppression of knowledge indicating that a certain course of action will lead to disaster. In this respect, Janis's groups behaved no less irrationally than the would-be bird men who jump off high buildings with feathers attached to their arms. The tragedy of the Somme in 1916, or the fall of Singapore in 1941, hints at similar processes operating among groups of military planners. Such blunders, as Dixon (1976) demonstrated in his analysis of military incompetence, demand the involvement of both psycho-dynamic and cognitive considerations in order to provide adequate explanations.

Another reason for not foreclosing on irrationality is that it forces us to continue grappling with the many problems inherent in this term. It is full of paradox. Pursuing the logic of Simon's definition of rationality, given earlier, it follows that a non-rational plan is one that directs action towards some undesirable goal, or which contrives to thwart the achievement of desirable ends. But to be truly irrational in this sense, one has to know what one is doing, otherwise these acts are merely the product of limited or flawed cognition. And yet such knowledge implies some degree of rationality, albeit of a rather warped and self-defeating kind.

Other difficulties are raised by the fact that we have many coexisting plans at any one time. Is it irrational to plan and successfully carry out a sequence of actions whose end result prevents or seriously delays the attainment of some longer term objective? Is the dieter behaving irrationally when he gives in to his stomach pangs and treats himself to a large calorie-laden meal? Many would say yes. But a closer examination of his circumstances might reveal that this was the wiser course: perhaps his diet was causing hypogly-caemia, or was seriously impairing his efficiency at some critical task. In short, the question of irrationality could well turn out to be a matter of opinion, something that is likely to change according to one's viewpoint, degree of 'inside knowledge', or time perspective. And the same also applies to the reverse situation: when someone engages in a planned sequence of actions that appear self-damaging in the short term, but which may promote the achievement of some longer term advantage.

The aim here is not to muddy this already cloudy pool still further, but to highlight some unresolved issues concerning the matter of human irrationality. It is interesting to note that most systems of criminal law generally cope with these difficulties by requiring a majority judgement from twelve ordinary men and women on the basis of the evidence before them. In 1843, Daniel M'Naghten intended to murder Sir Robert Peel, but killed his secretary instead. This gave rise to the famous M'Naghten Rules which, in common law, define the criterion of criminal responsibility. Their basic propositions are as follows:

> . . . the jurors ought to be told in all cases that every man is presumed to be sane, and to possess a sufficient degree of reason to be responsible for his crimes, until the contrary be proved to their satisfaction; and that to establish a defence on the ground of insanity, it must be clearly proved that, at the time of committing the act, the party accused was labouring under such defect of reason, from disease of the mind, as not to know the nature and quality of the act he was doing, or, if he did know it, that he did not know he was doing what was wrong. (Smith and Hogan, 1973, p. 134)

Thus, the law makes a very subtle distinction. If the accused claims to have been unaware of the nature and consequences of his or her act because of some 'defect of reason' or 'disease of the mind', the burden of proof shifts to the defence. But if he or she does not claim insanity, but attributes this unawareness to other factors, then the burden of proof remains with the prosecution, and if the evidence brought by the prosecution was inadequate to convince the jury, the accused would be entitled to acquittal on the grounds that he or she lacked the necessary *mens rea*, or 'guilty intent'. In other words, the accused is considered to have behaved rationally, with or without criminal intent, unless contrary proof is offered. This is a position which is comparable to that adopted by a number of contemporary psychologists in regard to mistakes (see Nisbett and Ross, 1980), and is in sharp contrast to earlier psychodynamic views that emphasized the irrational basis of human error.

REFERENCES

Anderson, F. H. (1960) *Bacon: The New Organon*. Indianapolis: Bobbs-Merrill.

Bruner, J. S., Goodnow, J. J., and Austin, G. A. (1956) *A Study of Thinking*. New York: Wiley.

Dennett, D. C. (1979) *Brainstorms*. Sussex: Harvester.

Dixon, N. F. (1976) *On the Psychology of Military Incompetence*. London: Jonathan Cape.

Harrison, E. F. (1975) *The Managerial Decision-Making Process*. Boston: Houghton Mifflin Company.

James, W. (1890) *Principles of Psychology*. New York: Holt.

James, W. (1908) *Talks to Teachers on Psychology*. London: Longmans, Green & Co.

Kahneman, D. (1973) *Attention and Effort*. Englewood Cliffs, NJ: Prentice-Hall.

Nisbett, R., and Ross, L. (1980) *Human Inference: Strategies and Shortcomings of Social Judgment*. Englewood Cliffs, NJ: Prentice-Hall.

Norman, D. A. (1981) Categorization of action slips. *Psychological Review*, **88**, 1–15.

Reason, J. T., and Mycielska, K. (1982) *Absent-Minded? The Psychology of Mental Lapses and Everyday Errors*. Englewood Cliffs, NJ: Prentice-Hall.

Simon, H. A. (1957) *Models of Man*. New York: Wiley.

Smith, J. C., and Hogan, B. (1973) *Criminal Law*, 3rd edn. London: Butterworths.

Watkins, J. (1970) Imperfect rationality. In: R. Borger and F. Cioffi (Eds), *Explanation in the Behavioural Sciences*. Cambridge: Cambridge University Press.

---

*See Ch.5 for an account of the basic differences between slips and mistakes.

New Technology and Human Error
Edited by J. Rasmussen, K. Duncan and J. Leplat
© 1987 John Wiley & Sons Ltd

3. The Definition of Human Error and a Taxonomy for Technical System Design

Jens Rasmussen
Risø National Laboratory

SUMMARY

Analysis of industrial accidents and the role of human performance raise the question of the definition of human error. In the chapter, it is argued that the identification of an event as a human error depends entirely upon the stop rule applied for the explanatory search after the fact. Consequently, human errors are not events for which objective data can be collected, instead they should be considered occurrences of man–task mismatches which can only be characterized by a multifaceted description. The outline of a taxonomy to support analysis of event reports and the design of error tolerant systems is given.

INTRODUCTION

The need for human error data for various purposes has been discussed for decades, yet no acceptable human error data bank has emerged. What is the problem? Are there events which can objectively be considered human errors and for which data can be collected from real-life work situations? What attributes are necessary to characterize the human involvement in accidental chains of events? In the following sections, these questions are discussed, and it is argued that instead of focusing on human errors, data should be collected to represent situations of man–task mismatch and characterized accordingly. Furthermore, to support design of error-tolerant work situations, more emphasis should be put on analysis of error recovery features.

DEFINITION OF HUMAN ERROR

Analyses of incidents and accidents immediately make it evident that faults and errors cannot be defined objectively by considering the performance of humans or equipment in isolation. They can only be defined with reference to human intentions or expectations; they depend upon somebody's judgement of the specific situation. Faults and errors are not only caused by changes in performance with respect to the normal or accepted performance, but also by changes of the criteria of judgements, i.e., changes in requirements to system performance, in safety requirements, or in legal conventions, will be able to turn hitherto accepted performance into erroneous acts.

In other words, human error occurrences are defined by the behaviour of the total man–task system. Human intentions and the resulting actions may be correct from the performer's point of view, from the goal he selects — which may be inappropriate judged from system output.

Human errors: Causes of accidents?

In the present man–task context we can define faults and errors as causes of unfulfilled system purposes. If system performance is judged below the accepted standard, somebody will typically try to backtrack the causal chain to find the causes. How far back to seek is a rather open question; generally, the search will stop when one or more changes are found which are familiar and therefore acceptable as explanations, and to which something can be done for correction. In the case of a technical breakdown, a 'component' failure is generally accepted as the cause at that component level where replacement is convenient. In some cases, however, component failure will not be found an acceptable cause; for example, if it occurs more frequently than expected. In such cases, the search will often continue to find the 'root cause' of the component's malfunction. In summary, the characteristics of a fault are: (a) it is the cause of deviation from a standard; (b) it is found on the causal path backwards from this effect; (c) it is accepted as a familiar and therefore reasonable explanation; and (d) a cure is known.

This means that allocation of causes to people or technical parts in the system is a purely pragmatic question regarding the stop rule applied for analysis after the fact. There is no well-defined 'start' of the causal chain involved in accidents, and the link which is chosen to represent the 'cause' for which 'error data' are collected depends on the application of the data. This fact should, as will be discussed below, be reflected in the error data taxonomy.

Human errors: Man–machine mismatch situations?

For improvement of safety, a more fruitful point of view is to describe human errors as instances of man–machine or man–task misfits. In case of systematic or frequent misfits, the cause can then typically be considered a design error. Occasional misfits are either caused by variability on part of the system or the man and will typically be considered component failures or human errors, respectively.

The interaction can be seen as a complex, multidimensional demand/ resource fit. To discuss the misfits and evaluate means for improvement, it is more important to find the nature or dimensions of the misfits than to identify their causes. In other words, it is necessary to find *what* went wrong rather than *why*, i.e., to identify potential conflicts, rather than their predecessors in the course of events. Again, this consideration should be reflected in the error data taxonomy.

With respect to man–system misfits, human variability can play a role in two different ways. First, mismatch may occur when human variability brings human actions on the system outside the boundary allowing continued acceptable system function. Second, adaptability and variability of human behaviour may not be large enough to maintain a match, following changes in system behaviour. To explain man–system mismatch we must therefore look at the control of human behaviour, to find mechanisms behind variability during normal, familiar situations and mechanisms limiting adaptability in unfamiliar situations when the system changes. This point of view is discussed in more detail in Chapter 6.

Human errors: Experiments in an unkind environment?

Human variability is an important ingredient in adaptation and learning, and the ability to adapt to peculiarities in system performance and optimize interaction is the very reason for having people in a system. To optimize performance, to develop smooth and efficient skills, it is very important to have opportunities to 'cut corners', to perform trial and error experiments, and human errors can in a way be considered to be unsuccessful experiments with unacceptable consequences. When analysing incident reports, one rapidly gets the impression that human acts are only classified as human errors because they are performed in an 'unkind' work environment. An unkind work environment is then defined by the fact that it is not possible for a man to correct the effects of inappropriate variations in performance before they lead to unacceptable consequences. Typically, because he either cannot immediately observe the effects of his 'errors', or because they are irreversible.

A TAXONOMY OF HUMAN ERROR

It was argued above that human errors are events in the causal path followed when analysing the causes of system malfunctions. In order to extract data from reports on accidents and incidents, useful for design of error-tolerant systems, a consistent taxonomy is necessary.

There are, however, many possible ways to characterize human errors: it can be done with reference to task characteristics, to human psychological mechanisms, to environmental factors, etc. It turns out that a taxonomy should reflect several points of view if it is to be useful for design of reliable systems.

The dimensions of such a taxonomy can be identified from the factors it is necessary to consider in order to explain the human behaviour as found when backtracking the causal course of events after an incident. The result of this will be a multifacet description system, rather than an exclusive, generic classification tree.

The first element of a man–system mismatch met during backtracking will be an unacceptable state of a physical object or component due to a human act, i.e., features of the mismatch are described in terms of inappropriate task performance. In Figure 1 this dimension is called the *external mode of human malfunction*, in order to avoid the term 'human error' with its flavour of guilt. In this category, mismatch is expressed in terms of omission of acts in procedural sequences, acts on wrong components, reversals in a sequence, wrong timing, etc. Data from this category will be sufficient for design of work conditions when applying a technology and tools very similar to the environment from which data are collected, i.e., during slow technological changes. When new technological means are introduced, however, data are needed which relate mismatches also to psychological mechanisms.

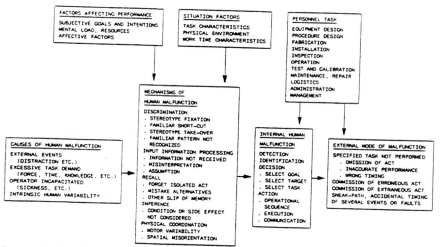

Figure 1. Multifacet taxonomy for description and analysis of events involving human malfunction. (From Rasmussen, 1982, with permission from Elsevier Scientific Publishing Company.)

To do this, it is necessary first to characterize the mental task which has been involved in the event. A cognitive task analysis is therefore necessary to identify the internal mode of malfunction, i.e., the element of the internal cognitive decision process which was affected, either by not being properly performed or by being improperly bypassed by a habitual short-cut. In practice, this analysis is possible to the level of detail represented in the decision sequence of Figure 2, but only by a person familiar with the task content and the level of training of the performer. Given the knowledge of the task and the particular external error mode found, it is in general possible *for the more familiar routine tasks* to judge the internal mode of malfunction from a case story (Rasmussen, 1980). For performance in unfamiliar situations requiring proper problem solving, a cognitive task analysis, if at all possible, requires interviews and discussions with the performer (see for instance Pew *et al.*, 1981).

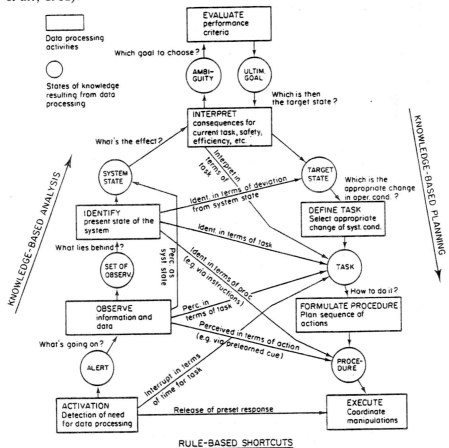

Figure 2. Schematic map of the sequence of mental activities used between initiation of response and the manual action. Rational, causal reasoning connects the 'states of knowledge' in the basic sequence. Stereotyped mental processes can bypass intermediate states. (From Rasmussen, 1976, with permission from Plenum Publishing Corp.)

To further characterize an event with reference to psychological mechanisms, as is done in the category *mechanisms of human malfunctions*, it is necessary to refer to a model of the mechanisms of cognitive control which

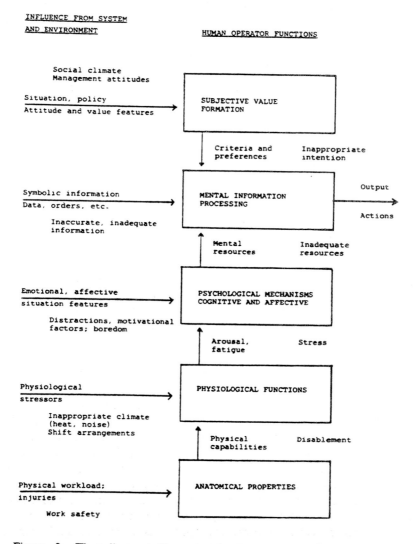

Figure 3. The diagram illustrates the complex interaction in a man–machine system which controls the mismatch features in an error situation. (From Rasmussen, 1982, with permission from Elsevier Scientific Publishing Company.)

can explain the mismatch characterized so far. The elements of this category of the taxonomy are related to the model discussed in Chapter 6.

Frequently, the human–system mismatch will not be due to spontaneous, inherent human variability, but events in the environment, which act as precursors, can be identified. Such events can be characterized in the taxonomy by the dimension *causes of human malfunction*, and the causal backtracking can be continued upstream from the human. In the taxonomy, only *events* recognizable at distinct locations in time are considered causes, such as for instance interference by messages from colleagues, telephone calls, events in the environment such as bursts of noise, etc. More persistent conditions, like generally stressing work environments, bad ergonomic designs, inadequate instruction, etc., are considered *performance affecting factors* and characterized separately. This dimension of the taxonomy is intended to take into consideration that the human system interaction cannot be described adequately only considering the cognitive information processing level (see Figure 3).

This taxonomy does not lead to a generic, hierarchical classification system, but to a multifacet system to characterize mismatch occurrences. This approach has several advantages. First of all, a very high resolution in the description of mismatch events can be obtained with only a manageable few elements in each of the dimensions of the taxonomy. Furthermore, the internal structure of an event is preserved in the description, and can be regenerated in another context for analysis during design of new systems. For instance, very complex, but likely, scenarios for mismatch events can be identified and studied by postulating an internal mismatch mechanism, which is then folded on to the different decision phases under the assumption of level of training of the person. The resulting relevant 'internal malfunctions' are then correlated with each of the steps in an assumed work procedure by careful consideration of potential interference in the different relevant elements of the decision sequence (see Figure 2), and the combined effects of possible inappropriate acts are assessed for different alternative system configurations. The probability of the significant courses of events could then be judged by identification of the likely causes and the quality of work situation in terms of performance affecting factors. The advantage is that complex scenarios can be identified directly from the underlying psychological mechanisms. If the analysis is based only on the consideration of human errors in terms of their external manifestations, as for instance omissions, commissions and inappropriate timing, search for complex and risky scenarios will be hindered by a combinatorial explosion (Rasmussen, 1982). The multi-facet taxonomy of Figure 1, supplemented by categories to characterize the technical system and component faults, has been considered for an event reporting system for nuclear installations by an OECD working group (Rasmussen *et al.*, 1981).

REFERENCES

Pew, R. W., Miller, D. C., and Feehrer, C. E. (1981) Evaluation of proposed control room improvements through analysis of critical operator decisions. Electric Power Research Institute. Research report NP-1982. Palo Alto, 1981.

Rasmussen, J. (1976) Outlines of a hybrid model of the process operator. In: Sheridan and Johannsen (Eds), *Monitoring Behaviour and Supervisory Control*. New York: Plenum Press.

Rasmussen, J. (1980) What can be learned from human error reports? In: K. Duncan, M. Gruneberg, and D. Wallis (Eds), *Changes in Working Life*. John Wiley.

Rasmussen, J., Pedersen, O. M., Mancini, G., Carnino, A., Griffon, M., and Gagnolet, P. (1981) Classification system for reporting events involving human malfunction. Risø-M-2240.

Rasmussen, J. (1982) Human errors. A taxonomy for describing human malfunction in industrial installations. *Journal of Occupational Accidents*, **4** (2–4), 311–35.

New Technology and Human Error
Edited by J. Rasmussen, K. Duncan and J. Leplat
© 1987 John Wiley & Sons Ltd

4. The Hermeneutics of Accidents and Safety

Donald H. Taylor
The University, Southampton
Now: Donald Taylor and Associates Ltd.

SUMMARY

Discusses *doctrine of mechanism* in the *philosophy of science* as the basis of *ergonomics*. Proposes recently revived doctrine of *hermeneutics* as alternative regarding *accidents* and *safety behaviour*. Hermeneutics is a search for *meanings of actions*. The basic hypothesis proposed is that accidents are by definition meaningless events.

THE DECLINE OF MECHANISM

The science of ergonomics, viewed as the study of man–machine systems, relies upon a deterministic, ultimately predictable, model of man if it is to succeed as a science. The doctrine of mechanism emphasizes the machine-like qualities of man, and underlies all of behavioural science, including ergonomics. To suggest in the journal *Ergonomics* that the basic doctrine of mechanism is in decline seems a dangerous and heretical thing to do. There has always been a school of thought that opposed mechanism as applied to humans, but scientists and engineers have had little trouble in ignoring it, since its achievements in terms of measurable human 'progress' have been slight. It is argued with increasing frequency, however, that the so-called human sciences have not achieved such rapid progress as had been hoped for, and that this is because of a fundamental weakness in the doctrine of mechanism. Certain aspects of human affairs, it is claimed, cannot logically be analysed using mechanism as a basis, and this is (or will prove to be) a limitation of the applicability of human science. It is argued in this paper that the field of accidents and safety is one in which this limitation is beginning to be felt, and that alternatives to mechanism need to be explored. One such alternative is introduced and its potential applications to accidents and safety are investigated.

In respect of health and safety, the environment of civilized man has improved beyond recognition in this century, mainly as a result of scientific advance and social amelioration. Although there is still a significant amount of death and suffering caused by accidents and diseases, it appears in the Western world at least to be reaching an asymptotically low level. Some causes of death and suffering have been virtually eliminated, such as infectious diseases, and many industrial hazards; the levels of those that remain, however, seem intractable and troubling. In the health field, the major killing diseases that remain are those which are linked to lifestyles, i.e., that people in a sense bring on themselves by the way that they choose to live. The 'hard core' of accidents, too, seems to be due to the way that people conduct themselves, rather than to technically preventable factors. Doctors find that their traditional role of curing disease has been changed into one of preventing disease (public health), and is now changing again into one of persuading people to adhere to healthy lifestyles. In the field of accidental injury, too, attention has expanded from merely repairing damage to environmental changes which reduce its severity, and those concerned with safety are reaching the same point as the doctors, in trying now to persuade people to behave in safe ways. In both fields, success is limited: the asymptotes that seemingly are being approached are non-zero, and high enough to cause continuing concern.

It is understandable that health and safety professionals should show irritation or even anger at the apparent perversity of the public in continuing, as they see it, to bring death and suffering upon itself through its own voluntary actions. It is at this point that the doctrine of mechanism is weakest: it would be easy enough to *control* machine-like people in such a way that they would avoid accidents and diseases, but only in the imagined world of B. F. Skinner does this seem at all practicable; most others would agree that voluntary action is an important basis of human life. Within certain social and cultural constraints, this implies freedom in how the body is treated, in respect of health, and what risks are taken, regarding accidents. If this is true at all, it is independent of how much medical techniques improve, and also of ergonomic design. Design engineers, too, could show anger and irritation at the way carefully designed man–machine systems are 'misused' with what seems like deliberate carelessness. It can seem almost as if the public is out to defeat safety measures by finding new ways of having accidents in an increasingly safer world, but this is of little use as an explanation. It may be, however, that there is truth in Herbert Spencer's (1820–1903) saying that 'the ultimate result of shielding men from the effects of folly is to fill the world with fools'.

In psychology generally, there has been some recent feeling that all is not well with mechanism. Here the ground is theoretical rather than practical, and amounts mostly to contending that the theoretical framework offered by a mechanistic view of man is not equal to the task of investigating human action. The most explicit case against mechanism on these grounds has been made by Gauld and Shotter (1977) who attempt to show that a view of man as a generalized machine cannot encompass aspects of human activity that they feel are the proper domain of psychology. For the present purpose of discussing accidents and safety, the argument hinges on whether it is more useful to retain the traditional psychological framework of causally determined behaviour, or to seek explanations in terms of reasons for people's actions, which is a rather different thing.

Taylor (1976) has pointed out that accidents resist attempts to define them causally, i.e., in mechanistic terms, and that some elaboration of theory is logically required to make sense of them. The present paper proceeds from the assumption that in respect of accidents the limit of mechanistic explanation has been reached; implying, as a working hypothesis, that *the man–machine interface cannot be further improved*. This, of course, cannot be literally or universally true, but it signifies that the way forward is to be sought in a somewhat different direction from the traditional preoccupations of ergonomics.

THE RISE OF HERMENEUTICS

The word *hermeneutics* refers to the interpretation of texts or text-like material. Like *ergonomics*, it is a Greek-derived word, but of much older origin, and seems to have been first used in an explicitly psychological sense by John Shotter. Gauld and Shotter (1977) explain its use thus:

> It has been proposed that the psychological and social sciences are essentially hermeneutical, that the proper task of the psychologist is not to formulate the laws of human behaviour, but to elucidate the 'meanings' of pieces of human behaviour (p. 25).

Ergonomists will immediately note two features of this observation: the explanations sought are not likely to be *generally* true, nor quantitatively expressed — qualities usually regarded as essential in laws of human behaviour. The author of catastrophe theory, René Thom, has taken up both of these points. The first will be discussed later; the second, Thom (1975), associates with Lord Rutherford's dictum: 'Qualitative is nothing but poor quantitative', which he disputes, proceeding to show that qualitative thinking need not be based on 'relentlessly naïve' ideas, but (in his hands at least) can become quite sophisticated. For Thom (who also used the word hermeneutical to describe his mode of thought) the goal of a transcendent qualitative analysis is a morphology which is free of intuitions derived from our experience in three-dimensional space; for Gauld and Shotter it is perhaps a 'model of man' that is free of the assumption that man is a 'generalized machine'. Shotter (1980) expresses the fear that we may become what we model ourselves upon; in particular that we might lose a moral sense of ourselves and others. He says:

> We forget . . . that what matters most is that people learn what it is to take responsibility for their actions . . . without that determination, that kind of self control, there can be no guarantee of order in the community at all (p. 21).

This sounds like a 'missing link' in health and safety, the need for which is discussed above, that the possibilities of an hermeneutical approach seem well worth exploring in this field.

The terms used in hermeneutical enquiry are reasons, meanings, intentions, actions, desires, etc., and although they are words used in common discourse, they are not the language of science. It is a mistake simply to try to add them on to a scientific discourse as extra terms to be taken into account: to do this would be to mix two levels of explanation, and leads instantly to chaos. Schutz (1960) warned of this as follows:

> If . . . the ramifications of your problem lead you in the progress of your work to the acceptance of other schemes of reference and interpretation, do not forget that with the change in the scheme all terms in the formerly used scheme undergo a shift of meaning. To preserve the consistency of your thought you have to see to it that the 'subscript' of all the terms and concepts that you use is the same! (p. 209).

A 'paradigm shift' in the study of accidents and safety is therefore not likely to be easy. There exists a rather large literature on alternative approaches to social enquiry, and the present paper can do no more than hint at its relevance to the topic in hand. A current overview of the field is provided by some of the contributors to Chapman and Jones (1980), and the works of Goffman and Harré are also very relevant.

Among the contributors to Chapman and Jones, Hargreaves (1980) speaks for a psychology of common sense, as Joynson (1974) did, but Shotter is inclined to argue that the potential use of the apparently simple language of hermeneutical discourse goes far beyond common sense, and that considerable conceptual analysis is required to realize its potential. Just as in conventional science, there are some situations which are so obvious as to need no further technical explanation, and others which are as yet very obscure; the task of both schemes of enquiry is to extend the area of what is understood, between those two extremes. As an example of this in hermeneutical terms, it has been suggested by Taylor (1976, 1980) that driver behaviour may usefully be regarded as if it were rule-governed. Some aspects of driving are so obvious to all who do or see them that no explanation is required (such as stopping the vehicle before getting out of it); there may be other aspects so rare, bizarre and unpredictable that no analysis of rules could ever elucidate them. In between, as Wilde (1976) notes, there are rule-governed systems about which more could be discovered.

Hermeneutical explanation is sought in the form of intersubjectively shared understanding of the meanings of actions: attempting systematically to characterize and share with others the sense which we have of ourselves as we act, which seems in some way to guide what we try to do (Shotter, 1975). This is not a matter of introspection of 'inner sense': if it were, we would know much more than we do what it is we have acquired when we have attained 'common sense'. (This is the same argument as is used against an introspective view of skill learning.) Above all, intersubjectivity involves considerations of morals and values, which are concepts inaccessible to conventional science, but essential to consideration of risk and safety.

ACCIDENTS AS MEANINGLESS EVENTS

What place can accidents have in a scheme of enquiry that is concerned with the meanings of human actions? Clearly, accidents can never *be* actions, but it may be said that they always *result from* actions. The meaning of an action which happens to lead to an accident cannot include any reference to the accident, because then to intend the action would be to intend the accident: a contradiction in terms. However, an action involving an increased probability of accident has a clear meaning: it is taking a risk. There is thus a paradox of meaning in the antecedents to accidents. The consequences of accidents have clear meanings in terms of damage, injury or death, but these are not actions, they are events contingent upon the accident. It is only the accident itself, the unpredictable event linking antecedents to consequences, that seems devoid of meaning. This is sometimes felt by accident victims or their close relatives, who may express anger simply at the happening of such a senseless event. It is proposed as an hypothesis that accidents uniquely comprise an anomaly of meaning: a kind of 'black hole' in the universe of meaning, which cannot be explained in the same terms as the rest of the space. Accidents may thus be regarded as truly *meaningless events*. Another analogy may be found in the actual discontinuity of catastrophe theory models (Zeeman, 1976). The surface itself is nowhere discontinuous, and until the moment of catastrophe gives no clue *locally* as to what may happen; the catastrophe itself is instantaneous and quite unlike the smooth rule-governed motion on the surface before and after it.

It seems to be the absence of meaning which troubles us about accidents, and much of the activity in the aftermath of an accident may be directed towards trying to ascribe some meaning to the event in a broader context. Looking for causes is one such activity, both in the particular case and in general. Many papers in the accident literature refer to the *causes* of accidents, as if this would explain why they happened, by linking them to meaningful antecedents in the framework of inductive generalization, i.e., to predict that other accidents would happen in similar circumstances. This type of causal analysis is useful in so far as it links the accident with events that could potentially be understood, but it does not explain how actions leading to those events came about. For example, to say that an accident was caused by faulty brakes is to say that vehicles with brakes in that condition are liable to accidents, that the accident would not have occurred if the brakes had not been faulty, etc.; but it is not to explain actions leading to the existence of the faulty brakes as being careless, unskilled, motivated by false economy, etc. The latter type of meaning ascription is often used in allocating blame: another kind of explanation of the accident. It is difficult to link the antecedents of accidents with their consequences, because exactly similar events can lead to widely different consequences (the property of 'divergence' noted in catastrophe theory). If, for example, a construction worker drops a block of concrete from a crane on a deserted spot, what no one sees no one cares about; if he drops it near someone, he is shouted at for being careless; if he drops it *on* someone, the consequences are quite different: the event is an accident. The seriousness of the consequence is not related in any sensible way to the antecedent, and this may be a property of the meaninglessness of the event itself.

We seek to understand events in the world by reference to their meaning, not usually in isolation, but with reference to the whole cultural environment in which they occur. If it is true that accidents are not connected with the meaningful environment by virtue of their having no meaning, some anomalous findings may be expected in the domain of accidents and safety. One such finding may be the extraordinary lack of power possessed by accidents and their consequences to persuade people to avoid them. Safety and health warnings do not in general have the desired effects, and the 'it's not going to happen to me' attitude is familiar to everyone. It is possible that this goes beyond mere optimism in low-probability risk situations, and beyond ignorance, avoidance or perversity; it may be *inability* to relate to the possible consequences, due to the definitional meaningless of the accidental event. In scientific terms, probabilistic contingency is allowed as causal explanation, and under this rule it is perfectly meaningful to link events antecedent to accidents with their consequences, and the apparent lack of public acceptance of these links, or at least their failure to act upon them, is very puzzling and annoying. If, however, the shift from understanding the world in statistical terms to understanding individual events is a shift of the *level* of explanation — a paradigm shift — then Schutz's warning may apply, and the rules of explanation may turn out to be quite different.

It is worth speculating upon what it is about accidents that might deprive them of meaning. Their stochastic property is one possibility, their harmful consequences another. Is *any* stochastic event fundamentally meaningless, or is any event with harmful consequences? Evidently not the latter, in view of Samuel Johnson's remark that to be hanged in a fortnight concentrates the mind wonderfully. Nor do stochastic events with favourable outcomes seem difficult to ascribe meaning to: they are part of the intention to take a risk. It therefore seems that only stochastic events with negative outcomes appear meaningless. Where actions can lead to both pleasant and harmful outcomes, the former can thus be understood, the latter may be in the 'black hole' and so cannot. Inability to comprehend possibly harmful outcomes may be a fundamental property of human existence. This does not of course prevent people learning from their own experience about the outcomes of their actions. Some actions contain their own 'natural signs' of danger, and in so far as they are perceived by the agents, the actions are understood as risky. For all of us, some events are naturally frightening, as judged for example by autonomic response, and we easily learn to respond to other events in this way. This does not interfere, however, with the corollary of the 'black hole' theory: that people will not in general believe in the *statistical* association between their actions and accidents, *unless* it is part of their experience.

THE SEARCH FOR MEANING

If accidents themselves are meaningless, where can we look for explanation of them in a conceptual framework which is centred on meaning as a basic concept? Presumably, we need to label certain actions or kinds of action as dangerous in the statistical sense, and to accept that this labelling will not in general be meaningful to the agents involved. We therefore need to seek the meanings of these actions as understood by the agents, which is an intersubjective process. Hermeneutical argument ascribes 'meaning' to actions in a sense similar to that in which words have meaning: for example, that both may be used conventionally and intentionally to indicate a state of affairs, and the meanings of both depend upon a shared understanding of the occasions on which it is appropriate to use them. As Winch (1958) argued, it is not possible to deduce the meanings of actions merely by observing them, i.e., by regarding them as behaviour. It is this, more than anything, which separates hermeneutical enquiry from conventional science. The meanings of actions have to be interpreted in the light of the agents' motives, purposes, principles and beliefs, indeed from the whole social context in which the actions take place.

There are some actions apparently leading to accidents which do not seem to need this process of interpretation. The 'actions not as planned' discussed by Reason (1979) are interesting because they are *not* actions in the present sense of meaningful intended activities; they may be amusing (when not tragic) because the 'agent' can offer no explanation for them. Other accidents result from inappropriate plans, based on miscalculation or use of inaccurate information; these (when not tragic) may be amusing because of the contrast between agent's understood intentions and expectations, and the unexpected outcome. However, both types of happening can raise questions of the agent's propriety in allowing such events to happen, knowing perhaps that such things could happen, or even that he was unusually prone to them.

Other types of antecedent action that contain no element of deliberate risk-taking are those where there is either ignorance or disbelief of what has been said by 'experts' about the possible consequences. For example, many motorcyclists still do not know that it is safer to ride with headlamp on even in daylight; some motorcyclists make a cult of disbelieving that helmets protect head injuries in a way meaningful to themselves. Actions resulting from these states of knowledge or belief raise moral questions of the extent to which it is justifiable to be ignorant of or disbelieve information from certain sources which are supposed to be credible.

Some actions involve a conscious element of risk-taking; others cause the agent some autonomic arousal and thus may feel risky. Although deliberate risk-taking might be generally frowned upon as undesirable, what is generally meant is the taking of unusual or unjustifiable risks in the social context. Taylor (1976) has argued that some awareness and intention of risk-taking is practically inevitable in road use, and that its existence should be acknowledged if such actions are to be understood. It is generally assumed (though on little real evidence) that taking risks involves balancing all the possible positive and negative consequences: true for rational decision making in formal circumstances, but not often consciously observable in driving situations. Assuming that such balance is ever attempted, how are negative consequences of actions to be included if they are to be defined as meaningless? The answer may be that the negative consequences have nothing to do with the probability of accident, but are fears of non-conformity to respected opinion, social deviance, or lawbreaking. For example, a driver venturing on a short journey at night without functioning lights probably does not feel that his life is at risk, but may well fear that the police will stop him, or that other drivers will protest, or that if an accident does happen he will be made to take the blame, or even that to behave in such a way is to act in a foolish and uncaring manner inconsistent with his image of himself. The balance may, in other words, be a moral one. In general, the more that drivers are trained to be aware of hazards, the more moral aspects there will be of their actions in relation to them. The 'hidden agenda' of driver training, at present, is how to deal with these moral problems.

It is still possible to argue for a socially determined explanation of driver behaviour within what seems like a scientific framework by invoking concepts of social norms as determinants of behaviour. However, Gauld and Shotter (1977, pp. 66–75) argue strongly against such a view, holding that there is more to moral and cultural values than can be embedded in a theory based on the behaviour of majorities. In particular, they feel that theories of social behaviour fall short of giving a credible account of the assimilation of children into the culture. Their general observations on this (1977, p. 73) translate interestingly into the more limited instance of how a person learns what his culture regards as a safe way in which to conduct himself.

DIRECTIONS FOR ENQUIRY

It must by now be evident to the reader that hermeneutical enquiry, based on meaning and morality, is most unlikely to yield universal quantitative truths: the *sine qua non* of scientific research. What may be even harder to accept is that fact-finding, data-based research does not provide the basic material for the conceptual analysis required in an hermeneutical approach. Any issue involving the meaning of actions which is generally true among humans is also probably generally obvious, and thus does not require explanation. Hermeneutical explanation is more likely to be local in character, linked more to what obtains in the particular culture and circumstances than in general. It is interesting to note that Thom (1977) has made similar points in relation to catastrophe theory: warning that hopes of fitting catastrophe models neatly into the quantitative framework of social sciences are probably misplaced, and showing what can be done with mathematical theories concerned with the *neighbourhood* of a point in space.

However it is regarded, the promulgation of safety is a matter of social influence. Assuming that safe behaviour is not innate, and that it should not be acquired only by direct experience (i.e., of accidents), some persuasive process must take place. The scientific paradigm emphasizes the acquisition of skills and knowledge of contingencies; the hermeneutical paradigm is more concerned with how to interpret and evaluate situations, and how certain actions are regarded by people in the culture. In either case there is a clear need for rationality in matters of safety and the consequences of actions; there is no point in basing rules for the preservation of life and health on mere magic. Research of an epidemiological type, concerning the antecedents of accidents, will always be required, but it must not shrink from investigating antecedents in terms of their meaning to the agents involved. A mere behavioural analysis, however detailed, will never be enough. Deehy (1968), reported by Wilde (1976), provided what seems to have been a useful discussion of conformity to informal and formal rule systems, and other (rather inaccessible) sources cited in the same paper seem to have made a promising start by looking at instances of accidents and road behaviour. Hargreaves (1980) provides a useful typology of rules, distinguishing normative, implemental, probabilistic, and interpretive types, which could serve as a conceptual basis for an exploration of rule-governed action systems in driving and road use.

Finally, in case the threat of the armchair should seem too much for the active seeker after knowledge, there may be comfort in noting that evaluation research is an active and growing field, which is both localized in its application and developmental in nature (Campbell, 1969; Morris and Fitz-Gibbon, 1978). This kind of research, though empirical, does not seek universal generalizations, but is concerned with providing information for decision makers about programmes of intervention. Its techniques focus on the provision of credible information to those who can most usefully employ it, and thus can get closer to the hermeneutical goal of intersubjectively shared understanding than does most scientific research. In the fields of both safety and health, interventions may at first need to be small scale, and the outcomes measured in terms of short time scales, i.e., safety or health related behaviour and attitudes rather than accidents or morbidity. However, small programmes that really achieve understanding of what is happening may well prove cumulatively to be more use than large-scale impersonal studies whose well-documented outcomes could reasonably have been expected before they were undertaken.

This paper has raised some difficult and perhaps unpalatable issues for ergonomists. Perhaps the last word should be Shotter's (1975, p. 135):

> The truth about people, about human nature, then, is not something that is awaiting discovery, ready made, like something under a stone on a beach: it can only be made by people in dialogue, as the product of a social act, in continual mutual interrogation and reply.

REFERENCES

Campbell, D. (1969) Reforms as experiments. *American Psychologist*, **24**, 409–29.

Chapman, A. J., and Jones, D. M. (1980) *Models of Man*. Leicester: British Psychological Society.

Deehy, P. T. (1968) Sociology and road safety. In: *Proceedings of a Seminar*, at Kingston, Ontario, The Engineering Institute of Canada, Committee on Road Safety Research.

Gauld, A., and Shotter, J. (1977) *Human Action and its Psychological Investigation*. London: Routledge & Kegan Paul.

Hargreaves, D. H. (1980) Common-sense models of action. In: A. J. Chapman and D. M. Jones (Eds), *Models of Man*. Leicester: British Psychological Society, pp. 215–25.

Joynson, R. L. (1974) *Psychology and Common Sense*. London: Routledge & Kegan Paul.

Morris, L. L., and Fitz-Gibbon, C. T. (1978) *Evaluator's Handbook*. Beverly Hills: Sage.

Reason, J. T. (1979) Actions not as planned: the price of automatization. In: G. Underwood and R. Stevens (Eds), *Aspects of Consciousness*, Vol. I. New York: Wiley, pp. 67–90.

Schutz, A. (1960) The social world and the theory of social action. *Social Research*, **27**, 203–21.

Shotter, J. (1975) *Images of Man in Psychological Research*. London: Methuen.

Shotter, J. (1980) Men the magicians: the duality of social being and the structure of moral worlds. In: A. J. Chapman and D. M. Jones (Eds), *Models of Man*. Leicester: British Psychological Society, pp. 13–34.

Taylor, D. H. (1976) Accidents, risks, and models of explanation. *Human Factors*, **18**, 371–80.

Taylor, D. H. (1980) The new psychology in transport research. In: *Proceedings of the World Conference on Transport Research*, London.

Thom, R. (1975) *Structural Stability and Morphogenesis* (translated by D. H. Fowler). Reading, Mass.: Benjamin.

Thom, R. (1977) Structural stability, catastrophe theory, and applied mathematics. *SIAM Review*, **19**, 189–201.

Wilde, G. J. S. (1976) Social interaction patterns in driver behaviour: an introductory review. *Human Factors*, **18**, 477–92.

Winch, P. (1958) *The Idea of a Social Science and its Relations to Philosophy*. London: Routledge & Kegan Paul.

Zeeman, E. C. (1976) Catastrophe theory. *Scientific American*, **234**, 65–70, 75–83.

New Technology and Human Error
Edited by J. Rasmussen, K. Duncan and J. Leplat
© 1987 John Wiley & Sons Ltd

Part 2: Cognitive Error Mechanisms and Error Control

INTRODUCTION

The discussion of the relationship between human error mechanisms and the control of cognitive processes in Chapters 5 and 6 of Part 2 is closely related to the discussion of taxonomies in Part 1.

The basic structure of the models of cognitive control discussed by Reason and Rasmussen in Part 1 is very similar. Reason describes control in terms of a volatile *database* and a set of *mental operations* on this database controlled by *schemata*. Rasmussen talks about *data* and *strategies* for operations on the data by means of an information-processing model. There is, however, no simple one-to-one mapping between these frameworks. Reason's distinctions relate to classical psychological concepts such as short- and long-term memory and Bartlett's schemata. Rasmussen's distinctions are derived from information processing and control concepts. This leads Rasmussen to distinguish between three levels of cognitive control: skill-based behaviour which is characterized by patterns of movements generated from an internal dynamic world model, the rule-based level where control depends on implicit models of the environment embedded in procedural rules, and the knowledge-based level depending on structural models, mental models, of the environment. This framework is directed towards a clear separation of the representation of structural or declarative from procedural information because this is important for the specification of requirements for interface design. In Reason's approach this distinction is not sought since the focus is on psychological mechanisms. Schemata, for instance, are related to the structure of memory and, therefore, will represent structural as well as procedural information.

In consequence, the mapping between the concepts of the two approaches is complicated and is as yet not resolved. Further exploration appears to be important for a better bridge between research and design of systems based on advanced information technology.

Two papers by de Keyser and Herry, which are introduced in Part 6, are touched on briefly here since they both focus upon the difference in cognitive control applied by different members of a work organization. These issues are again considered in the general discussion in Part 8. A key point made by de Keyser is the limited capability of formal knowledge to support the operator's interpretation of plant phenomena. Her paper (Chapter 22) provides important evidence on errors related to the transition between the novices' dependence on formal knowledge and the development with experience of know-how, or in Rasmussen's terms, the transition between knowledge-based and rule-based behaviour. This evidence should be compared to Rasmussen's discussion of the operators' difficulties in switching from their normally effective know-how to more functional reasoning during abnormal plant conditions, and to Reason's discussion of the interaction between the attentional processing mode and the default mode controlled by schemata. Difference in control is also found by Herry when comparing the cognitive structure revealed by explanations offered by her 'expert' and skilled workers. Again, the conceptual mapping from these two papers on to those of Reason and Rasmussen is not straightforward and a more detailed exploration should be made.

These clarifications of the relationships between the different conceptual frameworks are important in order to bridge the gap between psychological research and systems design. Research and systems design may very well need different conceptual frameworks but it is important that they are compatible.

The paper by Herry introduces the concept of 'an expert', which in her context is a term for the engineer, the designer, or another person with formal, functional knowledge of the processes of a plant to be controlled by operators. Very often, advanced information technology is introduced under the catch phrase of 'expert systems'. In this context, an expert whose knowledge is sought for implementation in an advisory computer system, is a skilled person with a large repertoire of routines and procedural rules within a particular professional domain. This point is also mentioned by Lucas in Part 8. In this sense, operators are as much experts as engineers, but in another domain. Indeed, some experienced industrial operators are experts while 'expert systems', as yet, are not.

Finally, the third paper (Chapter 7), by Reason, added after the workshop, illustrates the ongoing discussion in its attempt to combine the approaches of Reason and Rasmussen into a single framework for system design consideration and for planning experimental research.

New Technology and Human Error
Edited by J. Rasmussen, K. Duncan and J. Leplat
© 1987 John Wiley & Sons Ltd

5. The Psychology of Mistakes: A Brief Review of Planning Failures

James Reason
University of Manchester

SUMMARY

Three sources of bias in the planning process are discussed: (a) those intrinsic to the properties of the working database; (b) those emanating from mental operations; and (c) those arising from schema properties.

INTRODUCTION

Human error can be conveniently divided into two broad classes: slips and mistakes. Slips are defined as errors which result from some failure in the execution stage of an action sequence, whereas mistakes have their origins in the planning phase (Norman, 1981; Reason and Mycielska, 1982). Thus, mistakes are deficiencies or failures in the judgemental and/or inferential processes involved in the selection of an objective or in the specification of the means to achieve it, irrespective of whether or not the actions directed by this decision-scheme run according to plan.

Although the matter of slips is far from settled, there exist considerably more data and theory bearing upon their forms and underlying mechanisms than is the case for mistakes. Yet mistakes are likely to be more subtle, more complex, and, as a result, more dangerous than slips. The aim of this paper is to go some small way towards redressing this imbalance by focusing upon what has been learned over the past decade or so regarding the more predictable varieties of mistakes.

A BRIEF SKETCH OF THE PLANNING PROCESS

Below is presented a simple model of the psychological processes involved in planning. It has three major components: a working database, a set of mental operations that act upon this database, and the schemata, or the structures comprising the long-term knowledge base (Bartlett, 1932; Bobrow and Norman, 1975; Neisser, 1976; Bransford, 1979; Taylor and Crocker, 1981; Hastie, 1981; Brewer and Nakamura, 1984). Also assumed but not specified in any detail are the input and output functions linking the planner to the world.

The working database

This contains the information currently being used in the planning process, and corresponds to the working memory/attention/consciousness constructions of contemporary information-processing models. The database is limited in capacity and continuously variable in content. At least three kinds of information are likely to be present within it: that derived directly from the environment via the input function; that which has been intentionally called up from the schema base; and that which has been spontaneously thrown up by active, though not necessarily plan-relevant, schemata.

The mental operations

Three interrelated operations are involved: selection, judgement, and decision making. The contents of the working database may, in part at least, be selected by the planner, both from the immediate environment and from the long-term schema store. The judgements are of two kinds: those concerned with goal setting and those relating to goal achievement. In the former, various desired outcomes are considered and then assigned weightings according to the judged likelihood of their attainability. In the latter, a similar set of judgements is applied to the alternative means by which these outcomes could be achieved. Finally, decisions are made on the basis of these judgements as to the outcome to be pursued, and the sequence of future actions by which it is to be attained.

Taken in isolation, the planning process may be broken down into four stages: (a) the setting of objectives; (b) the search for alternative courses of action; (c) comparing and evaluating alternatives; and (d) deciding upon the appropriate course of action. This presents a static and idealized picture of the planning process; more often, it occurs in the context of ongoing behaviour in which the feedback generated by action demands a continual reassessment of the plan.

The schemata

Schemata are involved in all stages of the planning process. They contribute both selected (i.e., plan-relevant) and uncalled-for information to the working database. The latter will take the form of conscious fragments (images and words) thrown up by highly activated schemata. These fragments are likely to include emotionally charged material, stored information triggered by the environmental context, or through association with plan elements, or they may be the outputs from recently and/or frequently used schemata.

Since schemata generate the major part of the working database, their products will constitute the manipulanda of the mental operations discussed above. And, once formulated, the plan itself will consist of a sequence of schematically controlled operations. Although we cannot specify precisely how this occurs, it is reasonable to suppose that the completed plan is stored as a set of sequentially linked schemata that are primed to go into action at a given time, or when certain environmental conditions are met.

POSSIBLE SOURCES OF BIAS LEADING TO MISTAKES

From what is known of the heuristics influencing judgement, the limits of human information processing, and the generally agreed characteristics of schema function, it is possible to make a number of predictions about when distortions will be introduced into the planning process, and what form they will take. These can be summarized under three headings, each relating to a component of the planning model.

Sources of bias in the working database

1. At any one moment, the working database will 'display' only a small fraction of all the information potentially available and relevant to the plan in question (Simon, 1957).
2. Of the several factors (variables) that might potentially bear upon the planning process, not more than two or three of them are likely to be represented in the database at any one time (see Shepard, 1964; Slovic and Lichtenstein, 1971; Inbar, 1979).
3. Only a small proportion of the time available will be taken up with planning, and even in one time period, this activity is unlikely to be sustained for more than a few seconds. And, when planning is resumed, the contents of the working database will be different.
4. The information represented in the working database will be more congruent with existing schemata than is justified by the total amount of information that could bear upon the planning process. Or, to put it another way, planning is more shaped by past experience than is appropriate, given the possible variability of future events.
5. The information 'called' into the working database from the schema store will be biased in favour of those items that are most readily available (i.e., activated), a feature that may be more potent than the objective relevance of the information. This potential source of distortion is further enhanced by the fact that the database will also contain 'uncalled-for' fragments from activated schemata. This will mean that emotionally

charged material, contextually relevant information (irrespective of whether it is plan relevant), and recently or frequently used information will have privileged access to the working database, regardless of its bearing on the plan.

6. The information contained in the working database will be biased in favour of past successes rather than past failures. Thus plans are likely to include operations that have proved successful in the past, and these may have dubious utility in the present situation (Bruner *et al.*, 1956; Luchins and Luchins, 1959 — the Einstellung effect).

7. Some of the information contained in the working database will have been cued by local environmental factors. The more vivid and attention-grabbing this information, the more likely it is to be incorporated into the planning process, irrespective of its objective relevance (see Bacon's 'Idols' — Anderson, 1960).

Sources of bias in the mental operations

1. Planners, being guided primarily by past events, will underestimate the likelihood of the unexpected or chance intervention. As a consequence, they will plan for fewer contingencies than are likely to occur.

2. Planners will give inferential weight to information in proportion to its vividness, or emotional impact. This is likely to outweigh its objective value in the planning process (see Nisbett and Ross, 1980).

3. Planners' characterization of data is heavily influenced by their theories. Where these theories are inappropriate, systematic sources of bias will be introduced into the planning process. One predictable consequence of being 'theory-driven' is that planners will unconsciously fill in the missing details in the available evidence in accord with the dictates of their theories. Subsequently, they may be unable to distinguish in recollection between those data that were actually present and those supplied schematically (see Bransford, 1979).

4. Planners are not good at assessing population parameters on the basis of data samples. They are not aware that more available instances tend to bias their characterization of the sample unduly. They also have little appreciation of the unreliability of small samples or of the effects of bias in the sampling procedures (see Nisbett and Ross, 1980).

5. Planners are poor at detecting many types of covariation. Partly, they have little understanding of the basic logic of covariation, and partly they are disposed to detect covariation only when their theories of the world are likely to predict it (see Chapman and Chapman, 1967 — 'illusory correlation').

6. Planners will be subject to the 'halo effect'. That is, they will show a predilection for single orderings (De Soto, 1961), and an aversion to

discrepant orderings. They have difficulty independently processing two separate orderings of the same people or objects. Hence, they reduce these discrepant orderings to a single ordering by merit.

7. Planners tend to have an overly simplistic view of causality. Causal analysis is heavily influenced by both the representativeness and availability heuristics. The former indicates that they are likely to judge causality on the basis of perceived similarity between cause and effect. The latter means that causal explanations of events are at the mercy of arbitrary shifts in the salience of possible explanatory factors. This is also compounded by the belief that a given event can only have one sufficient cause (see Nisbett and Ross, 1980). Planners are also likely to suffer from what Fischhoff (1975) has called 'creeping determinism' or hindsight bias; that is, knowledge of the outcome of a past event increases the perceived likelihood of that outcome. It is possible that this may also lead planners to overestimate their ability to influence future events (Langer, 1975 — illusion of control).

8. Planners are likely to be over-confident in evaluating the correctness of their knowledge (Koriat *et al.*, 1980). Thus, they will tend to justify their chosen course of action by focusing on evidence which favours it, and by disregarding contradictory signs. This tendency is further compounded by the confirmation bias exerted by a completed plan (see below).

9. Planners are likely to perform poorly when predicting future events. This arises partly because of their failure to understand statistical principles, notably regression, and partly because they greatly over-utilize the representativeness heuristic. That is, they tend to match the features of the present evidence with those of a possible outcome, and predict that this evidence will lead to that outcome to the extent that its features resemble those of the outcome. They are also likely to make inadequate use of base-rate information (Tversky and Kahneman, 1974).

Schematic sources of bias

These have been largely covered in the preceding two sections. However, there is a further set of biases that comes into effect after the plan has been formulated and before it is executed. These stem primarily from the overwhelming urge to seek confirmatory evidence for the validity of the now established plan of action. The reverse side of this coin is the planner's inability to assimilate additional information which suggests that the plan might fail.

A completed plan is not only a set of directions for later action, it is also a theory concerning the future state of the world. It confers order and reduces anxiety. As such, it will be strongly resistant to change, even in the face of fresh information clearly indicating that the planned actions are unlikely to achieve their objective, or that the objective itself is unrealistic. This resistance of the completed plan to being modified or jettisoned is likely to be greatest under the following conditions.

1. When the plan is very elaborate, involving the detailed intermeshing of several different action sequences. That is, when the plan represents a complex theory.
2. When the plan was the product of considerable labour and emotional investment, and when its completion was associated with a marked reduction in tension or anxiety (Festinger, 1954 — dissonance reduction).
3. When the time interval separating its completion from its intended execution is relatively long.
4. When the plan is the brain child of many people.
5. When the plan has hidden objectives; that is, when it is conceived, either consciously or unconsciously, to satisfy a number of different needs or motives.

Nevertheless, even the most complacent of planners is likely to review his or her plans at some time prior to their execution. But here again, distortions creep in. One question they are likely to ask themselves is: 'Have I taken account of all the possible factors bearing upon my choice of action?' They will then review their recollections of the planning process to check on the factors they considered. This search will probably reveal what appears to be a satisfactory number; but as Shepard (1964) pointed out: '. . . although we remember that at some time or other we have attended to each of the different factors, we fail to notice that it is seldom more than one or two that we consider at any one time' (p. 266). Thus, in retrospect, we overlook that the working database was, at any one moment, limited in scope, and that its contents were rapidly changing fragments rather than systematic reviews of the relevant material. We can term this the 'check-off' illusion.

In summary, it can be seen that these various sources of distortion are likely to lead to an inadequate database, unrealistic goal setting, faulty judgements of the likely consequences of actions, and an unwarranted confidence in the efficacy of the resulting plan. These, in turn, stem from the following characteristics of the human planner.

1. A limited capacity working database whose contents are in continual flux.
2. An unwillingness or an inability to sustain an attentional–rational mode of thought for more than brief periods at a time.
3. A tendency for information processing to slip unawares into the 'default' or schematic mode.
4. The possession of a virtually limitless long-term memory that contains

theories or models of the world rather than isolated facts, and which is capable of processing information effortlessly and in parallel so long as the data conform to the theories.

5. And, dominating these features, is a powerful urge to make sense of all information, whether internally or externally generated. This 'effort after meaning' (Bartlett, 1932) is so overwhelming that we are prepared to be mistaken in particular instances as long as we can preserve order within the world at large (Nisbett and Ross, 1980).

REFERENCES

Anderson, F. H. (1960) *Bacon: The New Organon*. Indianopolis: Bobbs-Merill.

Bartlett, F. E. (1932) *Remembering*. Cambridge: Cambridge University Press.

Bobrow, D. G., and Normann, D. A. (1975) Some principles of memory schemata. In: D. Bobrow and A. Collins (Eds), Representation and Understanding: Studies in Cognitive Science. New York: Academic Press.

Bransford, J. D. (1979) *Human Cognition: Learning, Understanding and Remembering*. Belmont: Wadsworth.

Brewer, W. F., and Nakamura, G. U. (1984) The nature and function of schemas. In: R. Wyer and T. Srull (Eds), *Handbook of Social Cognition*. Hillsdale, NJ: Erlbaum.

Bruner, J. S., Goodnow, J. J., and Austin, G. A. (1956) *A Study of Thinking*. New York: Wiley.

Chapman, L. J., and Chapman, J. P. (1967) Genesis of popular but erroneous diagnostic observations. *Journal of Abnormal Psychology*, **72**, 193–204.

De Soto, C. B. (1961) The predilection for single orderings. *Journal of Abnormal and Social Psychology*, **62**, 16–23.

Festinger, L. (1954) A theory of social comparison process. *Human Relations*, **7**, 117–40.

Fischhoff, B. (1975) Hindsight does not equal foresight: the effect of outcome knowledge on judgement under uncertainty. *Journal of Experimental Psychology* (HP & P), **1**, 288–99.

Hastie, R. (1981) Schematic principles in human memory. In: E. T. Higgins, C. P. Herman, and M. P. Zanna (Eds), *Social Cognition: The Ontario Symposium*, Vol. 1. Hillsdale, NJ: Erlbaum.

Inbar, M. (1979) *Routine Decision-Making*. Beverly Hills: Sage.

James, W. (1908) *Talks to Teachers on Psychology and to Students on some of Life's Ideals*. London: Longmans, Green & Co.

Koriat, A., Lichtenstein, S., and Fischhoff, B. (1980) Reasons for confidence. *Journal of Experimental Psychology* (HL & M), **6**, 107–17.

Langer, E. J. (1975) The illusion of control. *Journal of Personality and Social Psychology*, **7**, 185–207.

Luchins, A. S., and Luchins, E. M. (1950) New experimental attempts at presenting mechanization. *Journal General Psychology*, **42**, 279–97.

Neisser, U. (1976) *Cognition and Reality*. San Francisco: Freeman.

Nisbett, R., and Ross, L. (1980) *Human Inference: Strategies and Shortcomings of Social Judgment*. Englewood Cliffs: Prentice-Hall.

Norman, D. A. (1981) Categorization of action slips. *Psychological Review*, **88**, 1–15.

Reason, J. T., and Mycielska, K. (1982) *Absent-Minded? The Psychology of Mental*

Lapses and Everyday Errors. Englewood Cliffs, NJ: Prentice-Hall.

Shepard, R. N. (1964) On the subjectively optimum selection among multiattribute alternatives. In: M. W. Shelly and G. L. Bryan (Eds), *Human Judgments and Optimality*. New York: Wiley.

Simon, H. A. (1957) *Models of Man*. New York: Wiley.

Slovic, R., and Lichtenstein, S. C. (1971) Comparison of Bayesian and regression approaches to the study of information processing in judgment. *Organizational Behaviour and Human Performance*, **6**, 649–744.

Taylor, S. E., and Crocker, J. C. (1981) Schematic bases of social information processing. In: E. T. Higgins, P. Herman, and M. P. Zanna (Eds), *Social Cognition: The Ontario Symposium*, Vol. 1. Hillsdale, NJ: Erlbaum.

Tversky, A., and Kahneman, D. (1974) Judgement and uncertainty: Heuristics and biases. *Science*, **185**, 1124–31.

New Technology and Human Error
Edited by J. Rasmussen, K. Duncan and J. Leplat
© 1987 John Wiley & Sons Ltd

6. Cognitive Control and Human Error Mechanisms

Jens Rasmussen
Risø National Laboratory

SUMMARY

Cognitive control domains are discussed in terms of skill-, rule-, and knowledge-based behaviour. This distinction is used to characterize the psychological mechanisms behind typical categories of errors considered as occurrences of man–task mismatches. The relationship of errors with human learning and adaptation is stressed.

INTRODUCTION

When analysing reports describing incidents and accidents in industrial installations, it becomes clear that different cognitive control mechanisms should be considered in order to explain the different types of 'human errors' which appear, depending on the familiarity of the work situation in question. From such an analysis, three levels of cognitive control can be identified which depend on different kinds of knowledge about the environment and different interpretation of the available information (Rasmussen, 1980, 1983).

THE SKILL–RULE–KNOWLEDGE FRAMEWORK

A model representing human control of behaviour in terms of a hierarchical control structure as the one illustrated in Figure 1 is well suited to discuss mismatches in the human interaction with a dynamic environment from a system engineering point of view. Quite naturally, however, the model appears to be compatible with psychological descriptions of the different phases of skill acquisition (Fitts and Posner, 1962).

The model distinguishes between three levels of cognitive control which are related to a decreasing familiarity with environment: the levels of skill-, rule-, and knowledge-based behaviour.

The *skill-based behaviour* represents sensori-motor performance during acts or activities which, following a statement of an intention take place without conscious control as smooth, automated and highly integrated patterns of behaviour.

At the *skill-based* level the perceptual-motor system acts as a multivariable, continuous control system synchronizing the physical activity such as navigating the body through the environment and manipulating external objects in a time–space domain. For this control the sensed information is perceived as time–space *signals*, continuous, quantitative indicators of the time–space behaviour of the environment. These signals have no 'meaning' or significance except as direct physical time–space data. The performance at the skill-based level may be released or guided by value features attached by prior experience to certain patterns in the information not taking part in the time–space control but acting as cues or *signs* activating the organism. Performance is based on feedforward control and depends upon a very flexible and efficient dynamic internal world model.

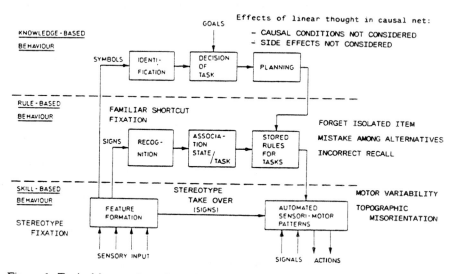

Figure 1. Typical human 'error' mechanisms and their relations to control of behaviour. (From Rasmussen, 1980, with permission from John Wiley & Sons Ltd.)

At the next level of *rule-based behaviour*, the composition of a sequence of subroutines in a familiar work situation is typically controlled by a *stored rule* or procedure which may have been derived empirically during previous occasions, communicated from other persons' know-how as an instruction or cookbook recipe, or it may be prepared on occasion by conscious problem solving and planning. The point is here that performance is goal oriented, but structured by 'feedforward control' through a stored rule. Very often, the goal is not even explicitly formulated, but is found implicitly in the situation releasing the stored rules. The control is teleological in the sense that the rule or control is selected from previous successful experiences. The control evolves by 'survival of the fittest' rule. Furthermore, in actual life, the goal will only be reached after a long sequence of acts, and direct feedback correction considering the goal may not be possible.

At the rule-based level, the information is typically perceived as *signs*. The information perceived is defined as a sign when it serves to activate or modify predetermined actions or manipulations. Signs refer to situations or proper behaviour by convention or prior experience; they do not refer to concepts or represent functional properties of the environment. Signs are generally labelled by names which may refer to states or situations in the environment or to goals and tasks of a person. Signs can only be used to select or modify the rules controlling the sequencing of skilled subroutines; they cannot be used for functional reasoning, to generate new rules, or to predict the response of an environment to unfamiliar disturbances. During unfamiliar situations, faced with an environment for which no know-how or rules for control are available from previous encounters, the control of performance must move to a higher conceptual level, in which performance is goal controlled, and *knowledge based*. In this situation, the goal is explicitly formulated, based on an analysis of the environment and the overall aims of the person. Then a useful plan is developed — by selection, such that different plans are considered and their effect tested against the goal, physically by trial and error, or conceptually by means of understanding of the functional properties of the environment and prediction of the effects of the plan considered. At this level of functional reasoning, the internal structure of the system is explicitly represented by a 'mental model' which may take several different forms.

To be useful for causal functional reasoning in order to predict or explain unfamiliar behaviour of the environment, information must be perceived as *symbols*. While signs refer to percepts and rules for action, symbols refer to concepts tied to functional properties and can be used for reasoning and computation by means of a suitable representation of such properties. Signs have external reference to states of and actions upon the environment, but symbols are defined by and refer to the internal, conceptual representation which is the basis for reasoning and planning.

During training in a particular task, control moves from the knowledge- or rule-based levels towards the skill-based control, as familiarity with the work scenarios is developed. An important point is that it is *not* the control processes of the higher levels that are automated. Automated manual skills are developing while they are controlled and supervised at the higher levels. When explicit knowledge or rules are no longer needed for behavioural control during normal work, they may eventually deteriorate. With respect to error observability, it is a problem at the skill- and rule-based levels that the goals are not explicitly controlling the activity. This means that errors during performance may only be evident at a very late stage — an error in the use of a recipe may not manifest itself until you taste the cake, i.e., when the *product* is present. Early detection of the effect of one's own variability (or of changes in system conditions) depends on an ability to monitor the *process*, i.e., on knowledge-based monitoring based on understanding of the underlying processes. For error detection it may therefore be important to maintain knowledge, even though high skill is developed.

Within this framework, different typical mechanisms which can lead to man–system mismatch are discussed on the following pages. A more thorough illustration by examples can be found in Rasmussen (1986).

MECHANISMS BEHIND MAN–SYSTEM MISMATCHES

Discussing these mechanisms, we are considering those occasions when a man–system interaction is judged a mismatch which needs correction. This judgement may be made by the person himself or by somebody else at a later instance. Typically, mismatches are corrected immediately by the person, but the success of the correction depends very much upon qualities of the task and environment, such as observability and reversibility, and should be discussed separately from the mechanisms behind the initial mismatch which led to a corrective action or adaptive change in behaviour.

Human variability during familiar tasks

We will first consider intrinsic human variability which leads to mismatches during normal work situations, i.e., we consider the effect of variability upon skill- and rule-based behaviour. Two types of mismatches are frequently found: (a) *motor variability* — the time–space precision of *skill-based* sensori-motor control may not be adequate for the task at hand, leading to occasional mismatches; (b) *topographic misorientation* is another mechanism of mismatches during sensori-motor performance, occurring when the internal world model of some cause loses synchronism with the external world.

These are mechanisms within a single motor schema; other mechanisms are related to the fact that skilled operators have a large repertoire of schemata, and that a schema may involve a long sequence of acts. A single conscious statement of intention may activate a schema, whereafter the attention may be directed towards planning of future activities or monitoring the past. The current, unmonitored schema will then be sensitive to inter-ference leading to *stereotype takeover*. This means another schema takes over the control, either because a part of current action sequence is also part of another frequently used schema, or due to interfering intentions of the detached attention.

Since the repertoire of automated sensori-motor schemata and their complexity increases with the skill which operators develop during their daily interaction with their system, the role of this kind of mismatch becomes more important with their experience, and can only be counteracted by making systems more 'error' tolerant.

At the *rule-based level*, human variability during performance of the normal, familiar tasks is most frequently found as incorrect recall of rules and know-how. A characteristic category is *forgetting an isolated item*, i.e., which is not an integrated part of a larger memory structure. Typical is *omission of an isolated act* which is not a necessary part of the main task sequence. Typical examples are forgetting to restore normal conditions after repair or calibrations. The fact that the omitted steps are frequently unrelated to the verbal label of the task may be a condition directly contributing to their frequency. Analysis of industrial fires led Whorf (1956) to the conclusion that 'the name of a situation affects behaviour'. A closely related mechanism is the *incorrect recall of isolated items*, such as quantitative figures, numbers, etc.

Another frequent mechanism of variability during familiar tasks is the *mistake among alternatives*, which frequently appears as incorrect choice of one of a couple of possible alternatives to use, such as left–right, up–down, plus–minus, A–B, etc.

These are all mismatch events caused by human variability in normal, familiar task situations. Other mechanisms lead to mismatch, when humans fail to adapt adequately to variations and changes in the task environment.

Improper human adaptation to system changes

The efficiency of human interaction with the environment at the skill-based level is due to a high degree of fine tuning of the sensori-motor schemata to the time–space features in the environment. Changes in the environment will often be met by an updating of the current schema by a subconscious reaction to cues or a consciously expressed intention: 'Now look, be careful, the road is icy'.

However, as mentioned above, frequently the updating of the current schema will not take place until a mismatch has occurred, for instance, when walking on to more uneven ground, adaptation of the current motor schema to the actual features of the environment may first happen after the feet have detected the mismatch by stumbling. The point here is that adaptation and fine tuning of sensori-motor schemata basically depend upon mismatch occurrences for optimal adjustments. The proper limits for fine tuning can only be found if surpassed once in a while. This means that mismatches cannot — and should not — be avoided, but a system must be tolerant and not respond irreversibly. This discussion relates to mismatches which are needed to control adaptation within the skill-based level. More serious mismatch categories are met when changes in the environment are not met by proper activation of higher level control of behaviour.

Two types of mismatch mechanisms are related to *improper activation of rule-based control*: stereotype fixation, and stereotype takeover, similar to that discussed on page 56.

Stereotype fixation represents the situation when a sensori-motor schema is activated in an improper context, and the person on afterthought very well knows what he should have done. He does not switch to proper rule-based control.

In other cases people realize the need for use of special procedures, but relapse to familiar routines, i.e., *stereotype takes over* because of overlapping sequence elements.

Similar difficulties in proper adaptation to system changes by switching to knowledge-based behaviour are caused by the reliance on *signs* during all familiar situations. The high efficiency of human interaction with objects and other persons of everyday life is due to a large repertoire of skilled subroutines and of rules, know-how for updating the routines and linking them together. The control is based on recognition of the state of affairs in the environment in terms of signs, which relates to the appropriate rules by convention or experience. Even in direct interaction with the physical environment, these signs will be convenient correlates in the given context rather than defining attributes. This makes the interaction susceptible to mistakes if the environment changes in a way which does not affect the signs, but makes the related behaviour inappropriate. This is basically the idea behind all kind of hunting traps.

In the direct interaction with a physical world, identification of signs takes place by perceptual categorization, which can be based on complex patterns and therefore also be rather sensitive to changes. This is typically not the case for human interaction with complex industrial systems, where operators are controlling more or less invisible processes. They have to infer the state and select proper actions from a set of physical measurements which is seldom presented in a way which allows perceptual identification of the state; operators are supposed to apply conceptual categorization based on rational reasoning, i.e., to exhibit knowledge-based reasoning. For several reasons, this leads to difficulties for human operators to adapt appropriately to changes in the system as for instance caused by technical faults.

The use of a set of measured variables requires knowledge of the system in terms of engineers' conception as a network of quantitative relations among variables. Natural language reasoning, which is typically used for control of the systems, is, however, not based on nets of relations among variables, but upon linear sequences of events in a system of interacting components or functions. To circumvent the need for mental effort to derive states and events from the sets of variables and their relations, operators generally use indications which are typical for the normal events and states, including informal signals as motor and relay noise, as convenient signs for familiar states in the system. This is a very effective and mentally economic strategy during normal and familiar periods, but leads the operator into traps when changes in plant conditions are not adequately reflected in his set of signs. Such mental traps often contribute significantly to the operator's misidentification of unfamiliar, complex plant states. Therefore, to adapt performance to the requirements of a system in a unique and unfamiliar state, the operators must not only switch to knowledge-based reasoning based on a mental model of the system's internal, functional properties; he must also replace his perception of information as signs with an analytical interpretation as symbols. This appears to be very difficult, since the use of signs basically means that information from the system is not really observed, but is obtained by 'asking questions' which are heavily biased by expectations based on a set of well-known situations.

Taken together, these aspects force one to draw the conclusion that there is a considerable probability that highly skilled operators with a large repertoire of convenient signs and related know-how will not switch to analytical reasoning when required, if they find a familiar subset of data during their reading of instruments. They will rather run into a 'procedural trap' and be caught by a *'familiar association short-cut'*.

Errors during knowledge-based reasoning

Once an operator has succeeded in shifting to analytical functional reasoning at the level of knowledge-based behaviour, it is very difficult to characterize his mental data processing and the related mechanisms leading to mismatch.

At the skill- and rule-based levels, behaviour is controlled by motor schemata and know-how rules, the goals are implicitly specified, and 'error' mechanisms are described in terms related to established, 'normal' action sequences in a rather behaviouristic way. At the knowledge-based level, this is not possible. The sequence of arguments an operator will use during problem solving cannot be described in general terms, the goal to pursue must be explicitly considered, and the actual choice depends on very subjective and situation-dependent features. At the skill- and rule-based levels, it is known per definition that adaptation to changes is within the human capability since we are considering familiar tasks. This is not the case when knowledge-based performance is required during complex disturbances. Therefore, different kinds of mismatch situations may occur:

1. Adaptation is outside the limits of capability, due to requirements for knowledge about system properties which is not available; for data which are not presented; or to excessive time or workload requirements.
2. Adaptation is possible, but unsuccessful due to inappropriate decisions, which result in acts upon the system, not conforming with actual require-

ments. It must be noted here that this is only 'errors' if they are not corrected timely; as discussed below actions not conforming with system requirements can be an important element during problem solving.

In the present context only the latter category is considered, and again different typical categories of mismatch situations can be found during any of the necessary phases of the decision making, such as identification of system state; evaluations and choice of ultimate goals; and planning of proper action sequence:

1. *Human variability in a cognitive task*, slips of memory, mistakes, interference from familiar lines of reasoning, etc. Mechanisms similar to those discussed above. They are difficult to identify or to use in prediction, when the problem-solving process is as unconstrained as it is in a real life task in a control room.
2. Errors caused by the difficulty of keeping track of sequential reasoning in a causal structure, which is in fact a complex network, unsuited for linear reasoning. The mental workload involved may lead to adoption of premature hypotheses from the influence of factors as the 'way of least resistance' and the 'point of no return', leading to *lack of consideration* of *important conditions* or *unacceptable side effects* by the ultimate decision.
3. Actions not conforming with system requirements may not be related to the ultimate result of erroneous decision making, but a reasonable act to *test a hypothesis* or get information which, however, may bring the system into a more complex and less controllable state.
4. The need for human decision making during disturbed system conditions basically depends on functional redundancy in the purpose/function/equipment relationships of the system. There is a complex many-to-many mapping between the levels in this hierarchy and during search for resources to resolve the various goals in a complex situation, operators may very likely be caught by familiar or proceduralized relationships serving goals which are not relevant in the present situation. Decision errors during complex disturbances are not stochastic events, but very often reasonable mistakes caused by interference in this mapping.

The conclusion is that in present-day control rooms based on individual presentation of the measured variables, the context in which operators make decisions at the knowledge-based level is far too unstructured to allow the development of a model of their problem-solving process, and hence, to identify typical 'error' modes, except in very general terms, such as 'lack of consideration of latent conditions or side effects' (Rasmussen, 1980).

As a basis for a useful model, the conceptual framework within which the operators have to make decision, has to be modelled in a consistent way in terms of the system's purpose/function/equipment hierarchy. As Simon notes (Simon, 1969) 'the complexity of human behaviour largely reflects the complexity of his environment . . .'. Before his behaviour can be modelled, a systematic description of his decision-making context must be found in order to identify likely interferences. Secondly, realistic models will probably only be possible, if his choice of goals and strategies is more constrained and controlled than is the case in present-day control rooms. This is possible if a computer-controlled presentation of a symbolic framework is developed, which may lead to skill- and rule-based problem solving in an externalized, mental model.

REFERENCES

Fitts, P. M., and Posner, M. I. (1962) *Human Performance*. Belmont, CA: Brooks/ Cole.

Rasmussen, J. (1980) What can be learned from human error reports? In: K. Duncan, M. Gruneberg, and D. Wallis (Eds), *Changes in Working Life*. John Wiley.

Rasmussen, J. (1983) Skills, rules, knowledge; signals, signs, and symbols; and other distinctions in human performance models. *IEEE Transactions on Systems, Man, and Cybernetics*, Vol. SMC-13, No. 3.

Rasmussen, J. (1986) *Information Processing and Human–machine Interaction: An Approach to Cognitive Engineering*. New York: Elsevier Scientific.

Simon, H. A. (1969) *The Sciences of the Artificial*. Cambridge, Mass.: MIT Press.

Whorf, B. L. (1956) The relation of habitual thought and behaviour to language. In: J. B. Carroll (Ed.), *Language, Thought and Reality, Selected Writings of Whorf*. Cambridge, Mass.: MIT Press.

New Technology and Human Error
Edited by J. Rasmussen, K. Duncan and J. Leplat
© 1987 John Wiley & Sons Ltd

7. Generic Error-Modelling System (GEMS): A Cognitive Framework for Locating Common Human Error Forms

James Reason
University of Manchester

SUMMARY

GEMS is a general framework for locating the principal limitations and biases giving rise to the more predictable varieties of human error. Three basic error types are identified: skill-based slips, rule-based mistakes, and knowledge-based mistakes.

AIMS

The purpose of GEMS is to provide a simple, generic (i.e., context-free) framework within which to locate the principal cognitive limitations and biases that give rise to the more predictable varieties of human error. It seeks to integrate two hitherto distinct areas of error research:

1. *Slips* Departures of action from intention, or execution failures (see Norman and Shallice, 1980; Norman, 1981; Reason and Mycielska, 1982).
2. *Mistakes* Errors in which the actions may run according to plan, but where the plan is inadequate to achieve its desired outcome (see Newell and Simon, 1972; Wason and Johnson-Laird, 1972; Rasmussen and Jensen, 1974; Nisbett and Ross, 1980; Rouse, 1981; Kahneman *et al.*, 1982; Evans, 1983; Hunt and Rouse, 1984).

BASIC ASSUMPTIONS

GEMS makes the following general assumptions concerning the 'architecture' of the cognitive system:

1. Cognitive control processes operate at various levels, and exert their influence simultaneously over widely differing time spans.
2. The higher levels of this control system can function over both long time

spans and a wide range of circumstances. These higher levels are primarily concerned with the setting of goals, with selecting the means to achieve them, and with monitoring progress towards these objectives. The products of this high-level planning and monitoring activity are available to consciousness. But since consciousness is a severely restricted 'window', it is usually the case that only one such high-level activity can be 'viewed' and modified at any one time. These resource limitations confer the important benefit of selectivity, since several high-level activities are likely to be potentially available to consciousness in a given period.

2. Higher level agencies can govern the order in which lower level processors are brought into play, but this control function is only intermittently exercised.

3. A substantial part of cognitive activity is governed by lower level processors (schemata, scripts, frames, heuristics, and rules) capable of independent function. Typically, these low-level processors operate over brief time spans in response to very specific data sets.

4. The successful repetition of any human activity results in the gradual devolution of control from the higher to the lower levels. Or, as William James (1890) succinctly put it: 'Habit diminishes the conscious attention with which our acts are performed.'

5. The control of human action arises from the interaction between two control modes: the *attentional* and the *schematic* modes. The former is closely identified with consciousness and working memory. It has powerful, analytical, feedback-driven, information-processing capabilities, and is essential for coping with novel or changed circumstances and for detecting and recovering slips. But it is also severely resource-limited, slow, laborious, sequential and difficult to sustain. The schematic mode, on the other hand, has no known limits on its capacity. It can process familiar information rapidly, in parallel, and without conscious involvement or effort. But it is ineffective in the face of novel or unforeseen circumstances.

6. Central to GEMS is Rasmussen's (1976, 1980) distinction between the *skill-based*, *rule-based*, and *knowledge-based* levels of performance. At the skill-based level, the informational content is in the form of *signals*, and performance is governed by stored patterns of preprogrammed instructions (schemata) represented as analogue structures in a time–space domain. At the rule-based level, performance is guided by *signs* relating to stored rules or productions (of the IF <situation> THEN <action> form). The knowledge-based level comes into play in novel situations for which actions must be planned on-line, through the manipulation of *symbols*. The skill- and rule-based levels most involve the schematic control mode, while the attentional mode predominates at the skill-based level.

7. The *predictable* varieties of human error have their origins in useful, functional, and adaptive processes. Systematic error forms are inextricably bound up with things at which the human cognitive system excels. Some aspects of this cognitive 'balance sheet' are summarized in Table 1. Correct performance and systematic errors are two sides of the same coin.

TABLE 1: *The cognitive 'balance sheet' showing the relationship between 'assets' (processes at which the cognitive system excels) and 'debits' (predictable error forms)*

ASSETS	DEBITS
Delegation of control to low-level automatic processors. This liberates resource-limited conscious processes for non-immediate concerns, e.g., planning future actions	'Strong-but-wrong' error forms
Selectivity: the limitations of the attentional resource permits focusing upon particular aspects of the world	Cognitive overload
Effort after meaning: long-term memory contains specialized 'theories' of the world rather than isolated facts	Confirmation bias
A *retrieval system* capable of locating items in an enormous knowledge base, usually performed both rapidly and accurately. This seems to relate to the user's metaknowledge or intuitive awareness of how the system works, e.g., the user knows what he/she doesn't know	Availability and matching biases. An over-reliance upon generally useful heuristics for accessing stored information

AN OVERVIEW OF GEMS

GEMS is a simplified composite of two sets of error theories: those of Norman (1981) and Reason and Mycielska (1982) relating to slips and lapses; and the GPS (Newell and Simon, 1972) tradition of problem-solving theorizing which has been applied to operator failures in high-risk technologies by Rasmussen (1983) and by Rouse (1981). Its operations divide conveniently into two areas: those which *precede* the detection of a problem (skill-based level); and those which *follow* it (the rule- and knowledge-based levels). Errors (slips) occurring prior to problem detection are primarily associated with *monitoring failures*, while those which appear in the subsequent phases (mistakes) are subsumed under the general heading of problem-solving failures. The main features of GEMS are summarized in Figure 1.

Monitoring failures

In its simplest form, routine action (i.e., well-practised tasks carried out in familiar surroundings by skilled operators) can be regarded as comprising segments of preprogrammed behavioural sequences interspersed with attentional checks upon progress, carried out either consciously or preconsciously. These checks involve bringing the higher levels of the cognitive system momentarily into the control loop and seek to establish: (a) whether the

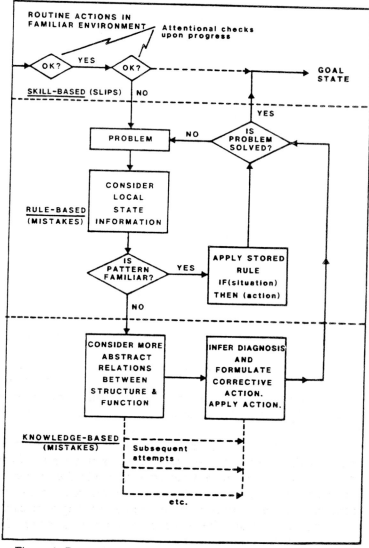

Figure 1. Dynamics of generic error-modelling system (GEMS)

actions are running according to plan; and (b) at a more complex level, whether the plan is still adequate to achieve the goal. The former are detected far more readily than the latter, since attention is reasonably adept at picking up deviations from the intended track (see Mandler, 1975).

It is also meaningful to regard action sequences as involving a series of nodes or choice points beyond which the subsequent actions can take a number of possible routes. For example, boiling a kettle can lead to a variety of outcomes: making tea, coffee and other beverages, cooking vegetables, preparing instant soups, hot-water bottles, and so forth. Post-nodal routes will vary widely in their frequency and recency of prior use. To be maximally effective, checks should be associated with these nodal points.

Diary studies of naturally occurring action slips (see Reason and Mycielska, 1982) clearly indicate the dependency of slips upon failures of attentional checking. These failures are basically of two kinds: the large proportion are associated with *inattention* (omitting to make a check), but a significant number of slips are also related to *overattention* (making an attentional check at an inappropriate moment in the sequence). Both could be termed *control-mode failures* in that errors arise as the result of being in the wrong control mode with respect to the demands of the current task (i.e., the higher levels of the control system are open-loop when they should have been closed-loop, and conversely). Detailed descriptions of the various forms these slips can take, together with actual examples, are given elsewhere (Reason, 1979, 1984; Reason and Mycielska, 1982; Norman, 1981).

Problem-solving failures

In purely psychological terms, a problem can be defined as some externally or internally produced change which requires a deviation from customary behaviour. In other words, problems demand the involvement of the resource-limited attentional mode; the schematic control mode can only operate satisfactorily when the current state conforms to its expectations. Departures from routine can range from relatively minor contingencies, rapidly dealt with by preprogrammed corrective procedures, to entirely novel circumstances or goals, requiring new plans and strategies to be derived from 'first principles'.

The problem-solving elements of GEMS employ a slightly modified version of Hunt and Rouse's (1984) 'fuzzy set' variant of Rasmussen's (1980) 'step-ladder' model, and are based upon a recurrent theme in the psychological literature, namely that '. . . humans, if given a choice, would prefer to act as context specific pattern recognizers rather than attempting to calculate or optimize' (Rouse, 1981). Thus, the sequence of operations within GEMS indicates that human problem solvers always confront an unplanned-for change by *first* deciding whether or not they have encountered this particular pattern of local signs and symptoms before. If the pattern is recognized, they then determine whether or not they have some corrective rule readily available. Only when this low-effort pattern-matching and rule-applying procedure fails will they move to the more laborious mode of making diagnostic inferences from knowledge-based mental models of the system in question, and, from these, go on to formulate and try out remedial possibilities.

This high priority given to the rule-based route is designed to reflect what Shepard (1964) described as '. . . the obvious disparity between the effortless speed and surety of most perceptual decisions and the painful hesitation and doubt characteristic of subsequent higher level decisions'.

Human beings are furious pattern matchers. They are strongly disposed to exploit the parallel and automatic operations of specialized, low-level processors: *schemata* (Bartlett, 1932), *frames* (knowledge structures for representing familiar scenes — see Minsky, 1975), and *scripts* (comparable structures for representing stereotyped episodes or scenarios — see Schank and Abelson, 1977). Knowledge structures are capable of 'filling in' the gaps in missing data on the basis of 'default values'. These default settings are provided by the memory system's remarkable ability to encode frequency-of-occurrence information without any intentional guidance or mental effort (see Hasher and Zacks, 1984). Higher level manipulations, however, require the slow, laborious, resource-limited involvement of the attentional control mode.

WHAT DETERMINES SWITCHING BETWEEN LEVELS?

The 'switching rules' governing the shifts of control between the skill-based, rule-based, and knowledge-based levels are summarized below.

Skill-based <--> rule-based

The skill-based level of GEMS relates to the execution of highly routinized activities in familiar (i.e., planned-for) surroundings. The rule-based level is engaged when an attentional check (--<OK?>--) upon progress detects a problem, i.e., a situation that cannot be handled by the routines set in train by the current plan. A primary feature of GEMS is that rule-based efforts at problem solution will always be tried first. If the deviation is minor, and appropriate corrective rules are readily found, this phase may be terminated by a rapid return to the skill-based level. With more difficult problems, however, the cycle (scanning local signs and symptoms, rule matching, and evaluating solution effectiveness) may be repeated several times.

Rule-base <-> knowledge-based

According to the simple logic of GEMS, the switch from the rule-based to the knowledge-based level occurs when the problem solver realizes that none of his or her repertoire of rule-based solutions is adequate to solve the problem. In reality, however, this is likely to be complicated by affective factors. Duncan (personal communication) has suggested that the decision to resort to the more abstract, laborious, and sequential consideration of structure–function relations will depend upon the complex interaction between subjective uncertainty and concern. Both will increase rapidly as successive rule-based attempts to solve the problem are recognized as failures.

With knowledge-based processing, the focus of problem solving shifts away from immediate state considerations to some mental model of the system as a whole. Progress at this level tends to involve the search for suitable analogies, or diagnostic theories, to fit the current situation. The discovery of such an analogy usually brings with it a set of remedial possibilities (e.g., IF <it's like situation X> THEN <I should try action Y>, and so on). A well-understood analogy is likely to entail a set of remedial rules which will switch the focus of activity back to the rule-based level of performance so long as that particular analogy or theory continues to be entertained. This cycling between the knowledge-based and rule-based levels can be repeated several times as various theories are explored.

Knowledge-based → skill-based

Activity at the knowledge-based level can be terminated by the discovery of an adequate (or an apparently adequate) solution to the problem. This solution is likely to constitute a new plan of action involving a fresh set of skill-based routines. This is indicated in Figure 1 by the affirmative route from the <Is the problem solved?> decision element. There are powerful cognitive forces at work to encourage the problem solver to accept inadequate or incomplete solutions as being satisfactory at this point. In other words, confirming biases will lead to the acceptance of inappropriate solutions and result in the premature termination of problem-solving behaviour. The consequences of this error may or may not be detected rapidly by an <OK?> check. Once such an error has been detected, however, the system will again switch into the rule-based mode. By this time, the local signs and symptoms will have changed as a consequence of the previous activity, allowing the possibility of new rule-based solutions to be applied — and so on. In this way, the focus of control will shift continuously between all three performance levels.

THREE BASIC ERROR TYPES

One of the difficulties with the simple distinction between slips and mistakes is that both slips and certain kinds of mistakes take the same 'strong-but-wrong' forms. GEMS allows us to circumvent this problem by yielding three distinct error types: skill-based slips, rule-based mistakes, and knowledge-based mistakes. These three basic types can be differentiated along a number of different dimensions, as summarized in Table 2.

TABLE 2: *Distinctions between the three basic error types*

FACTORS:	SKILL-BASED SLIPS	RULE-BASED MISTAKES	KNOWLEDGE-BASED MISTAKES
ACTIVITY	Routine actions	Problem solving	
CONTROL	Mainly automatic processors		Resource-limited conscious processes
	(Schemata)	(Rules)	
FOCUS OF ATTENTION	On something other than present task	Directed at problem-related issues	
FORMS	Largely predictable 'Strong-but-wrong' error forms		Variable
	(Actions)	(Rules)	
DETECTION	Usually fairly rapid	Hard, and often only achieved with help from others	

EXPERTISE AND THE PREDICTABILITY OF ERROR FORMS

At both the skill-based and the rule-based levels, errors are most likely to take the form of *'strong-but-wrong'* routines. At the former level, the guidance of action tends to be snatched by the most active motor schema in the 'vicinity' of the node when an attentional check is omitted or mistimed. Similarly, the most probable error at the rule-based level involves the inappropriate matching of readily available but irrelevant patterns, scripts or frames (i.e., making a false-positive at the decision point). In both cases, the error forms are *already available* within the individual's stored repertoire of action sequences or rules. But the same is not necessarily true for errors at the knowledge-based level. When the problem space is largely uncharted territory, it is less easy to specify in advance the short-cuts that might be taken in error. Thus, knowledge-based mistakes, arising from a complex interaction between bounded rationality and incomplete mental models, are likely to be less predictable in their forms. At best, it is only possible to indicate the general cognitive and situational factors that conspire to create knowledge-based mistakes.

In this sense, mistakes at the knowledge-based level have hit-and-miss qualities not dissimilar to the errors of beginners. No matter how expert people are in coping with familiar problems, their performance will begin to approximate to that of novices once their repertoire of schemata and rules has been exhausted by the demands of a novel situation. The important differences between the novice and the expert are to be found at the skill- and rule-based levels of GEMS. Expertise consists of having a large stock of appropriate routines to deal with a wide variety of contingencies.

There is now a large body of research evidence (see Adelson, 1984) to show that in skilled problem solving, the crucial differences between experts and novices lie in both the level and the complexity of their knowledge representations and rules. Repeatedly it is found that experts represent the problem space at a more abstract level than non-experts. The latter focus more on the surface features of the problem. The classic result on the abstract representations of experts was obtained by Chase and Simon (1973) who demonstrated the marked superiority of chess masters in reconstructing meaningful midgame boards after a five second presentation. They found that chess masters' recall clusters frequently consisted of pieces that formed attack or defence configurations. Thus individual chess pieces were 'chunked' as integral parts of larger meaningful units. Comparable findings have been obtained for master 'Go' players (Reitman, 1976), physicists (Chi *et al.*, 1981), mathematicians (Lewis, 1981), and computer programmers (Adelson, 1981, 1984).

The application of these findings to GEMS means that experts, in comparison with novices, will have a much larger collection of rules which are formulated at a more abstract level of representation. Taken to an unlikely extreme, this argues that the ultimate in expertise means never having to resort to the knowledge-based mode of problem solving. More realistically, however, it establishes a close relationship between the predictability of error and the degree of expertise: the more skilled an individual is in carrying out a particular task, the more likely it is that his or her errors will take 'strong-but-wrong' forms at the skill-based and rule-based levels of performance.

TASK CHARACTERISTICS AND PERFORMANCE LEVEL

Of late, there has been a marked resurgence of Brunswikian thinking (Brunswik, 1957) in the related fields of judgement, problem solving and decision making (see Brehmer, 1980, 1981; Hammond, 1982; Payne, 1982; Hammond *et al.*, 1984). This approach lays great stress on the potency of task characteristics in determining the kind of cognitive activity that is employed. Hammond's cognitive continuum theory locates these various types of activity along a dimension ranging from *intuition* at one extreme to *analysis* at the other, with 'quasi-rationality', or everyday common-sense thinking, lying in between. The properties of these polar states correspond closely to those described earlier for the schematic and attentional modes of control. Thus, if a task presents '(a) *many redundant* cues with (b) *continuous* values displayed (c) *simultaneously* that must be measured (d) *perceptually*, and for which the subject has available no (e) *explicit principle* or method for organizing cues into a judgement, then the subject will employ intuitive cognition' (Hammond *et al.*, 1984). A task with opposite attributes will call forth an analytic mode of cognition. Tasks with properties from each pole of the continuum may induce the compromise state of quasi-rationality.

The point of alluding to this approach here is to emphasize that task characteristics and intrinsic cognitive factors (i.e., the existence of appropriate stored routines) function as a total system in determining the focus of activity within GEMS. Very approximately, Hammond's intuitive mode will predominate at the rule-based level, while knowledge-based performance is likely to implicate both the quasi-rational and the analytic modes of judgement.

ERROR-SHAPING FACTORS AT EACH OF THE THREE LEVELS

Errors at the three levels of performance are further distinguished by the nature of the psychological and situational factors which combine to shape characteristic error forms. However, these distinctions are quite subtle since many of these error-shaping factors operate at more than two levels. As a rough guide, it seems likely that the error-shaping factors which prevail at the skill-based level also exert an influence at the rule-based level, and many of those which come into play at the rule-based level also affect operations at the knowledge-based level. The major error-shaping factors at each level are summarized in Table 3, and are discussed further below.

I. Error-shaping factors at the skill-based level

Given that an attentional check upon the progress of routine actions has been omitted or applied inappropriately, what factors are most likely to influence the form taken by a slip? In other words, what are the non-intentional factors that can bring 'strong' schemata into play against the dictates of the current plan of action? A careful examination of the circumstances under which slips occur (see Reason and Mycielska, 1982) suggests that the following are of primary importance.

Recency and frequency of prior employment:

The more recently and frequently a particular routine is set in motion and

TABLE 3: *The major error-shaping factors at each level of performance*

PERFORMANCE LEVEL	ERROR-SHAPING FACTORS
SKILL-BASED I	1. Recency and frequency of previous use 2. Environmental control signals 3. Shared schema properties 4. Concurrent plans
RULE-BASED II	1. Mind set ('It's always worked before') 2. Availability ('First come best preferred') 3. Matching bias ('like relates to like') 4. Over-simplification (e.g., 'halo effect') 5. Over-confidence ('I'm sure I'm right')
KNOWLEDGE-BASED III	1. Selectivity (bounded rationality) 2. Working memory overload (bounded rationality) 3. Out of sight out of mind (bounded rationality) 4. Thematic 'vagabonding' and 'encysting' 5. Memory cueing/reasoning by analogy 6. Matching bias revisited 7. Incomplete/incorrect mental model

achieves its desired outcome, the greater its likelihood of recurring univited as a slip of habit. William James (1890) compared habits to 'great flywheels'. Once set in motion, they require very little additional energy to keep them going. But the penalty for this momentum is a reluctance to change direction when altered circumstances or new destinations demand it.

Environmental control signals:

The slips and lapses data (Reason, 1979; Norman, 1981) reveal the potency of environmental cues in eliciting unintentional actions. Familiar environments trigger associated action routines, particularly in moments of reduced intentionality. These erroneous actions obey local rules even though they are out of step with the current plan. Much handled objects and frequently visited places possess a large measure of control over well-established action sequences (Reason and Mycielska, 1982).

Shared schema features:

From the pattern of slips observed in everyday life, it is evident that the intentional activation of a given set of action schemata also has the effect of increasing the activation of other schemata possessing shared features. For example, beginning to take off one's clothes is likely to increase the activation of all other action schemata that could be subsequently employed in an undressing scenario. Thus, intentionally activating a schema that is common to many different outcomes will increase the likelihood of one of these subsequent action sequences appearing unbidden.

Concurrent plans:

Many slips betray the influence of concurrent plans or intentions. These can take the form of *blends* in which two active plans become intermingled in the same action sequence (e.g., 'I was making tea when the cat appeared at the kitchen door clamouring to be fed. I opened a tin of catfood and starting spooning its contents into the teapot which I had left empty waiting for the tea.'). Alternatively, they can involve *reversals* in which the right actions are applied to the wrong objects (e.g., 'In a hurried effort to finish the housework and have a bath, I put the plants meant for the lounge in the bedroom and my underwear on the lounge window sill.').

Schema activation — a schema's readiness to do its particular thing — is likely to be a complex function of all of these factors, plus whatever intentional activity (top–down processing) and emotional influences are being directed at it. GEMS predicts that when an attentional check is omitted at a branch-point (node) in a behavioural sequence, the subsequent actions will be governed by the most active schema beyond that node. The control of routine action is thus like a rather curious railway system where all the points are set by default to follow the most popular routes. To change these settings requires a *positive attentional act* on the part of the 'driver'. It is the omission of this positive act which gives rise to the vast majority of slips.

II. Error-shaping factors at the rule-based level

The primary interest here is in those factors which bias a problem solver to decide that the situational component of a stored rule (IF <situation> THEN <action>) is appropriate to the local system state when, in fact, it is not. It is assumed that false-negatives (rejecting an appropriate rule), though logically possible, are most likely to result from the prior selection of a wrong rule rather than from the failure to recognize the suitability of a correct and available rule.

Mind set (Einstellung):

The most convincing demonstration of the potential rigidity of rule-bound thinking was made by Luchins. There can be little doubt about the robustness of his findings since he used the same basic technique — the Jars Test — on over 9000 adults and children. Luchins was concerned with the blinding effects of past experience, and with what happens when a habit '. . . ceases to be a tool discriminantly applied but becomes a procrustean bed to which the situation must conform; when, in a word, instead of the individual mastering the habit, the habit masters the individual (Luchins and Luchins, 1950).

The Jars Test and other comparable techniques demonstrated a strong and remarkably unshakeable bias toward applying the familiar, clumsy solution when simpler and more effective solutions were available. This mechanization of thinking is quick to develop and hard to dislodge. If a rule has been employed successfully in the past, then there is a strong tendency to apply it again, even though the circumstances no longer warrant its use. To a person with just a hammer, every problem looks like a nail.

Availability:

People's personal knowledge (metaknowledge) of the workings of their cognitive systems becomes encapsulated in a few intuitive rules of thumb or heuristics. The usually unconscious application of these heuristics directly colours the interpretation placed upon certain pieces of evidence in judgemental tasks in which the information is incomplete or uncertain (Tversky and Kahneman, 1973). For the most part, these heuristics work to our advantage by reducing the cognitive load. But they can also lead to predictable errors when over-utilized. One of the most potent and pervasive of these is the *availability heuristic*. This can be summarized as follows: 'Things that come readily to mind are likely to be more frequent, more probable, more important, more useful, and better understood than less readily available items'. The error-inducing effects of this heuristic have been demonstrated in a wide variety of tasks (see Kahneman *et al.*, 1982).

The most likely effect of the availability heuristic in rule matching is to bias the problem solver in favour of rules that spring quickly to mind, even though they may not always be relevant or applicable. In short, there will be a 'first come best preferred' bias at work. And, most importantly, people are *not* consciously aware of the operation of these heuristic biases (Nisbett and Ross, 1980).

Matching bias:

Tversky and Kahneman (1974) have shown that when people are asked to decide upon the likely class membership of given data set, they tend to base their judgements upon the perceived similarity between a salient characteristic of the sample and some stereotypic impression of its assumed parent population, disregarding other more relevant factors which, in any case, they poorly understand. This process is governed by the *representativeness heuristic* which assumes that 'like causes like', or that 'like goes along with like'. A similar matching bias will be at work in rule-finding situations. Inappropriate matches are likely to be made on the basis of the similarity between one prominent aspect of the current system state and a stored situational representation which also possesses that feature. This is especially probable in view of the human predilection for rendering down complex multi-attribute judgements to single global impressions.

Over-simplification:

Studies by De Soto (1961), and by Osgood *et al.* (1957), in which people are asked to rate objects or other people on each of several specified dimensions, reveal a striking inability to take account of the independent way in which these entities vary along the different dimensions. Instead, there seems to be an overwhelming tendency to collapse all these dimensions into a single ordering by merit or 'good versus bad' dimension, thus losing valuable information about the pattern of attributes unique to a single object or individual. Thus, people show a marked preference for single orderings and a strong aversion to discrepant orderings.

Over-confidence:

Problem solvers have a marked tendency to be over-confident in evaluating the correctness of both their rule selections and their knowledge of the system (Koriat *et al.*, 1980). They will tend to justify their chosen course of action by focusing upon evidence that favours it, and by disregarding contradictory signs. These confirming biases are likely to result in the continued acceptance of an inappropriate rule, despite the presence of counter-indications. This bias pervades all aspects of human cognition.

III. Error-shaping factors at the knowledge-based level

Aside from those due to inadequate knowledge, the bulk of the error factors at this level relate to Simon's (1957) *principle of bounded rationality*: 'The capacity of the human mind for formulating and solving complex problems is very small compared with the size of the problems whose solution is required for objectively rational behaviour in the real world — or even for a reasonable approximation of such objective rationality.' This fundamental limitation gives rise to 'satisficing' behaviour, or the tendency to select manageable rather than optimal courses of action. Problem solvers compromise in their goal setting by choosing minimal objectives rather than those likely to yield the best possible outcome.

A useful image to conjure up when considering the problem of bounded rationality is that of a beam of light (the working database of the attentional resource) being directed on to a large screen (the problem space). The difficulties are that the illuminated portion of the screen is very small compared to its total area, that the information potentially available on the screen is inadequately and inefficiently sampled by the tracking of the light beam, and that, in any case, the beam is continually changing its direction in a manner that is only partially under the control of its operator. The beam is repeatedly drawn to certain parts of the screen, while other parts remain in darkness. Nor is it obvious that these favoured portions are necessarily those most required for finding a problem solution. The beam will be drawn to salient but irrelevant data and to fragments from activated schemata that may or may not bear upon the problem.

Selectivity:

There is now a wealth of evidence (see Evans, 1983) to show that an important source of reasoning errors lies in the selective processing of task information. Errors will arise if attention is given to the wrong features or not given to the right features. Accuracy of reasoning performance is a consequence of whether the problem solver's attention is directed to the *logically important* rather than to the psychologically salient aspects of the problem.

Working memory limitations:

Reasoners at the knowledge-based level interpret data by constructing an integrated mental model of them (Johnson-Laird, 1983). In order to check whether an inference is valid it is necessary to search for different mental models of the situation that will explain the available data. This activity of integrating several possible models places a heavy burden upon the limited capacity of working memory. The evidence from a variety of reasoning studies indicates that working memory operates on 'first in first out' basis. Thus, it is easier to recall the premises of a syllogism in the order in which they were presented than in the opposite order. Similarly, it is easier to formulate a conclusion in which the terms occur in the order in which they entered working memory. The forms in which problems are presented vary considerably in the load they impose upon memory. When the load is excessive, false inferences will be made. Rasmussen (1981) observed that in electronic trouble shooting the most important factor determining the route of least resistance was the desire to minimize the load upon working memory.

Out of sight out of mind:

Availability has two faces. One gives undue weight to those facts that come readily to mind. The other ignores that which is not immediately present (see Fischhoff *et al.*, 1978).

Thematic 'vagabonding' and 'encystment':

Doerner (1984) described two maladaptive strategies that some people adopt when coping with a complex, dynamic control task at the knowledge-based level. One — thematic vagabonding — involves flitting from issue to issue quickly, treating each one superficially. No one theme is pursued to its natural conclusion. The other — encystment — appears to be the exact opposite of vagabonding. Topics are lingered over and small details attended to lovingly. Other more important issues are disregarded. However, the differences between vagabonding and encystment are only on the surface. Both manifest bounded rationality and escapist tendencies.

Memory cueing/reasoning by analogy:

This is a process which has both useful and error-producing features. There is considerable evidence to show that problem content can cue familiar information in long-term memory, which is then used to reach a solution. If not directly applicable, situational cues lead to problem-solving strategies based upon reasoning by analogy with more familiar systems (Griggs, 1983). Such processes can lead to startling successes and dismal failures. The benign aspects of this strategy were described by Rumelhart (1980) as follows: 'Once we can "understand" the situation by encoding it in terms of a relatively rich set of schemata, the conceptual constraints of the schemata can be brought into play and the problem readily solved.' Failures arise when the wrong schemata are instantiated or an inappropriate analogy invoked.

Matching bias revisited:

In summarizing their extensive investigations of the way people draw inferences from evidence, Wason and Johnson-Laird (1972) reduced a variety of error-shaping factors down to a single principle: '*Whenever two different items, or classes, can be matched in a one-to-one fashion, then the process of inference is readily made, whether it be logically valid or invalid.*' As they pointed out, the notion that a one-to-one relation is easy is so fundamental as to need no psychological justification.

Incorrect and incomplete knowledge:

This needs little amplification except to remark upon the frequency with which this factor contributes to mistakes in dealing with emergencies in nuclear power plants (Pew *et al.*, 1981; Woods *et al.*, 1982). Detailed case studies of nuclear power plant emergencies (e.g., Three Mile Island, Oyster Creek, North Anna, and Ginna) provide some of the best available data regarding the limitations of knowledge-based problem solving.

INTRINSIC VERSUS EXTRINSIC ERROR-SHAPING FACTORS

GEMS is context-free. It assumes that certain error-shaping factors are intrinsic to the way the cognitive system functions, and that human beings are prone to make certain kinds of error irrespective of the task or the situation. But it is equally clear, from the preceding discussion that these intrinsic error-shaping tendencies are not equally influential in determining the precise forms taken by the three basic error types described above. This raises two questions. First, what — in very general terms — can be said about the relative contributions of intrinsic (cognitive biases, attentional limitations, etc.) and extrinsic factors (the structural characteristics of the task, context effects, etc.) to shaping the particular forms taken by each of the three error types? Second, given a reasonable knowledge of these intrinsic and extrinsic factors, what can be said about the relative predictability of each of these three basic error types? Very tentative guesses concerning the answer to the first question are given in Table 4.

TABLE 4: *Relative contributions of intrinsic and extrinsic factors in shaping specific error forms*

	INTRINSIC	EXTRINSIC
SKILL-BASED SLIPS	High	Moderate
RULE-BASED MISTAKES	Moderate	High
KNOWLEDGE-BASED MISTAKES	Low	Very high

In skill-based slips, the primary error-shaping factors are attentional 'capture' and the 'strength' of the associated action schemata — where 'strength' is, in large part, determined by the relative frequency of successful execution. All that is required to elicit a 'strong-but-wrong' action sequence is the omission (or misapplication) of an attentional check in circumstances where some departure from previous routine was intended. For rule-based mistakes, the story is somewhat similar. It is reasonable to assume that rules too are arranged in an ordered priority list (see Payne, 1982), where the most available production is also the one whose conditions are most frequently satisfied by the prevailing state indications. In this case, however, we need to know more about the nature of the task in order to predict which rule the person is likely to apply in error. With rule-based mistakes, it is necessary to understand what alternative rules could be satisfied, either wholly or partially, by the current state indicators, and for this a detailed knowledge of both the task and the person's training is required.

At the knowledge-based level, however, mistakes can take a wide variety of forms, none of which is necessarily predictable on the basis of the individual's past experience. Of particular importance here is the way in which both the task and other situational variables direct the limited attentional resource to relevant or non-relevant areas of the problem space (see Payne, 1982). The bulk of the evidence relating to activity at this level stresses the extent to which cognitive performance is dependent upon '. . . seemingly minor changes in tasks' (Einhorn and Hogarth, 1981). All that can be said with any confidence is that people are extremely error prone at this level of operation — which is hardly surprising since, in ecologically valid activities, making errors and recovering from them is an essential part of coping with novel situations. But operations in high-risk technology emergencies are not always so forgiving of this trial and error exploration of the problem space.

In considering the relative predictability of the three basic error types, it is necessary to differentiate between the quantity and the quality (i.e., the specific forms taken) of the errors. Since both the skill-based and rule-based levels of performance are characteristic of skilled individuals, it is reasonable to assume that the quantity of the errors in both cases will be small, but that when errors do occur they will take 'strong-but-wrong' forms (i.e., will be recognizable as well-used parts of the person's repertoire in that context). At the knowledge-based level, however, we can only say at present that a relatively large number of errors are likely to be committed, and that their forms will be highly variable. To achieve more precise qualitative predictions at this level, we need a better understanding of the complex interaction between task variables and problem-solving strategies, and of the way in which the latter change as a consequence of continued efforts at finding a solution.

REFERENCES

Adelson, B. (1981) Knowledge structures of computer programmers. *Proceedings of the Fourth Annual Meeting of the Cognitive Science Society*, **4**, 243–8.

Adelson, B. (1984) When novices surpass experts: The difficulty of a task may increase with expertise. *Journal of Experimental Psychology: Learning, Memory, and Cognition*, **10**, 483–95.

Bartlett, F. J. (1932) *Remembering*. Cambridge: Cambridge University Press.

Brehmer, B. (1980) In one word: Not from experience. *Acta Psychologica*, **45**, 223–41.

Brehmer, B. (1981) Models of diagnostic judgments. In: J. Rasmussen and W. Rouse (Eds), *Human Detection and Diagnosis of System Failures*. New York: Plenum.

Brunswik, E. (1957) Scope and aspects of the cognitive problem. In: H. Gruber, R. Jessor, and K. Hammond (Eds), *Cognition: The Colorado Symposium*. Cambridge, Mass.: Harvard University Press.

Chapman, L. J., and Chapman, J. P. (1967) Genesis of popular but erroneous diagnostic observations. *Journal of Abnormal Psychology*, **72**, 193–204.

Chase, W. C., and Simon, H. A. (1973) Perception in chess. *Cognitive Psychology*, **4**, 55–81.

Chi, M., Glaser, R., and Rees, E. (1981) Expertise in problem-solving. In: *Advances in the Psychology of Human Intelligence*, Vol. 1. Hillsdale, NJ: Erlbaum.

Combs, B., and Slovic, P. (1979) Causes of death: Biased newspaper coverage and biased judgements. *Journalism Quarterly*, **56**, 837–43.

De Soto, C. B. (1961) The predilection for single orderings. *Journal of Abnormal and Social Psychology*, **62**, 16–23.

Dörner, D. (1984) Of the difficulties people have in dealing with complexity. *Simulation and Games*, **11**, 67–106.

Einhorn, H. J., and Hogarth, R. M. (1981) Behavioral decision theory: Processes of judgment and choice. *Annual Review of Psychology*, **32**, 52–88.

Evans, J. St. B. T. (1983) *Thinking and Reasoning: Psychological Approaches*. London: Routledge & Kegan Paul.

Fischhoff, B. (1977) Perceived informativeness of facts. *Journal of Experimental Psychology: Human Perception and Performance*, **3**, 349–58.

Fischhoff, B., Slovic, P., and Lichtenstein (1978) Fault trees: sensitising of estimated failure probabilities to problem representation. *Journal of Experimental Psychology: Human Perception and Performance*, **4**, 330–334.

Griggs, R. A. (1983) The role of problem content in the selection task and in the THOG problem. In: J. Evans (Ed.), *Thinking and Reasoning: Psychological Approaches*. London: Routledge & Kegan Paul.

Hammond, K. R. (1982) *Unification of Theory and Research in Judgment and Decision Making*. Boulder: University of Colorado, Center for Research on Judgement and Policy.

Hammond, K. R., Hamm, R. M., Grassia, J., and Pearson, T. (1984) The relative efficacy of intuitive and analytical cognition: A second direct comparison. Report No. 252. Center for Research on Judgment and Policy. Boulder, Co: University of Colorado.

Hasher, L., and Zacks, R. T. (1984) Automatic processing of fundamental information: The case of frequency of occurrence. *American Psychologist*, **39**, 1372–88.

Hunt, R. M., and Rouse, W. B. (1984) A fuzzy rule-based model of human problem solving. *IEEE Transactions on Systems, Man, and Cybernetics*, SMC-14, 112–20.

James, W. (1890) *The Principles of Psychology*. New York: Henry Holt.

Johnson-Laird, P. N. (1983) *Mental Models*. Cambridge: Cambridge University Press.

Kahneman, D., Slovic, P., and Tversky, A. (1982) *Judgement under Uncertainty: Heuristics and Biases*. Cambridge: Cambridge University Press.

Koriat, A., Lichtenstein, S., and Fischhoff, B. (1980) Reasons for confidence. *Journal of Experimental Psychology: Human Learning and Memory*, **6**, 107–17.

Lewis, C. (1981) Skill in algebra. In: J. R. Anderson (Ed.), *Cognitive Skills and their Acquisition*. Hillsdale, NJ: Erlbaum.

Lichtenstein, S., Slovic, P., Fischhoff, B., Layman, M., and Combs, B. (1978) Judged frequency of lethal events. *Journal of Experimental Psychology: Human Learning and Memory*, **4**, 551–78.

Luchins, A. S., and Luchins, E. H. (1950) New experimental attempts at preventing mechanization in problem solving. *Journal of General Psychology*, **42**, 279–97.

Mandler, G. (1975) *Mind and Emotion*. New York: Wiley.

Minsky, M. (1975) A framework for representing knowledge. In: P. Winston (Ed.), *The Psychology of Computer Vision*. New York: McGraw-Hill.

Newell, A., and Simon, H. A. (1972) *Human Problem Solving*. Englewood Cliffs, NJ: Prentice-Hall.

Nisbett, R., and Ross, L. (1980) *Human Inference: Strategies and Shortcomings of Social Judgement*. Englewood Cliffs, NJ: Prentice-Hall.

Norman, D. A. (1981) Categorization of action slips. *Psychological Review*, **88**, 1–15.

Norman, D. A., and Shallice, T. (1980) *Attention to Action: Willed and Automatic Control of Behavior*, CHIP 99, Center for Human Information Processing, University of California, San Diego, La Jolla, California.

Osgood, C. S., Suci, G. J., and Tannenbaum, P. H. (1957) *The Measurement of Meaning*. Urbana, Illinois: University of Illinois Press.

Payne, J. W. (1982) Contingent decision behavior. *Psychological Bulletin*, **92**, 382–402.

Pew, R. W., Miller, D. C., and Feeher, C. E. (1981) *Evaluation of Proposed Control Room Improvements through Analysis of Critical Operator Decisions*. NP-1982, Research Project 891, Cambridge, Mass: Bolt Baranek & Newman Inc.

Rasmussen, J. (1976) Outlines of a hybrid model of the process operator. In: T. Sheridan and G. Johannsen (Eds), *Monitoring Behavior and Supervisory Control*. New York: Plenum Press.

Rasmussen, J. (1980) What can be learned from human error reports? In: K. Duncan, M. Gruneberg, and D. Wallis (Eds), *Changes in Working Life*. London: Wiley.

Rasmussen, J. (1981) Models of mental strategies in process plant diagnosis. In: J. Rasmussen, and W. Rouse (Eds), *Human Detection and Diagnosis of System Failures*. New York: Plenum.

Rasmussen, J. (1983) Skills, rules, knowledge; signals, signs and symbols; and other distinctions in human performance models. *Institute of Electrical and Electronic Engineers Transactions on Systems, Man and Cybernetics*, SMC-13, No. 3.

Rasmussen, J., and Jensen, A. (1974) Mental procedures in real life tasks: A case study of electronic troubleshooting. *Ergonomics*, **17**, 293–307.

Reason, J. T. (1979) Actions not as planned: The price of automatization. In: G. Underwood and R. Stevens (Eds), *Aspects of Consciousness*, Vol. 1. London: Academic Press.

Reason, J. T. (1984) Lapses of attention. In: R. Parasuraman and D. Davies (Eds), *Varieties of Attention*. New York: Academic Press.

Reason, J. T., and Mycielska, K. (1982) *Absent-Minded? The Psychology of Mental Lapses and Everyday Errors*. Englewood Cliffs, NJ: Prentice-Hall.

Reitman, J. S. (1976) Skilled perception in go: Deducing memory structures from inter-response times. *Cognitive Psychology*, **8**, 336–56.

Rouse, W. B. (1981) Models of human problem solving: detection, diagnosis, and compensation for system failures. Preprint for *Proceedings of IFAC Conference on Analysis, Design and Evaluation of Man–Machine Systems*. Baden-Baden, F. R. Germany, September 1982.

Rumelhart, D. E. (1980) Schemata: The building blocks of cognition. In: R. Spiro, B. Bruce, and W. Brewer (Eds), *Theoretical Issues in Reading Comprehension*. Hillsdale, NJ: Erlbaum.

Schank, R. C., and Abelson, R. P. (1977) *Scripts, Plans, Goals, and Understanding*. Hillsdale, NJ: Erlbaum.

Shepard, R. N. (1964) On subjectively optimum selections among multiattribute alternatives. In: M. Shelley, and G. Bryan (Eds), *Human Judgements and Optimality*. New York: Wiley.

Simon, H. A. (1957) *Models of Man*. New York: Wiley.

Slovic, P., Fischhoff, B., and Lichtenstein, S. (1982) Facts versus fears: Understanding perceived risk. In: D. Kahneman, P. Slovic, and A. Tversky (Eds), *Judgement under Uncertainty: Heuristics and Biases*. Cambridge: Cambridge University Press.

Tversky, A., and Kahneman, D. (1973) Availability: A heuristic for judging frequency and probability. *Cognitive Science*, **5**, 207–32.

Tversky, A., and Kahneman, D. (1974) Judgement under uncertainty: Heuristics and biases. *Science*, **185**, 1124–31.

Wason, P. C. (1966) Reasoning. In: B. Foss (Ed.), *New Horizons in Psychology*. London: Penguin.

Wason, P. C., and Johnson-Laird, P. N. (1972) *Psychology of Reasoning: Structure and Content*. London: Batsford.

Woods, D. D., Wise, J. A., and Hanes, L. F. (1982) *Evaluation of Safety Parameter Display Concepts* NP-2239, Palo Alto, California: Electric Power Research Institute.

New Technology and Human Error
Edited by J. Rasmussen, K. Duncan and J. Leplat
© 1987 John Wiley & Sons Ltd

Part 3: Errors of Judgement and the Social Context

INTRODUCTION

It is questionable whether there are major differences between the mechanisms and sources of error discussed in Parts 1 and 2 and those discussed in Part 3, although the different approaches have different frames of reference and have evolved in different, primarily social, contexts. Certainly, as the contributions show, the problem-solving situations involve different methodologies.

The discussion of human errors in Parts 1 and 2 emphasized performance, and its failings, for which individual cognitive control mechanisms or value systems can be advanced. The concern was primarily with individual errors — in two senses. Firstly, the actions performed by one person and their consequences were considered for the most part without reference to those of other people. Secondly, the isolated act received more attention than the action sequence or sequence of decisions.

In Part 3, besides involving more than one person in transactions which often consist of extended action sequences, the problems which may be the subject of human error tend to be more complex. Moreover, errors are not defined solely in terms of acts or decisions which bring the state of affairs to an unacceptable end.

In both his papers (Chapters 8 and 10), Brehmer stresses the uncertainty and delayed feedback in social situations, e.g., in medical diagnoses, the clinician cannot consult the plans of the system designer, and some time will elapse before the consequences become clear of whatever treatment is prescribed.

Dörner (Chapter 9) describes the difficulties people have in dealing with complex planning situations calling for more or less intuitive judgements.

His studies are based on simulated, complex task environments such as those of a city mayor. He identifies errors which, at least in some cases, may be peculiar to this task with its social pressures and social consequences, for instance, decreasing willingness to make decisions, and 'thematic vaga-bonding' or the tendency, in the face of difficulties, to jump from one topic to another.

The question of errors peculiar to group problem solving and decision making is taken up by both Reason and Quintanilla. Both contributors refer to the tendency to risky decisions by groups. Reason cites the 'groupthink' syndrome described by Janis, for example, the illusory experiences of shared invulnerability and of shared unanimity among group members. Such erroneous impressions can lead to 'fiascos' of international importance. But these, and other similar processes in decision-making groups, sometimes have the reverse effect as, according to Janis, in the successful defusing of the Cuban Missiles Crisis.

When it comes to the important question of design for error tolerance, we have to reckon that biases may be countered by 'bias discount' in the propagation of information within some present-day organizations, as Cyert and March observed. This may be particularly important when communication by face-to-face encounter is replaced by information retrieval from computer terminals. Interpreting or misinterpreting implicit intentions in the sender of a message is only one of the possible effects of the removal of non-verbal cues, not to mention the host of signals which are loosely described as 'body language'. At any rate we should not neglect the possibility that the organization may be better served, and errors more easily averted, by direct personal interaction of those involved. But neither should we forget that formality in a communication system may be associated with settlements in favour of the stronger case when an issue is in dispute (Morley and Stephenson, 1977, p. 135).

REFERENCES

Cyert, R. M., and J. G. March. (1963). *A Behavioral Theory of the Firm*. Englewood Cliffs, NJ: Prentice-Hall.

Morley, I. E., and Stephenson, G. M. (1977) *The Social Psychology of Bargaining*. London: George Allen and Unwin.

New Technology and Human Error
Edited by J. Rasmussen, K. Duncan and J. Leplat
© 1987 John Wiley & Sons Ltd

8. Models of Diagnostic Judgements*

Berndt Brehmer
University of Uppsala

SUMMARY

This chapter reviews the results from studies using the regression approach to the modelling of diagnostic judgements. The results show that people use few symptoms, that they integrate information additively, that they are inconsistent, and that there are wide interindividual differences even among experienced diagnosticians.

The diagnostic process may be divided into three stages: data collection, information integration, and feedback. The present paper is concerned only with the second of these stages: the information integration stage. This is not because the other stages are unimportant, but because most of the research on human judgement has been aimed at this stage. One reason for this may be that it provides a particular challenge, for whereas the other two stages in the diagnostic process are overt and public, the information integration stage tends to be covert and private: the diagnostician often is not able to describe how he arrives at his judgements (e.g., Hoffman, 1960).

The challenge to research, then, is this: How do we describe a mental process of which the person himself is not aware? Fortunately, there is a simple solution to this problem. This solution takes as its point of departure that although a person may not be able to describe how he makes his judgements, he is nevertheless able to make them when he is given the relevant information. If we know what judgements a person has made, and the information upon which the judgements are based, it is possible to construct a model that relates the judgements to the input information. If our model is successful, it will produce the same judgement as the person does when given the same information. The model is then a simulation of the mental process, and we will be able to learn about this covert and private process by studying the overt and public simulation.

The problem, then, is to choose an appropriate model for this simulation. Psychologists studying human judgement processes have found that linear statistical models, such as multiple regression, are useful in this context. This is not the place to discuss the reasons for this particular kind of model: I have done so at length elsewhere (Brehmer, 1979a). It is sufficient to point out two important features of these models. First, they can be used for describing systems that contain uncertainty. Thus, they can be used, not only to describe the mental process involved in diagnosis but also the diagnostic tasks. That is, the same model can be used to describe both the person and the task, and this enables us to compare them. This is important, because it makes it possible to determine the extent to which the person uses the information available for his judgements in an adequate way. This reveals how well the person performs, and will suggest how he would have to change to improve.

A second advantage of linear models is that they describe the process in terms that are readily understood by the person being analysed. This is, of course, a necessary condition if we want the person to use the information to change his mental system to improve his judgements.

Linear models have now been used to analyse diagnostic judgements in a wide variety of circumstances. The subjects studied include stockbrokers, clinical psychologists, and physicians (see, e.g., Slovic Lichtenstein, 1971 for a review). In an as yet unpublished series of studies, we have used linear models to study a variety of judgements by psychiatrists, psychologists, and nurses.

These studies are carried out in a series of standardized steps. The aim of the first step is to set up the judgement task. In this step, the subjects for the study are interviewed to ascertain what information they require for making the judgements under investigation. For example, if the purpose of the study is to investigate how the psychiatrists make judgements about the risk that a patient will commit suicide, each psychiatrist will first be asked what things he or she will need to know about the patient to decide whether or not the patient will commit suicide. These interviews will yield a list of symptoms, most of which are usually common to all of the subjects, although some, of course, may be idiosyncratic. In the second step, a subset of the symptoms on the list is selected. If the purpose of the study is to analyse the group of subjects, this list may comprise those symptoms that are common to all of the subjects. It is, however, also possible to work with each individual subject's list of symptoms, doing all analyses on a single subject basis. Whatever the approach the next step is to construct a set of 'patients' by combining the symptoms according to some set of principles. This step is critical for the success of the study in two respects. Firstly, the cases resulting from the combination of symptoms must be credible. Therefore, the set of cases should be screened by the prospective subjects. Secondly, the method used for constructing the set of cases determines what analyses may be performed. If the symptoms are combined orthogonally, it is possible to use analysis of variance procedures, but if the symptoms are correlated, multiple regression procedures must be used.

This has some consequences when it comes to testing for deviations from additivity in the combination of the information from the various symptoms (see Anderson, 1968), and for the indices of weight that are used, see below. The 'patients' are then given to the subjects who make a judgement about each case. In most studies, subjects judge each case twice, so that it becomes possible to ascertain the reliability of their judgements. The judgements are then analysed for each subject separately by analysis of variance, multiple regression or some other variety of the linear model. This analysis then yields information about five important aspects of the judgement process:

1. *The symptoms* actually used by each subject. This is shown by the presence or absence of significant main effects for the symptoms in the analyses.
2. *The relative weights* given to the symptoms. This is shown by the weight indices calculated, such as the beta weights in the multiple regression, or the ω^2 calculated from the analysis of variance results.
3. *The form of the functions relating the judgements to each symptom*, i.e., whether a symptom is used in a linear way, so that the higher the value of symptom, the higher the judgement, or whether it is used in a non-linear way, e.g., so that there is an optimum value, which leads to a high judgement, while departures from this optimum value in either direction lead to lower judgements. This information can, of course, be obtained only when the symptoms are quantitative.
4. *How the subject integrates information from different symptoms into a judgement.* He may integrate the information additively, e.g., by adding or averaging it, or configuratively, i.e., in such a way that the weight given to one symptom varies with the value of another symptom. Alternatively, he may use a multiplicative, rather than additive, rule. This aspect of the process is assessed by first examining the analysis results for significant deviations from additivity, and if there are such deviations, determining the exact form of the non-additive rule used by the subject.

    These four aspects of the judgement process — what symptoms are used, their relative importance, the functional relations between each symptom and the judgements, and the rule is used for integration of information from the symptoms into unitary judgements — are aspects of the process that are readily understood by a subject, so these aspects of the process are thus easily communicated to the subject. This, however, is not true of the fifth aspect of the process revealed by this kind of analysis:

5. *The reliability*, or consistency, *of the process.* This is the extent to which the subject uses the same rule from case to case. It is shown by the error variance in his system as estimated, for example, by the test–retest reliability of his judgements, i.e., the correlations between the judgements

made at two different occasions, or by the residual, or error variance. Whereas the analysis of actual judgement regularly shows that the process is inconsistent, people seem to have no subjective awareness of this.

The results of studies using this methodology are easy to summarize because the results are essentially the same, regardless of what kind of subjects have been studied or what kinds of judgements have been investigated. There are four main results.

The first of these is that the form of the judgement process tends to be very simple. It is simple in two aspects. Firstly, very little information seems to be used for the judgements. A person may ask for ten different symptoms for making his judgements about suicide risk, but the results of the analysis of his actual judgements then shows that he uses very few, usually only two or three. Secondly, the process is simple in that it tends to be additive rather than configural. Few studies have yielded any deviations from additivity, and when such deviations have been found, they are usually small and of little systematic importance in the process.

A second result from studies of judgement is that the process is generally found to be inconsistent. The subjects in these studies usually do not seem to use exactly the same rule from case to case, and when the same case is presented a second time, the judgement may differ considerably from what it was the first time.

A third finding in judgement studies is that there are wide individual differences in judgements. The correlation between the judgements made by two subjects for the same cases is often quite low, even though the subjects are experts with years of experience in their field. In part, this disagreement in judgements is due to lack of consistency; when the processes that produce the judgements are not perfectly reliable, the judgements cannot, of course, be perfectly correlated. However, not all of the disagreement is due to lack of reliability. There are also systematic differences between subjects in many cases. They may differ both in which symptoms they use, and in the relative weights they give to the symptoms they use.

A fourth important finding is that the subjects are not very good at describing how they make their judgements. When a model of the process is constructed from subjective descriptions of the process, the judgements produced by this model usually do not correlate very highly with those actually made by the subject (see, e.g., Hoffman, 1960).

Two results are of particular importance here. The first is that the process lacks consistency. Inconsistency of this kind seems to be a general feature of cognitive systems faced with tasks that contain uncertainty. It is not a simple matter of lack of reliability, for the degree of consistency is systematically related to the nature of the judgement task. Two aspects of the judgement task are especially important: its predictability and its complexity.

As for predictability, as defined, for example, by the multiple correlation between the cues and the variable to be judged, the results show that the degree of reliability in the subject's cognitive system varies monotonically with the predictability of the task. Thus, the higher the predictability of the task, the more consistent the subjects tend to be. This is true of various laboratory tasks, as well as of judgements collected from experts performing tasks with which they have years of experience (Brehmer, 1976). The explanation for this result is not known, but its implication is clear: the characteristics of human judgement processes depart in systematic ways from what is required for optimality according to statistical decision theory.

As for complexity, the results suggest that as the complexity of the judgement task increases, the consistency decreases. Thus, when the subjects are required to use information from few symptoms, they are more consistent than when they have to use many symptoms, and when the task requires the subjects to use non-linear rules, they are less consistent than when they have to use linear rules (Brehmer, 1971). To some extent, the subjects improve with training, but these effects seem to be rather limited (Brehmer, 1979b). These results have been interpreted to mean that, in some respects, judgement is like a motor skill. Just because a person knows what rule to use for his judgements, it is not certain that the judgements will actually follow this rule, and the subject will, of course, not detect that his judgements do not follow the rules he intends to use (Brehmer et al., 1980).

The second general result of importance in this context is that there are wide individual differences, also among experts. At first, this may be surprising, because we would expect that experts, having essentially the same kind of experience, ought to have learned about the same things. Thus, they ought to make their judgements in the same way. Analyses of the circumstances under which experts have to learn show, however, that the possibilities of learning anything from the kind of the experience provided in these settings is rather limited (Brehmer, 1980). In short, the argument is that to learn from experience in these settings, people have to have hypotheses relevant to their task. These hypotheses must be statistical hypotheses, because the tasks often contain a large measure of uncertainty. But people generally do not employ these kinds of hypotheses, and they are therefore not able to profit from experience as they should. When subjects are given statistical hypotheses, their ability to use them is severely limited, presumably because they cannot process the amount of information needed to test these statistical hypotheses in an adequate way (Brehmer, 1979c). To learn the same thing from experience, people would have to have adequate hypotheses, and use them correctly. Since they do not, it is no longer surprising that they do not learn the same thing.

These and other results (see Brehmer, 1980, for a review) show that when the task has some complexity, and when it requires the subjects to handle relations which contain some uncertainty, experience does not guarantee good judgement. The alternative would be to teach people to make good judgements. However, great problems are involved in trying to teach judgement. We have already remarked that people seem to have only limited ability to describe how they make judgements. Consequently, it is very hard for an expert to teach a novice how to make judgements in the same way he does. The problems are further exacerbated because the teacher will not understand what the pupil is doing. Consequently, the pupil is likely to be left to his own devices, and he will have to acquire whatever expertise he can get from his own experience. This means that he will have to learn on the basis of largely unintelligible remarks from his older and more experienced colleagues, and from the feedback he may receive from the system he is trying to learn. Such feedback, when provided at all, may be very rare, thus providing little information. Furthermore, the feedback will contain error, thus making it hard to use for learning. These considerations show that to teach judgement, we cannot rely on the traditional approaches to teaching. A new approach is needed.

A NEW APPROACH TO TEACHING JUDGEMENT

The most important problem in teaching judgement is to provide adequate feedback to the learner. Since diagnostic tasks are often probabilistic in nature, the feedback provided contains error, and in addition, the feedback actually provided is often very infrequent and it may occur after a considerable delay, it may not be of much use. Furthermore, it is not particularly informative even under the best of circumstances. This is because it gives only indirect information about what is to be learned. The feedback usually informs the learner only whether he was right or wrong, or, at best, about the direction of his error. It does not tell him why he made an error. Therefore, he must use the feedback information to infer why his judgement was correct or why it was not correct. This may lead to problems. A typical diagnostic task requires the person to learn relations between symptoms and judgements, and single instances of outcome feedback telling the subject that he was wrong do not inform the learner how he should change the relations between the symptoms and his judgements. If the task is probabilistic, an error may not even mean that he should change the relations between the symptoms and his judgements. Having a teacher may not help much because the teacher faces the same problem as the learner: he has to infer what was wrong with what the pupil did, since the pupil may not be able to tell him exactly what he did.

A second problem in teaching judgement is to create a good description of the task to be learned. For many judgement tasks, there may exist no objective account of the tasks; all the relevant knowledge about the task is in the heads of experts, and the experts may not be able to describe what they know in such a way that it can be used to teach a person to make judgements. Consequently, to obtain the knowledge needed, it may be necessary to analyse judgements of experts to determine what they know. An approach to the solution of this problem has already been outlined in this paper. We now turn to the problem of providing feedback.

As a step towards the solution of this problem, we (Hammond and Brehmer, 1973) have developed a computer-based system. This system presents information to the learner in the form of a series of cases. For each case, the learner makes a judgement. After a sufficient number of cases, the system performs an analysis of the judgements of the learner, and then displays the results graphically on a screen. These displays allow the learner to compare the characteristics of his cognitive system with those of the task. Thus, the system will display the relative weights given to the symptoms by the learner next to the weights he should use, so that the learner is informed of any discrepancies. Furthermore, the system displays the functional relations between each cue and the judgements together with the correct functional relations, so that the learner may compare his way of using the cue with the correct way. The system also provides information about the consistency of the judgements. Furthermore, it is also possible to display individual cases for which the learner has made especially grave errors for discussion and analysis with a teacher.

The system, then, provides exactly the kind of information needed for learning a judgement task. It does not require the learner to infer how he should change, but shows exactly what changes are needed in the parameters of his cognitive system. As might be expected, this system leads to rapid learning also when the task has considerable complexity (e.g., Hammond, 1971).

The actual experiments in using the system for training in practical situations is, as yet, rather limited, although some attempts have been made. On theoretical grounds, the system has considerable promise, and as it is tried out in new circumstances, we will know more about its practical usefulness.

APPLICATIONS TO OTHER SYSTEMS

The general approach to diagnostic judgement described in this paper is, of course, developed mainly for handling the problems related to psychological and medical diagnosis. It has not been developed for the problem of trouble shooting or assessment of mechanical and electronic systems. There is at least one important difference between the diagnostic problem facing a psychiatrist and that facing an engineer. This is that the system with which the engineer is concerned has been created by other engineers. The system facing the psychiatrist, on the other hand, has been created by forces that are unknown to him. This makes a difference. For the electronic or mechanical system, plans and specifications are available, so that it is possible, at least in principle, to find whatever is wrong with the system when it is not functioning properly. For the task facing the psychiatrist, there is no such guarantee that he will find the real problem with the patient. Thus, the psychiatrist works under genuine uncertainty, but the engineer does not.

However, it seems that the difference between the task facing the engineer and that facing the psychiatrist may be diminishing as the complexity of the technical systems increases. As these systems become more complex (say on the order of a nuclear plant or a computer), it no longer seems possible to predict the systems perfectly, and it becomes harder and harder to decide when the system is functioning properly. The task facing those who take care of these systems thus seems to approach that facing psychiatrists, or others who take care of systems not created by man. This suggests that the cognitive processes of engineers in these tasks would become similar to those of physicians and psychologists, and that the general approach developed for the study of diagnostic judgement in these areas would become applicable also to the tasks facing the engineer.

REFERENCES

Anderson, N. H. (1968) A simple model for information integration. In: R. P. Abelson, E. Aronson, W. J. McGuire, T. M. Newcomb, M. J. Rosenberg, and P. E. Tannenbaum (Eds), *Theories of Cognitive Consistency: A Sourcebook*. Chicago: Rand McNally, pp. 731–43.

Brehmer, B. (1971) Subjects' ability to use functional rules. *Psychonomic Science*, **24**, 259–60.

Brehmer, B. (1976) Note on clinical judgment and the formal characteristics of clinical tasks. *Psychological Bulletin*, **83**, 778–82.

Brehmer, B. (1979a) Preliminaries to a psychology of inference. *Scandinavian Journal of Psychology*, **20**, 193–210.

Brehmer, B. (1979b) Effect of practice on utilization of nonlinear rules in inference tasks. *Scandinavian Journal of Psychology*, **20**, 141–9.

Brehmer, B. (1979c) Note on hypothesis testing in probabilitic inference tasks. *Scandinavian Journal of Psychology*, **20**, 155–8.

Brehmer, B. (1980) In one word: Not from experience. *Acta Psychologica*, **45**, 223–41.

Brehmer, B., Hagafors, R., and Johansson, R. (1980) Cognitive skills in judgment: Subjects' ability to use information about weights, function forms, and organizational principles. *Organizational Behavior and Human Performance*, **26**, 373–85.

Hammond, K. R. (1971) Computer graphics as an aid to learning. *Science*, **172**, 903–8.

Hammond, K. R., and Brehmer, B. (1973) Quasi-rationality and distrust: Implications for international conflict. In: D. Summers, and L. Rappoport (Eds), *Human Judgment and Social Interaction*. New York: Holt, Rinehart and Winston, pp. 338–91.

Hoffman, P. J. (1960) Paramorphic representation of clinical judgment. *Psychological Bulletin*, **57**, 116–31.

Slovic, P., and Lichtenstein, S. (1971) Comparison of Bayesian and regression approaches to the study of information processing in judgment. *Organizational Behavior and Human Performance*, **6**, 649–744.

*Preparation of this paper was supported by grants from the Swedish National Defence Institute and the Swedish Council for Social Science Research.

New Technology and Human Error
Edited by J. Rasmussen, K. Duncan and J. Leplat
© 1987 John Wiley & Sons Ltd

9. On the Difficulties People Have in Dealing with Complexity

Dietrich Dörner
University of Bamberg

SUMMARY

In this chapter we analyse the mistakes of human subjects when tackling problems in complex, non-transparent, and dynamic environments. Behaviour of subjects in a complex planning and decision-making task has been observed and analysed for regularities. Distinct differences between good and weak subjects have been found, throwing a light on the strengths and weaknesses of human cognition when confronted with complex problems.

INTRODUCTION

Human thinking and action in very complex areas is not easy to analyse. In reality it drags on over long periods of time and is only casuistically observable; one does not know to what extent the results can be generalized and whether the results represent general laws of human behaviour.

We sought a way out of this difficulty by transferring complex environments to the laboratory. One can use computers to simulate reality by programming them to represent models of political or economic systems, for example. It is possible to define the social, psychological, economic, and ecological relations of a small city as a network of interrelations and then simulate this with a computer. The computer acts then — more or less in accordance with reality — like a small town.

Such a simulation of reality makes it possible to analyse psychological processes in great detail and for many individuals, such as can otherwise only be superficially observed in a limited number of people. In one of our experiments we gave subjects the task of ruling the fate of a small mid-European town named Lohhausen as mayor. Figure 1 shows the map of Lohhausen.

The town had approximately 3500 residents and lived mainly from a municipal industrial enterprise, a manufacturing plant producing watches.

In addition, there was a city administration, doctors' practices, retail stores and shops, a bank, schools, kindergardens, etc. This system existed as a

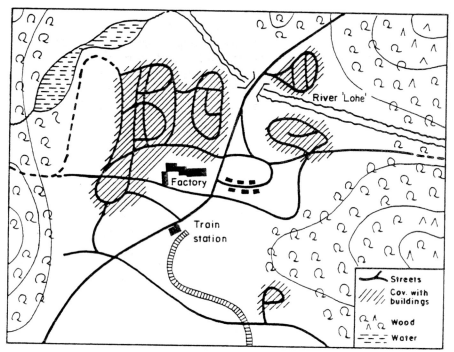

Figure 1. The map of the town of Lohhausen

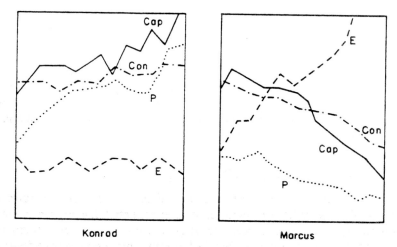

Konrad   Marcus

Figure 2. The development of Lohhausen for a very good subject
(Konrad) and a very bad subject (Marcus) with regard to some important
variables. CAP = capital, CON = contentment, P = production, E =
number of unemployed people

computer model. In this system there were many different measures possible. Subjects were able to influence production and sales policies of the city factory, to vary rates of taxation, to create employment positions for school and kindergarden teachers, to establish and lease doctors' practices, to urge on housing construction, to provide for leisure time arrangements, etc.

Many subjects accomplished this task very well, others not as well. Figure 2 shows the development of the town for a very good subject (Konrad) and a very bad one (Marcus).

It is an interesting question, why some people apparently are able to deal with such complex structures without prior training, while others, in certain cases *with* relevant pretraining, only master the task in an unsatisfactory manner. I don't want to pursue this question at this time, however.

I shall now be concerned mainly with the mistakes of the bad subjects and I shall try to systematize these mistakes to find out the psychological background of the behaviour of the subjects. First I shall discuss some primary mistakes which nearly all subjects make as they begin, and then review especially the mistakes of subjects with poor performances.

PRIMARY MISTAKES

There is a series of mistakes which almost all subjects make when dealing with complex systems.

The insufficient consideration of processes in time

When solving such complex tasks, most people are not interested in finding out the existent trends and developmental tendencies at first, but are interested instead in the *status quo*. For example, they are not interested in the way in which city assets have developed in recent years, but rather the amount of money in the city treasury at the moment. This information is practically meaningless, however, without knowledge of developmental tendencies and their determinants.

Difficulties in dealing with exponential developments

In connection with the judgement of processes in time it is also significant that almost all subjects have difficulties with exponential developments. For certain reasons, exponential curves are of great significance in all systems in which growth or decline appears. People have absolutely no intuitive feeling for processes which develop exponentially, although they are surrounded by such. When subjects are asked to estimate such curves, something like the result depicted in Figure 3 typically appears.

This implies that someone who reads in the newspaper, for instance that 6% growth is possible in the long run, is not in the position to understand this piece of information. The dynamic and almost explosive acceleration which exponential curves display is assessed in a completely false way. This inability to deal with exponential functions when working with complex material causes unbelievable amazement and astonishment over developments which are unforeseen in the eyes of the subjects, but which in reality are precisely predictable at closer view.

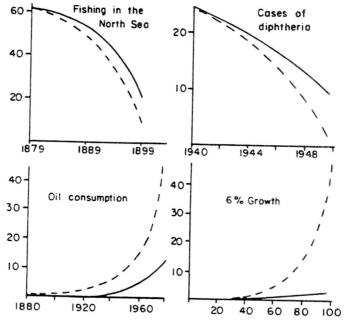

Figure 3. Average estimated values (———) and actual exponential curves (------) for some examples of exponential growth and dedim. Data from Bürkle (1978)

Thinking in causal series instead of in causal nets

A third, quite general mistake is the tendency to think in causal *series*, not in causal nets. Subjects who are not accustomed to dealing with complexity usually only see the aspired main effect of the measure, and not the side effects which also appear. There are several examples of this type stemming from the early days of policy making involving aid to developing countries, for example, and not only in this area.

People make these and other mistakes. Some can learn from them and adapt their thinking to the challenges of the situation, others don't succeed in doing this.

MISTAKES OF SUBJECTS WITH POOR PERFORMANCES

Poor performers show a low assessment of their own ability to act. There exists a statistically significant relationship between the self-assessment of the subjects and their performance (Kreuzig, 1978). It is, however, not clear whether the self-assessment of poor performers is low, *a priori*, or whether the low self-assessment develops in the course of the experiment. We assume, that there exists a low self-assessment of the bad subjects, *a priori*, which in a positive feedback loop is weakened further by the experience of failure.

Some consequences of low self-assessment (resulting from data of Stäudel (1979) and Reither (1979)) are depicted in Figure 4.

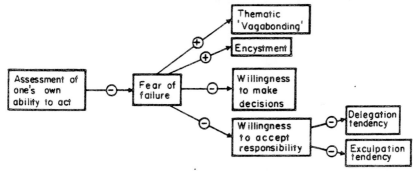

Figure 4. Consequences of the fear of failure. —⊕→ implies a 'positive' relationship: 'if more . . . then more' resp. 'if less . . . then less'. —⊖→ implies a negative relation: 'if more . . . then less . . .' resp. 'if less . . . then more'

Failure, despite efforts to get control of the situation, threatens the individual. The continual failure of one's action in a certain area implies that one doesn't have control over this area. Continuous failure induces a *loss of control*. One begins to estimate one's own ability to act as being very low. The loss of control implies *fear*; above all, a fear of a further loss of control, fear of failure, the consequences of which are given below.

Thematic vagabonding

This is manifested in the fact that individuals change the topic under consideration relatively quickly and often, without thinking a theme out to the end and ending it. People jump from one topic to the next, treating all superficially, in certain cases picking up again topics dealt with earlier; they don't go beneath the surface with any topic and seldom finish any. This intellectual vagabonding has already been superficially demonstrated (Dörner, 1979) and we interpret it as escape behaviour. Whenever subjects have difficulties dealing with a topic, they leave it alone, so that they don't have to face their own helplessness more than necessary.

Encystment

At first glance this tendency seems to be the opposite of the one mentioned above. Subjects stick to a subject matter, enclose themselves in it, treating small details very fondly, and don't take on anything else. This tendency is only apparently opposite to the tendency to thematic vagabonding. In reality subjects enclose themselves in those areas which don't seem to offer them any difficulty. These are usually the least problematic and therefore unimportant areas.

Decreasing willingness to make decisions

The number of decisions decreases. Figure 5 shows this clearly. One sees here that the number of decisions made by poor subjects increases up to the fourth session, then sinks, however, to stagnate on a low level.

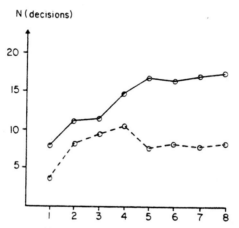

Figure 5. Average number of decisions in each of the eight sessions of the Lohhausen experiment. (————): good subjects; (------): poor subjects

In addition, subjects postpone the decisions for a later time; they begin to fear having to make decisions and try to avoid them.

Tendency to delegate

This is closely related to the previous heading. Subjects try to shift decisions which they are responsible for, to other decision-making authorities. 'The head of the housing department should worry about that!' said one subject after his efforts to finance housing construction were in vain.

Exculpation tendency

This tendency is closely related to the delegation tendency. Subjects try to find external reasons for their failure, in order to free themselves from responsibility. Many subjects expressed something like 'You've intentionally programmed the system in such a way that it is not *possible* to succeed in dealing with it!' Others blamed the workers' laziness or the management's inability for the deplorable failure.

EMERGENCY SITUATIONS

A situation which proves to be inaccessible to the efforts of the subjects, which becomes more and more uncontrollable with time, not only induces fear because it endangers the individual's self-confidence, but is also threatening because one doesn't know everything that can happen.

Such a situation is therefore not only a danger to the subjective estimation of one's own competence; the danger extends and attacks the physical intactness and existence in some cases. (Our game situations were naturally harmless in this respect; we presume, however, that general situations which elude one's own control can be detrimental in quite a general way and not only harmful in respect to the individual feeling of well-being.)

A critical situation causes an *intellectual emergency reaction*. The entire system of action becomes adapted to a *quick readiness to react*. A quick readiness to act is hindered by an intellectual level which is too high.

Searching for *new* possibilities of action is out of place in a dangerous situation; it takes up too much time. It is better to employ the secure 'programmed' inventory of reactions which is available from acquired stimulus–reaction sequences. In extreme cases 'thinking' becomes totally eliminated in danger situations. One turns into a reflexive being who acts 'automatically'; anyone who has been in an extremely dangerous situation, for example while driving, can confirm this.

The sinking of the intellectual level, which we observed in our experiments whenever subjects lost control of the situation, is the result of such a general emergency reaction, we believe. One observes the following details.

Reduction in the number of self-reflections

Phases of self-reflection, in which subjects recapitulate and critically analyse their own past action and thought, are of great significance for changing and improving one's own thinking. The number of such elements making up the cognitive process decreases under conditions of failure. This indicates, we believe, that a certain cognitive emergency reaction occurs. Closely related to a decrease in those phases of the thinking process which contain a critical self-analysis of the procedure employed is a series of other symptoms, depicted in Figure 6.

Reduction in the number of plans

Subjects usually 'programme' their behaviour more or less by means of 'plans'. They say: 'First I must do this, then that; if that is the case, then I must take care of . . .', etc.,.. These programmes are a rather important part of the cognitive process, as they guarantee a systematic progression of thought; accordingly, their temporary loss results in a less coherent cognitive process. Furthermore, loss implies the decompensation of thinking, the dissipation of thinking in disconnected individual actions (see Reither, 1979). The fact that this dissipation of thinking actually occurs is supported by the fact that thinking becomes increasingly characterized by stereotyping.

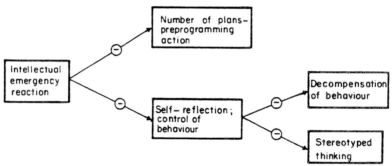

Figure 6. Consequences of reduced self-reflection. Further explanations to be found in the text

Increasing stereotyping

With an increasing rate of failure it is possible to observe that subjects become less and less aware that they are following the same thought sequence once again. It occurs more and more frequently that subjects think over the same sequence as before all over again. The fact that they don't notice this points to a decreased amount of self-control.

Decreasing control over the realization of plans

This is a further index for the decrease in self-control. We have already shown that the number of programs represented in the number of expressed plans clearly sinks when subjects tend to face failure. If one compares the relative number of realized intentions of good subjects to the corresponding number of subjects who tend to fail, one can see that the number of *realized* intentions clearly sinks in relation to the number of suggested plans. That implies that subjects facing failure don't even control whether those plans which they themselves have considered have been realized.

The cognitive emergency reaction which we have described above doesn't only involve lowering the intellectual level. In addition, it is important to master the situation. A dangerous situation must be quickly overcome; we presume that for this reason the emergency reaction creates a readiness for quick action. This tendency has a series of consequences which we have depicted in Figure 7. It is not possible to act quickly when one takes too many conditions for one's own action into account. The intellectual emergency reaction causes a reduction in the number of conditions considered before decision making.

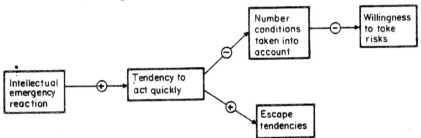

Figure 7. Consequences resulting from the tendency to (re)act quickly. Further explanations to be found in the text

CONDITIONS CONSIDERED BEFORE DECISION MAKING

Increase in risky behaviour

Subjects are prepared to put up with a greater number of risks if they have previously experienced failure. A tendency to master the situation 'at any price' seems to appear.

Increase in the number of violations against rules and regulations

This is closely related to the increase in risky behaviour. The more subjects are exposed to failures, the less their willingness to stick to given rules or regulations. One can generally say that subjects' behaviour becomes more 'absolute'. Peripheral conditions for limiting behaviour to certain forms are increasingly disregarded. It is no longer of interest whether or not a certain type of behaviour is allowed or forbidden; the only important thing is whether or not it can help to achieve the aspired goal. It would probably be very easy for the unsuccessful subjects in our experiment to accept the saying that 'the end justifies the means'.

Increase in the tendency to escape

It is therefore not surprising, that under these conditions it is also possible to report an increase in escapism. One can clearly observe that the number of attempts to escape from the situation increases. This is expressed for example in the fact that subjects facing failure tend to lengthen their pauses to a greater extent or begin to talk with the experimenter about topics having nothing to do with the experiment. It is not possible to decide whether the tendency to escape really is due merely to the intellectual emergency reaction, or whether the attempt to avoid failure is an additional factor; one can assume that both are important.

THE NATURE OF THE SITUATION

It is not only important to act in *any way* in a situation; it is important to behave adequately for the respective situation. Therefore, it is important to have a clear picture of the situation. One must know the character of the situation to be able to act wisely.

It is characteristic of complex situations that one doesn't have complete knowledge of the situation, but rather that one must acquire this information while acting. An additional cognitive task for a complex situation is thus the formation of hypotheses. One can observe subjects' characteristic deformations under the influence of failure with respect to the formation of hypotheses, which we summarize in Figure 8.

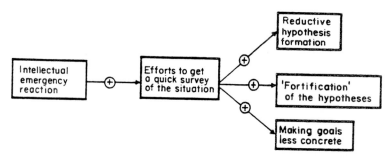

Figure 8. Results of the attempt to get a survey quickly. Explanations in the text

Hypothesis formation becomes increasingly more global

This fact implies that subjects try to reduce more and more characteristics to fewer and fewer causes. A differentiated system of individual hypotheses, which one — for lack of knowledge — neglects to integrate, when an integration doesn't simply result by itself, yields a rough, radially organized general hypothesis, in which all 'phenomena' are attributed to a central cause. Figure 8 shows this development.

Subjects usually make partial hypotheses about existing relationships on the basis of past experience, which do not necessarily become integrated. Figure 9(a) shows an example of this. Under conditions of failure the pressure to integrate and build a general hypothesis apparently rises, which takes on a reductive form, as depicted in Figure 9(b). All facts are attributed to a central motive here ('contentment of the population'). Such total hypotheses are also well known to us from other sources, moreover, and take on the form of the following examples: 'Only the profit greediness of the big business and the multis . . .' 'Only the subversive activity of the imperialistic Soviet Communism . . .' 'Only the international Judaism . . .', etc.

Reductive hypotheses are very attractive for the simple reason that they reduce insecurity with one stroke and encourage the feeling that things are understood. (They can even be right — why not, that can be proved. The probability is rather low, however, that organic structures are monocausal and radially organized.) The degeneration of hypothesis formation is accompanied by a deformation of the *methods* of testing the hypotheses.

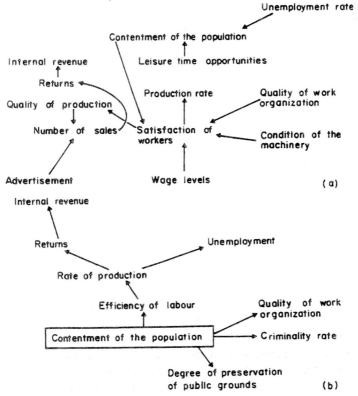

Figure 9. 'Normal' network hypotheses (Figure 9a) and reductive hypotheses (Figure 9b)

'Fortification' tendency

The strictest way to test the validity of an hypothesis is to attempt to disprove it. Subjects don't display this tendency at first; they don't look for disproof, but rather for confirmation. In the course of the experiment good subjects change to a strategy involving refutation of their hypotheses, whereas poor subjects continue looking for confirming information. This is a dangerous tendency and is the same as an 'entrenchment' of previously formed hypotheses. By ignoring or rationalizing information which could refute an hypothesis, it is possible to maintain each hypothesis as long as desired. This can be observed by unsuccessful subjects.

Goals become less concrete

A further effect of the tendency to deal quickly with a situation is the fact that goals become less concrete.

At the beginning of the experiment, subjects mostly pursue very concrete goals which are very precisely specified. This picture changes with increasing failure. One can also keep the number of proposed goals lower by being abstract as many concrete goals can be subsumed by one abstract one. On the other hand, the ability of concrete goals to guide action decreases as goals become more abstract. One can still deduce what must be done to reach the following goal from the sentence: 'Increase sales/returns from the city watch factory!' This goal can function as a directing force. It is a different story with the goal 'Increase residents' happiness!' The assertion of this goal is indeed praiseworthy and certifies the individual's humanitarian intentions; it is rather difficult, however, to deduce concrete measures from this goal.

Both a decrease in the amount of self-control and the building of less concrete goals are responsible for the fact that in the face of increasing failure subjects' general behaviour becomes increasingly decompensated and decomposes more and more into unconnected individual actions (Reither, 1979).

CONCLUSIONS

The total sum of tendencies brewed here together apparently makes up quite a troublesome mixture. Although each tendency taken alone doesn't always seem to be an unreasonable consequence to the situation, taken collectively they result in a combination which gives occasion for consideration. This becomes clear upon intensifying the depicted tendencies somewhat.

In the extreme situation the tendency to become less willing to make decisions and the tendency to shift responsibility, for example, change to a state of indecisive semiconsciousness, into which the person lethargically drifts at random, as it were, standing next to or outside of things. This state is by all means compatible with the fact that the same person, upon being urged to act, tends to resort to extremely hard measures and to take extreme risks at the next moment, not feeling responsible for any negative consequences.

Let's turn to other possible consequences of behaviour tendencies described above: isn't it possible to deduce from the tendency to shift responsibility and the exculpation tendency, along with a simultaneous reduction in the willingness to act, the existence of an increased willingness to subordinate to the leadership of individuals or institutions which claim or verify that they have the correct plan of action? We believe that this is in accordance with the depicted behavioural tendencies, especially when one additionally considers the tendency to build reductive hypotheses, which we have described above. Reductive hypotheses are those which explain the phenomena of an area in terms of a single motive.

The tendency to shift responsibility and the fear of acting, coupled with the simultaneous feeling that one must act, and the tendency to build reductive hypotheses, build, in short, a potential which induces the acceptance of totalitarian theories and ideologies coupled with a simultaneous willingness to resign from acting and let other (more competent?) institutions do so.

If one includes the tendency to test hypotheses exclusively by verifying them, i.e., to exclude all falsifying information, then an additional ingredient appears in the cocktail described thus far, namely the tendency to entrench one's own opinions, in short, the tendency to become obstinate and dogmatic.

It must be stressed that all these conclusions are generalizations from generally observable behaviour tendencies. We therefore believe that certain deformations and degenerations of reason are to a certain extent natural effects of general human behaviour patterns.

REFERENCES

Bürkle, A. (1978) Die Bedingungsabhängigkeit der Schätzung exponentieller Verläufe. Diploma thesis, FB 06, Psychologie, Universität Gießen.

Dörner, D. (1978) Merkmale der kognitiven Struktur 'guter' und 'schlechter' Versuchspersonen beim Umgang mit einem sehr komplexen System. In: H. Ueckert and D. Rhenius (Eds), *Komplexe menschliche Informationsverarbeitung*. Bern: Huber.

Dörner, D. and Stäudel, T. (1979) Planen und Entscheiden in sehr komplexen Systemen. In: H. Eckensberger (Ed.), *Bericht über den 31*. Kongreß der Deutschen Gesellschaft für Psychologie in Mannheim, 1978. Hogrefe Göttingen.

Kreuzig, H. W. (1978) Möglichkeiten zur Prognose der Güte komplexer geistiger Abläufe. In: H. Eckensberger (Ed.), *Bericht über den 31*. Kongreß der Deutschen Gesellschaft für Psychologie in Mannheim, 1978. Hogrefe, Göttingen.

Reither, F. (1979) Über die Selbstreflexion beim Problem-lösen. Dissertation am Fachbereich 06, Psychologie, Universität Gießen.

Stäudel, T. (1979) Das Entscheidungsverhalten in sehr komplexen Realitätsbereichen. Diploma thesis, FB 06, Psychologie, Universität Gießen.

New Technology and Human Error
Edited by J. Rasmussen, K. Duncan and J. Leplat
© 1987 John Wiley & Sons Ltd

10. Development of Mental Models for Decision in Technological Systems

Berndt Brehmer*
University of Uppsala

SUMMARY

Decision making in technological systems is discussed from a control perspective. In this perspective, the models of the system which the operators develop are the central problem. Results on mental models for statistic and dynamic systems are reviewed which indicate that operators may have problems also under common circumstances.

INTRODUCTION

The object of decision making is control, and to control a system, a person must develop a model of the system he wishes to control (Conant and Ashby, 1970). Before the advent of modern technology, such mental models could usually be developed on the basis of direct experience of the system to be controlled. That is, models for systems could be developed on the basis of concrete information about all of the steps in the process to be controlled.

Modern technology makes this impossible. It changes man's relation to his environment both on the output side and the input side, and this has important consequences for his ability to develop adequate mental models to guide him when making decisions.

On the output side, technology changes man's powers to act, both with respect to the magnitude of the consequences of the actions and with respect to the temporal and spatial reach of these actions. This, of course, creates needs for planning and careful decision making that just did not exist, say, 100 years ago, or even 50 years ago, for that matter.

However, technology makes the relation between actions and outcomes opaque, because this relation is often hidden in complex and interdependent processes. In many cases, we literally do not know how the effects of our decisions are brought about. This is not only true in the proverbial case of the ordinary person using a TV set, but also of workers operating process plants, and of politicians who attempt to control inflation by this or that means which has been suggested to them by economic technology.* In all these cases, the decision makers are limited to observing the relation between their actions and the outcomes of these actions, but they do not see much of the process that mediates this relation. Clearly, these are not conditions that are conducive to finding a good model of the system which will help the decision makers cope with unexpected chains of events.

The effects on the input side are as drastic as those on the output side. At first, the main effect of technology may seem to be to facilitate decision making in that it provides new and convenient ways of supplying huge masses of information for a given decision. Such wealth of information leads to the problem of information overload, however, and it creates a need for ways of condensing the information into a more manageable form.

More important, however, is that technology changes the basic character of the information available for decision. Information technology does, of course, not transmit reality itself, it transmits only a representation of reality. Representations are, of course, not only indirect and abstract, they are also models, models that have been created by the designers of the information system for the explicit or implicit purpose of facilitating a foreseeable range of decisions. This means that an important part of the decision-making power in the system is in the hands of these designers, rather than in the hands of the decision maker proper, because by designing the system to give certain information, the range of possible decisions has been limited. This is true both for the operator of a process plant, who will get only that information about the state of the plant through his displays that the designer of these displays has decided to give him, and for the manager of the plant who will get only the information about the state of the market and his sales that his economists have decided to give him. Moreover, the information in both cases will be highly abstract, and bear little direct relation to the process that the decision maker seeks to control. We could thus think of the designer of the information systems as akin to the bureaucrat who prepares the background information for a political or administrative decision, and who supplies the information *he* thinks that the decision maker needs. There is, however, one important difference: the information system of, say, a process plant cannot be asked to supply additional information, while the bureaucrat certainly can be asked to provide more and different kinds of information if the decision maker thinks of a new option not foreseen by the bureaucrat. This does not mean that the process plant operator will not try to get more information from the system than it was designed to give. He does so by manipulating the system, trying to figure out how it works. Thereby he builds a mental model of the system that he cannot do from the information provided by the displays only. Such system manipulation is a serious problem in many kinds of plants, but it should surprise no one that it occurs because it may be the only way in which the operator can develop the model he needs to control the system. To conclude, then, it is clear that technology makes man's relation to the system he seeks to control abstract and indirect.

Both the information he receives and the outcomes he creates are mediated by complex processes that are hidden from direct view. Work thus becomes mental and abstract, rather than physical and concrete. Decision making becomes the very essence of this mental work, for work in the control room of a process plant is similar to that in the board room in that it is a question of selecting actions rather than of performing actions. The problem, then, is how people are able to form those mental models that can help them to make these decisions under conditions where they have little insight into the process they want to control. In the remainder of this paper we will report some results from studies involving two rather different kinds of decision problems, which may shed some light on this problem.

STATIC DECISIONS TASKS: THE CASE OF DIAGNOSIS

A *static* decision task is defined as one that allows only one decision, and where the decision problem does not change while the decision is being made. The archetypical example of such a decision problem is whether or not to buy a ticket in a lottery. Here, however, we will discuss the problem of diagnosis in clinical psychology as an example of such a static task.

Diagnosis in clinical psychology utilizes a particular technology, that of mental tests. A mental test is a perfect example of how technology creates large amounts of abstract and indirect information for decision making. Thus, in a test, the personality of a living person is captured in a number of (usually quantitative) scales of an abstract nature, and these scales comprise more information about the patient, considered as an instance of the patient population, than the clinician could collect if he knew the patient for many years. At the same time, the test only gives information about those aspects of the patient deemed important by the test constructor, and as a representation of the living person, the test profile is indirect and abstract, to say the least.

Mental tests usually have manuals that define how they should be used, but, of course, a clinician often develops his own ideas about how the test scores should be interpreted. This is, of course, what we should expect, first because even when the tests are used according to the manual, they are less than perfect, and the clinician will therefore seek to improve upon the manual from his own experience and, second, because the clinician may want to make decisions that the test designer has not foreseen. However, the clinicians are usually not too successful in their attempts to improve the manual. There has been considerable research on how clinicians use tests. In 1954, Meehl demonstrated that a simple statistical combination of test results usually outperformed clinicians. Later research has confirmed these findings. These results have also shown that there are considerable individual differences among clinicians in how they use a given test (e.g., Goldberg, 1970). Moreover, clinicians are found to be inconsistent, i.e., their judgements lack reliability, and the reliability of their judgement processes has proved to be a monotone function of the predictability of the test (Brehmer, 1976). Finally, the results showed that experience with a given test often fails to improve the clinicians' judgements (see, for example, Brehmer, 1980; Goldberg, 1959).

An attempt to simulate the conditions under which clinicians learn to use tests has been created in the psychological laboratory in the form of the multiple-cue probability learning experiment. In these experiments, subjects are required to learn to use a set of cues (symptoms) to make judgements (diagnoses) about a criterion variable (the disease) that is probabilistically related to the cues. The simulation has met with some success for the results from studies with this paradigm are similar to those obtained in studies on clinical judgement (Brehmer, 1976, 1980).

The results suggest that multiple-cue probability learning tasks are learned by a hypothesis testing process where subjects sample hypotheses from an established hierarchy of hypotheses about possible cue criterion relations (Brehmer, 1980). Some hypotheses, such as the hypothesis that a relation is a positive linear function, are dominant and tried first by the subjects. If this hypothesis is found inadequate, they proceed to try other hypotheses but the set of possible hypotheses seems highly limited. Most subjects seem to lack any notion that the relations between cues and criterion may be probabilistic, and they therefore fail to develop the statistical prediction rules suitable for these tasks. Instead, they go on switching hypotheses for hundreds of trials (Brehmer, 1980). That is, they become inconsistent, just as the clinicians, and there are wide individual differences in actual utilization, depending on what hypotheses the individual had available just as there is in clinical judgement. However, that the subjects do not have an adequate statistical strategy does not mean that their performance is totally unsuccessful. The deterministic systems they develop in multiple-cue probability learning often provide a good approximation to the optical statistical strategy, at least if the task is mainly linear, and this is, of course, true in many cases of clinical judgement also (Brehmer, 1984). It is just that the decisions are not quite as good as they could have been. Reading the manual for the test they are asked to learn to use does not seem to protect the subjects from being affected by the probabilistic feedback. Subjects who have been given full information about the nature of the cue–criterion relations nevertheless become inconsistent in a multiple-cue probability learning task, and when interviewed about their rules after the experiment, they have often found new rules that they consider better than the (actually) optimal rules given by the experimenter (Ekegren, 1983). In this, our subjects are obviously quite similar to the clinicians who devise their own rules for using a test, even though they have studied the manual that gives them the optimal rules for using the test.

The results obtained with psychiatrists and clinical psychologists have now been replicated with many other professional groups (see, e.g., Slovic and Lichtenstein, 1971). There are thus grounds for assuming that these results have some generality for static diagnostic tasks where decisions are made from abstract information, where there is noise in the relations between this information and the outcome, and where the actual process connecting symptoms and outcomes is hidden from view. Under these conditions, then, we can expect that people will develop their own rules, that these rules will be constrained by the hypotheses they can come up with, and that they will end up making judgements with less than perfect reliability. To some extent, having groups, rather than individuals working with these kinds of tasks will lead to more efficient learning. This is because it increases the probability that at least one of the persons in the group will have the correct hypothesis for the tasks. However, groups have a number of problems of their own, and communication failures may lead the group to be less efficient than the individual persons (Andersson, 1978).

DYNAMIC DECISION PROBLEMS: THE CASE OF FIRE FIGHTING

A dynamic decision problem is characterized by: (a) that a series of interdependent decisions are required to reach the goal; (b) that the environment changes over time; (c) that the decisions change the state of the world, thus creating a new decision problem (Edwards, 1962).

Dynamic problems differ from static problems in that there is no recognized normative theory for the dynamic problems comparable to statistical decision theory that provides the normative theory for statistic decision problems. Yet, people obviously cope with these dynamic problems despite that there is no normative theory to guide them. By studying how they do that, we may not only learn what factors affect their ability to cope with these problems but also perhaps get some helpful hints concerning how tasks of this kind should be performed. That is, perhaps some steps towards a normative theory could be taken from descriptive data.

To study these kinds of problems, we (Brehmer et al., 1983; Karlsson et al., 1984) have developed DESSY: The Dynamic Environmental Simulation System. DESSY is a general computer program for simulating dynamic decision problems. The current version, DESSY-F, is concerned with fire fighting. The general features of the system that we simulate are illustrated in Figure 1. As can be seen from the figure, DESSY-F simulates the decision problems facing a fire chief who obtains information about forest fires from a reconnaissance plane. The information is displayed on a graphics terminal in front of him. Fires are reported accurately and without delay by the plane. When a fire breaks out the fire chief can send his fire fighting units to the fire by means of one of two commands: either an unconditional command to go to a given place regardless of whether a fire is encountered *en route*;

or by a command which enables the fire fighting unit to move towards a given location and start fighting those fires they may meet on their way to this location. The fire fighting units report back to the fire chief about their location and the results of their actions, but these reports may be delayed. As the fire chief is fighting one fire, a new fire might start. The fires spread according to weather conditions such as direction of the wind. In fighting the fires he has two goals. The one with the highest priority is to prevent the fire from reaching the base where he himself is located. The second goal is to minimize the area that is burned down.

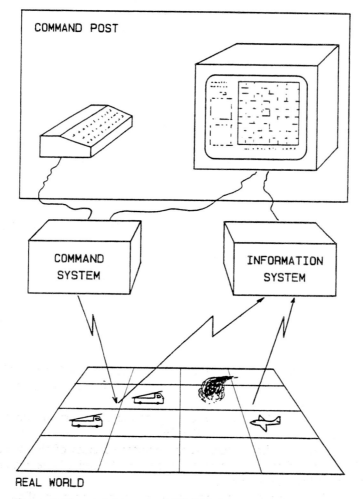

Figure 1. General features of DESSY-F, the version simulating the decision problems facing a fire chief. For explanation, see text

The fire chief receives information about fires, locations of his fire fighting units, their actions and the weather conditions on the display (see Figure 2).

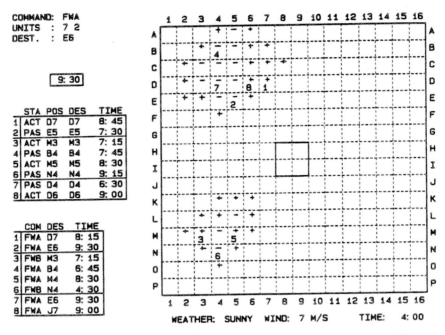

Figure 2. The display facing the 'fire chief' in the DESSY-F experiments. The + signs indicate fire, the − signs fire that has been put out, the numbers indicate the location of the various fire fighting units, and the outline rectangle in the middle the base that must be protected. The weather report is given under the 'map', and the displays to the left give information about the actions of the units, when they reported, and what commands have been given and at what time

DESSY makes it possible to vary the seven fundamental characteristics of a dynamic system:

1. *Complexity* which is defined in terms of number of possible actions (number of fire fighting units) and their relative efficiency, and the number of fires.
2. *Quality of information*, i.e., the quality of the information about the process being controlled, that is, the fire(s).
3. *Quality of feedback*, i.e., information about the results of the decision maker's actions, that is, what parts of the fire the units have managed to put out and where they are.
4. *Cycle time*, i.e., the rate of change in the process being controlled.
5. *Relation between the process being controlled and the means used for this control*. In the case of fire fighting, the process (fires) spreads

exponentially while the fire fighting units work linearly, and this defines the problem for the decision maker, but of course many other kinds of relations can be envisaged.

6. *Distribution of power*, i.e., whether all decision-making power is concentrated to one central decision maker, or if it is distributed so that local units are allowed to make decisions on their own.

7. *Probabilism or determinism*, i.e., whether some relations in the system are inherently probabilistic, or deterministic.

In the fire fighting application, complexity is set at eight fire fighting units in most experiments, with all units being equally efficient (both of these factors have been varied, however). The quality of information is made perfect; the quality of feedback has been varied with no delay being compared to a minimum delay of feedback, cycle time is rather slow, the relation between process and means is that the fire spreads exponentially while the units work linearly, distribution of power is optional; the subjects may choose between two kinds of commands as stated above, and the system is perfectly deterministic.

The DESSY experiments capture many of the features of decision making in technological systems as described in the introduction. Thus, all information is indirect and abstract, both on the input and output side. No actions are performed, the decision maker only has to choose between various possible actions and issue commands, and there is no direct insight into the actual process. That is, neither the fire nor the work of the fire fighting units is ever seen.

Clearly, DESSY could be used to simulate a variety of control tasks, i.e., working in a process plant, fighting a battle, running a business, or fighting disease.

For the experiments performed this far, our principal research question has been that of what affects subjects' ability to develop an adequate mental model for controlling a dynamic system. So far, we have concentrated on two variables: *complexity*, defined in terms of the number of units the subject has at his disposal for fighting the fires, and in terms of the relative efficiency of these units; and *feedback delay*.

In the experiments, the subjects solve eight different problems, two a day for four different days. Solving a problem requires between 15 and 20 minutes, on the average.

The results (Brehmer *et al.*, 1983) are reasonably clear. Complexity has little, or no, effect on performance, so long as the total efficiency of the units as a whole is kept constant. The subjects do not learn to differentiate between more efficient and less efficient fire fighting units, even when the more efficient units put out fires four times as fast as the less efficient units. They do form beliefs about the relative efficiency of the units, however, but the correlations between their estimates of efficiency and actual efficiency are virtually zero.

Delay of feedback, on the other hand, has truly disastrous effects on subjects' ability to control the system. Even when the delay is minimal, there is virtually no improvement over problems. When feedback delay was introduced for only some of the units, the subjects were unable to distinguish those units that reported with some delay from those that did not.

These results suggest that the subjects do not manage to form any truly predictive model of the system. Instead, they only react on direct feedback. This works reasonably well when there is no feedback delay, but is, of course, disastrous when feedback is delayed, because the subjects will then always be behind in their actions.

Another indication that the subjects do not realize the implications of feedback delay is that they do not use the commands which give some freedom of action to the units themselves. Such delegation of responsibility is, of course, the only possible way in which they could cope with the effects of feedback delay. When there is such delay, the local unit commanders will always have better information about what needs to be done than the centrally placed decision maker who always receives his information too late. It is interesting to note that as things get more difficult near the end of a problem when most of the forest has burned down and the fire threatens the base, the subjects are less willing to delegate responsibility. This suggests that stress may lead to attempts at overcontrol, a finding consistent with some of the results of Dörner (this volume).

Our work on dynamic decision making is only at the beginning. Much more needs to be done before more solid generalizations can be made. Nevertheless, we feel that the results with respect to the effects of feedback delay can be trusted to generalize also to other systems. This is important because feedback delay is presumably much more common than immediate feedback. The results suggest that if feedback delays cannot be engineered out of the system, the decision-making powers in the system will have to be distributed throughout the system, and that steps must be taken to prevent the central decision maker from assuming the total control that he cannot exercise with any success.

CONCLUSIONS

The results presented above suggest that developing adequate mental models for even moderately complex tasks is no easy matter, regardless of whether the task is a static, or a dynamic one. Clearly, we have to expect less than perfect decisions from those who have to make decisions on the basis of experience with such systems. At the present time, there are no obvious ways of training decision makers to become very much better. The only solution, therefore, is to design systems which do not require perfect decisions.

REFERENCES

Andersson, H. (1978) *Studies in Interpersonal Learning*. Umeå University: Unpublished Ph.D. thesis.

Brehmer, B. (1976) Note on clinical judgment and the formal characteristics of clinical tasks. *Psychological Bulletin*, **83**, 778–83.

Brehmer, B. (1980) In one word: Not from experience. *Acta Psychologica*, **45**, 223–41.

Brehmer, B. (1984) Social judgment theory and the psychology of prediction. Paper presented at the 4th Int. Symp. Forecast., London.

Brehmer, B., Allard, R., and Lind, M. (1983) Fire fighting: A paradigm for the study of dynamic decision making. Paper presented at the 9th Res. Conf. on Subject. Prob., Util. and Dec. Mak., Groningen.

Conant, R. R., and Ashby, W. R. (1970) Every good regulator of a system must be a model of that system. *International Journal of System Science*, **1**, 59–74.

Edwards, W. (1962) Dynamic decision theory and probabilistic information processing. *Human Factors*, **4**, 59–74.

Ekegren, G. (1983) *Verbal Reports about Strategies in Probabilistic Inference Learning Tasks*. Acta Universitatis Upsalienses, Studia Psychologica No. 8, Uppsala.

Goldberg, L. R. (1959) The effectiveness of clinicians' judgments: The diagnosis of organic brain damage from the Bender Gestal Test. *Journal of Consulting Psychology*, **23**, 25–33.

Goldberg, L. R. (1970) Man versus model of man: A rationale, plus some evidence, for a method of improving on clinical judgment. *Psychological Bulletin*, **73**, 422–32.

Karlsson, R., Lind, M., and Brehmer, B. (1984) Dynamiskt beslutsfattande. Swed. Nat. Def. Res. Inst. Rep. C-53015-M2, Linköping, Sweden.

Meehl, P. E. (1954) *Clinical vs. Statistical Prediction*. Minneapolis: University of Minnesota Press.

Slovic, P., and Lichtenstein, S. (1971) Comparison of Bayesian and regression approaches to the study of information processing in judgment. *Organ of Behaviour and Human Performance*, **6**, 644–749.

*Work on this paper was supported by a grant from the Swedish Council for Research in the Humanities and Social Sciences.

*The term 'economic technology' may strike some as strange, but in fact, the activities of professional economists who serve as advisers have all the marks of technology. Thus, they offer a set of procedures for solving practical problems, procedures that are (at least to some extent) based on scientific research. In this paper, the term 'technology' is used in this very wide sense to underline similarity of problems facing people in a variety of professions where mental models must be developed to aid decisions.

New Technology and Human Error
Edited by J. Rasmussen, K. Duncan and J. Leplat
© 1987 John Wiley & Sons Ltd

11.   Collective Planning and its Failures

James Reason
University of Manchester

SUMMARY

Errors in collective planning: organizational planning failures; planning failures in small cohesive groups; groupthink.

INTRODUCTION

Considering the planner as if he or she functioned in isolation has the advantage of allowing us to pinpoint the potential trouble-spots in the psychological processes, but it does not necessarily correspond with the reality. Most of the plans that affect our lives and our well-being are the product of many minds: politicians, civil servants, military staffs, and bureaucrats of all persuasions. In this chapter, I will briefly examine collective planning within two contexts: the organization and the group.

ORGANIZATIONAL PLANNING

An extremely influential theory of organizational planning was developed by the Carnegie-Mellon group of behavioural analysts, headed by Herbert Simon. This theory, known as the 'Behavioural Theory of the Firm' (Cyert and March, 1963), was founded in part upon Simon's principle of 'bounded rationality':

> The capacity of the human mind for formulating and solving complex problems is very small compared with the size of the problems whose solution is required for objectively rational behaviour in the real world — or even for a reasonable approximation of such objective rationality (Simon, 1957, p. 198).

This fundamental limitation gives rise to 'satisficing behaviour', or the tendency to select satisfactory rather than optimal courses of action. In other words, organizational planners are inclined to compromise in their goal setting by choosing minimal objectives rather than those likely to yield the best possible outcome.

Just as Tversky and Kahneman's (1974) research challenged normative models of human judgement, so also did Cyert and March's theory of the firm bring into question economic models of decision making that assumed omniscient rationality on the part of organizational planners (see also Simon, 1983). And as Tversky and Kahneman did subsequently, they argued that the psychological processes were better understood in terms of general heuristics than normative models. Four such heuristics were identified: quasi-resolution of conflict, uncertainty avoidance, problemistic search, and selective organizational learning.

Are the systematic errors generated through the over-utilization of these heuristics likely to be further exaggerated by being diffused throughout the organization? Cyert and March (1963) investigated this question experimentally, and came up with a negative answer. They explained their results as follows:

> The anomaly that variations in behaviour at the micro level can exist actively without being reflected at the macro level is a common enough phenomenon. It does not elicit surprise after the fact . . . it seems clear that in an organization of individuals having about the same intelligence, adaptation to the falsification of data occurs fast enough to maintain a more or less stable organizational performance. For the bulk of our subjects in both experiments, the idea that estimates communicated from other individuals should be taken at face value (or that their own estimates would be so taken) was not really viewed as reasonable. *For every bias, there was a bias discount.* (Cyert and March, 1963, p. 77; my italics)

Kaplan (1964) has applied a similar kind of analysis to planning in the arena of international politics. Like Cyert and March, he emphasized the significance of the sub-units within large organizations. With time, these units come to acquire increasing internal solidarity and insulation against inputs from other units. The longer such a unit has been in existence, the more likely it is that this solidarity and insularity will lead to inertia and an inadequate perception of new and disturbing factors within its area of concern. A recent example of this tendency was the combined failure of the British Foreign Office and the Joint Intelligence Committee to interpret the clear signs of an impending Argentinian invasion of the Falklands (Report of the Franks Committee, 1983).

Downs (1967) elaborated a theory of decision making within large and essentially non-profit-making organizations. Although his arguments are framed within the economic–rational tradition (his initial hypothesis is that bureaucrats seek to attain their goals rationally), he is heavily influenced by the Carnegie–Mellon theorists in recognizing the biases which deflect plans from their rational course. In addition to reiterating the inherent limitations of human decision making covered by the principle of 'bounded rationality', he identified four self-serving biases common to all officials:

> 1. Each official tends to distort the information he passes upward in the hierarchy, exaggerating those data favorable to himself and minimizing those unfavorable to himself.

2. Each official is biased in favor of those policies or actions that advance his own interests or the programs he advocates, and against those that injure or simply fail to advance those interests or programs.

3. Each official will vary the degree to which he complies with directives from his superiors, depending upon whether those directives favor or oppose his own interests.

4. The degree to which each individual will seek out additional responsibilities and accept risks in performing his duties will vary directly with the extent to which such initiative is likely to help him achieve his own personal goals (Downs, 1967, p. 266).

Other biases depend upon the nature of the official. One important distinction is between 'climbers' and 'conservers'. Thus, climbers are strongly motivated to invent new functions for their bureaux and to avoid economies (except where these will finance an expansion of their functions). Conservers, on the other hand, are biased against any changes in the *status quo*. Officials become conservers the longer they hold a given position, the older they become, and the more authority and responsibility they have. But in all bureaux, there is a strong pressure upon the vast majority of individuals to become conservers sooner or later. The middle levels of the hierarchy are likely to contain more conservers than either the lowest or the highest levels, and the proportion of conservers among older officials is usually higher than among younger ones. The more extensively a bureau relies on formal rules, the more conservers it is likely to contain.

Obviously, organizations, being coalitions of many people, are subject to more potential sources of planning failure than single individuals, and one must be wary of over-facile comparisons. None the less, there are some compelling similarities in the underlying error tendencies. The planning of both organizations and individuals clearly manifests the limitations imposed by 'bounded rationality'. Despite the involvement of many minds, organizations, like individuals, plan on the basis of extremely restricted databases. Similarly, biases in both individual and organizational planning can be traced to the over-utilization of labour-saving heuristics. Both show themselves to be the prisoners of past experience in their preference for well-tried routines rather than new departures. This tendency of both organizations and individuals to err in a conservative direction was neatly summed up by Barbara Tuchman (1963) in her comment on the Schlieffen Plan: 'Dead battles, like dead generals, hold the military mind in their dead grip, and Germans, no less than other peoples, prepare for the last war' (p. 38).

PLANNING IN SMALL GROUPS

Many of the analyses of organizational planning have stressed the importance of the sub-unit as a source of faulty perception and inadequate decision making. The behaviour of small groups of highly influential planners was investigated by Janis (1972). His reason for focusing upon the small group rather than upon the individual or the organization was because '. . . all the well-known errors stemming from the limitations of an individual and of a large organization can be greatly augmented by group processes that produce shared miscalculations' (p. 7).

The term 'groupthink' was used to describe the deterioration of mental efficiency, reality testing, and moral judgement that results from belonging to a relatively small, highly cohesive, and often elite planning group. His data were detailed case studies of foreign policy disasters, ranging from the Bay of Pigs invasion to the escalation of the Vietnam War. The criteria for the selection of these case studies were twofold. First, that the decisions were made principally by small cohesive groups; and, secondly, that the decisions had catastrophic consequences.

The 'groupthink' syndrome was characterized by eight main symptoms: (a) an illusion of invulnerability, creating extreme optimism and the willingness to take excessive risks; (b) collective efforts to rationalize away warnings that might have led to reconsiderations of the plan; (c) an unswerving belief in the rightness of the group's intentions; (d) stereotyped perceptions of the opposition as being either too evil to negotiate with, or too stupid to counter the planned actions; (e) the exertion of direct group pressure on any member that deviated from the collective stereotypes, illusions or commitments; (f) self-censorship of any doubts felt by individual members; (g) a shared illusion of unanimity, arising both from self-censorship of doubts and the assumption that silence means consent; (h) the emergence of self-appointed 'mindguards' — members who saw it as their duty to protect the group from any contrary signs or adverse information.

These group dynamics appear to add an emotional dimension to the distortion of the planning processes, and this serves not only to bring certain of the individual biases into greater prominence, but also contributes some that are unique to group membership. The powerful forces of perceived 'togetherness' act in concert to render the possibility of failure unthinkable — and if not unthinkable, then certainly unspeakable.

REFERENCES

Cyert, R. M., and March, J. G. (1963) *A Behavioural Theory of the Firm*. Englewood Cliffs, NJ: Prentice-Hall.
Downs, A. (1967) *Inside Bureaucracy*. Boston: Little, Brown and Company.
Janis, I. L. (1972) *Victims of Groupthink*. Boston: Houghton Mifflin.
Kaplan, A. (1964) *The Conduct of Enquiry*. San Francisco: Chandler.
Simon, H. A. (1957) *Models of Man*. New York: Wiley.
Simon, H. A. (1983) *Reason in Human Affairs*. Oxford: Blackwell.
Tuchman, B. (1963) *The Guns of August*. London: Four Square.
Tversky, A., and Kahneman, D. (1974) Judgment under uncertainty: Heuristics and biases. *Science*, **195**, 1124–31.

New Technology and Human Error
Edited by J. Rasmussen, K. Duncan and J. Leplat
© 1987 John Wiley & Sons Ltd

12. New Technologies and Human Error: Social and Organizational Factors

S. Antonio Ruiz Quintanilla
Berlin University of Technology

SUMMARY

This chapter starts out by evoking the danger that psychology in connection with human error research might end up with an individualistic myopia. It presents a four-level analytic approach to the study of social factors relating to new technologies and human error by discussing individual, group, organizational and societal level issues derived from received theory and research paradigms.

It has been claimed that the history of psychology is marked by an astounding neglect of the world of things, a neglect that is due to the discipline's 'organismic preoccupation' (Graumann, 1974). The author goes on to argue that almost all things/objects of our daily life have an important social significance. While it may be true that psychology as a whole has paid little attention to the world of things, the same cannot be claimed for engineering psychology and ergonomics which exclusively address the problems of man and his work environment, the interaction between man and machine, man and technology. However, it appears that in these disciplinary contexts we face another danger — a preoccupation with the individual and his or her work environment at the expense of neglecting its social implications: the danger of an individualistic myopia.

The rest of this chapter will address some of the social factors relating to new technologies and human error by considering four analytic levels: the individual, the work group, the organizational system as a whole, and the societal level.

INDIVIDUAL LEVEL PERSPECTIVE

The lion's share of publications in recent years which treat man–machine interaction problems are guided by theoretical approaches that might be considered as deriving from a general psychological (software psychology/

ergonomy, cognitive ergonomy, cognitive engineering etc.) or physiological framework (e.g., Feigenbaum and McCorduck, 1983). The very nature of such frameworks suggests an individualistic bias of focus and attention. Saying this is not to belittle their important contributions to the analysis and understanding of man–machine interactions and human error occurrence. It is only to say that already on the individual level analysis it may be necessary to introduce a social–psychological theoretical framework.

Any technological device — whether a simple instrument or a complex computing system — is part of the world of things and as such is an 'agendum' (Graumann, 1974) which due to its specific technical features presents itself with a specific demand structure that has been incorporated into it by its designer. As such it might be considered as 'frozen action structure'. Man–machine interaction, by virtue of this imputed action structure becomes a virtual social interaction between the operator and the machine's designer. It follows that all such interaction can be conceptualized as a communication process, liable to the same differential degrees of understanding, comprehension or misunderstanding as all communication — however, with the added complication that feedback processes are less feasible and simple as direct face-to-face interaction.

GROUP LEVEL PERSPECTIVE

Considering work groups and their interactions with technical systems it becomes more readily self-evident that social processes play an important part in error generation and error-free operation of technical systems. As a case in point may be considered the development of informal group norms that deviate from behaviour norms prescribed by the designer or a safety agent. The phenomenon is well documented in the literature and must be considered as an important factor in error generation and error control. Theorizing on group norm development has long traditions (Asch, 1964) and its relevance for our context has been made abundantly plain — as for instance in the case of the risky-shift paradigm (Cartwright, 1973) or the groupthink phenomenon (Janis, 1972) — but has hardly found its way into conceptualizations of social aspects of new technologies and error.

Little known in Western countries is another action-oriented approach by Misumi (1978; Wilpert, 1984). Based on Lewinian concepts of group dynamics he has strikingly demonstrated that group centred approaches to the reduction of safety and accident risks can be considered as a significant strategy to accident prevention in large-scale, technologically highly developed industrial contexts (shipyards, transport agencies). Lewin's 'unfreeze — move — refreeze' model of group decision making has here once again shown its capacity to serve as a powerful social change technique.

ORGANIZATIONAL LEVEL PERSPECTIVE

The discussion of new technologies as imposing new and rigid technological and organizational imperatives versus their inherent flexibility as opening up new organizational and structural degrees of freedom for the division of labour and job designs has by no means come to an end, although the balance of arguments seems to tend towards the increased freedom thesis (IDE, 1981).

Wherever the discussion will lead us, the introduction of new technologies in work organizations poses ever more strongly the issue as to how the needs of those who are affected can adequately be taken into account. The provision of appropriate structures for an adequate articulation of employee interests in all phases of the introductory process is by no means free of error relevance. Growing numbers of instances of obstructionism are in all likelihood symptoms of total systems strain and failure. It is quite conceivable that new technologies will bring about or even require fundamental changes in long-established bargaining patterns on the company level and possibly also beyond in the industrial relations systems. Implicit in such a perspective is the plea to widen drastically our received conceptualizations of human error problems to include more comprehensive systemic aspects as well.

SOCIETAL LEVEL PERSPECTIVE

Recent studies regarding social value changes (Strümpel, and Von Klipstein, 1984) and on the meaning of working in different social groups and strata (Ruiz Quintanilla, 1984) show that people continue to identify strongly with their work and profession and consider working as a significant part of their life, provided their work setting meets certain criteria. Such criteria may be described as discretionary freedom or the potential for self-regulatory work activities in organizations. As Triebe (1980) has shown, identical tasks can be solved by different individuals with comparable efficiency via different action strategies. The possibility to leave the optimal choice of problem-solving strategies to the individual operator, therefore, presents itself as conducive to the avoidance of monotony, satiation, and error proneness.

Similar advantages can be deduced for a systematic taking into account of work-related value orientations and cognitions for adequate job design strategies. The implementation of design options for new technologies in terms of an 'optimal fit' with preference structures and job expectations as they can presently be observed as emerging in many societal groups, so can be argued, will lead to higher levels of job identification, responsibility, and problem solution capacities which, in turn, should result in appreciable effects of reducing human error.

REFERENCES

Asch, S. E. (1964) Opinions and social pressure. In: H. J. Lewitt, and C. R. Pondy (Eds), *Readings in Managerial Psychology*. Chicago, London: The University of Chicago Press, pp. 304–14.

Cartwright, D. (1973) Determinants of scientific progress. *American Psychologist*, **28**, 222–31.

Feigenbaum, E. A., and McCorduck, P. (1983) *The Fifth Generation*. Reading, Mass.: Addison-Wesley.

Graumann, Carl F. (1974) Psychology and the world of things. *Journal of Phenomenological Psychology*, **4**, 389–404.

IDE-Research Group (1981) *Industrial Democracy in Europe (IDE)*. London: Oxford University Press.

Janis, Irving L. (1972) *Victims of Groupthink*. Boston: Houghton Mifflin.

Misumi, J. (1978) The effects of organizational climate variables, particularly leadership variable and group decision making on accident prevention. 19th International Congress for Applied Psychology, München.

Ruiz Quintanilla, S. A. (1984) Bedeutung des Arbeitens. Entwicklung und empirische Erprobung eines sozialwissenschaftlichen Modells zur Erfassung arbeitsrelevanter Werthaltungen und Kognitionen. Berlin: Eigenverlag.

Strümpel, B., and Klipstein, M. Von. (1984) *Der Überdruß am Überfluß*. München: Olzog Verlag.

Triebe, J. K. (1980) Untersuchung zum Lernprozeß während des Erwerbs der Grundqualifikation. In: Arbeits- und sozialpsychologische Untersuchung von Arbeitsstrukturen im Bereich der Aggregate-Fertigung der Volkswagen AG.Band 3. Bonn: Forschungsbericht des Bundesministeriums f. Forschung und Technologie.

Wilpert, B. (1984) Führungsforschung à la Japonaise. *Psychologie und Praxis – Organisations und Arbeitspsychologie*, **1**, 39–40.

New Technology and Human Error
Edited by J. Rasmussen, K. Duncan and J. Leplat
© 1987 John Wiley & Sons Ltd

Part 4: Human Error and Safety at Work

INTRODUCTION

The study of the relations between errors and accidents and between reliability and safety has been the subject of much research over the past years. Special mention must be made of the studies carried out by Faverge (1982) in the context of the research programmes financed by the Coal and Steel Community, and Apostolakis *et al.* (1980) recently edited a collection of articles in which Rasmussen, in particular, has tried to bring out the connection between the two sets of notions. It was therefore important that this present work, which is particularly concerned with human error, should include research more directly centred on accidents, as human error often plays an important role in their genesis.

While an engineer who has designed a technical system can define, at least in principle, the characteristics of its elements and clearly tackle the problems of reliability, the same cannot be done for socio-technical systems as their operation depends on operator and operator group characteristics which are much harder to define. In this case any *a priori* prediction of reliability or safety becomes much more difficult and, consequently, research is necessary in order to try and identify the mechanisms and factors on which reliability and safety can be based.

Because accidents undermine the workers' physical integrity, they have for a long time been the object of enquiries aimed at discovering the origins – but often with the limited aim of evaluating legal responsibility. Progressively, the inadequacy of ordinary analysis became apparent and procedures have now been developed to systematize the research into describing the conditions of the accident. The texts of Leplat and Kjellén present some of these methods. As shown in Leplat's and Rasmussen's text, the analyses reveal the role played by human activity and error in producing accidents and suggest, in consequence, a way of analysing the error.

Accident analysis, like system analysis, has brought to the fore the idea of *change or variation*. Johnson (1980), who devoted many studies to accidents, entitled a chapter of his synthesis 'Change is the mother of trouble' and wrote, 'it is intuitively obvious that if tasks and jobs comparable to those involved in an accident have been conducted in the past without incident, changes and differences provide a logical focal point in accident investigations' (p. 57). Change is conceived as the destabilizing element in a system which has not an adequate response for it. It will be seen in Leplat's text how this idea is implemented in elaborating an analysis chart.

But, this notion of change must itself be defined and this definition presents several problems which will be evoked by Kjellen. The most important of these is the definition of the terms of reference whereby a given event will or will not be considered as a change. The term of reference most often selected is the habitual situation (this definition must itself be clarified) but other terms can be considered (for example, the situation as stipulated by its organization) which would cast a different light on the analysis: there is here an opportunity for further research. It is also possible to attempt to classify the variations with a view to future statistical exploitation. Leplat's text gives an example of such classifications.

It must be noted that the changes or variations are not sufficient in themselves to establish the production of the accident or error. Habitual events and factors play an important role and can be integrated in the variations chart. Two steps can therefore be distinguished in the study of accident production: the development of the variation chart and then how it is complemented with normal events.

Any analysis *a posteriori* of accidents and errors must be able to single out the potential factors of the accident or error, factors which could be used for a diagnosis of safety and reliability. The systematization of this kind of analysis is still far from advanced: an example will be found in the text of Leplat and Rasmussen.

Human errors appearing on accident charts are analysable by reference to activity models of human operators (cf., previous chapters). Leplat's and Rasmussen's text shows a possible exploitation of Rasmussen's model for diagnosing sources of error.

The development of new technologies makes new relations appear between incidents and accidents because the effects of operator action are more indirect and mediated by more and more complex technical devices. Kjellén's text (Chapter 16) shows some consequences of the introduction of new technologies on safety. He emphasizes the growing importance of technical and organizational conditions of safety which will be developed in Parts 5 and 6. He stresses the necessity of a systematic and multidisciplinary approach for achieving noticeable improvements in safety evaluation and control.

The set of contributions in Part 4 shows that new technologies place safety problems in a new light and link them to reliability problems. This should lead in the near future to specialists in these domains working more closely together and to an increasing coordination of their different activities.

Error analysis and accident analysis must, at the same time, be separate and related. They can, in any case, be mutually enriching, and much progress still remains to be achieved in the direction undertaken by the previous research activities.

REFERENCES

Apostolakis, Garribba and Volk (1980) *Synthesis and Analysis Methods for Safety and Reliability Studies*. New York: Plenum.

Faverge, J. M. (1982) *Le Travail Humain*, **45**, 1–136.

Johnson, W. G. (1980) *MORT Safety Assurance Systems*. New York: M. Decker Inc.

New Technology and Human Error
Edited by J. Rasmussen, K. Duncan and J. Leplat
© 1987 John Wiley & Sons Ltd

13. Accidents and Incidents Production: Methods of Analysis

Jacques Leplat
École Pratique des Hautes Études — Paris

:

SUMMARY

From the error to its consequences: the case of well-defined systems with clear functioning, identification of procedure and errors, estimation of probability. From the error to its sources: the case of poorly defined systems: principles and characteristics of the method of variations diagram, rules of the system functioning, vicarious activities, statistical use.

INTRODUCTION

Accidents as well as incidents and errors may be considered as products of the system in which they occur, the man–machine system or, in more general terms, the socio-technical system. Consequently, any analysis of risks depends on the extraction of factors and mechanisms responsible for accident production. Such an analysis may be carried out at different levels; the choice of a particular level depends on the nature of the system, the accident, the analyst's qualifications and the possibilities of investigation available to him. Rasmussen presented a refined method of analysis that he applied to rather homogeneous conditions. I would like, from the perspective of work psychology, to suggest other approaches that might also yield useful information on risks. My contribution is based on studies conducted in collaboration with other researchers in various organizations (Communauté Charbon-Acier, Institut National de Recherches et de Sécurité, and a group of the OECD chaired by Rasmussen).

GENERAL FRAMEWORK

By definition, errors, incidents, and accidents are events that are not programmed in the functioning of the system. When they occur, they reveal that functioning did not work in conformity with expectations. Characterizing these events in this negative way is generally unfruitful for risk analysis.

Errors and incidents are at the same time cause and consequence (cf., for example Nielsen, 1975). They are the cause in the sense that they generate effects, i.e., other errors, incidents or accidents. Conversely, they are consequence, the result of a genesis. Errors may be analysed from two different perspectives (cf., Figure 1): one focuses on their sources (it is sometimes called the 'top–down analysis' because of the orientation of the tree representing it), the other on their consequences. Concerning accidents, one will speak of primary safety when one acts upon their causes, and of secondary safety when one acts upon their consequences.

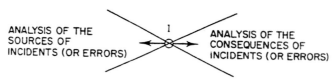

Figure 1. Two types of analysis. In the centre: the incident or error; on the left: the various factors having contributed to incident production; on the right: the various consequences of incident

In order to understand the production of error, incident or accident, it is necessary to know the properties of the system in which they occur, whether these properties are normal or result from anomalies. If man assumes functions within this system, the analysis of error, incident or accident will be correlative with a work analysis (Leplat and Cuny, 1974) the aim of which will be to reveal the sources of malfunctioning inherent in poor interaction between man and his working conditions (in the broader sense). One should, however, take care not to adopt a technician's view of a human operator's functioning. The first part of this paper will emphasize this point.

FROM THE ERROR TO ITS CONSEQUENCES: THE CASE OF WELL-DEFINED SYSTEMS WITH CLEAR FUNCTIONING

As is well known, reliability methods have been very successful in the study of technical systems. It was tempting to try to use them in the study of systems in which man fulfils some functions. This has been done in technologically advanced sectors (nuclear power plants, military and spatial systems). In these cases, the system is strictly delimited, its components and objectives are well identified, and knowledge of technical functioning quite satisfactory.

Swain's (1976) attempt is typical of such an approach which aims at estimating 'the operator's contribution to system reliability' (p. 11) and, more precisely, 'to predict human error rates and to evaluate the degradation to man–machine system likely to be caused by human errors in association with equipment functioning, operational procedures and practices, and other system and human characteristics which influence system behavior' (ibid.). Such a method is appealing but applying it raises many problems; a survey of these will permit us to apprehend the particularities of man as an element of the system and the status of human error. Swain (1976) himself acknowledged the crucial and general difficulty raised by the greater variability and unpredictability of human performance as compared with equipment performance (p. 12). This difficulty underlies several issues that impose limits on the possibility of applying this method and these I shall now review.

Identifying the procedure actually adopted by the operator

It would not be cautious and safe to assimilate the procedure adopted by the operator to the prescribed and standardized procedure defined by the expert (on the indispensable distinction between prescribed task and real task, cf., Herbst, 1974; Leplat and Cuny, 1977; Hoc, 1980). Such an assimilation might be all the more suspect as the operator's procedure is less stereotyped and more goal orientated, i.e., in general, operator is more qualified and capable of finding several solutions for the same problem, according to his knowledge of equipment and to working conditions. Operators can use their representation of phenomena in working out solutions; they can anticipate errors and prevent them.

In some cases, a qualified operator is capable of rectifying errors that he made or that are due to equipment defects so that human error will no longer have detrimental consequences on system outcomes and will keep reliability unchanged. This self-regulated role of the operator that many authors have described (Rasmussen, 1980) invalidates any strict prediction based on a stable procedure.

Reliability methods would be valid only in the case of strictly standardized procedures such as those intervening in calibration tasks for which a checklist is used; but these procedures have disadvantages that may sometimes be very serious (rigidness, inadequacy in relation to unexpected events, etc.) and they reduce the functions of the operator to the function of a simple executant. Current tendencies in the evolution of types of work organization reveal the decline of such a view of activity.

The division of the global task into sub-tasks

Applying reliability methods requires that elementary tasks and their chaining are determined. The often implicit hypothesis is that there exists a unique procedure to reach a specified goal, whereas more refined work analyses show that procedures often differ either in the nature of collected information or in the way in which it is collected (for instance directly or through an instrument) or in the functional properties called into play to reach the goal in view. Fluency graphs reveal that in many cases there are several ways of obtaining the same effect in the control of industrial processes (Leplat and

Cuny, 1977, Chs. IV and V). Another type of difficulty raised by task division is the correspondence between task division and activity division. It is a question of knowing whether units distinguished in the task correspond in their effects to those of the operator's activity involved in meeting the requirement of this task. This is reminiscent of the problems encountered by initiators of time and motion studies that Abruzzi (1952) has so well shown. The issue was then to divide a global task into elementary operations to which were attributed elementary times. The time taken for performing the global task was estimated by summing elementary times. Experimental studies revealed that activity did not conform to this model. In particular, activities corresponding to elementary operations are not independent, contrary to the model. In other words, the organization of activity does not follow the standardized activity assumed by the model. Furthermore, this method requires stable working conditions, which is far from being the case, especially due to frequent hazards (equipment or stock defects).

As is known, with training some parts of activity become automatic and the organization of global activity involves broader and broader units of behaviour. Conversely, fatigue or stressful conditions often result in a reversal to more elementary units. Consequently, any standardized division of task may be inadequate in numerous conditions and/or for many operators.

Identifying errors and estimating their probability

Assuming that a human operator adopts the designed procedure, he may make a mistake and each elementary task may be performed without conforming to the determined norms. Reliability studies require that this error should be estimated, a step that has been attempted as shown in Table 1 which is an excerpt from a table designed for this purpose. It can be seen that errors have been classified into more or less general categories, as illustrated by the selected examples.

Table 1: *Excerpt from a table entitled 'General error rate estimates' in* Failure Data, *WASH-1400, US Nuclear Regulatory Commission. Oct. 1975*

Estimated rates	Activity
10^{-4}	Selection of a key operated switch rather than a non-key-switch (this value does not include the error of decision where the operator misinterprets situation and believes key choice is correct (choice))
3×10^{-3}	General error of commission, e.g., misreading label and therefore selecting wrong switch
10^{-2}	Operator fails to act correctly after the first several hours in a high stress condition

Probability assessment 'can vary from a rather impressionistic subjective assessment to one involving considerably more rigor, depending upon importance and available data' (Swain, 1976, p. 8).

The identification of errors and the assessment of probabilities is very difficult, whether experts, experiments or statistics are involved. Furthermore, the apparent rigour of quantification may block the research, since one might believe that the problems of human error are solved. These dangers are all the more acute as it is not possible to validate probability estimates since in the technological systems in which they are used actual errors that are recorded have generally (and fortunately) a low frequency.

FROM THE ERROR TO ITS SOURCES: THE CASE OF POORLY DEFINED SYSTEMS

To trace the source of error, there exists a method very familiar to reliability specialists, the 'fault tree analysis'. 'The goal of fault tree construction is to model the system conditions that can result in the undesired event (. . .). A fault tree is a model that graphically and logically represents the various combinations of possible events, both fault and normal, occurring in a system that leads to the top event' (Barlow and Lambert, 1975, p. 8), i.e., for us, the fault event, error or accident. Applying this method to socio-technical systems raises the same difficulties as the ones mentioned above. I would like to present now the principles of another method (1) which does not raise these difficulties and which is quite widespread in France.

Like the preceding method, this involves retracing the source of an accident (it might as well be an incident or error) but, contrary to it, it starts from a real accident. Consequently, the resulting tree (or diagram) will not include all possible branches leading to this type of accident but only the branch leading to a real accident. From a formal viewpoint, the tree is a sub-tree of the fault tree characterized by the fact that it does not present 'OR gates'. As will be seen, it also differs from the fault tree in the nature of the elements considered.

Main principles of the INRS method

The analysis of an error or an accident in which an operator or a group of operators have a share may be performed at various levels of refinement and precision. The greater the accuracy sought, the more qualified specialists will be needed. The INRS method devised for widespread application has been designed for agents with average qualifications. It should lead to a sort of basic tree that might later be enriched if necessary.

This method rests upon some principles that I shall now present briefly. The basic idea is that error production results from changes in the 'usual' condition. An accident originates in changes or variations (also called variation antecedents or incidents) that the analyst will first have to locate in order to list. These variation antecedents will then be organized into a diagram, following certain rules from which I shall select the main ones.

The *event chain relationship*, noted $X \rightarrow Y$, indicates that if X event had not occurred Y event would not have occurred.

The *confluence relationship*, noted

$$\left.\begin{array}{l} X_1 \\ X_2 \end{array}\right\} \rightarrow Y$$

indicates that in the absence of two independent events, X_1 and X_2, Y event would not have occurred.

Figure 2 gives a simplified example of the diagram obtained with these principles.(2)

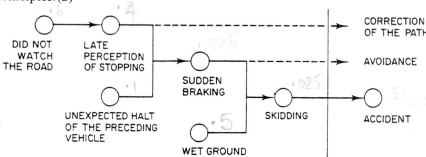

Figure 2. Simplified diagram of the analysis of an accident. In unbroken lines: the chaining of vicarious actions (or actions of 'recuperation'); in dashed lines: the possible consequences of these actions (if these had succeeded)

Some characteristics of the INRS method

The properties of these diagrams having been presented in detail elsewhere (Leplat, 1978), I shall mention only some of their distinctive features.

The diagram of variations is not the diagram of causes

Variations — or variation events — represent only a subset of the causes intervening in the genesis of an accident (or an error).

Variations represented on the left of the arrow are only conditions necessary to the production of the event represented on the right of the arrow but generally are not sufficient conditions. Let us consider the combination of sudden braking and wet ground.

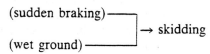

Other factors than the variations mentioned above may have contributed to skidding, for instance tyre wear, poorly balanced braking system, etc.; they should be considered if skidding is to be entirely explained. Variations constitute only conditional factors of the resulting event: they imply the presence of other factors which are not represented since they are permanent elements of the system. In some cases, the analyst may represent some of them in order to improve diagram comprehension; they are called 'state antecedents' or 'permanent antecedents'.

The ideal arrangement of 'variation antecedents' and 'state antecedents' would constitute the diagram of the genesis of an accident. On the basis of the diagram of variations, the analysis may be continued and one may try to approach the diagram of genesis by introducing permanent antecedents and refining the activity and system analysis.

Identifying variations

Identifying variations requires that working conditions are known accurately in order that the analyst might determine unusual events. Even though this notion cannot be defined in rigorous terms, it is not crucial for applying the INRS method. On the other hand, it is sometimes difficult — or even impossible — to identify subtle variations that are hard to observe directly. This is the case with some variations in the subject's state which cannot be analysed by this method.

Knowledge of the rules of system functioning

Establishing relationships between events necessitates knowledge of system functioning but this knowledge is less deep than that necessary to build the diagram of accident genesis. The elaboration of the variation diagram — the conditional diagram — is based on a model of functioning which may be rather rudimentary (but not wrong), and which thus permits the use of this method by personnel who are not highly qualified. The counterpart is that the analysis will be succinct; concerning operators, the analysis will be more of a behavioural than a cognitive type.

'Recuperation' of incidents and vicarious methods

The sequence of a subject's actions leading to error or accident may be represented on the variation diagram. If these actions had worked, the terminal error would have been avoided. For instance, the diagram representing the sequence of actions shows that even late perception of the danger would normally have permitted the driver to rectify the route and that sudden braking would have permitted him to avoid the obstacle. The failure of these actions is due to concomitant variations in the conditions under which they were performed, e.g., the sudden braking resulted in skidding because of the wet ground (even if this factor is not the only one). These successive corrective actions, which attempt to mitigate a series of disturbances, aim at reaching the final goal; if they succeeded, they would reach the goal by other means than those used in normal conditions. Moyen *et al.* (1980) who have investigated this question systematically proposed the term *vicarious* to qualify these corrective actions. The failure of vicarious actions (or actions of 'recuperation') entails other vicarious actions. Faverge (1967) and his colleagues were the first to show that many accidents occurred at the end of a sequence of unsuccessful recuperations.

Use of variation diagrams

These diagrams may be used within a clinical or a statistical perspective. From the clinical perspective, the study of the diagram gives a certain amount of information. The INRS proposed models for such analyses. The method consists of extracting from the diagram a list of the factors involved in the accident, to define the possible curative actions and the potential factors of accidents which constitute a sort of generalization of the concrete factors of accidents (X, 1977).

Diagrams may also be used from a statistical perspective once their components are coded. For instance, Krawsky *et al.* (1972) used a coding derived from socio-technical studies and classified the variations as a function

Table 2: *Matrix of occurrence frequency of factor classified into j category or of A accident following occurrence of factor classified into i category or during normal N* task

Category 1: defect; 2: lack of reliability; 3: misconception of the machine or the task; 4: individual factors disturbing the task; 5: omission or partial execution of a task element; 6: dangerous situation in itself (which does not depend on the task). (From Moyen *et al.*, 1980)

i	P(i,1)	P(i,2)	P(i,3)	P(i,4)	P(i,5)	P(i,6)	P(i,A)
1	4.5	13.7	4.5	4.5	13.7	50.0	9.1
2	8.3	4.8	9.5	6.0	42.8	23.8	4.8
3		5.4	8.1	5.4	2.7	29.7	48.7
4		10.5				26.3	63.2
5	3.2		4.8	3.2	9.7	29.1	50.0
6	2.1		2.1	1.1	2.1	8.5	84.1
P(N,j)	7	50	14	5	10	14	

of their nature into one of the following categories: individual, task, equipment, environment. This procedure permits one to extract categories of potential factors of accidents. Recently, Moyen *et al.* (1980) analysed factors triggering vicarious actions into 146 accidents, using a classification of these factors into six categories (see Table 2). Moyen *et al.* have shown that the sequence of factors is not random and that their frequency distribution differs with their rank of occurrence and their proximity to the accident. Szekely and de Keyser (1980) characterized the diagrams with an index of complexity and analysed the evolution of this index over time.

CONCLUSION

An accident constitutes the ultimate (negative) criterion of safety studies, but it is not the only possible one. If one considers an accident as an indicator of system malfunctioning, one is led to search for other indicators of this malfunctioning; errors and incidents may contribute to their discovery. Knowledge of malfunctioning permits one to identify factors of risk, thus enabling a diagnosis of safety before the occurrence of an accident. Many methods may be used to tackle such problems; they depend on the nature of the systems concerned, on the role of human operators and on the analyst's competence. In any case, the analysis requires one to refer to a model of system functioning in normal and disturbed conditions. The model will be more or less detailed. The definition of the system concerned may vary since one may want to trace back to more or less distant sources, i.e., to refer to more or less extended systems (from the job to the firm and even beyond it).

The two types of cases selected in this report have shown that the analyst cannot restrict himself to a knowledge of the prescribed functioning but that he has to collect detailed information concerning the real functioning which often differs from what is prescribed, especially when man intervenes in the system. To this end, reliable methods with well-defined conditions of validity should be available. There remains a great deal of work to be done in this area.

REFERENCES

Abruzzi, A. (1952) *Work Measurement*. Columbia University Press, New York.
Barlow, R. E., and Lamber, H. E. (1975) Introduction to fault tree analysis. In: R. E. Barlow, J. B. Fussel, and N. D. Singpurwalla (Eds), *Reliability and Fault Tree Analysis*. Society for industrial and applied mathematics, Philadelphia US.
Faverge, J. M. (1967) *Recherche dans les charbonnages belges*. C.E.C.A. Luxembourg. Service des publications des communautés européennes.
Herbst, P. G. (1974) *Socio-Technical Design*. Tavistock Publications.

Hoc, J. M. (1980) L'articulation entre la description de la tâche et la caractérisation de la conduite dans l'analyse du travail. *Bulletin de Psychologie*, **33**, 207–12.

Krawsky, G., Monteau, M., and Cuny, X. (1972) Méthode pratique de recherche de facteurs d'accidents. Rapport No. 024/RE/A, I.N.R.S. Vandoeuvre.

Leplat, J. (1976) Origin of accidents and risk factors. In: *Occupational Accident Research*. The Swedish work environment fund. pp. 146–56.

Leplat, J. (1978) Accident analyses and work analyses. *Journal of Occupational Accidents*, **1**, 331–40.

Leplat, J., and Cuny, X. (1974) *Les accidents du travail*. P.U.F., Coll. Que Sais-Je?, Paris.

Leplat, J., and Cuny, X. (1977) *Introduction à la psychologie du travail*. P.U.F., Coll. SUP, Paris.

Meric, M., Monteau, M., and Szekely, J. (1976) Techniques de gestion de la sécurité. Rapport No. 234/RE, I.N.R.S., 54500 Vandoeuvre.

Moyen, D., Quinot, E., and Heimfert, M. (1980) Exploitation d'analyses d'accidents du travail à des fins de prévention. Essai méthodologique. *Travail Humain*, **43** (2), 255–75.

Nielsen, D. (1975) Use of cause–consequences charts in practical systems analysis. In: R. E. Barlow *et al.* (Eds), *Reliability and Fault Tree Analysis*. Society for industrial and applied mathematics, Philadelphia, US, pp. 849–80.

Quinot, E., Meric, M., Monteau, M., and Szekely, J. (1977) Occupational accident prevention: research and description of potential factors of accidents. In: Liber Tryck (Ed.), *Research of Occupational Prevention*. Stockholm, pp. 45–65.

Rasmussen, J. (1980) Notes on human error analysis and prediction. In: G. Apostoiakis, S. Garribba, and G. Volta (Eds), *Synthesis and Analysis Methods for Safety and Reliability Studies*. Plenum Publishing Corporation.

Swain, A. D. (1976) *Sandia Human Factors Program for Weapon Development*. Sandia Laboratories. Albuquerque New Mexico, SAND 76.0326.

Szekely, J., and de Keyser, V. (1980) *La sécurité dans deux usines de textile*. ANACT, Collection Etudes et Recherches, Paris.

X (1975) — Failure data. Appendix III to reactor safety study. WASH-1400 US Nuclear regulatory commission.

X (1977) — L'arbre des causes du mois. Travail et Sécurité No. 4, pp. 177–9, No. 5, pp. 251–3.

(1) This method is often called 'INRS method' termed after the 'Institut National de Recherche et de Sécurité' which devised it; it is also called 'causes tree' (Méric *et al.*, 1976; Quinot *et al.*, 1977).

(2) Other examples are presented in Chapter 15.

New Technology and Human Error
Edited by J. Rasmussen, K. Duncan and J. Leplat
© 1987 John Wiley & Sons Ltd

14. Deviations and the Feedback Control of Accidents

Urban Kjellén
Royal Institute of Technology, Stockholm

SUMMARY

The purpose of this chapter is to assess the potentialities and limitations of the deviation concept as applied to occupational accident control. Accident research literature on definitions and taxonomies of deviations, on theories and models of human deviations, on the collection of data on deviations, and on relations between deviations and accidents, is reviewed. It is concluded that deviations must be defined and structured in relation to the systems view of those responsible for the design and operation of a production system, in order to provide a valid basis for the feedback control of accidents in the system in question.

INTRODUCTION

The field of occupational accident research is characterized by a continuing growth in the number of different theories, models, and analytic frameworks of accidents (for an overview, see, e.g., Surry, 1969; Hale and Hale, 1972; Kjellén and Larsson, 1981). This manifoldness is beneficial and even necessary for the theoretical understanding of the nature and determinants of accidents. It has, however, at present produced a widening gap between research and professional practice.

The concept of a systems variable deviating from a norm is a common element in a number of different theories, models and analytic frameworks of accidents. It is thus possible to reduce this apparent manifoldness. This chapter reviews research literature, particularly from the field of occupational accidents, that is pertinent to the analysis of deviations. The aim is to assess the potentialities and limitations of the deviation concept as applied to the control of occupational accidents.

DEFINITION OF DEVIATIONS

A systems variable is here classified as a *deviation* when its value falls outside a norm.

Two basic elements included in the definition of deviations are 'systems variable' and 'norm'. A review of terms used in the accident research literature has shown that variations of these two elements are included in many of the definitions (Kjellén, 1984). Examples of such terms are 'near accident', 'critical incident', 'human error', 'unsafe act', 'unsafe condition', and 'disturbance'.

Different types of norms appear in the accident research literature, for example: (a) standard, rule or regulation; (b) adequate or acceptable; (c) normal or usual; and (d) planned or intended.

The type of process, by which the norm is established, is a basic feature which distinguishes the different types of norms. On the other hand, there is no general relationship between the type of norm and the level of risk.

In accident investigations, the norm acts as a filter in order to reduce the volume of information to a manageable size. The aim is to improve the effectiveness and efficiency of information systems inside companies for the feedback control of accidents. However, the above-mentioned types of norms suffer from problems of a limited applicability and/or fuzziness.

The *standard, rule or regulation* is of great practical significance. It is often operationally defined in detail, which makes a reliable data collection possible. However, for practical reasons only a limited set of systems variables may be controlled by such norms and it is rarely possible to specify in detail to what context the norm is valid.

Norms which require judgement, e.g., at the data collection phase (i.e., after the occurrence of an accident) of what is *adequate or acceptable* involve problems of intersubjectivity.

Norms relating to what is *normal or usual* suffer from two different types of uncertainty. The first one is of a statistical nature and has to do with the data collector's knowledge about the distribution of the appearance of the systems variable in question. The second type of uncertainty depends on the 'fuzziness' of the criterion of what share of the distribution ought to be considered as normal (e.g. 50% or 90%).

Norms that are based on what is *planned or intended* have the advantage of being in accordance with the main goals of the production activities. They build upon the assumption that plans for the activities have been established and communicated to the concerned operators. In practice these two conditions are rarely fulfilled. For example, norms are lacking at the systems level for unstructured tasks. These are typically non-productive tasks, e.g., removal of disturbance or cleaning or fetching of tools, machines or materials. They are characterized by a higher risk of accidents than productive tasks, which have been planned in advance (Saari and Lahtela, 1981).

It is here suggested, that deviations are defined in relation to the planned production process. The motives are as follows:

1. Differences in opinion, for example, between workers on the one hand and management and systems designers on the other hand, as to what constitutes the faultless production process, may in themselves constitute an accident risk. These differences should be identified and resolved, for example in group settings, by establishing shared norms that produce reasonable risk levels.
2. Data on deviations are fed back to the organization for corrective and preventive actions. The established information systems for operational planning and control should be utilized for this purpose. For these systems to be reliable and compatible, data must be collected on the basis of a uniform and generally accepted set of norms.
3. Information about relations between accidents and deviations are identified and communicated to the various levels and functions of the organization. Consequently, this information is used as a tool in the development of more valid and comprehensive accident risk perceptions of the members of the organization.

In cases where norms are lacking at the systems level, these could be related to the individual worker's judgement of what is the expected or planned sequence of his work. However, this solution is not available in work situations, which are characterized by the solving of problems that have not been encountered before. The significance to occupational accidents of tasks that involve true problem solving is, in general, not known and deserves further attention.

HUMAN DEVIATIONS

Theories and models of human deviations or errors (i.e., human actions which fall outside a norm) constitute important subsets of theories and models which are related to the analysis of accidents. Research has shown that human operators are actively involved in a substantial share of the occupational accidents (CIS, 1967; Heinrich et al., 1980). This is because man plays a fundamental role as a systems operator in industrial production systems.

Theories and models of human errors are here sub-divided into two categories: (a) theories and models of relations between characteristics of the production system and the probability of human errors; and (b) theories and models of maladaptive human responses to deviations in the production process.

Human errors induced by the resources of the production system

Classical *information ergonomics* or *human factors theory* is concerned with the effects of the characteristics of equipment, environment, and task structure on the probability of human errors (see, e.g., Swain, 1977; Corlett and Gilbank, 1978). Examples of so-called performance shaping factors which increase the probability of human errors are violations of population stereotypes in the design of displays and controls, high work load and excessive heat, noise, or other physical stressors.

According to the *adjustment-stress-theory* an individual is more likely to initiate a hazardous incident if he is failing to adjust to the psychological stresses of the work (Kerr, 1950, 1957). In contrast, freedom for the individual to set goals will result in high quality work performance.

Learning theory is rooted in behaviourism. According to this theory, the development of unsafe habits as well as safe habits is the result of a learning process involving different types of motivations (Sundström-Frisk, 1978; Burkardt, 1981).

Human responses (e.g., hand movements) are subject to *fluctuations or variations* with respect to speed and accuracy around an ideal path (Branton, 1970). These fluctuations are, e.g., normally distributed or skewed. An error or incident arises when the fluctuations exceed a boundary (i.e., a norm), set by the working conditions (Surry, 1969). The probability of a human error is according to this model dependent on the distribution of the fluctuation and the tolerance limits of the system.

Maladaptive response to deviations

A study of punching machine accidents showed that the model of fluctuating human responses (in this case hand movements) is not suited for the prediction of these accidents (Winsemius, 1965). The only possibility of having an accident lies in the disturbance of the normal work rhythm and the impulsive response by the operator to restore the desired course of events. These have been called *recovery accidents* (Faverge, 1967), and may be explained by the tendency to completion (Mandler, 1975). The attempts by the operator to restore the desired course of events is a means of avoiding the negative emotional consequences of an interruption of the organized goal-oriented work sequence.

On the basis of empirical studies of human performance in disturbed systems, *stress reactions* such as adherence to a false hypothesis about the situation, preoccupation with one task, and emergency mechanisms have been identified (Russel Davis, 1958).

Other theoretical approaches to human actions in disturbed systems focus on the *information processing* of the operator.

The human operator has been modelled as a noisy information channel with a limited information transmission rate (Singleton, 1973). The adaptive responses to a deviation may involve the interruption of highly organized behaviour in accordance with stored patterns or rules and the switching to a mode of operation that involves problem solving (Simon, 1967; Kay, 1971; Rasmussen, 1982). Failure to recognize the deviation and to adapt may be due to information overload, i.e., the individual has too much information to process in too little time. The information load is chiefly determined by the complexity of the ordinary task and the perceptibility and controllability of the deviation (Saari, 1976/77).

According to a sequential model of the human information processing, this includes the following phases; perception, recognition, assessment, decision, and execution (Gagne, 1962). This model, or variations of it, has been applied to the processing of information about the work situation (Hale and Hale, 1970) and of information about deviations such as warnings (Lawrence, 1974), or dangers (Andersson *et al.*, 1978; Surry, 1969). Failure in any of the phases of information processing will accordingly result in maladaptive response and as a consequence in increased risk of injury.

Models and theories of *risk-taking behaviour* focus on the decision-making phase of human information processing. Whenever a human operator faces a deviation he may choose between a set of alternative actions to deal with the deviation. Each of these alternatives is associated with certain costs and benefits such as pay or recognition, increased or reduced risk of accidents, and cognitive and emotional stimuli (Rockwell *et al.*, 1961; Näätänen and Summala, 1982). The individual's choice of action is dependent on his assessment of the relative costs and benefits associated with each choice. According to the theory of risk compensation, the individual attempts to maintain a constant risk and consequently adapts his behaviour to the exposure to hazards in the environment (Wilde, 1976).

Socio-technical systems theory is concerned with the joint optimization of the technical and social systems in the production organization (Robinson, 1982). This general theoretical framework has been applied to the analysis of the 'variance' or deviation control processes in production; i.e., the members of the organization monitoring, diagnosing, and correcting variables of the techical system that go beyond some tolerance limit (Herbst, 1974). By applying a technique of analysing the transmission of variances through the production process of a pulp and paper mill, a number of technical and organizational factors, having a dysfunctional effect on the variance control process, were identified (Engelstad, 1979). These included lack of feedback, segregation of individual operators' jobs, division of labour and wage and bonus system.

It emerges from this review, which does not pretend to be complete, that the role of the human operator in accident processes is very complex. There is no single theory or model which predicts the occurrence of human errors and their effects that may serve as a sole basis for data collection and analysis. A comprehensive approach involves different theories and models which consider (cf. Rasmussen, 1982): (a) the effects of physiological and motivational factors of the working environment on the probability of human errors; and (b) the human processing of information on deviations and the prerequisites for the identification and correction of these deviations by the human operator.

CLASSIFICATION OF DEVIATIONS

Taxonomies are applied in information systems in order to reduce the complexity of data collection, processing, and feedback (Samuelson, 1978). Taxonomies of deviations thus act as filters in the collection of data about accidents and as a basis for organizing these data, for setting priorities, and for designing and implementing counter-measures.

Different taxonomies, that are applicable to the classification of deviations, have been suggested in the research literature (Table 1). The features or variables that represent the classes of these taxonomies are related to different theories and models of accidents.

Table 1: *Examples of taxonomies for the classification of deviations*

THEORY/MODEL/ VARIABLE	CLASSES	AUTHOR
PROCESS MODEL		
Emergence	Sudden; deterioration over time/ gradual	Johnson, 1973; Monteau, 1977
Duration	Event/act; state/condition	ANSI, 1962; Heinrich, 1959
Phase of the accident sequence	First phase; second phase; third phase	Haddon, 1968
	Initial phase; concluding phase; injury phase	Kjellén and Larsson, 1981
	Preceding events; contact event; injury event	Andersson and Lagerlöf, 1983
SYSTEMS THEORY		
Subject-object	(Act of) person; mechanical or physical (condition)	ANSI, 1962; Heinrich, 1959
	Human; environment	Skiba, 1973
	Internal; external	Van de Putte, 1981
Epidemiological model	Host/victim; agent; environment	Gordon, 1949
	Man; vehicle; environment	Haddon, 1968
Systems ergonomics	Individual; task; equipment; environment	Monteau, 1977
Industrial engineering	Specific control factors; management system's factors	Johnson, 1975

	Technical; organizational; human	Hagenkötter and Schröder, 1970
	Materials; labor power; information; technical; human; intersecting/parallell activity; environment; stationary guard; personal protective equipment	Kjellén and Larsson, 1981
ENERGY MODEL Type of energy	Thermal; radiation; mechanical; electrical; chemical	Haddon, 1968
HUMAN ERRORS Human information processing	Reception; central processing; effector	Dunn, 1972
	Presented information; expected information; perceived information; decision; action	Hale and Hale, 1970
Human skills	Omission; commission; extraneous act; sequential error; time error	Swain, 1977
Stress reactions	False hypothesis; preoccupation; emergency mechanism	Russel Davis, 1958
Type of remedy	Design; incentives; selection; training; monitoring	Singleton, 1972
CONSEQUENCES	No significant consequence; time loss; degraded output quality; equipment damage; material loss; personal injury	Altman, 1970
	Negligible; marginal; critical; catastrophic	Hammer, 1972

Time is the basic variable in taxonomies that are related to the *process model* of accidents. The accident is seen as a flow of events (Figure 1). The domino theory is an early variant which models an accident as an one-dimensional sequence of events (Heinrich, 1959). A later variant is the 'multilinear events sequencing method', which models the process resulting in injury as an events sequence made up of interactions between various actors of a system (Benner, 1975). This model is based on the so-called P-theory, according to which an injury is the result of the inability of an actor of the system to adapt to disturbances from the environment of the system and the subsequent loss of control.

Deviations may be classified with respect to their emergence, their duration, or the phase of the accident process during which they occur. Taxonomies related to the process model of accidents have a firm theoretical basis. They are suitable for the operationalization of such concepts in common use as unsafe act/condition, and near accident and critical incident. Classification with respect to the phase of the accident sequence may support the analysis of the direction of interactions and the design and implementation of counter-measures.

According to *systems theory*, an injury is one of several abnormal or unwanted effects of a system. An injury is a consequence of a dysfunction in the system which does not work as planned (Leplat, 1984).

Taxonomies which are related to systems theory include features such as type of component/subsystem or type of interaction between subsystems/components. These are used to classify the systems variable element of a deviation.

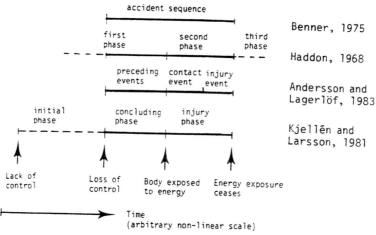

Figure 1. Relation between the phases of different process models of accidents. The Swedish information system of occupational injuries classifies accidents in accordance with the model by Andersson and Lagerlöf (1983)

The subject–object dichotomy is embraced in many taxonomies in common use. They differ with respect to where the boundary has been drawn.

The epidemiological model is a variant of the subject–object dichotomy where the object has been split into agent (i.e., the object that directly gives rise to the injury) and environment.

The man–machine–environment taxonomy is related to the fields of systems ergonomics. According to the INRS model (Monteau, 1977) deviations are assigned to one of the following classes: (a) the individual, i.e., the systems operator; (b) the machine he is operating; (c) the surrounding environment; and (d) the task, i.e., the interaction between the operator and the machine.

On the basis of industrial engineering systems views, taxonomies have been developed which focus on the control of the production system from management's point of view. They differ with respect to at what system's level they are applicable. Taxonomies which are relevant to the managerial/

organizational level sub-divide a production organization into a management subsystem and a production subsystem (Johnson, 1975). Other taxonomies are relevant to the subsystem or component level of a production system and are related to the various systems of controlling these subsystems and components (Kjellén and Larsson, 1981).

Taxonomies based on systems theory make possible a filtering of data with respect to the boundaries of the production system. The analysis of data with respect to deficiencies of single components and of hazardous interactions between components of a production system is facilitated by such taxonomies.

The *energy model* limits the scope to the energy processes that result in injury (Haddon, 1968). Taxonomies that are based on this model are relevant to the classification of deviations which are characterized by an uncontrolled flow of energy. The type of energy is an important variable in predicting the expected consequences of these types of deviations (Shannon and Manning, 1980) and in designing safety measures (e.g., of a traditional type such as guards).

Various taxonomies for the classification of human deviations or errors are based on sequential models of *human information processing*. The classification of human errors is, e.g., made in accordance with where the blockage of information within the operator is likely to have occurred (Singleton, 1972). Taxonomies based on models of human skilled performance consider the effect of the blockage of the information flow through the operator. The classification of errors is in this case related to the task that the operator was supposed to perform. Other types of human error taxonomies are related to knowledge about human stress reactions and to the different types of remedies which are available.

Taxonomies of human errors have contributed to the efficient control of such errors in systems of high potential accident risks, e.g., commercial aviation (Singleton, 1972), as well as in traditional types of industrial environments (Komaki *et al.*, 1978). In the latter case, the bases of the taxonomies have been pragmatic rather than theoretical.

Deviations are also classified with respect to the expected or real *consequences* (i.e., severity). This type of classification is a form of measurement, and the scale chosen is either nominal (Altman, 1970), or ordinal (Hammer, 1972). It is a means of setting priority in decisions about remedial action.

COLLECTION OF DATA ON DEVIATIONS

Data on deviations are collected in accident and near-accident investigations. Safety inspections map deviations in the production system on a sampling basis.

There are two main problems associated with these three different types of data sources; i.e., the systematic suppression or filtering of data on certain types of deviations and incidents, and unreliability in data collection.

Data on deviations usually must be derived from the free text description of the sequence of events of the accident or near-accident report. Reports not particularily enquiring about deviations of the initial phase of the accident sequence (see Figure 1) often do not include data on these deviations (see also Edwards, 1981; Kjellén, 1982). Different studies have shown that data from near-accident reporting are filtered and mainly concern technical deviations (Vasilas et al., 1953; Hammarsten, 1979; Kjellén, 1982).

An evaluation of routine safety inspections within companies showed that the information included in the protocols from these inspections was of a limited variety (Kjellén, 1982). The safety inspections mainly identified a limited number of categories of deviations, i.e., defective safety guards, technical failures, and inadequate cleaning.

The various filters in accident and near-accident investigations prevent the comprehensive mapping and description of deviations.

Further, the routine reporting of accidents and near accidents and routine safety inspection inside companies usually do not generate reliable data for the estimation of the probabilities of deviations. Neither do these data sources generate reliable data for the assessment of the expected or potential consequences of these deviations. For example, experiences indicate that it is difficult to maintain a reliable reporting of incidents for an extended period of time. A negative correlation between the reporting intensity of first-aid and near accidents and the time from the initiation of the reporting has been found in a number of research studies (Gustafsson et al., 1970; Kjellén and Baneryd, 1976; Nilsson, 1976; Saari, 1976; Hammarsten, 1979;).

In various research studies, it has been possible to improve the comprehensiveness and reliability in data collection. For a review of this research, see Kjellén (1984). The measures that have been introduced include the application of checklists, special training of data collectors, feedback of results to the data collector and fixed routines. In addition, improvements in near-accident reporting have been accomplished through anonymous reporting, directive reporting, and reporting during a limited time period.

Further research will show whether it is possible to develop reliable and valid predictors of the accident risk of specific industrial systems on the basis of the occurrence of deviations in these systems. This would require improvements of the current corporate safety information systems and a long-term systematic accumulation of experience, for example, through the aid of computers.

CONCLUSIONS

The analysis of the deviation concept gives support to the conclusion, that this concept provides a valid basis for the design of corporate information systems for the efficient control of accidents. Deviations is a systems concept that integrates theories and models of accidents emanating from various basic sciences. It is applicable to a wide range of production systems and accident types. Further, the concept provides an opportunity for the integration of production and safety management.

The general definition of deviations is subject to interpretation in relation to the conditions of the specific production systems, to which it is applied. Consequently, there is a general lack of scientific evidence on the validity of deviations with respect to the risk of accidents. Operational definitions of deviations and of taxonomies for the classification of deviations should be closely related to the systems view of those designing and managing the industrial systems. Enquiries about the significance of deviations with respect to the risk of accidents should be made through a combination of logical analyses and judgements made by members of the industrial organization.

REFERENCES

Altman, J. W. (1970) Behavior and accidents. *Journal of Safety Research*, 2, 109–22.

Andersson, R., Johansson, B., Linden, K., Svanström, K., and Svanström, L. (1978) Development of a model for research on occupational accidents. *Journal of Occupational Accidents*, 1, 341–52.

Andersson, R., and Lagerlöf, E. (1983) Accident data in the new Swedish information system on occupational injuries. *Ergonomics*, 26, 33–42.

ANSI, (1962) *Method of recording basic facts relating to the nature and occurrence of work injuries: Z-16.2*, American National Standards Institute, New York.

Benner, L. (1975) Accident investigations — multilinear events sequencing methods. *Journal of Safety Research*, 7, 67–73.

Branton, P. (1970) A field study of repetitive manual work in relation to accidents at the work place. *International Journal of Production Research*, 8(2), 93–107.

Burkardt, F. (1981) *Information und Motivation zur Arbeitssicherheit*. Universum Verlag, Wiesbaden.

CIS (1967) *Human Factors and Safety*. CIS Information Sheet No. 15, Geneva.

Corlett, E., and Gilbank, G. (1978) A systemic technique for accident analysis. *Journal of Occupational Accidents*, 2, 25–38.

Dunn, J. (1972) A safety analysis technique derived from skills analysis. *Applied Ergonomics*, 3, 30–6.

Edwards, M. (1981) The design of an accident investigation procedure. *Applied Ergonomics*, 12, 111–15.

Engelstad, P. H. (1979) Sociotechnical approach to problems of process control. In: L. E. Davis and J. C. Taylor (Eds), *Design of Jobs*, 2nd edn. Santa Monica, California: Goodyear Publishing Company.

Faverge, J. M. (1967) *Psychologie des accidents du travail*. Presses Universitaires de France, Paris.

Gagne, R. M. (1962) *Psychological Principles in System Development*. New York: Holt, Rinehart, and Winston.

Gordon, J. E. (1949) The epidemiology of accidents. *American Journal of Public Health*, 39, 504–15.

Gustafsson, L., Lagerlöf, E., and Pettersson, B. (1970) *Analys av olyckstillbud vid huggning.* Royal College of Forestry, Department of Operational Efficiency, Report No. 37, Stockholm.

Haddon, W. (1968) The changing approach to the epidemiology, prevention, and amelioration of trauma: The transition to approaches ethologically rather than descriptively based. *American Journal of Public Health,* **58,** 1431–8.

Hagenkötter, M., and Schröder, O. E. (1970) *Unfallursachenanalyse. Der Mensch in der betrieblichen Umwelt,* Herne, as quoted by Thiele, B., and Gottschalk, F. (1973). Litteraturexpertise über theoretische Grundlagen des Arbeitsschutzes, Bundesanstalt für Arbeitsschutz and Unfallforschung, Forschungsbericht Nr. 111, Dortmund.

Hale, A., and Hale, M. (1970) Accidents in perspective. *Occupational Psychology,* **44,** 115–21.

Hale, A. R., and Hale, M. (1972) *A Review of the Industrial Accident Research Literature.* London: Her Majesty's Stationery Office.

Hammarsten, B. (1979) *Tillbudsrapportering och olycksfallsfrekvens inom verkstadsindustrin.* Unpublished paper, Göteborgs Universitet, Psykologiska institutionen, Göteborg.

Hammer, W. (1972) *Handbook of System and Product Safety.* Englewood Cliffs, NJ: Prentice-Hall.

Heinrich, H. W. (1959) *Industrial Accident Prevention.* New York: McGraw-Hill.

Heinrich, H., Petersen, D., and Roos, N. (1980) *Industrial Accident Prevention.* New York: McGraw-Hill.

Herbst, P. G. (1974) *Socio-technical Design. Strategies in Multidisciplinary Research.* London: Tavistock Publications.

Johnson, W. G. (1973) The role of change in accidents. *National Safety News,* November, 90–102.

Johnson, W. G. (1975) MORT — the management oversight and risk tree. *Journal of Safety Research,* **7,** 4–125.

Kay, H. (1971) Accidents — some facts and theories. In: P. B. Warr (Ed.), *Psychology at Work.* Harmondsworth: Penguin.

Kerr, W. (1950) Accident proneness of factory departments. *Journal of Applied Psychology,* **34,** 167–70.

Kerr, W. (1957) Complementary theories of safety psychology. *Journal of Social Psychology,* **45,** 3–9.

Kjellén, U. (1982) An evaluation of safety information systems at six medium-sized and large firms. *Journal of Occupational Accidents,* **3,** 273–88.

Kjellén, U. (1984) The deviation concept in occupational accident control — I & II. *Accident Analysis and Prevention,* **16,** 289–323.

Kjellén, U., and Baneryd, K. (1976) *Undersökning av störningar vid tillverkning av explosivämnen — inrapportering, analys och åtgärder,* National Defence Research Institute, Report No. A20020-D1, Stockholm.

Kjellén, U., and Larsson, T. J. (1981) Investigating accidents and reducing risks – a dynamic approach. *Journal of Occupational Accidents,* **3,** 129–40.

Komaki, J., Barwick, K. D., and Scott, L. R. (1978) A behavioral approach to occupational safety – pinpointing and reinforcing safe performance in a food manufacturing plant. *Journal of Applied Psychology,* **63,** 434–45.

Lawrence, A. C. (1974) Human error as a cause of accidents in gold mining. *Journal of Safety Research,* **6,** 78–88.

Leplat, J. (1984) Occupational accident research and systems approach. *Journal of Occupational Accidents,* **6,** 77–89.

Mandler, G. (1975) *Mind and Emotion.* New York: Wiley.

Miller, J. G. (1978) *Living Systems*. New York: McGraw-Hill.

Monteau, M. (1977) *A Practical Method of Investigating Accident Factors. Principles and Experimental Application*, Commission of the European Communities, Luxemburg.

Näätänen, R., and Summala, H. (1982) Progress of technology and traffic accidents. *Journal of Occupational Accidents*, 4, 145–56.

Nilsson, B.-C. (1976) *Att förebygga olycksfall*, Department of Sociology, University of Uppsala, Uppsala.

Rasmussen, J. (1982) Human errors. A taxonomy for describing human malfunction in industrial installations. *Journal of Occupational Accidents*, 4, 311–33.

Robinson, G. H. (1982) Accident and sociotechnical systems. Principles for design. *Accident Analysis and Prevention*, 14, 121–30.

Rockwell, T. H., Galbraith, F. D., and Center, D. H. (1961) *Risk-Acceptance Research in Man–Machine Systems*. Ohio State University, Engineering Experimental Station, Bulletin No. 187, Columbus.

Russel Davis, D. (1958) Human errors and transport accidents. *Ergonomics*, 2(24), 24–33.

Saari, J. (1976) Efficiency of three techniques for gathering data on near accidents. *Control*, May, 65–9.

Saari, J. (1976/77) Characteristics of tasks associated with the occurrence of accidents. *Journal of Occupational Accidents*, 1, 273–9.

Saari, J., and Lahtela, J. (1981) Work conditions and accidents in three industries. *Scandinavian Journal of Environmental Health*, 7, suppl. 4, 97–105.

Samuelsson, K. (1978) *Informatics by General Systems and Cybernetics*. The Royal Institute of Technology, Report No. TRITA-IBADB-5011, Stockholm.

Shannon, H., and Manning, D. (1980) The use of a model to record and store data on industrial accidents resulting in injury. *Journal of Occupational Accidents*, 3, 57–65.

Simon, H. A. (1967) Motivational and emotional controls of cognition. *Psychological Review*, 74, 29–39.

Singleton, W. T. (1972) Techniques for determining the causes of error. *Applied Ergonomics*, 3, 126–31.

Singleton, W. T. (1973) Theoretical approaches to human error. *Ergonomics*, 16, 727–37.

Skiba, R. (1973) *Die Gefahrenträgertheorie*. Forschungsbericht Nr. 106, Bundesanstalt für Arbeitsschutz und Unfallforschung, Dortmund.

Sundström-Frisk, C. (1978) Styrfaktorer vid riskfyllt arbetsbeteende. *Sveriges Skogsförbunds Tidskrift*, 76(1–2), 57–62.

Surry, J. (1969) *Industrial Accident Research. A Human Engineering Appraisal*. Toronto, Ontario: University of Toronto.

Swain, A. D. (1977) Estimating human error rates and their effects on system reliability. Paper presented at the CEA – EDF cycles de conferences sur la fialibilite et disponibilite des systemes mecanique et de leurs composants, Jouy-en Josas, 3–7 October 1977.

Van de Putte, T. (1981) Purpose and framework of a safety study in the process industry. *Journal of Hazardous Materials*, 4, 225–34.

Vasilas, J., Fitzpatrick, R., Dubois, P. H., and Youtz, R. P. (1953) Human factors in near accidents. Air University, US Forces School of Aviation Medicine, Report No. 1, Project No. 21-1207-0001, as quoted by W. E. Tarrants (1963). An evaluation of the critical incident technique as a method for identifying industrial accident causal factors. Unpublished doctoral dissertation, New York University, New York.

Wilde, G. J. S. (1976) Social interaction patterns in driver behavior: an introduction review. *Human Factors*, **18**, 477–92.

Winsemius, W. (1965) Some ergonomic aspects of safety. *Ergonomics*, **8**, 151–62.

New Technology and Human Error
Edited by J. Rasmussen, K. Duncan and J. Leplat

15. Analysis of Human Errors in Industrial Incidents and Accidents for Improvement of Work Safety

Jacques Leplat
Ecole Pratique des Hautes Etudes, Paris
and
Jens Rasmussen
Risø National Laboratory

SUMMARY

Methods for the analysis of work accidents are discussed, and a description is given of a causal situation analysis in terms of a 'variation tree' in order to explain the course of events of the individual cases and to identify possible improvements. The difficulties in identifying 'causes' of accidents are discussed, and it is proposed to analyse accident reports with the specific aim of identifying potential for future improvements rather than causes of past events. The use of a model of cognitive control mechanisms is proposed for identification of the human decisions which are most sensitive to improvements.

INTRODUCTION

In different branches of industry, different methods have been developed for analysis of incidents and accidents in order to identify their causes and propose improvements for safety. Within process industries characterized by large production units and high levels of automation, risk and accident analysis is focused on avoidance of low probability events with large consequences to the plant and its environment. Analysis is here based on causal models of the accidental chains of events which can serve to identify deficiencies in the design of the plant and its protective systems, as well as to predict the level of risk involved in operation. Detailed analysis of the actual, individual incidents and accidents is normally performed to identify these possible weak spots in the plant and its operation. It is a general experience that human acts play an important role in such industrial accidents, and much effort is spent to include human performance in the causal accident models. This approach is feasible because of the well-structured nature of industrial process plants, which also leads to a well-defined task structure for the operators involved.

The situation is quite different for safety aspects related to workshops and construction sites, characterized by much less structured work situations and a high number of reported cases. Consequently, analysis is typically based on statistical and epidemiological methods rather than detailed causal analyses of the individual cases. Such analyses are generally based on an analysis of the routine reports collected by safety authorities which give only sparse information on the individual events and, in particular, on the work conditions and the normal routines which led to the case (Leplat, 1978, 1982). Typically, such data are used for management and insurance purposes, rather than design of counter-measures.

During recent years, several attempts have been made to use the causal situation analysis on work accidents; a promising approach has been the INRS method described below. However, the aims of this method as well as other attempts have often been to explain the individual cases; to identify the causes of the accidents.

The present paper suggests an analysis which focuses on the identification of points in the sequence which are sensitive to future improvements rather than causes of past events. It is based on the 'analysis of variations' developed for analysis of work accidents, combined with a model of human decision making based on analysis of human performance and errors in process plants.

ANALYSIS OF INCIDENTS AND ACCIDENTS

A method which is useful for shedding some light upon the causation of incidents and accidents is described here. Reliability specialists have long been interested in this problem and typically will use fault tree analysis. The application of this method presupposes a number of conditions, typically related to the well-defined structure of process plants and other technical machinery, which are rarely found in socio-technical systems. The method presented here is certainly less systematic, but its possibilities of use are much broader, for instance for study of work accidents in workshops and construction sites. In particular, when used for *post hoc* analysis, it differs from the fault tree on one specific point: the top event is not a class of events but one particular event — incident or accident — which actually occurred and for which the antecedent chain of events must be discovered. The tree obtained is, formally, a sub-tree of the fault tree (which would include a family of possible chains of events leading to the same type of accident). This sub-tree is peculiar in having no 'OR gates'. Combining a number of such sub-trees for a given type of accident would lead to a fault tree, defined after the fact.

The method of variation tree

This method is based on the idea that the occurrence of an accident results from aberrations or variations happening in the normal or 'habitual' work situation. During the analysis of an incident or accident, it is first necessary to identify such changes, i.e., to establish a list of changes and then to organize them in order to define their interrelationship. The method is described and the symbols used in the following figures defined in Chapter 13.

:

An example — A driving accident

To illustrate the diagram of variations and to have a case for further discussion in subsequent sections, the following accident is considered.

A lorry driver is ordered to deliver a cargo at a certain destination. As his usual lorry has had a breakdown, he picks up a replacement lorry, which is unfamiliar to him and, as it turns out, has faulty brakes. The lorry is then loaded and in fact overloaded. It appears that the route the driver usually takes is closed due to road repair. The driver takes a detour which turns out to have an unexpected steep slope. Due to slope, load, and bad brakes, the driver loses control and is unable to follow the curve in the road. He runs the lorry into a wall and is severely injured. The diagram of variations is shown on Figure 1.

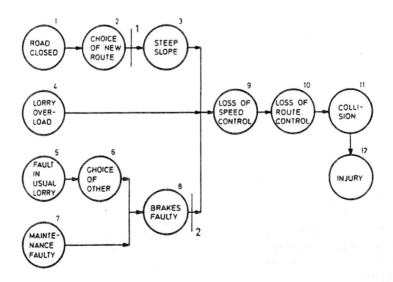

Figure 1. Diagram of variation of a driving accident

The Combination of the Diagrams of Variations

When a number of incidents or accidents have been analysed on the same system, for example on the same type of machine, we can try to merge the corresponding diagrams of variations. This has been done by Bruun *et al.* (1979) by means of cause–consequence charts, proposed by Nielsen (1975). Figure 2 gives the main elements of such a diagram. Figure 3 shows the principle of the combination of diagrams from a simple example. Bruun *et al.* give more complete examples obtained from a set of accidents which occurred on drilling machines.

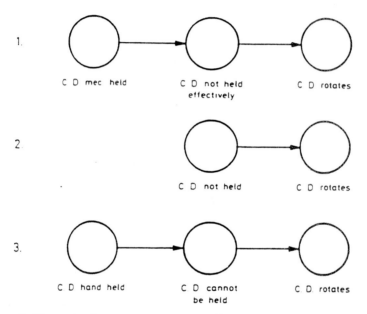

Figure 2. Elements of a cause–consequence diagram for accidents during drilling. C. D. refers to the clamping device for holding work piece

In order that a set of diagrams can be merged, a number of conditions of homogeneity must be met which are expressed by Bruun *et al.* (p. 7) as follows:

Choose the same starting point for analysis of similar accidents.
Choose the same level of detail for recording each accident.
Trace the causes of accidents backwards to the same stage in causation.
Use the same terms at each stage in the accident descriptions to describe identical events or conditions.

One can add 'Have a consistent concept of variation'. To merge the diagrams, it will sometimes be necessary to complete them with elements which are not variations (but normal states, activities, or events). The formation of merged (or synthetic) diagrams permits the evaluation of the risk presented by some characteristics of the operator and machine (from the frequency of incidents and accidents) and the identification of critical routes leading to the accident: in consequence, its usefulness for preventive safety measures is quite clear.

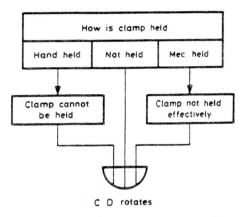

Figure 3. A merged cause–consequence diagram

ANALYSIS OF HUMAN ERRORS

The analysis of human errors and their role in industrial accidents is an important part of the development of systematic methods for industrial reliability and risk prediction. In order to obtain data for such predictive analyses, for instance by means of fault trees, as previously mentioned, it is necessary to analyse accidents and incidents to identify their *causes* in terms of component failures and human errors, since data on the frequency of such causes will make it possible to estimate the probability of the related chains of events during design of new systems.

However, the determination of how far back in an accidental chain of events it is necessary to go in order to find its causes is a matter of practical judgement and depends on the purpose of the analysis.

In consequence, the definition of human errors becomes ambiguous and — as discussed in detail in chapter 3 (page 23) — it appears to be a more fruitful point of view to consider human errors as instances of man–machine misfits, i.e., instances when human variability is not within the span acceptable for successful task performance. Variations in performance become human errors only in an 'unkind' environment which does not allow immediate correction. This means that to characterize human 'errors', one has to determine the variability of human behaviour *and* the acceptance limits for variation which hold for the work situation.

Generally, human errors are defined in terms of the faulty, *external task* element and data are collected correspondingly. If, however, the point of view of variability of human behaviour is taken, it is necessary to identify the varying element of human behaviour in terms referring to the internal human properties.

There is no one-to-one relationship between the external task performance and the internal human functions which are used. Consequently, to characterize the human role in an accidental chain of events, it is necessary also to consider the internal mental decision functions which are required in the task (see Chapter 3, Figure 2), the related internal psychological mechanisms which are involved in the error (discussed in Chapter 6, see Figure 1), and the possible presence of external causes to the particular human response. The internal decision functions and error mechanisms depend on the psychological functions and the accesses to knowledge which are activated by subjective factors in a particular situation.

The models and the error taxonomy described in Part 2 have been used for data collection from analysis of event reports (Rasmussen, 1980, 1982). For reliability prediction, this approach may be useful during design of man–machine interface systems for industrial process plants. The highly structured functional properties of such systems lead to a fairly well defined anatomy of accidents, in which causes and latent failure conditions can be reasonably well defined and identified by *post hoc* analysis.

For less structured work situations and hence for the study of common work accidents, this approach is not immediately attractive, since the causal net and its topology are not so well defined, and the reference situations used to define errors and causes are therefore questionable. It appears, however, that a promising approach can be found if the analysis of accidents is oriented more to the identification of future improvements than towards past causes. This will be discussed in more detail below.

ANALYSIS OF ACCIDENTS FOR POINTS OF CRITICAL DECISIONS

A common feature of the two approaches to the analysis of accidents and incidents discussed in the two preceding sections is the view of such events as the consequences of chains of events released and/or conditioned by a number of 'variations' with respect to a normally successful performance. It appeared to us that this view, if carried further in its consequences, could lead to a more fruitful approach to the *post hoc* analysis of accidents. Rather than identifying causes of accidents in order to collect data for their frequency or to find means for their removal — or, as is frequently the case, to find someone to blame — it appears to be more appropriate to map an accident as a tree of variations and to look for the effect of variations towards safety which might be introduced. It may be much more fruitful to introduce a variation that will break the accidental sequence than to try to remove its cause(s). In the following we discuss this approach in more detail. In effect, it amounts to finding critical decision points where conditions for existing decisions or acts can be improved or new decisions can be inserted to change the route of events in a safe direction.

The basis for the analysis will be a variation diagram, as discussed on page 159. This diagram should be prepared very carefully in order to identify 'variation' antecedents to the accidental event as well as 'state' antecedents. State antecedents are states which act by conditioning the work context and therefore prepare the route of events. They are very likely latent effects of previous variations with respect to a safe condition, since the nodes of the diagram are typically variations from normal.

What kind of changes can be introduced to break the flow of events in the variation diagram? It appears immediately that the course of events is broken if the conditions producing a variation are removed or the effects cancelled. However, since the release condition for one node of variation is the effect of an antecedent variation, it appears that a general rule will be *to cancel a variation node*, either by changing the physical condition (replace a worn tyre on a car), or changing the basis for a human act (by training, better information in the situation, or more tolerant work conditions). In case of confluence relationships, it suffices to cancel one of the necessary events (see Figure 1) or state antecedents. In other words, the problem is to identify those changes or improvements which will eliminate the effect of human variability during the course of events, or will counteract prior variations or decisions, for instance during the design phase, which lead to antecedent states preparing the route of the accident.

Another possibility will be to *break the flow of events* between nodes in the diagram of variations. What change can sensibly be introduced that will activate a human being to make a decision in the sequence which breaks or corrects the flow of events? How can the mental state of human beings or the work condition be changed so as to lead a person involved to detect and correct the risky conditions?

To develop this approach into a practical method, at least two major problems should be considered.

First, considering a single accident case, it is very easy to suggest many changes *ad hoc* which would break the sequence. Therefore a screening method must be found to select the reasonable candidates. One such method could be to superimpose a number of variation diagrams with suggestions for changes, derived for similar accident sequences or similar work conditions, in order to identify changes which have recurrent effect, and thus reject *ad hoc* candidates which are only relevant for a single case.

It is by no means a new idea to try to identify factors which can be changed in order to break accident sequences. However, this is typically done by generalizing into a few categories of improvement during the analysis of the individual cases, or by making correlation analyses between accident statistics and a number of general factors as level of education, weather conditions, etc. Typically, this analysis is performed as standard statistical analysis directly on the data contained in the accident reports collected by work safety authorities. In practice this leads to very general recommendations like better education, more effective maintenance, etc., which are very difficult to implement or make operational. In the approach proposed here, the changes are identified very explicitly and in detail for every case, and generalization is only made after a high number of cases have been merged. This makes the identified changes very specific and operational. However, this kind of analysis cannot be undertaken in the same way as standard statistical analyses of the data in accident reports. It is necessary to convert the data in routine reports into diagrams of variations, i.e., the accident reports should be related to knowledge of the normal, successful performance. This means that information should be added to the reports which is only available from persons intimately familiar with the normal work routine, as for instance supervisors or work safety representatives on site.

Secondly, we have to identify the changes in work conditions or in human disposition which will cause the proper decisions to be made. It is a general observation that motivation programmes or requests that people should 'try harder' have limited effect. This problem will be discussed in more detail in relation to the human performance model, but first we have to identify the kind of decisions we want to influence.

In general, analysis of accidents and the resulting diagram of variations will be expressed as a sequence or tree including observable physical events or human acts. In order to identify means for breaking the sequence we will be looking for nodes in the diagram which are sensitive to *cancelling*. For nodes representing inappropriate acts, this must be done by improving conditions for human decision and acting during the situation. For nodes representing abnormal states of the physical work environment, cancelling involves improvement of this physical condition, i.e., the conditions for decision making during work planning or system design must be evaluated for possible improvements.

Looking for suitable means for *breaking the sequence* by removing the causal relation among nodes, we can also look for reasonable points when people during the event can be made aware of the risky course of events and enabled to make decisions which can break the sequence or change its course. In addition, we can look for suitable locations for physical changes which will act as barriers against the flow of events. This means to look for suitable decision points during work or system design.

It will be seen that the analysis focuses attention on decisions related to variations at all levels in an organization, not only the worker directly involved. For overloading the truck in the example of Figure 1, not only the loading itself, but also driving schedules, payment policies, and supervisory control must be considered.

It will in all cases be necessary to evaluate all phases of the sequence involved in human decision making and acting in order to identify the sensitivity to improvement, i.e., whether support should be given to *detection* of the course of event under way, to *identification* of the problem, to *evaluation of goals* and priorities, or to *planning and execution* of the intervention. In some cases, just making the person aware that the potential for a risky chain of events is present will activate proper decisions. In other cases, support of proper identification of the circumstances will be vital, sometimes the consideration of conflicting goals must be considered, and so forth.

To be able to judge the appropriate means for changing the decisions of human beings involved in the accidental chain of events or the planning of work conditions, it is necessary to consider the level of cognitive awareness of the persons during the situations in which it is planned to change their decisions. The rational decision sequence involving all phases is illustrated in Figure 4 which also shows how their relevance depends on the level of cognitive activity involved in the performance, i.e., upon the training of the person. During highly trained, skill-based routines, the decision sequence is not at all activated; and during familiar tasks based on know-how, the higher level decision phases are bypassed by stereotype rules and habits. The point here is that it will not be reasonable to base improvements on support of decision phases which are in fact bypassed during the actual situation. If an activity is controlled by highly skilled routines, it will be less effective to change it by improving the knowledge of the persons involved or by asking them to be more careful. The most effective influence will be through changes of the work situation. This means that it is necessary to identify a person in the work planning or design phase who will work at a level of cognitive awareness and whose decisions can be affected.

To conclude, we propose that the traditional search for means to improve work safety through epidemiological analysis of accident records based on statistical data and very general characteristics of the work situation should be supplemented by detailed analysis of the diagram of variations for each accident which includes experts' knowledge of the normally successful work performance. Improvements are identified for each case separately, carefully considering the level of conscious awareness of the people involved in the specific situations in order to eliminate psychologically infeasible *ad hoc* proposals. Candidates for serious consideration as proposals for improvements are then identified by an 'overlay' of sets of variation diagrams for similar work situations and types of accident in order to have a screening against singular *ad hoc* proposals. The approach can be illustrated by the following example.

Analysis of Driving Example, Figure 1

First, we consider the possibility of cancelling the nodes of variation in the diagram given in Figure 1. The phases in the decision sequence which are judged to be sensitive to improvements are indicated in Figure 4 by the number of node to cancel indicated by (n) or path to break indicated by 1^n.

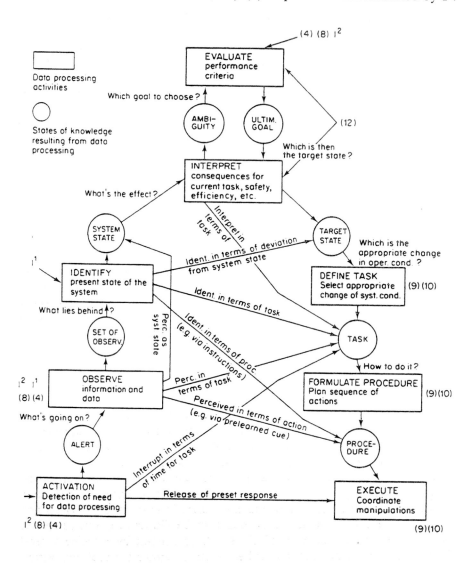

Figure 4. Illustration of the phases in decision process which can be supported in driving accident, see example in text

Cancelling nodes

(1), (2), and (3) (Figure 1). These relate to road conditions and do not lend themselves to control in the present context. To propose a decreased slope appears to be an *ad hoc* solution of low generality.

(4) Overload. Changes towards safety may involve:
—Detection, makes driver alert by some kind of overload alarm.
—Observation, easy access to weight information.
—Evaluation, change criteria for judgement. It will probably be difficult to influence highly skilled people at this level by motivational programmes, etc. Therefore, changes involve changes in work condition and social context, i.e., decisions in work planning context related to company policy, payment, penalties, etc.

(5) and (6). Faulty truck and replacement. Change the rules of allocation of trucks.

(7) Inadequate maintenance. Reorganize the maintenance department.

(8) Brakes faulty.
—Detection; worn brake alarm devices; regular inspection.
—Evaluation; changing criteria, penalties.

(9), (10), and (11). Loss of control. Since the driver at this point is well aware of the problem, cancelling will be related to defining the task to pursue (to save the car/load/people/himself) and to find the proper procedures. Since skilled drivers do not depend on conscious planning, verbal instruction will probably be less efficient than real training in emergency procedures.

(12). Avoid injury. Cancelling here involves introduction of protective devices such as safety belt, absorbent lorry bodies, etc. This involves high level decisions during lorry design.

Breaking paths

1^1 Avoiding steep slope route. Better slope information on route (sign?); better understanding of slope/load relations (probably not feasible for highly skilled driver who will not perform rational evaluations).

1^2 Driver does not accept lorry with faulty brakes, as (8).

The general rule is that when an improvement can be envisaged involving a certain decision phase, it will be necessary to find a person in the system for whom that phase is active and not normally by-passed by habits and routines. The list given above is meant to be illustrative, not complete. Further screening of *ad hoc* solutions will be needed by merging several diagrams for traffic accidents with heavy trucks, either for accidents within the company or for accidents in particular areas, depending on the purpose of the analysis.

CONCLUSION

This chapter proposes the general outline of an approach to the analysis of work accidents with the specific aim of safety improvement, rather than the evaluation and understanding of past events. Further development is needed to evaluate its practical value. For this purpose, a tight cooperation between several professional areas is necessary in the analysis of events. The analysis requires access to a representative number of uniform cases which is only possible for a central safety authority. On the other hand, the analysis requires that the routine event reports are studied by persons with an intimate knowledge of the work situation, the normal work routines and the tools and equipment used, as well as the organizational and socio-technical relationships. This information is available only to persons who participate in the particular industrial work situations and, therefore, can identify 'variations'. Finally, the analysis requires psychological expertise and knowledge about relevant models of human decision making.

Development of the method therefore requires a mutual and positive cooperation among representatives of industrial workers, authorities, and academic research — a cooperation which has its own problems and conflicts. From the test cases, however, it is our experience that such a cooperation can be established, and that the approach is worth pursuing.

The approach would serve to improve the skill of the safety officer and, in general, contribute to a better management of reliability and safety in socio-technical systems. In addition, it is worth while to emphasize the amenability of the proposed method to further improvements as the result of experience.

REFERENCES

Bruun, O., Rasmussen, A., and Taylor, J. R. (1979) *Cause–Consequence Reporting for Accident Reduction.* Risø-M-2206.

Leplat, J. (1978) Accident analyses and work analyses. *Journal of Occupational Accidents,* 1, 331–40.

Leplat, J. (1982) Fiabilité et sécurité. *Le Travail Humain,* 45, 101–8.

Nielsen, D. S. (1975) Use of cause–consequence charts in practical systems analysis. In: *Reliability and Fault Tree Analysis, Theoretical and Applied Aspects of Systems Reliability and Safety Assessment.* Philadelphia: Society for Industrial and Applied Mathematics, pp. 849–80.

Rasmussen, J. (1980) What can be learned from human error reports? In: Duncan, Gruneberg, and Wallis (Eds), *Changes in Working Life.* New York: Wiley.

Rasmussen, J. (1982) Human errors. A taxonomy for describing human malfunction in industrial installations. *Journal of Occupational Accidents,* 4, 311–33.

New Technology and Human Error
Edited by J. Rasmussen, K. Duncan and J. Leplat
© 1987 John Wiley & Sons Ltd

16. A Changing Role of Human Actors in Accident Control — Implications for New Technology Systems

Urban Kjellén
Royal Institute of Technology, Stockholm

SUMMARY

The paper discusses research needs in accident control of new technology systems. Various motives for shifting the focus of research from the behaviour of the individual operator to the information processing and decision making of the higher levels of the organizational hierarchy, responsible for design and operation of production systems, are presented. The development of the necessary decision aids requires a multidisciplinary approach and close cooperation between theory and practice.

BASIC VIEW OF ACCIDENTS AND PREVENTICE PHILOSOPHY

An accident includes an exchange of energy between the body and the environment in excess of body injury thresholds (Haddon, 1968). Basic accident preventive strategies in industry include controls of energies in the production system and barriers between the body and the possible harmful energy flow. Whereas energy barriers represent specific safety measures, the energy controls usually are the concern of the general production planning and control system.

THE SIGNIFICANCE OF HUMAN ACTIONS IN ACCIDENT OCCURENCES

According to Heinrich (1950), 88% of all accidents are caused primarily by dangerous acts on the part of the individual worker. This frequently quoted figure indicates the significant role of human actions in accident sequences. It is, however, based on a simplistic model of accidents. For example, the model does not take into account the multiple causality of accidents and the interaction between human actions and the context in which they occur.

169

Heinrich's study is cited here because of its great effect on the accident perceptions of researchers as well as safety practicians.

More recent studies by the Occupational Accident Research Unit (OARU) show that 60–80% of accidents in various industries (i.e., steel and rolling mills, construction, mechanical industry and railway) were the direct result of the operator's loss of control of energies in the system (Kjellén, 1981). Further, various malfunctions of production and safety control systems preceded these events in three-quarters of the accidents. The control systems were designed and operated by members of the industrial organization. Consequently, this modulated interpretation of Heinrich's conclusion about the significant role of human acts in accidents is valid in these industries.

This conclusion is further supported by evidence from a Finnish study (Saari, 1984). This study showed that there is no simple relation between the exposure to energies in a system and the risk of accidents. The interpretation was made that man behaves differently in an environment with many and few energy concentrations respectively. This compensatory behaviour in relation to a new risk level has also been identified in traffic safety research (Wilde, 1976). The implications are that an accident reduction strategy must take the motives and value systems of the persons exposed to hazards into account.

DEFINITION OF HUMAN DEVIATIONS

In the research carried out by OARU, accidents are analysed in relation to deviations. A *deviation* is the classification of a systems variable, when the variable takes values that fall outside a norm (Kjellén, 1984).

A taxonomy of deviations has been developed. One class of deviations is made up of human acts (i.e., human errors). Other classes of deviations include material, information and instructions, technical equipment, relation between activities, the environment and energy barriers. The classes of deviations are related to various corporate systems of production planning and control.

The class 'human deviations' has not been structured further. This is due to the practical aim of the research, i.e., the application of the taxonomy in the development of tools for use inside companies in the feedback control of accidents.

All different classes of deviations are defined in relation to *norms* at the systems level, i.e., with respect to the planned, expected or intended production process. There are problems associated with the use of this type of norm in defining human errors. For example, the way in which a task is executed frequently varies from the way it was planned according to task descriptions, etc. Further, norms are lacking at the systems level for unstructured tasks. These are typically non-productive tasks, e.g., removal of disturbance or cleaning or fetching of tools, machines or materials. They are characterized by a higher risk of accidents than productive tasks, which have been planned in advance (Saari and Lahtela, 1981).

We have defined deviations, including human errors, in relation to the planned production process for various reasons:

1. Differences in opinion, for example, between workers on the one hand (the informal system) and management and systems designers on the other hand (the formal system), as to what constitutes the faultless production process, may in themselves constitute an accident risk. These differences should be identified and resolved, for example in group settings, by establishing shared norms that produce reasonable risk levels.
2. Data on deviations are fed back to the organization for corrective and preventive actions. The established information systems for operational planning and control should be utilized for this purpose. For these systems to be reliable and compatible, data must be collected on the basis of a uniform and generally accepted set of norms.
3. Information about relations between accidents and deviations are identified and communicated to the various levels and functions of the organization. Consequently, this information is used as a tool in the development of more valid and comprehensive accident risk perceptions of the members of the organization.

The norms of unstructured tasks are operationally defined in relation to the individual worker's judgement of what is the expected or planned sequence of his work. However, this definition does not apply to work situations, which are characterized by information processing in the knowledge-based domain, e.g., the solving of problems that have not been encountered before (Rasmussen, 1982). Results from critical incident studies show that many so-called unstructured tasks, e.g., the removal of disturbances, do actually occur frequently. It follows that it should be possible to establish norms at the systems level for many of these tasks. Tasks that involve true problem solving are becoming an increasing safety problem, especially in new technology systems, and deserve further attention.

TRENDS IN ACCIDENT OCCURRENCE

During the last decades, Sweden and many other industrialized countries have experienced a steady state in the rate at which accidents have been reported to insurance companies for compensation purposes. During the same period, the frequency of work-related fatalities has declined (Singleton, 1984). Whereas the accident frequency is affected by a number of extraneous factors, i.e., compensation scheme and employee attitude, the occurrence of fatalities is more closely linked to the real risk level.

The reduction of the risk of accidents, as indicated by the decrease in the fatality rate, can be attributed to a number of factors. These include, for example, increased investments in accident control at the national and industry levels, and a flow of labour power from high risk jobs in production industry to low risk jobs in service and information processing industries; the general economic recession during the last years has also influenced the accident figures. At the present state of knowledge, it is not possible to separate and rate the relative importance of these and other factors.

A breakdown of the accident statistics by industry and occupation reveals an unequal distribution of the risk of accidents, i.e., parts of the working population have not benefited from this general risk reduction.

Effects of new technology

It is probable that the occupational fatality rate in Sweden will stabilize at a level close to the one at present experienced. This situation would be characterized by a balance between counteracting forces. Factors affecting the risk of accidents in a positive direction, as indicated above, would still be present (possibly with the exception of a declining economy). However, these factors may be counteracted by factors which, for example, have to do with the rapid transformation of industry.

At present, industry experiences a high rate of change and even discontinuities in the technological development. A high rate of change is associated with an increased risk of accidents. This has to do with the fact that the possibilities of learning from experience and of developing heuristics to solve safety problems is reduced during periods of rapid changes in production technology.

New technologies are characterized by a high degree of automization and hence a removal of the operators from the energy flows during normal operational conditions. However, many manual and semi-mechanized tasks will still be carried out in direct contact with the energy flows of the system. These include construction, maintenance and modification of industrial system and materials handling and transportation. It will be increasingly difficult to control the accident risks of these tasks due to a number of conditions:

1. Traditional safety measures such as guards, will in many cases be unfeasible.
2. High technology is associated with an increased complexity, i.e., systems are made up of networks of closely related subsystems. Accident problems emerge in interfaces between subsystems and when disturbances progress from one subsystem to the other (Leplat, 1984).

3. Automized systems leave the human operator outside the immediate control of the energies of the system. Consequently, it is difficult for the individual who moves inside the physical system to anticipate the possible energy flows.
4. This difficulty in anticipating the performance and effects of the system is enhanced in systems which utilize exotic chemical and physical processes.
5. Many new technology systems are characterized by the existence of substantial amounts of energy, and consequently, of a high potential severity of accidents.

The systematic control of the energies of the system will be a basic accident control strategy in new technologies; this relates to all phases of the system's lifecycle, including design, construction, operation, maintenance, and modification. Uncontrolled energy flows may yield various outcomes, including personal injury, property damage, damage to the environment, etc. The prevention of each of these various unwanted outcomes should not be handled as a separate control problem.

HUMAN INFORMATION PROCESSING IN ACCIDENT CONTROL IN NEW TECHNOLOGY SYSTEMS

A classical approach in safety research has been to study the effects of the characteristics of the production system on human information processing and the probability of human errors. A current approach is to study human responses to deviations or disturbances in the system. Human actions in disturbed systems both prevent and contribute to the occurrence of accidents in high technology plants. For example, a study of accidents related to malfunctions of technical control systems showed that about one-third of the accident sequences included a human intervention in the control loop of the disturbed system (Backström and Harms-Ringdahl, 1984). For industrial robot systems, this figure was about two-thirds.

There are severe limitations to man's ability to process information, in particular during time constrains. In complex, automatized plants, the individual operator will to a large extent be at the mercy of the system, i.e., the way it is designed and operated. The constrains of the system will also affect his morale and motivation (Kjellén and Baneryd, 1983). Consequently, the attribution of accident causes to the operator will be an outdated accident perception. This doesn't imply that man will be uninteresting as a point for intervention in accident control; however, the focus of attention must shift to the higher levels of the organizational hierarchy. At these levels, the necessary competence, resources and authority should be available.

However, the limitations in information processing capacity also relate to persons responsible for systems design and operation. Certain of these limitations have severe implications for the possibilities of controlling accidents in high technology systems; for example, difficulties in assessing probabilities of rare events, a bias against considering side effects and a limited capacity to comprehend complex relations.

The *design* of high technology systems requires the coordination and integration of various expertise. The total systems performance becomes increasingly difficult to comprehend and anticipate. Various strategies are adopted by systems designers in order to delimit the complexity of the problem, e.g., by concentrating on the hardware part of the system and/or by overlooking contingencies. As a consequence, the distribution of roles and tasks between the operators and the hardware of the system is rarely optimized, for example, from a safety point of view.

Analytic and conceptual tools have been developed to remedy these problems. These include, for example, risk analysis, methods to identify and assess deviations and methods of bringing together information to display the state of the total system. The methods have been developed as research tools. The diffusion of knowledge in how to use these methods as applied to industry has been slow.

During the *operational phase*, data on deviations including human errors are needed for corrective and preventive control measures. Research into safety information systems of various companies shows that, in general, these systems were inadequate to meet the requirements of a systematic accident control (Kjellén, 1982). For example, filters in the collection of data on human deviations in accident and near-accident investigations were identified. Methods were lacking for the analysis and summarization of causal data on accidents. Information was not presented to decision makers in a way that was meaningful to them. As a consequence, learning from previous experiences of accidents and deviations was delayed and fragmentary.

The introduction of high technology implies higher demands on the ability of companies to identify, assess, and control risks during the design and operational phases of production.

Research is needed to map the institutional and psychological obstacles to the introduction of tools, for example, for risk analysis and assessment. The tools and the necessary organizational support structure should be developed and evaluated in experiments in industry. The risk analyses and assessments must integrate the knowledge and value systems of the users (i.e., operators, maintenance personnel, etc.).

Further, the whole process from data collection through distribution of information in corporate safety information systems needs to be evaluated and redesigned. This includes the integration of various existing information systems inside the company. The means of presenting information should be adapted to the cognitive schemata of the various user categories. The dissemination of information should be integrated into the context in which safety related decisions are made; for example, systems for computer aided design, activity planning, scheduling and follow up (including maintenance), and resource allocation could be utilized for this purpose. This would facilitate the making of proper decisions at the right time.

CONCLUSIONS

Industry has experienced a decline in the risk of accidents during the last decades. A continuation of this trend requires substantial systematic efforts in accident control. The development of the necessary means involves a multidisciplinary approach and a close cooperation between theory and practice.

REFERENCES

Backström, T., and Harms-Ringdahl, L. (1984). A statistical study of control systems and accidents at work. *J. Occupational Accidents*, **6**, 201–10.

Haddon, W. (1968) The changing approach to the epidemiology, prevention and amelioration of trauma: The transition to approaches ethologically rather than descriptively based. *American Journal of Public Health*, **58**, 1431–8.

Heinrich, W. W. (1950) *Industrial Accident Prevention*. New York: McGraw-Hill.

Kjellén, U. (1981) *Collection and use of information on accident risks. Results of a study of the safety activities at six companies*. Royal Institute of Technology, Report No. Trita-AOG-0012, Stockholm.

Kjellén, U. (1982) An evaluation of safety information systems of six medium-sized and large firms. *J. Occupational Accidents*, **3**, 273–88.

Kjellén, U. (1984) The deviation concept in occupational accident control. *Accident Analysis and Prevention*, **16**, 289–323.

Kjellén, U., and Baneryd, K. (1983) Changing local health and safety practices at work within the explosives industry. *Ergonomics*, **26**, 863–77.

Leplat, J. (1984). Occupational accident research and systems approach. *J. Occupational Accidents*, **6**, 77–89.

Rasmussen, J. (1982) Human errors. A taxonomy for describing human malfunctions in industrial installations. *J. Occupational Accidents*, **4**, 311–33.

Saari, J. (1984) Accidents and disturbances in the flow of information. *J. Occupational Accidents*, **6**, 91–105.

Saari, J., and Lahtela, J. (1981) Work conditions and accidents in three industries. *Scandinavian Journal of Work Environment Health*, **7**, suppl. 4, 97–105.

Singleton, T. (1984) 'Future trends in accident research in European countries'. *J. Occupational Accidents*, **6**, 3–12.

Wilde, G. J. (1976) Social interaction patterns in driver behavior: an introductory review. *Human Factors*, **18**, 477–92.

New Technology and Human Error
Edited by J. Rasmussen, K. Duncan and J. Leplat
© 1987 John Wiley & Sons Ltd

Part 5: Industrial Studies of Human Error — I

INTRODUCTION

In the paper by Leplat (Chapter 17) we return to the need for a systems perspective. In Part 1 Rasmussen emphasized system objectives as central to much industrial use of the term human error, and analysed operator interaction with process plant in system terms. Leplat goes beyond this comparatively well-structured case and employs the theory of systems to analyse work safety in complex industrial organizations. The primary purpose of his analysis is to identify the 'system dysfunctions', which can have unacceptable consequences, and put in jeopardy the achievement of system objectives. From this standpoint, the study of accidents must seek to specify the system dysfunction which lies behind their occurrence. Indeed the investigator should regard accidents as symptoms of dysfunction, and regard system dysfunctions as the proper objectives of study.

This general approach leads naturally to a consideration of other symptoms which may identify system dysfunction and thereby anticipate the risk of accidents. Among the examples provided by Leplat is the site of removal of blast furnace products, where accidents and other incidents are frequent and which, in system terms, lie at an ill-defined boundary between two subsystems, in this case the blast furnace department and the transport department. The importance of identifying the conditions for this, and other types of dysfunction distinguished by Leplat, is that it prompts the search for preventive measures and for measures which, as he puts it, are curative since they are directed to the dysfunction and not merely symptomatic, as would be measures directed solely to avoid repetition of a particular accident.

Like Leplat, Griffon-Fouco and Ghertman (Chapter 18) emphasize the misleading nature of global statistics in their account of human error data obtained in the nuclear power generation industry. They distinguish different purposes which may drive data collection and describe three levels of data analysis. First, a survey technique is employed which can detect the rank order of the main factors influencing human errors, such as, training, procedures, documentation; the effects of combinations of factors; and changes in ranking resulting from, e.g., plant changes or preventive measures.

The second level of analysis is also statistical, oriented to short-term estimates and to rank ordering the causes of human error with a view to local preventive measures. Two people complete questionnaires: a person on-site who first discovers the event; and a person off-site who verifies, encourages a dispassionate attitude, and guarantees confidentiality. This intuitively sensible method of employing two people to improve data reliability yields interesting quantitative findings, e.g., control room errors are more likely to be detected; of these half are discovered by the author of the error; a disproportionate number of errors are observed during the first two shift hours; all errors of omission are observed during the last six shift hours and most occur at the end of a task sequence.

The third level of analysis addresses the multicausality and complexity of human error, and explicitly attempts to establish event sequences (which are lost in the statistical analyses). To enable the construction of an 'event tree', a 'fault tree', and a tree of 'human error causes', it is noteworthy that the authors specify a clear stop rule. The need for a stop rule is pointed out in the earlier paper by Rasmussen (Chapter 3), and others have insisted on the importance of a clear stop rule if a method of analysis is to be both manageable and rigorous, (e.g., Annett and Duncan, 1967).

The stop rule applied by Griffon-Fouco and Ghertman leaves three possible fault tree 'roots': design condition, equipment failure, and human error. In an analysis of emergency core cooling, they identify one equipment failure and two human errors, one of which, 'too lengthy start-up steps', is used to illustrate the technique in detail. The lengthy start-up is attributed to: control room-to-plant telephone problems; failures to reset a control by the operating crew who had not been informed of a valve strap; and failure of a piece of equipment with a long-standing record of troubles calling for maintenance attention (to no avail). The authors chose, or chanced upon, an especially apposite case, consisting as it largely does of communication breakdown at several points. This is a source of error which is frequently emphasized by researcher and practitioner alike — including several other contributors to this volume.

Like De Keyser and Bainbridge, Duncan (Chapter 19) is pessimistic about the impact of formal or 'theoretical' training in how plant or equipment works. He also draws attention to the dangers of algorithmic procedures and regulations, what Rasmussen would call rule-based behaviour, when the task is fault diagnosis. He argues that experienced operators may be a source of powerful diagnostic heuristics on which fault diagnosis training may be based — powerful in the sense that they enable accurate diagnosis of faults not previously encountered.

Because it is heuristic, the diagnostic training described by Duncan is fallible. This point is taken up in Part 6, in the light of Reason's discussion of the dangers inherent in human predilections for heuristic solutions. Also the subject of further discussion in Part 6 is the significance of the need to employ the technique of withholding plant information. At this stage it is more important to note that an important source of powerful diagnostics were operators of a generation who had enjoyed previous experience of less automated plant. The point is a matter for concern, as Bainbridge points out. To the extent that training schemes, or other attempts to reduce errors, rely on earlier generations of operators, we are living on borrowed time.

Finally, for the human operator, the advent of high technology with its associated high capital costs, means working round the clock. All too often, little or no consideration is given to the physiological basis of cognitive processes which, however, may have important implications. This point of view is represented by Yvon Queinnec and Gilbert de Terssac in Chapter 20, who are concerned with the influence of circadian rhythms upon performance, and in particular their interactions with different schemes of shift work. This question is an important topic for the organization of work and, in common with the other chapters in Part 5, underlines the importance of field studies of human functions in the work setting.

REFERENCE

Annett, J., and Duncan, K. D. (1967) Task analysis and training design. *Occupational Psychology*, **41**, 211–21.

New Technology and Human Error
Edited by J. Rasmussen, K. Duncan and J. Leplat
© 1987 John Wiley & Sons Ltd

17. Occupational Accident Research and Systems Approach

Jacques Leplat
École Practique des Hautes Études, Paris

SUMMARY

Accident in terms of a symptom of a system dysfunctioning. Types of dysfunctioning: deficiencies in the articulation of subsystems (boundary areas, zones of overlapping, asynchronous evolution of the subsystems); lack of link-up between the elements. Accidents and other clues to dysfunctioning. Various systems of reference of accidents in individual appreciation.

INTRODUCTION

The theory of systems has inspired many scientific disciplines which, however, quite often just borrowed some general concepts from it. For example, only a few scientists working in the field of the psychology or sociology of organizations used the formalized aspects of this theory even though they were influenced by what some researchers (Emery, 1969) have called 'systems thinking'. Some scientists approached the study of socio-technical systems with this new mode of thinking (Emery and Trist, 1960). The present analysis of work accidents is also done within this perspective. This short paper will not specifically mention the other system approaches which, in fact, consider only part of the socio-technical system — for example, industrial engineering and human factors. This more complete system integrates the partial technical and human subsystems and their interactions.

On such a large subject, it is only possible to emphasize some points. I shall first mention some characteristics of systems which, in my view, should orient studies on accidents. I shall then present some studies conducted within the system perspective. Finally, I shall show how the study of accidents can benefit from such a perspective.

THE SYSTEM PERSPECTIVE IN STUDIES ON ACCIDENTS

There are many definitions of a system, each one emphasizing the features considered as typical. Ashby's (1970) definition is one of the most general:

he considers that to define a system is 'to list the variables that are to be taken into account' (p. 40). This apparently banal definition underlines that it is indispensable in every case to list precisely the variables or elements constituting the system considered. A system is indeed always a model, an abstraction conceived by the analyst. Within the same object one might distinguish different systems of variables, depending on the aim of the study; analogously, the boundary of a system, what separates the system from its environment, has to be defined. A system is never given: it has to be built and this construction is often the most difficult part of a study.

Socio-technical systems, man–machine systems, also named 'living organization' (Faverge *et al.*, 1970) which I shall often mention here, are open systems; their elements or variables are both human and technical. These systems are very diverse, from the elementary system constituted by the individual work place and possibly its components, to the whole plant, the workshop, the production unit, etc. One may also become interested in the social systems constituted by variably sized sets of individuals: the team, the department, a professional group.

It is important to note that in any socio-technical system, whether elementary or complete, human elements have a particular status. This particular status is expressed by the fact that individuals may consider their activity as serving aims that do not necessarily coincide with the aims of the whole system. Individuals and groups may redefine their goals as well as the means of attaining them (Hackman, 1969); hence, the distinction between prescribed task and real task (Herbst, 1974; Leplat and Hoc, 1983) is quite necessary.

Within this perspective, what is an accident? Before answering this question, I want to make it clear that an accident will be considered as an immediate injury to the bodily integrity of the human element in the system. The notion of immediate injury permits differentiation between accidents and long-term disorders (deafness, professional diseases . . .) caused by nuisances due to working conditions. An accident is an undesired — hence unplanned — consequence of the system functioning(what is possibly planned is prevention and/or remedial measures). An accident is therefore a consequence of a dysfunctioning in the system which does not work as planned (Leplat and Cuny, 1979). Consequently, the study of accidents may be envisaged as the study of the dysfunction(s) that caused them.

Conceiving an accident in terms of a symptom of a system dysfunctioning has several consequences:

1. It provides an objective in the study of accidents, i.e., the identification of the dysfunctionings, and an objective for safety measures, i.e., the reduction of the dysfunctionings. It is no longer a question of acting only upon the accident symptom (symptomatic treatment) but rather of acting upon the dysfunctions that caused it (curative treatment).

2. It leads to the investigation of various symptoms of the same dysfunctionings, i.e., other accidents or incidents which constitute additional indicators of danger.

3. Accidents may be studied by reference to several types of system: the composition of the considered systems, the relations between them, and their relative importance should be defined very precisely.

4. It runs counter to a simplified causal conception of the origin of accidents.

5. When accidents are considered as the result of the system's functioning, one is led to investigate the mechanisms of their production (one might say of their genesis).

TYPES OF DYSFUNCTIONING

Within the system perspective, an essential task is to identify and classify dysfunctionings. The notion of dysfunctioning is to be compared with the notion of risk factor or potential factor of accident. It should also be noted that one may trace back from the dysfunctioning to its origin. The same event may be considered as a dysfunction when paying attention to its origins, and as a source of dysfunctioning when paying attention to its consequences. With Cuny (Leplat and Cuny, 1979), I analysed in detail different categories of dysfunctionings. These categories were mostly defined on the basis of studies conducted in the iron and steel industry (X, 1969). Some of these categories will now be presented.

Deficiencies in the articulation of subsystems

A system may be divided into subsystems. The functioning of the global system depends not only on the functioning of these subsystems but also on the manner in which these functionings are coordinated to meet the aims of the global system. Several dysfunctions generating accidents which are ascribable to failures in this coordination can be mentioned.

Boundary areas as zones of insecurity:

When considering departments of a factory as types of subsystems, boundary areas between departments often constitute zones of uncertainty in which the functions of each department are poorly defined; thus, they constitute zones of insecurity.

As an illustration, there is the fact that, in an iron and steel plant, frequent accidents and incidents occurred in places of evacuation of blast furnace products. It was found that these places were at the boundary of the blast furnace department and the transport department. The distribution of the functions to be exercised in these places not being satisfactory, this gave rise to conflicts. For example: (a) the floor was not cleaned properly because each department considered the other to be responsible for cleaning; (b) a signal informing transport workers of the state of the blast furnace did not work and was not repaired because the members of each department were waiting for the members of the other department to repair it.

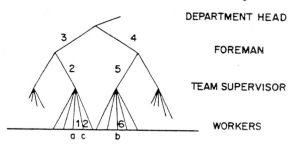

Figure 1. Hierarchic chart representing distances between individuals (the distance between individuals a and b is 6 since there are 6 transitions from one hierarchical level to another when information passes from a to b; between a and c there are only 2)

Faverge (1967) proposed interpreting some dysfunctionings observed in these boundary zones in terms of the hierarchic distance of the workers to the common executive. This distance is evaluated (Figure 1) by the number of lines of the hierarchic chart separating one individual from another (or by the number of transitions from one hierarchical level to another). The greater this distance, the more difficult the communication and the higher the level of uncertainty and insecurity.

There are also boundary zones between other subsystems, for instance, between teams, operators, professional groups, and it would be easy to find examples of studies revealing that accidents occurred in these zones.

Zones of overlapping as zones of insecurity:

Systems present overlappings. One of the many definitions of overlapping underlines that the same function is realized by the cooperation of two subsystems, another that the activity of two (or more) systems is exerted on the same site. I shall deal only with the second case and refer to it as co-activity. At the department level, this case is illustrated by the presence on the same site of a construction of maintenance department which is external to the plant and of a department belonging to the plant. The activities of the two departments often seem to be poorly coordinated; for instance, the safety rules observed by one department are ignored by the other. An investigation (X, 1969) in the steel industry (transport department and external construction service) revealed that 67% of technical incidents with material damage occurred in zones of co-activity representing only a small amount of the zones assigned to transport. Such conditions are frequent in modern industry which often use external enterprises to deal with some aspects of maintenance, repair, cleaning, building, etc. The organization of situations of co-activity is an important task for safety.

It should be noted that situations of co-activity may also be found at the interindividual level.

Asynchronous evolution of the subsystems of a system:

Changes are sometimes introduced into subsystems, due to the modernization of some equipment. Such changes are often carefully designed but their consequences on other parts of the system are sometimes totally neglected. For instance, a production procedure is modified in order to increase production greatly, but no change in the means for removing the products is planned, leading to pile-ups, and to temporal constraints on workers, both factors which impair safety.

Cases in which a properly designed part of a system deteriorates may also be considered as belonging to this class of dysfunction. For instance, a poor stretch in an otherwise good road or a faulty element in a new system. In these cases, the erroneous expectations of the user, the inaccurate appreciation of the situation, may lead to accidents.

Lack of link-up between the elements of a system

The quality of the link-up between the elements of a system is not only the condition of efficiency but can also be the condition of safety. This phenomenon may be observed at different levels of the systems, as illustrated by the following examples.

The link-up may concern firstly the members of a group: in this case, team or group cohesion. Several studies gave evidence of the relationship between lack of cohesion and safety (X, 1969). This relationship may be explained because a lack of cohesion is often an obstacle to the circulation of information within the group; information is indispensable when the actions of an individual depend on what another individual says or does.

The link-up may also concern the relations between the individuals and the material elements. The quality of this link-up is determined by reference to the task. When the capacities of the individual do not correspond to the task requirements, the result is quite often impaired safety (Johnson, 1980). However, the reverse is equally true. For instance, links between the displacements of a signal and the moves of a command which do not follow the sensori-motor stereotypes of users may lead to accidents. The notion of compatibility in ergonomics provides us with very useful data on this issue.

ACCIDENTS AND OTHER CLUES TO DYSFUNCTIONING

When considering an accident as a symptom of system dysfunctioning, the analyst is led to search for other symptoms, particularly symptoms of the same dysfunctioning which do not constitute accidents. Incidents, breakdowns and near-accidents belong to this latter category. A decisive issue for safety is to know to what extent such symptoms can give clues to the same dysfunctions as accidents. The question in this case is the determination of the relationship between reliability and safety. Does the former embrace the latter? Does any action which favours reliability necessarily favour safety? This question was examined in detail elsewhere (Leplat, 1982); consequently, I shall just mention some of its essential aspects. Three cases can be mentioned among the possible relationships between dysfunctions, incident and accident. In the first case, incidents are only the symptoms of dysfunctioning. A starter which does not work properly (dysfunctions) is the source of possible incidents (repeated attempts at starting the engine, which exhausts the battery) but does not result in an accident.

In the second case, the dysfunctioning generates incidents which themselves create accidents. There are several examples in the literature showing that accidents occurred at the end of a series of incidents (Faverge, 1967). The mechanisms through which incidents result in accidents are diverse. An accident may be a direct consequent of an incident (for instance a trolley leaves the track and a worker is thrown down) or an indirect one. The latter category includes accidents which occur when attempting to counteract an incident (for instance, a worker gets hurt when putting the trolley back on its track).

Finally, the same dysfunctioning may result both in incidents and accidents which are not related to each other. For instance, in some cases, the fact that the sling of a crane is not properly hooked (dysfunctioning) may result in some cases in material damages (damaged objects), in other cases in physical demage to the workers on the ground.

Simple schematic appreciations of this type will often have to be made more complex in order to take into account observed accidents. The same dysfunctioning may in fact result in the three different cases just mentioned.

In practice, the important point is to establish a link between incident and accident in order to use incidents — which are always more frequent — as predictors of accidents and to reveal dysfunctionings. The most systematic studies undertaken within this perspective concern road safety and aim at evaluating the danger of certain road configurations (intersections particularly), as well as providing us with elements of diagnosis of these situations.

Incidents or near-accidents considered here are called traffic conflicts. The definition of this conflict is difficult. Malaterre and Muhlrad (1976) defined it as follows: 'There is a conflict when at least a utilizer is obliged to undertake an avoidance action, such as braking, or accelerating, or changing lane or direction in order to avoid a probable accident' (p. 8). Identifying as well as evaluating a conflict raises difficult problems which cannot be dealt with here. I shall just report some characteristic results of these studies.

1. The correlation between the number of conflicts and the number of accidents varies with the severity of the conflict: it increases as more severe conflicts are taken into consideration (Malaterre et al., 1978; Russam et al., 1972).
2. The relationships between conflicts and accidents vary with the types of utilizers, the types of conflicts (Table 1) and the types of intervention.
3. In some cases, accidents and conflicts seem to belong to different types. 'These cases are observed on some difficult sites where the dangerous character of the cross-road is not due to the frequency of conflictual manoeuvres, but to a very particular dysfunctioning which is difficult to discover, which becomes evident in certain conditions and in an environment which is generally already structured to avoid conflicts' (Malaterre and Muhlrad, 1978, p. 18).

Table 1: *Relationships between conflicts and accidents as function of the type of utilizers and conflicts (1, 2, 3). The arrows represent the direction of the vehicles involved in the conflict (after Malaterre and Muhlrad, 1978)*

	Light vehicles	Heavy lorries	2 wheels	Pedestrians	1 → →	2 → ↑	3 → ↓
% conflicts	54	10	27	9	19	27	11
% accidents	23	3	68	6	8	44	22

These examples all point to the fact that if incidents may provide us with clues to safety which are sometimes very useful, it is always necessary to examine very carefully their real relationships with accidents, by using either clinical studies or statistical studies. An example of the exploitation of incidents (that the author called 'non-injury accidents') in the steel industry was recently given by Laitinen (1982).

ACCIDENTS AND CHANGES IN THE SYSTEM

Change and deviation are important concepts both in systems theory and in accident theories. Kjellén pointed to the usefulness and scope of these notions in a detailed way in Chapters 14 and 16 of this book: they will not be discussed further here.

SYSTEMS OF REFERENCE OF ACCIDENTS IN INDIVIDUAL APPRECIATION

The systems within which an accident may be inserted are numerous. An accident may be attributed to a dysfunctioning at the organization level, or at the socio-technical level constituted by the workshop of the workteam and their technical environment, or at the level of the elementary man–machine system. But an accident may also be related to the history of the individual, his personality, his abilities, etc., which also constitute systems interacting with the former. The relative importance of each of these systems varies from one accident to another. A historical review of studies on accidents reveals that the systems of reference which are preferred vary with the period. For a long time, psychologists considered individual characteristics as the main determinant of accidents, and the question of a predisposition to accidents was widely discussed. Later on, different systems appeared. If we now consider no longer the history but the different persons and groups in our society, we may observe an analogous phenomenon, namely that although each person's appreciation of the causes of an accident is different, it does not follow that they are completely wrong. A not-very-recent enquiry (Vibert, 1957) on modernization, involving 310 French workers and 7 industries asked the following question: 'In your opinion, what is the cause of an accident? Workers' lack of attention, too fast a work-pace, disregard of safety instructions, hazard, bad functioning of machines, fatigue, or lack of work coordination within a team'. It appeared that 'workers satisfied with their job, integrated into and participating in the enterprise, attribute accidents mainly to personal causes' (workers' lack of attention, disregard of safety instructions). Contrarily, workers who are not very satisfied, with a low degree of integration and participation invoke more often non-personal causes that imply that the enterprise is responsible. This enquiry revealed a relationship between the attitude towards the enterprise and workers' appreciation of the causes of accidents.

More recently, Sundbo (1980) showed differences in the attribution of the causes of accidents with the identity of the person questioned: victims, safety executives, management.

A systematic study of causal attribution was conducted in our laboratory by Kouabenan (1982): 320 workers from a public factory were asked questions analogous to the questions asked in the above-mentioned enquiry. Furthermore, workers were requested to interpret reports of accidents. Kouabenan distinguished three groups of subjects, depending on their qualification. The results show that the lower the position in the hierarchy, the greater the tendency to attribute the causes of accidents to factors linked to work organization (inadequacy or lack of safety measures, faulty materials, bad working conditions, etc.); individuals who have a high position in the hierarchy tend to attribute responsibility for accidents to the workers (lack of attention, of caution, inexperience, disregard of safety rules). It seems that accidents are attributed to the factors in which individuals are less directly involved. In his conclusion, the author underlines that the causal attribution of an accident seems to depend on some characteristics of the victim and of the analyst (hierarchical status, degree of involvement, satisfaction), as well as on the relationships between the victim and the analyst, and on the severity of the accident. This study was elaborated and analysed within the framework of the attribution theory (Kelley, 1972). The same theory inspired several experimental studies which aimed at a better specification of the factors and mechanisms of attribution.

When dealing with safety problems, the variation in the systems preferred by individuals when making their analysis should be taken into account.

1. In order to avoid bias which might distort or impoverish the analysis, it is necessary that persons having diverse professional status and different training participate in the analysis. In this way, there will be more opportunity to take into account the whole set of factors affecting the genesis of an accident.

2. It is possible — but experiments should investigate this point to confirm it — that operators' behaviour depends partly on their appreciation of the work situation and that, by modifying this appreciation through adequate training, one will contribute to the development of safety behaviour. It was shown in some studies that the attribution of accidents to hazard was more frequent in individuals having a low degree of training; it would be interesting to see if the same individuals are also less cautious. It would also be useful to have the means to evaluate the influence upon safety behaviour of training in the analysis of accidents, particularly of training in an analysis showing the role of the different intervening systems.

CONCLUSIONS

I have attempted to present some orientations suggested by the 'systems-thinking' approach in the study of accidents. I shall now try to extract the main general characteristics of this approach. At first, it seems that the systems theory in the analysis of accidents does not diverge fundamentally from other theories advanced. All theories extract and organize certain variables that may be considered as defining a system. In my view, systems theory is an invitation to coordinate the various theories of accidents which are always partial theories. An accident is a phenomenon resulting from the intervention of a set of variables for which there is no simple model. Their study will often necessitate the combination of several models, and the concepts of the systems theory may help towards this combination and organization.

However, systems theory does not specify the variables to be taken into account, and the components of the system that will be investigated, as well as its boundaries and functioning, remain to be defined. For this, partial models which are already well known may be useful.

The systems theory approach underlines the limitations of all interpretations in terms of a unique cause. Accidents do not have one single cause but rather a network of causes. The problem is not only to identify these causes, to locate them in terms of their distance from an accident (on a proximal/distal axis) but also to evaluate their respective importance. Multiple causes are always present, quite often very intricate, but their role is not equivalent either in a given accident or in a set of accidents.

One should also note that the systems approach emphasizes the problems of functioning and production. To think of an accident in terms of a system is to search for the mechanisms which produced it and for the characteristics of the system which may give an account of this process.

Finally, it should be kept in mind that systems explaining occupational accidents involve either one or several individuals or the variables which characterize them. In itself this characteristic is the source of great complexity, not only because of the interindividual variability, but also because individuals and groups may adopt their own goals which are not necessarily the same for all and which do not necessarily coincide with the goal of the enterprise. Men's activities in their work are oriented and directed by the appreciation they have of personal, technical or organizational systems which characterize them or into which they are inserted. This appreciation is quite often more difficult to apprehend and to control than their objective itself.

I hope I have been able to outline several orientations which may enable an approach to be made to this complexity and facilitate the analysis. Unfortunately, however, there is no simple recipe for doing so.

REFERENCES

Ashby, W. R. (1970) *An Introduction to Cybernetics*. London: Chapman and Hall, pp. 295.

Cuny, X. (1977) An accident analysis method. In: *Research on Occupational Accident*. Swedish Work Environment Fund, Stockholm, pp. 37–41.

Emery, F. E. (1969) *Systems Thinking*. Harmondsworth: Penguin Books, 398 pp.

Emery, F. E., and Trist, E. L. (1960) Socio-technical systems. In: F. E. Emery (Ed.), *Systems Thinking*. Harmondsworth: Penguin Books, pp. 281–96.

Faverge, J. M. (1967) Psychosociologie des Accidents du Travail. Paris: P.U.F., 160 pp.

Faverge, J. M., Houyoux, A., Olivier, M., Querton, A., Laporta, J., Poncin, A., and Salengros, P. (1970) *L'Organisation Vivante*. Editions de l'Institut de Sociologie, Bruxelles, 198 pp.

Hackman, J. R. (1969) Toward understanding the role of tasks in behavioral research. *Acta Psychologica*, **31**, 97–128.

Herbst, P. G. (1974) *Socio-Technical Design*. London: Tavistock Publications, 242 pp.

Johnson, W. G. (1980) *MORT Safety Assurance Systems*. New York: M. Decker Inc., 525 pp.

Kelley, H. H. (1972) Causal schemata and the attribution process. In: E. A. Jones *et al.*, (Eds), *Attribution: Perceiving the Causes of Behavior*. Morristown, NJ: General Learning Press, pp. 151–74.

Kjellén, U. (1983) The deviation concept in occupational accident control — theory and method. Royal Institute of Technology, Report No. Trita-AOG-0019, Stockholm.

Kouabenan, D. R. (1982) Représentation de la genèse des accidents du travail: déterminants des attributions causales. Thèse de 3ème cycle, E.P.H.E., Paris V, 345 pp.

Laitinen, H. (1982) Reporting non-injury accidents: a tool in accident prevention. *Journal of Occupational Accidents*, **4** (2–4), 275–80.

Leplat, J. (1982) Fiabilité et sécurité. *Le Travail Humain*, **45** (1), 101–8.

Leplat, J., and Cuny, X. (1979) *Les Accidents du Travail*. Coll. 'Que Sais-Je' No. 1591, Paris: P.U.F., 126 pp.

Leplat, J., and Hoc, J. M. (1983) Tâche et activité dans l'analyse psychologique des situations. *Cahiers de Psychologie Cognitive*, **3** (1), 49–64.

Leplat, J., and Rasmussen, J. (1983) Analysis of human errors in industrial incidents and accidents for improvement of work safety. Report to be published.

Malaterre, G., and Muhlrad (1976) Intérêt et limite du concept de conflit de trafic et quasi-accident dans les études de sécurité. Document interne, Monthlery, ONSER, 37 pp.

Malaterre, G., and Muhlrad (1978) Mise au point d'une méthodologie des conflits de trafic. Document interne, 79.41.034, Monthléry, ONSER, 39 pp.

Meric, M., and Szekely, J. (1980) Diagnostic de sécurité préalable à la définition d'actions de prévention. Rapport No. 399/RE et annexe I.N.R.S., Vandoeuvre.

Russam, K., and Sabey, B. E. (1972) Accidents and traffic conflicts at junctions. Report L.R. 146, Road Research Laboratory, Crowthorne.

Sundbo, J. (1980) Tilskadekomoster — forekomst of risitofaktorer. I Kommission hos teknisk forlag, København.

Vibert, P. (1957) La représentation des causes d'accidents du travail. *Bull. du CERP*, **VI** (4), 423–8.

X (1969) Recherche communautaire sur la sécurité dans les mines et la sidérurgie A — Sidérurgie. Etude de physiologie et de psychologie du travail No. 4, CECA, Service des publications des communautés européennes, Luxembourg.

New Technology and Human Error
Edited by J. Rasmussen, K. Duncan and J. Leplat
© 1987 John Wiley & Sons Ltd

18. Data Collection on Human Factors

M. Griffon-Fouco and F. Ghertman
Electricité de France

SUMMARY

Three collection methods are described, each relating to a different level of analysis:

1. Simplified statistical analysis.
2. In-depth statistical analysis by means of a detailed classification and questionnaires.
3. In-depth analysis by means of a method which reconstitutes the multi-causal aspect of the events and of each human error.

INTRODUCTION

The currently available statistics highlight that 15 to 30% of reported events have a human component. However, these figures give but a rough estimate rather than an efficient understanding of the factors generating human errors.

In a desire to reduce in number and importance such events affecting, in various degrees, availability, safety and security in its nuclear plants, Electricité de France was prompted to introduce a system of data collection concerning human errors.

Data are collected in two fields:

1. Training simulators: analysis of operator behaviour in incident or accident operating conditions.
2. Power plants in operation: analysis of events involving a human error component which occurred during operation.

This paper is concerned with the method of data collection in the latter field, namely, power plants in operation.

Actually three collection methods are used, each relating to a different level of analysis (see Figure 1):

1. Simplified statistical analysis of the causes of human error.
2. In-depth statistical analysis of the causes of certain human errors.
3. In-depth analysis of certain events involving a human component.

For each level of analysis a description is given of the selection criteria retained, of the methods used, and of some examples selected.

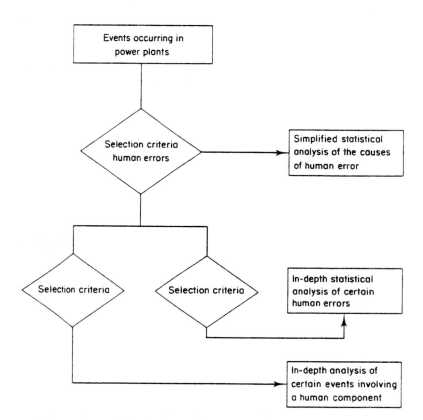

Figure 1. The three levels of data collection

SIMPLIFIED STATISTICAL ANALYSIS OF THE CAUSES OF HUMAN ERROR

Selection Criteria

In the initial stages, among events that occurred in nuclear power plants during operation, those involving human error are selected. Human error is defined as 'any human action revealing a deviation from the action that would have averted the event or reduced its seriousness'.

Method

Once human errors have thus been selected, they are succinctly analysed, distinction being made according to the following classification:

1. Type of activity: operations (start-up in particular), periodic test or maintenance.
2. Location of the error: control room or in-plant.
3. Actors of the error: automaticians–electricians, operating staff, maintenance staff, contract personnel.
4. Task type: performance, checking or communication.
5. Nature of the error: omission, transposition, inappropriate action, action performed too late or too soon.
6. Level of the task at which the error occurred: perception, information treatment, action.
7. Factors of the error: task characteristics, workstation characteristics, work time, work organization, training, format of procedures, individual factors.

A statistical analysis of human errors, classified in this way, makes it possible to determine the main factors of occurrence of these errors.

Example

At first, an analysis has been conducted on a particular category of events, here, the case of reactor trips that occurred in 900 MWe, PWR during 1982. For this purpose, use has been made of the information supplied in the event reports written by the power plants.

Sixty-two scrams involving human error have been numbered, which represents about one-third of the recorded scrams. Among these scrams, five involve two human errors so that our analysis covers 67 human errors.

Table 1 gives the percentage of human error attributable to each classification heading mentioned above.

Table 1: *Simplified statistical analysis of the causes of human errors*

Causes	Number of the errors concerned	percentage %
Activity		
Operations	26	39
(start-up)	(14)	(54)
Periodic tests	28	42
Maintenance	13	19
Location		
Control room	37	55
In-plant	30	45
Actors		
Operators	42	63
Automaticians–Electricians	18	27
Maintenance	3	4
Contractors	4	6
Task type		
Performance	61	91
Checking	4	6
Communication	2	3
Kind of error		
Omission	21	31
Transposition	14	21
Inappropriate action	26	39
Too late, or too early action	6	9
Level of the task when error occurred		
Detection	26	39
Interpretation	9	13
Action	32	48
Factors of error *		
Task characteristics	12	18
Workstation characteristics	14	21
Work organization	8	12
Training	36	54
Procedure	10	15
Individual factors	3	5

*The sum of percentages exceeds 100%, as a human error may be due to several factors.

The following main results emerge from this statistical analysis (considering that such results relate only to scrams and that the sample is of a restrictive and partial nature, these results should be handled with cautions):

1. About 40% of human errors occur during operation activities, 40% during periodic tests, and 20% in maintenance work.

2. 60% of the errors originate from operating staff, 30% from automaticians and electricians, 10% from maintenance and contract staff.
3. Over 50% of human operational errors occur during start-up or power escalation.
4. About 50% of human errors occur in the control room and 50% locally, in the plant.

Human error may often be attributable to a combination of factors which break down as follows, in order of importance:

1. Training provided to operators to perform their task.
2. Ergonomic characteristics of the workstation.
3. Format of the documents available to the operator.
4. Work organization.

By crossing factors, it is possible to refine the data provided by Table 1; e.g., it is possible to try to determine, for each personnel category, how many errors are partly attributable to training: 57% for operating staff, 39% for automaticians and electricians, 67% for maintenance staff and, at last, 75% for contract personnel.

IN-DEPTH STATISTICAL ANALYSIS OF THE CAUSES OF CERTAIN HUMAN ERRORS

Selection criteria

One can easily understand that an in-depth analysis of all the events occurring during operation is not feasible. Therefore, the field of investigation has to be limited to some human errors only. Hence the decision to group data collections according to campaign and to theme.

Initially, a validation of the collection method used was planned. It was completed, in cooperation with the Institute of Nuclear Power Operations (INPO), over a period of six months or so and within three nuclear plants (a French one and two in the USA). It focused on human errors that occurred during periodic tests.

Method

Classification used:

For each of the selected errors the following items are identified:

1. Circumstances of the error.

(a) Associated failures (equipment, procedure).
(b) Unit concerned.
(c) Systems concerned.
2. Circumstances of the discovery (where, when, how, by whom).
3. Identification of the error itself.
   (a) Nature of the error (omission, transposition, non-required action).
   (b) Level of the task at which the error occurred (perception, information, action).
   (c) Type of error (reflex action, lapse of memory).
4. Factors of the error
   (a) Tasks characteristics (activity in progress, purpose of the task, associated checking).
   (b) Workstation characteristics (location, display, tools).
   (c) Workstation environment (physical, socio-professional).
   (d) 'Time' in connection with work organization (date of the error, schedule).
   (e) Qualification, professional training of the personnel involved in the error.

Such items of information are collected thanks to two additional questionnaires:

1. Questionnaire A, compiling elements of information immediately accessible to the person concerned with the error: circumstances of the error and of its discovery (time, date, operating state of the unit), and individual data (professional status, age, sex).
2. Questionnaire B, compiling information depending on an analysis which, however succinct, necessitates resorting to specific concepts: error characterization (reflex action, lapse of memory), factors of error survey (as linked with workstation design, training).

Implementing mode of data collection:

The operating staff concerned must contribute to and cooperate with the development of a collection of data relating to human factors. Prior to starting the collection, all the people involved have, therefore, to be sensitized, from the plant management down to operations personnel, including trade union organizations.
   Then, data collection is achieved by two categories of persons:

1. 'Detectors' — i.e., people from whom the error originates or/and who have discovered it — in charge of filling out Questionnaire A.
2. The 'collector' — i.e., an offsite person — in charge of verifying whether

Questionnaire A has been properly completed and required to fill out
Questionnaire B.
Figure 2 shows the data flow diagram.

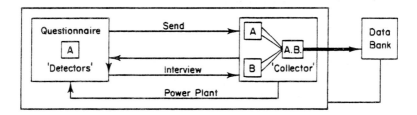

Figure 2. Data flow diagram

It is very useful that an external collector should be instrumental in the
process. Not only can such assistance ensure an efficient chain of steps (for
speed, document safeguard) but it has proved to be a stimulating element.
Sensitization as achieved prior to collection is not sufficient to maintain
the unflagging interest of personnel throughout the implementation of data
collection. Whenever he can intervene in order to highlight or stress the
importance of collecting data, to help select the appropriate answers, to
guarantee confidentiality, in sum to lead everyone, as is claimed by the
analysis, to look more dispassionately over human error, the collector enables
the problems raised by any work on these kinds of data to be overcome.

Example

As has been mentioned, a joint campaign has been engaged in together with
INPO to collect human errors having occurred during periodic tests. This
campaign is over now and the collected data are currently being processed.
All the same, it is already possible in order to illustrate our approach, to
present a few of the results obtained in the French power plant, without
taking into account those achieved in the two USA plants.

Twenty-one events due to human error have been collected. Data
processing has achieved results already supplied by simplified analysis.

For example:

1. 50% of the errors occur in the control room and 50% locally in the
   plant.
2. 70% of the errors originate from operators and 25% from automaticians
   and electricians.

Besides, more precise results can be obtained. By way of example:

1. 70% of the errors are discovered in the control room against 30% locally, in the plant.
2. 50% of the errors are discovered by the author of the error and 50% by somebody else.
3. For a period of work lasting eight hours, there are twice as many errors during the first two hours as during the six following hours.
4. Two-thirds of transpositions occur at the beginning of task sequence; one-third in the middle of task sequence; in the same connection, there are more mistakes during the first two hours, than during the six following ones.
5. Three-quarters of omissions occur by the end of task sequence and one-quarter in the middle; similarly the whole of the recorded omissions occur during the last six hours of work.

These results are given in the rough, without any interpretation, for the currently available data are too sparce to allow it. Indeed it should be kept in mind that this implementation of data collection aims at validating a method rather than at drawing conclusions concerning the results obtained.

IN-DEPTH ANALYSIS OF CERTAIN EVENTS INVOLVING A HUMAN COMPONENT

Selection Criteria

Events are selected according to:

1. Their actual or potential seriousness, or their being a precursor event.
2. The human factors they are made up of, particularly when these factors coincide with EDF ongoing studies, e.g., diagnosis error, error due to defective communication.

Analysis method

As analysis covers an event, no longer human error solely, it is preferably conducted by a multidisciplinary team consisting of a technician and a human factor specialist.

They are external people, carrying out the analysis on the basis of interviews with the various persons involved in the event.

First, the analysis consists in reconstituting the sequence of the events preceding the analysed event.

They are listed depending on time, on performed actions, on their location (locally or in the control room), on automatic actions and, lastly, on the different plant parameters (levels, temperature).

Then the tree of the events having generating the event is drawn up, differentiating between physical states, technical actions, and human actions.

Whenever a branch of the tree, built up in this way, reveals a permanent physical state or a primary human action or else a primary technical action, the tree building is stopped at this level.

The event tree is then changed into a fault tree:

1. Transient physical states vanish.
2. Permanent physical states are called 'design'.
3. Primary technical actions become 'equipment failures'.
4. Primary human actions become 'human errors'.

Then human errors and equipment failures can be better analysed in detail. Concerning human error, as in the case of in-depth statistical analysis (see page 197) the investigation centres on how the error has appeared (omission), what phase is concerned (detection, etc.) and, at last, what are the factors of the error (task characteristics etc.). Thus a tree of the causes of human error is built.

Example

Let us examine, as an example, an event analysed following this method: the case of an emergency core cooling required at a 900 MWe PWR plant.

The various stages of the analysis are set out in the form of sequence of events (see Table 2), event tree (see Figure 3) or fault tree (see Figure 4).

Next, each human error can be the subject of a detailed analysis: 'too lengthy start-up steps' may here be described as an example of error analysis.

Among the steps that have to be performed to start up, a few have been more time consuming than usual, because of the occurrence of a number of problems. These problems have affected the following steps:

1. *Trip breakers resetting* These steps necessitate coordination between the installation and the control room; due to telephone problems, the operator in charge of performing locally had to walk three times to and back from the control room, which caused the performance to last longer.
2. *Feedwater pumps resetting* After a few attempts to reset, first from the control room, then locally, the operators have looked for a malfunction in the relaying circuitry and have discovered a strap on a valve; once this strap had been removed, it has been possible to reset. Such a waste of time during these steps raises the question of shift team information about straps being placed on the systems.

Table 2: Sequence of the events leading to safety injection

| TIME | OPERATOR ACTIONS | Location | | Automatic Actions | PARAMETER | | | | |
		Control Room	Locally		SG level	CVCS level	Pressure level	Flow rate	Primary average temperature (Tm)
11.14.38s				AFW start-up	Low Low Level				
11.14.39s	Switch to pressure mode SG level off	—	—						
From 11.17									
11.19	Reset full length rod control system	—	—	Intermittent actuation of reactor boron and water make up system without flow rate Valve 15 VD locked		Low Level	Low Low Level		283 °C
11.21	Actuation of dilution	—							
From 11.28 to 11.38	Reset of turbine driven feedwater pump	—	—						278 °C 270 °C

| | | Location | | | PARAMETER | | | | |
TIME	OPERATOR ACTIONS	Control Room	Locally	Automatic Actions	SG level	CVCS level	Pressure level	Flow rate	Primary average temperature (Tm)
11.40	Switch to CVCS	–							260 °C
11.52	Stop of dilution	–							259 °C
	opening of valve 15 VD reactor boron and water makeup system		—						
11.59				Reactor boron and water make up supply control on automatic					261 °C
12	Switch from auxiliary feedwater system to main feedwater control system								
Around 12.30	Steam pressure Pv setpoint drop								
12.58				Turbine bypass (opened abruptly to 60%) SI				High	284 °C

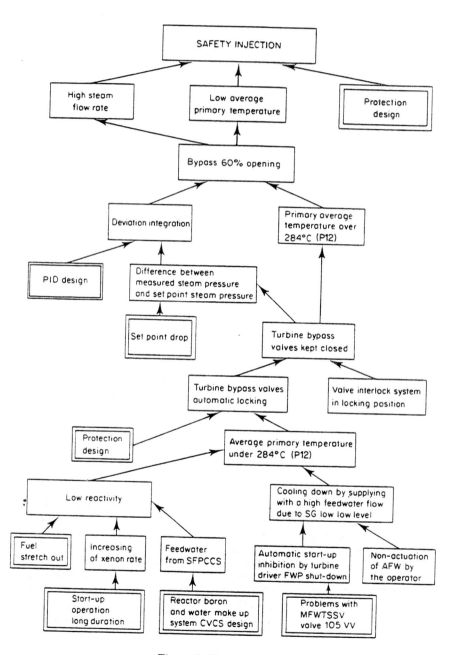

Figure 3. Events tree

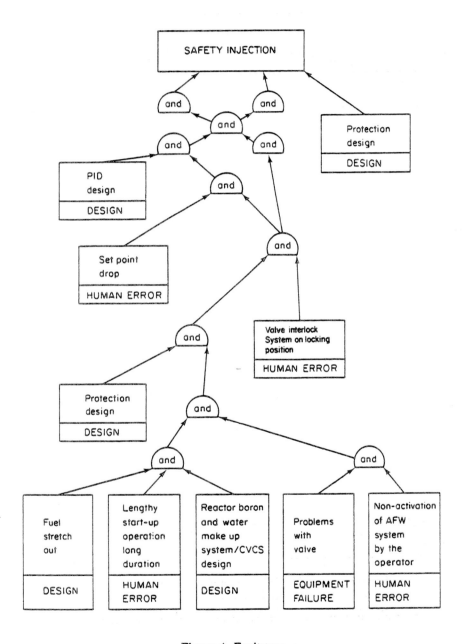

Figure 4. Fault tree

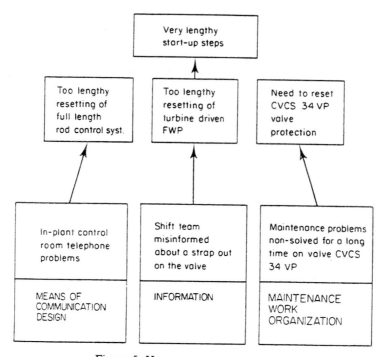

Figure 5. Human error — causes tree

3. *Valve shield resetting*   As a valve contactor had suddenly become inoperable, the operator had to go on the installation to exchange this valve rack for that of another valve, to allow its actuation from the control room. Now, this valve had been showing maintenance problems for some time, which brings in the question of maintenance work organization.

The tree of causes (Figure 5) can supplement the fault tree (Figure 4).

CONCLUSION

The data collection system, as defined in the present chapter, must not be regarded as fixed, on the contrary it has to remain very flexible.

First level analysis, i.e., simplified statistical analysis of the causes of human error is systematically used.

Thus it can play its role:

1. Of detector: in ranking the main factors of error.
2. Of trend indicator: in bringing out changes in the rank of factors of error, as a result of improvements in work situation.

The other two levels of analysis, i.e., in-depth statistical analysis of the causes of certain events involving a human component, are used in a non-exhaustive way:

1. In-depth statistical analysis as a short-term probing tool and on a limited sample with a view to ranking the causes of certain human errors (e.g., those occurring during periodic tests) and to initiating local corrective actions.
2. In-depth analysis of events involving a human component as a diagnosis tool to help reconstitute the complexity and multicausal aspect of an event and thereby determine adequate lines of action likely to improve the system.

The interest of the latter analysis compared with the former ones lies in the fact that it is not destructive of the event structure as, on the contrary, it brings out the chain of events through the faults tree and the causes tree; whereas statistical approaches may have the harmful effect of being destructive of the event structure and of depicting it in too linear and there-fore too simplifying a way.

New Technology and Human Error
Edited by J. Rasmussen, K. Duncan and J. Leplat
© 1987 John Wiley & Sons Ltd

19. Fault Diagnosis Training for Advanced Continuous Process Installations

K. D. Duncan

University of Wales Institute of Science and Technology

SUMMARY

The effects of formal knowledge, of inflexible or algorithmic procedures, and of diagnostic rules of thumb on identification of process plant faults; effects on diagnostic accuracy of withholding information during laboratory training schemes and operator training in a hazardous installation; diagnosis of faults not encountered during training as a criterion of skill or versatility.

INTRODUCTION

When considering the potential effects of new technology on work, it may be unwise to place too much reliance on the 'lessons of history', nevertheless one can look over the last two decades at those industries which could afford information processing devices, industries like petrochemicals and steel, at a time when information processing machines were relatively expensive, or beyond the means of most other industries, that is to say in the 1960s and 1970s. What happened in those industries was that the routine components of tasks tended to be replaced, and what was left for the operator to do was to cope with tasks of problem solving and decision making. So there is a precedent, or a warning or, at the very least, a question as to whether history might repeat itself.

In some petrochemical plants there may be little to do except perhaps once every six months, but then a difficult diagnosis within the order of three minutes may be needed and, if the operator does not solve the problem, the plant will be shut down, always provided the fail-safe devices do not themselves fail.

APPROACHES TO DIAGNOSIS TRAINING

Formal knowledge

What, then, do we know about how to enable people to solve problems such

209

as this? The approach of classical vocational educational often claims, if only implicitly, that teaching, for instance, the hydrodynamics and physical chemistry of the plant, should enable people to operate it or trouble-shoot it. This philosophy enjoys widespread support although the approach has had very limited success, when studied empirically. There is a quite extensive literature, albeit in a different technology, fault finding in electronic, especially complex military systems (Duncan, 1981). Nevertheless, those in charge of training who accept this kind of evidence, still invariably incorporate some technical story in their courses, usually on the grounds that operators would not tolerate operating plant unless they are given some account of how it works. It may be that more functionally directed theory or technical story might be more readily 'compiled' from a declarative mode into effective courses of action (Duncan and Gray, 1975a).

Procedures

A quite different approach prescribes routines or procedures, sometimes quite elaborate procedures with branching structures, or algorithms which, in the case of diagnosis, guarantee to distinguish between a set of faults provided that a series of questions are correctly answered — Figure 1 is an example. This too is an approach which does not lack supporters, persisting, perhaps, because of the intrinsic attraction of a guaranteed solution. Nevertheless the specification of branching procedures, of whatever sophistication, has the intrinsic limitation that, by definition, an algorithm will only distinguish the set of conditions which have been foreseen. If an unforeseen event occurs, the operator is not helped by algorithmic procedures.

Nowadays there are legal pressures to specify procedures, sometimes in the form of mandatory regulations, with the kind of complication that is nicely illustrated by the incident at North Anna in 1979. The operators at this plant had to contend with a US NRC regulation laid down after the Three Mile Island incident. The regulation stipulated that, after a reactor scram, the high head charging pumps or emergency cooling pumps must be left on for at least twenty minutes. But the North Anna operators could see that to obey this regulation would lead to a dangerous temperature shut-down profile. So how did they resolve the dilemma? Fortunately, they decided to break the regulation and turned off one of the two pumps for four minutes, 'without knowing precisely what reduction in total input could be expected, and what the net result on pressure and level might be, but it was considered a step in the right direction'! (Pew et al., 1982). This incident underlines the danger of trying to prescribe regulations, procedures or algorithms, especially when these prescriptions are backed by legal sanctions.

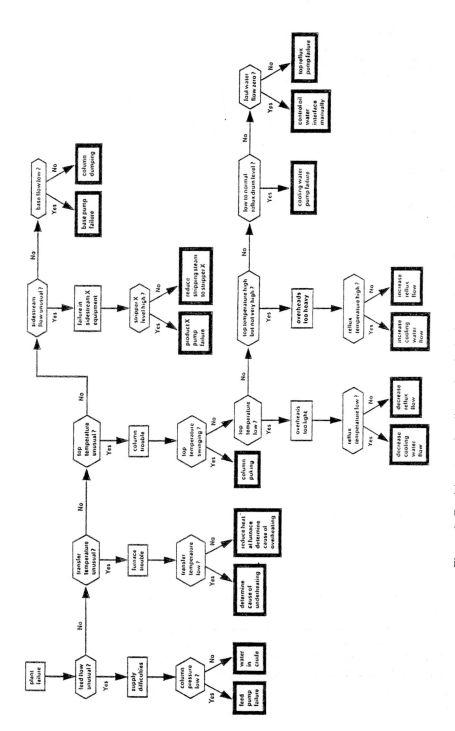

Figure 1. Decision tree for diagnosing faults in crude destillation units

Diagnostic rules

We have for some time used an approach to problem-solving training which is based on the diagnostic techniques which skilled operators employ. These techniques are powerful and flexible, but their formulation and application in training schemes needs caution, and is still a matter for research.

To begin our field and laboratory studies we needed a plant to serve as a basis for exploring fault diagnosis and the feasibility of training people to acquire this skill. Our purpose was to 'design' a fictitious plant which would incorporate as many as possible of the difficulties that are encountered when diagnosing faults in continuous processes. We checked out the fictitious plant in Figure 2 with chemical engineers, who agreed that it was conceivable that such a plant might exist, and that it was not implausible. It probably presents more different kinds of diagnostic difficulty than would be likely in any single real process plant.

Among other things, there are many control loops. Later (in Part 6), it is argued that there may be an important difference between the designer's model and the operator's model of a loop. For the moment, suffice it to say that, from the point of view of diagnostic problem solving, a control loop, by its very nature, masks the occurrence and subsequent development of a malfunction precisely because it copes with the immediate effects of a failure, at least for a time. Thus, one indication that the feed to a vessel falls or fails completely would be a lowering of the level, but a level control loop might maintain the level by automatically closing a valve or valves on the drain line, thereby masking the primary signal. This masking of a problem in the process would continue, but not indefinitely.

Another feature of petrochemical plant design is a response to social and other pressures, particularly in the 1970s, to conserve energy, and especially to improve thermal economy. For instance, if the process includes an exothermic reaction system (i.e., a reaction producing heat), the plant designer would attempt to recover as much as possible of that heat, often through a rather complicated exchange system, like the heat exchange section in Figure 2, and to transfer the recovered heat to other units in plant needing heat energy, e.g., to feed the reboiler driving a distillation column, as in the case of the fictitious plant in Figure 2. This makes good sense, but it introduces another, and I suspect unforeseen, diagnostic difficulty, namely the problem which doctors designate as 'referred symptoms' in medical diagnosis.

To illustrate the point in the case of our fictitious system, if trouble developed in the reactor, it might not appear first, and certainly would not appear only in the reactor instrumentation. The first indications of malfunction on the control panel might be loss of 'boil-up' in the column (although the failure was in fact in the reactor, and therefore in the loss of heat generation), and from the operator's viewpoint, the place in the plant where

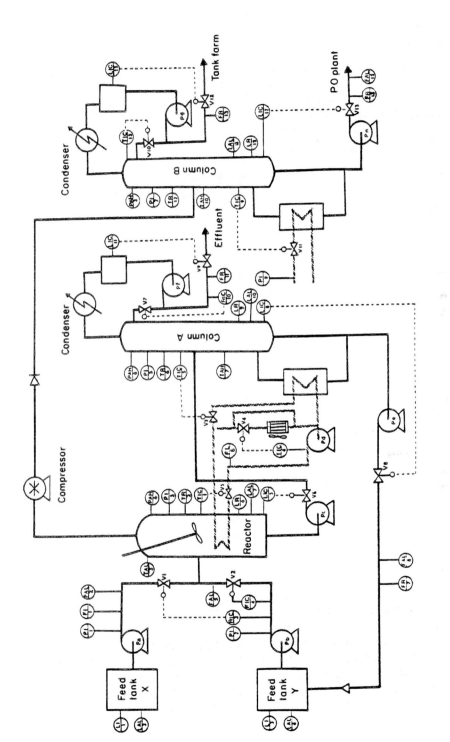

Figure 2. Flow diagram of fictitious chemical process plant

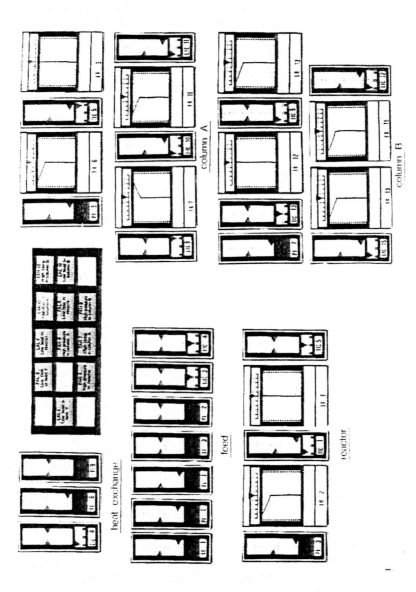

Figure 3. A simulated instrument panel showing symptoms of a fault

signs of trouble first emerge may not necessarily be the place where trouble or failures have occurred.

The next step was to develop fault arrays like those in Figures 3 and 4 which show the instrument panel with alarm block and the sort of indications which would confront an operator if things were to go wrong with our fictitious FP1 plant. Using these arrays, process operators and other people working in the process industries have attempted to diagnose faults on the fictitious FP1 plant and to talk about the ways in which they went about it. Among those who have attempted the task in this way are 'relief operators' from a large petrochemical site comprising several different processes and installations. Relief operators are rather versatile people who are required to go to a variety of different plants on the site and take over the control and fault diagnosis problems of an operator who is away because he is sick, or absent for other reasons. If anyone has powerful diagnostic techniques, these operators should have them.

EXPERIMENTAL TRAINING SCHEMES

We have incorporated diagnostic rules, verbally formulated in this way, into training programmes for novices (Duncan and Shepherd, 1975; Shepherd et al., 1977). Whether the rules reflect something of diagnostic skill, per se, is an issue which will be taken up in Part 6. For the moment the question is simply do these rules improve training?

The population of novices we have trained in our laboratory, includes both operators and people who would never go into a chemical factory in the ordinary course of events, such as housewives, bus drivers, students with time on their hands, and so forth. Figure 5 shows the results of a training experiment in which there were three conditions: no story, where subjects are not told anything about how the plant works; a 'theory' condition, where we explained how the plant works, in terms of its inputs, outputs, the flow between the two, the drives, the control loops, using as simple language as we possibly could, so that we might give this instructional condition a fair chance of success; and then we had a third condition in which we incorporated diagnostic rules.

Now there are two points about criteria which must first be made, and Figure 5 should highlight these. It is not particularly impressive if people are able correctly to diagnose faults or failures which they have previously encountered. These are referred to as 'old' faults in Figure 5, that is to say panel arrays which had previously been seen during training. This is a useful but 'weak' criterion. A 'strong' criterion, which should ideally be applied to any method of diagnosis training, is the extent to which it enables people to cope with faults which they have not previously seen, i.e., with panel arrays, which did not occur during training, referred to as 'new' faults in Figure 5.

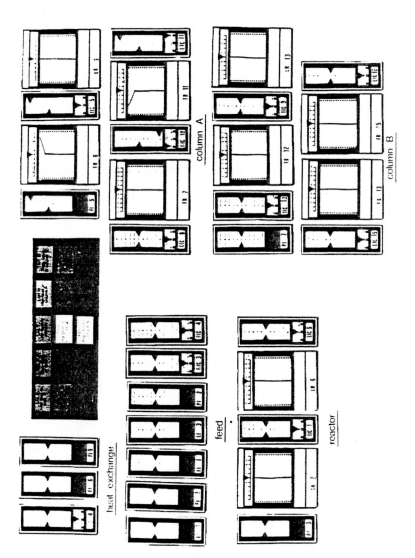

Figure 4. A simulated instrument panel showing symptoms of a fault

Trainees under each condition were given a post test of 16 failures, 8 of which they had previously encountered during training. It can be seen that the rules condition had a considerable advantage in terms of novel failures.

In a subsequent study, the technique of withholding plant information was introduced as a training technique (Marshall *et al.*, 1981a). Trainees practised fault diagnosis with paper and pencil exercises consisting of a drawing of the control panel, but with no indications or readings on the instruments. Indications were provided only when the trainee asked for them. This enabled the instructor to check to what extent the diagnostic rules were being applied, and indeed to intervene when they patently were not.

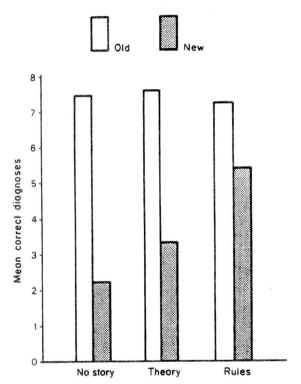

Figure 5. Mean correct diagnoses under three different training regimes — see text

Although information was withheld during training, the performance criteria during testing remained the same as in the earlier study, namely diagnosis of the complete panel array. This combination of withholding information and diagnostic rules further enhanced performance, the former presumably ensuring that the rules are at least to some extent applied. By now (Figure 6) novel failure correct diagnoses are not too far off correct diagnoses of failures previously encountered. It should be noted that the first condition in Figure 6 is identical to the third condition in Figure 5. It seemed advisable to repeat this condition, since the second experiment was carried out some 18 months later by different research associates, and after moving some distance to a different university. There were therefore various reasons for wanting to be sure that we had a comparable base line.

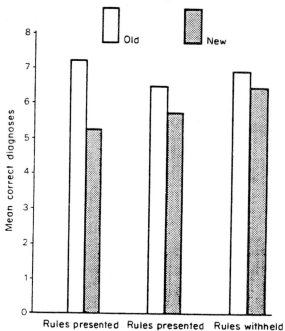

Figure 6. Comparison of training with information presented and information withheld

PANEL DIAGNOSIS OF FAULTS IN A HAZARDOUS PROCESS

During the course of our laboratory studies of diagnosis, we were consulted by line managers responsible for the ICI cyclohexane oxidation process. Cyclohexane is a very volatile hydrocarbon. Its oxidation is part of the route to produce nylon which achieved notoriety, at least in Britain, in the Flixborough disaster. It was agreed that we would collaborate in producing fault diagnostic training for this plant.

We began informally with two- to three-day discussions in which we first asked supervisors and managers to consider what would happen in terms of indications on their control room panels if various serious failures occurred. We then put them in the situation of arguing about what sorts of rules an operator might use if he had the problem of interpreting these indications, but not knowing the origin of the fault. In effect, we supported ICI personnel in applying to their plant the techniques of training by: (a) diagnostic rules; and (b) withholding plant information, for which we had already developed exemplars in the laboratory.

Both trainees and those who administered the training were enthusiastic about the technique of withholding plant information to ensure that diagnostic rules were first elicited and scrutinized and finally applied in diagnosis.

Some different diagnostic rules were produced by ICI personnel for their plant and the order of the rules was to some extent plant-specific. At this point it should be emphasized that we are not so naïve as to seek to establish universal diagnostic rules for problem solving in all chemical process plants. On the contrary we recognize that there will be some diagnostic rules which are plant-specific while some may be general to a number of plants. Examples of these would be scanning the panel and considering the possibility of symptoms referred forward or referred back. Effective plant-specific rules may occur at an early stage in the list or later on, e.g., the rule we observed in diagnosis at the ICI plant of looking for 'step changes' to identify the area in which the problem or fault lies. A sharp step change on a pen recorder was the target of initial scanning of the panel since, in a pressurized system, it would be very diagnostic of the area in which the fault might be found.

All the development of diagnostic rules and the subsequent training course was conducted by ICI personnel. Although research staff were always present when trainees were tested, we did not otherwise intervene during training. Both instructors and operators took to the training process, when plant information is withheld and diagnostic rules have been articulated. If, for example, operators asked questions about control loops before they had first scanned the panel for step changes, the instructor would intervene and ask why this question was being put and suggest that a more important question might first be asked.

Table 1: *Diagnostic accuracy of process operators at different stages of training*

	Mean % Diagnostic Accuracy	
	Failures practised during training	Novel failures
Test A: Initial test (6 faults)	–	33
Test B: Following introduction to fault finding and account of the process (6 faults)	–	40
Test C: Following withheld practice and diagnosis training (10 faults)	99	–
Test D: Following Test C (20 faults)	94	93
Test E: Final test (10 novel and more difficult faults)	–	63

Table 1 shows how effective the ICI training programme was. The initial frighteningly low score of experienced operators on novel failures was a surprise. The Test C result is gratifying, but rather what we expected, since it consists of failures which operators have previously encountered. Test D on the other hand shows that ICI has in effect achieved rather better results than we had achieved in the laboratory, i.e., training has resulted in fault diagnosis accuracy for novel failures approximating that of failures previously encountered during training.

During the course of this fieldwork, various people — managers, supervisors, and some operators — suggested failures, and the indications which would go with them, which they had not considered before the exercise began. They also thought of solutions, or diagnostic rules which might be applied, but which of course had not been included in the training scheme. So these were failures which the rules probably did not cope with at all well, but since, as a spin-off, we now had these failures specified, it seemed worth while to test trainees on what, by any standards, would be difficult, novel problems. On these diagnostic tasks, performance was much less accurate, but still substantially better than initial performance, i.e., 66% versus 33% before the course was introduced.

CONCLUSION

These field and laboratory results are encouraging but any optimism is best qualified. It is certainly possible to train people to solve this kind of problem by the application of diagnostic rules. However, training in itself is almost certainly not going to be enough, and we are now reaching diminishing returns. Of course, we have employed a very strict criterion of problems not previously encountered — but that is as it should be. Improving on first line panel diagnosis of novel failures beyond the 90% or mid-90% level is unlikely by developments in training. This of course leaves a high probability of failure, which in many industries is quite unacceptable.

REFERENCES

Duncan, K. D. (1981) Training for fault diagnosis in industrial process plant. In: W. B. Rouse and J. Rasmussen (Eds), *Human Detection and Diagnosis of System Failures*. New York: Plenum.

Duncan, K. D., and Gray, M. J. (1975a) Functional context training: a review and an application to a refinery control task. *Le Travail Humain*, **38**, 81–96.

Duncan, K. D., and Gray, M. J. (1975b) An evaluation of a fault finding training course for refinery process operators. *Journal of Occupational Psychology*, **48**, 199–218.

Duncan, K. D., and Shepherd, A. (1975) A simulator and training technique for diagnosing plant failures from control panels. *Ergonomics*, **18**, 627–41.

Marshall, E. C., Baker, S. M., and Duncan, K. D. (1981a) The role of withheld information in the training of process plant fault diagnosis. *Ergonomics*, **24**, 711–24.

Marshall, E. C., Scanlon, K. E., Shepherd, A., and Duncan, K. D. (1981b) Panel diagnosis training for major-hazard continuous process installations. *The Chemical Engineer*, February 1981.

Pew, R. W., Miller, D. C., and Feehler, C. E. (1982) Evaluation of proposed control room improvements through analysis of critical operator decisions. EPRI NP-1982, Project 891, Final Report.

Shepherd, A., Marshall, E. C., Turner, A., and Duncan, K. D. (1977) Diagnosis of plant failures from a control panel: a comparison of three training methods. *Ergonomics*, **20**, 347–61.

New Technology and Human Error
Edited by J. Rasmussen, K. Duncan and J. Leplat
© 1987 John Wiley & Sons Ltd

20. Chronobiological Approach of Human Errors in Complex Systems

Y. Queinnec
Université Paul Sabatier, TOULOUSE
and
G. de Terssac
Laboratoire d'Automatique et d'Analyse des Systèmes, TOULOUSE

SUMMARY

Human reliability analysis in process control. The reliability of complex systems depends on human responses. This chapter deals with the structure of the activity and its determinants: variations in the work context and structural variations as an intrinsic psychophysiological factor. Such knowledge will allow us to discuss the improvement of reliability of man–machine systems.

RELIABILITY OF COMPONENTS

For optimal operation, continuous production systems of ever increasing complexity demand reliability from their components. Here, reliability designates 'the characteristic of an apparatus expressed as the probability that it will carry out a required function in set conditions over a given period of time' (International Electrotechnology Commission). It is relatively easy to determine the probability of a hardware component carrying out its functions without failure over a fixed time in defined conditions. It is, however, much more difficult to determine the average level and average duration of 'correct operation' of human elements and impossible to evaluate the probability of human error.

This situation can be explained by the great variation in human operator responses. First of all it should be noted that human behaviour is always expressed in an environment which is itself unstable. This already contradicts the idea of a 'normal' work situation with stability as its characteristic.

Also, the operator's response is similarly dependent on intrinsic physiological and psychological factors and notably on 'structural variations' which are not dependent on the tasks performed. Finally, the types of interaction

223

which are set up between individuals are also factors and consequences of individual fluctuations. These different sources of variation make the human operator into a regulation system.

As a regulation system, the human operator is an essential element in the reliability of 'man–machine' systems. Indeed, certain functions are entrusted to men and others to automatic systems. The optimization of function sharing and the setting up of man–machine relationships require knowledge of the real operational modalities of human operators. In this way, the study of human failures over a long period of time (including especially the nocturnal portion of the nycthemer) can efficiently contribute to the comprehension and reduction of human errors (Leplat, 1985).

The functioning of a system can be evaluated by its performance, i.e., by estimation of the difference between the assigned aims and the actual results. As we are dealing with the 'man–machine' system two large categories of performance will be considered.

The first includes the responses of the operators for whom we shall attempt to define the 'non-desired results of work' (Leplat and Cuny, 1977). The second concerns the consequences of these responses on the production, on the installations, and also on the operators themselves.

Our aim in the present report is to show the existence of variations in performance over 24 hours, variations which arise from fluctuations in the work situation and also from modifications of the functional capacities of human operators. We shall then investigate the processes giving rise to these variations — the analysis dealing with the structure of the activity and its determinants. Finally, the elements concerning the zones of human failure will allow us to debate the actions to be undertaken to improve the reliability of man–machine systems.

CIRCADIAN PERFORMANCE VARIATIONS

Various studies devoted to continuous processes, especially involving a night shift, have investigated the fluctuation of performance and the appearance of errors over the 24-hour period.

On the whole, recent reviews of the existing literature (Folkard, 1981; Gadbois and Queinnec, 1984) show that almost all the categories of error (Fitts and Jones, 1947; de Montmollin, 1967) have been the object of research. So, the errors firstly concern the *operator responses* (e.g., errors in reading meters, Bjerner *et al.*, 1955; assaying errors, Meers 1977; delayed response, Browne 1949; absence of response, Hildebrandt *et al.*, 1974). These responses have been examined quantitatively (e.g., frequency, duration, delay) and qualitatively (e.g., substitution error, forgetfulness, inversion). These errors can also be identified by their *consequences on production* either directly (e.g., quantity of product produced, Meers, 1977; rejects, energy consumption) or indirectly (e.g., incidents, Folkard *et al.*, 1978; stoppages, Hildebrandt *et al.*, 1974; start-up time after incident Wojtczak-Jaroszowa and Pawlowska-Skyba, 1967). Here again the quantitative approach is backed up by the qualitative aspect.

Finally, in a few cases, the authors have examined the *consequences of the errors on the operators* (especially the hourly distribution of accidents, Kubler, 1956; Andlauer and Fourre, 1965; Harris, 1977). This point, however, has not received the attention it deserves.

All these investigations were oriented towards demonstrating the general phenomenon of the circadian rhythmicity of performance in a real work situation — a phenomenon widely established in laboratory experiments since the now classical studies of Kleitman (1963). So, whatever the situations studied, there is a certain similarity in the sinusoidal performance curves. There are almost always two dips: one which is short and shallow at the beginning of the afternoon (post-lunch dip); and another which is deeper and longer at around 3 to 4 o'clock in the morning. Although these studies show the existence of a clear drop in efficiency at night, it is also clear that the performance does not exactly follow the circadian variations affecting the operator's capacities. Steady performance does not necessarily signify a stable functional state: circadian variations of the capacities do not have direct and constant repercussions on performance (Gadbois and Queinnec, 1984). Indeed, the alteration in efficiency is mediated by the nature of the work to be done and the conditions in which it is carried out. Thus, reduced capacities do not imply that the capacities are lower than the level required by the task. On the one hand the demands of the task vary and do not

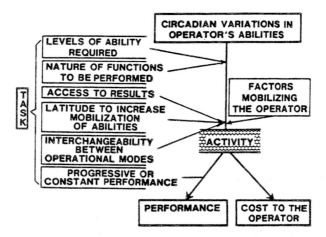

Figure 1. Factors with potential for influencing the impact of biopsychological rhythms on the organization of working activity (from Gadbois and Queinnec, 1984)

always require maximal capacity from the subjects, and on the other hand the degree of mobilization of the subjects can rise strongly even with a considerable increase in the operator's workload.

These different elements contribute to the modulation — to a greater or lesser extent — of the circadian rhythmicity and thus increase or reduce the probability of error appearance. It is therefore useful to investigate the psychophysiological functions actually used by the operators and so to go beyond analysis limited by performance criteria alone (Figure 1).

CIRCADIAN RHYTHMICITY AND TEMPORAL ACTIVITY ORGANIZATION

Task demands constitute one of the factors susceptible to vary performance fluctuations in the type of work required or the conditions in which the human operators readjust their 'degree of mobilization' or 'fraction of capacity used' (Leplat, 1972). Examination of the data collected by Browne (1949) shows that during a period theoretically corresponding to reduced efficiency — i.e., between midnight and 3.00 a.m. — although the number of calls received by the switchboard is high, the response time tends to be faster than that observed between 9.00 p.m. and midnight if the number of calls is low. Such an influence of work organization on workers' performance is also observed in the composing area of a newspaper (Queinnec et al., 1986).

Nevertheless, the task demands are far from making up the only factor explaining variations in performance. The existence of biological rhythms gives man a veritable 'temporal structure' (Reinberg, 1974). This constitutes a variable determinant of the fluctuations of performance. It is on the influence of the circadian biological rhythms on the organization of work activities that we shall focus our attention here.

The night worker: an individual with capacities which are reduced but mainly differently organized

The case of process controllers in the chemical industry:

The data presented were collected in a continuous process industry (with continental rota). The task of the operators was that of process control (Queinnec and de Terssac, 1981; Queinnec et al., 1984).

Circadian variations of activity

Various activities, not directly linked with work, such as changes in posture, locomotor activity, conversation, reading or writing activities, etc., show that the behaviour of the operators is subject to a high degree of circadian rhythmicity with minimum activity at night and high activity at the beginning of the afternoon ($P < 0.01$). Considering work activities, the hourly frequency of line of sight changes varies considerably over 24 hours (de Terssac *et al.*, 1983) (Figure 2).

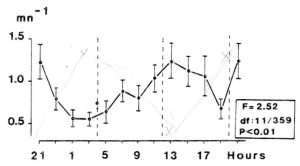

Figure 2. Hourly variation of the frequency, per minute, of line of sight changes (mean for six controllers). The broken lines indicate shift changes. The dispersion index represents the standard deviation (values from 360 observations of 30 minutes each). (From de Terssac *et al.*, 1983.)

Supervision organization

Whatever the shift considered, the operators do not look at the various informational zones of the control room evenly. Certain zones are frequently watched whereas others are almost never looked at: 2 glances out of 3 are directed towards 4 informational zones (out of 17).

However, the hierarchization of information collected is different in the afternoon, morning, and at night (Figure 3). The image of the functioning of the process which the operators make for themselves depends, at least partly, on the time. These variations cannot be attributed totally either to the presence or absence of day staff (persistence of the week-end rhythm) or to fluctuations in production, which overall is seen to remain stable, or even to the random changes in the operation of the process (absence of rhythmicity in the appearance of incidents). The variations of the human capacities would therefore seem to be an essential factor (de Terssac and Queinnec 1982; de Terssac *et al.*, 1983).

Observation strategies during the nycthemer

The nature of the zones looked at presents differences between the day and the night as do the procedures used by the operators in their observation. In most cases the controllers observe by taking information from an isolated zone. However, other techniques of surveying involving several zones can be observed, the temporal distribution of these various strategies varies during the nycthemer (de Terssac *et al.*, 1983).

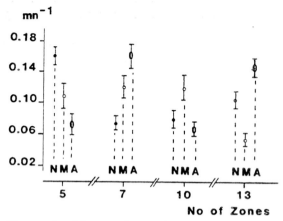

Figure 3. Mean values of controllers' glance frequencies (per minute) towards the four most important informational zones of the control room. The dispersion index represents the standard deviation. (Adapted from de Terssac *et al.*, 1983.)

Regulations in the work team

Usually, the control room is permanently occupied by two controllers. However, from time to time a controller can be alone or other workers can also be present. The presence or absence of a team-mate strongly influences the activity of the controllers (Queinnec *et al.*, 1981). In the same way, the presence of a third member in certain teams tends to reduce the amplitude of the circadian rhythmicity (Queinnec *et al.*, 1984) and also to create a certain task sharing between controllers (Figure 4).

Night workers in general

In general, at night there is a certain reduction in the activity of the operators but more particularly there is a reorganization of their operation. The latter result is not surprising if we refer to the data in the literature concerning circadian rhythms of various biological, physiological, and also psychological functions. From the experimental data existing in this field the idea appears that the night worker is above all an individual with differently structured capacities (Gadbois and Queinnec, 1984) and not an individual with reduced possibilities. Such a conclusion appears in research dealing with memory-loaded cognitive tasks (Monk and Embrey, 1981, Folkard, 1981). Thus

Folkard writes 'the information processing demands of a task may determine the *phase* of the circadian rhythm in performance'. Subsequently the task demands (such as high or low memory load, short-term or delayed retention of information, perceptual-motor or cognitive tasks . . .) may influence the time of day variation of errors. In their study on supervisory programs in a process control computer, Monk and Embrey (1981) found that 'over twice as many errors were made on the day shift as on the night shift'. This unusual result clearly demonstrates the interaction of functional capacities of shiftworkers and tasks to be carried out.

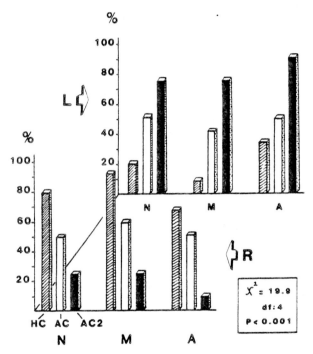

Figure 4. Relative distribution (in per cent) of glances towards the displays of the right (R) or the left (L) half of a control room (192 displays) during the three shifts, in teams with three controllers. HC: head controller, AC: first assistant controller, AC2: second assistant controller. N: night, M: morning, A: afternoon shifts (see Figure 1)

The night worker and the resolution of incidents

Although the above reasoning seems to be valid when the task demands are relatively stable the question arises as to what happens when the task requirements increase — for example when an incident occurs. In order to meet a sharp increase in task demands especially at night, how do the human operators adjust their activity to the new situation? Do they 'overcome' their rhythms or do they organize their behaviour with respect to their capacities at a given moment?

Abnormal conditions

In the context of abnormal conditions (large failures recorded in the log-book) we have observed a strong effect on controllers' activity during the afternoon and the morning shifts but not at night (Figure 5). So, in a situation of potential risk without immediate consequences, operators' behaviour is sustained more by the circadian rhythmicity than by the task context. This is not the case when an incident occurs.

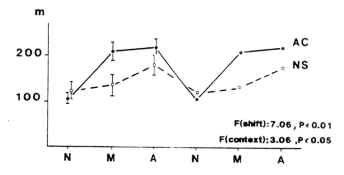

Figure 5. Shift variation of six controllers' locomotor activity in a control room (distance covered in metres per hour) during 'normal' situation (NS) and abnormal conditions (AC). N: night, M: morning, A: afternoon shifts. The dispersion index represents the standard deviation

Temporarily disturbed working conditions

In temporarily disturbed working conditions indicated by audio-warnings and lights the effects of incidents on the supervising activity (Queinnec and de Terssac, 1985) cause: (a) firstly, a quantitative modification of the activity which increases very strongly; (b) secondly, different consequences of the incident according to the time of occurrence: so at night the level of activity increases fourfold during the five minutes after the incident whereas in the afternoon the change in activity is quite minimal; (c) thirdly, analysing the activity minute by minute shows two phenomena: the increase in activity is stronger during the first minute after the incident and then a decrease can be observed but at night the decrease is very slow — even after six minutes, at night, the mean level before the incident was not reached; (d) moreover, the occurrence of an incident strongly modifies the distribution of the focusing towards the different panels: not only did the human operators abandon the night work procedure but when an incident occurred they adopted a 'day' type procedure. The observations show that at night when the human operator is at a low level of alertness, he is poorly prepared to make a diagnosis in a very short time and to solve an incident.

The different elements demonstrate a reorganization of the supervisory activity during the day and at night when an incident occurs; they also reveal the much greater impact of an incident when it appears at night.

SUGGESTIONS FOR THE PREVENTION OF CERTAIN HUMAN ERRORS

Certain human errors present a temporal distribution indicating the existence of circadian rhythms under-running the behavioural organization of the man at work. Even though the nature of the tasks and the conditions in which they are performed can modulate the rhythmicity, the phenomenon still persists, especially in tasks of high mental demands. The rhythmicity is clearly due to the 'temporal structure' of the human operator and appears to be a fundamental consideration in the conception, development, and running of a complex technical and organizational set-up. The data mentioned above show that the response of the human operators depends on their capacity to become mobilized, on the structure of the team, and also on the information available concerning the state of the process (Queinnec *et al.*, 1985b). The reliability of the man–machine system depends on the consideration of these factors. Three questions arise:

1. How should the shift times be organized?
2. How should the teams be structured?
3. How should the technical set-up be designed?

For the times of work, the number of shifts and their duration should derive from knowledge of the temporal dimension of man's functional state: so, night shifts would not necessarily have to be of the same length as day shifts. Similarly, the overlap between two shifts is reduced to the time necessary to exchange instructions: as if the worker were able to operate efficiently as soon as he steps into a control room. Would it not be preferable to increase the time of contact between operators so that a new arrival actually has the opportunity of acquiring up-to-the-minute knowledge of the state of the system and comparing it with that of his counterpart on the previous shift? One could also envisage a progressive changeover instead of the whole team going off at the same time.

For the size of the team, it is most common to find that whatever the shift, the number of members is the same: this would imply that the modalities of real activity were the same for all shifts and for all operators.

In opposition to this custom, it could be possible to have teams of varying sizes and in particular with larger teams at night. Similarly, an informal distribution of the functions within a team would be all the more probable considering the problems to be solved: is polycompetence not a means of facilitating the mobile distribution of activity?

Finally, in the design of technical set-ups, the idea that the human operator is a supercalculator capable of supplying an appropriate response in all circumstances and at all times should be dropped. The technical structure should be developed taking the risks of human failure into consideration. Should the operator not be helped in his diagnostic activity? For example by presenting him with all the symptoms which could be of use in checking a hypothesis on the probable causes for a given symptomatology.

Should the operator not be helped in his search for solutions? For example by presenting him with the range of actions possible considering the state of the system at a given moment or by indicating the repercussions of a certain action on a set of parameters.

These proposals are the outlines of an overall approach to human error which show their full importance as soon as the work situation involves a night shift or at least a prolonged requirement for stable work from human operators.

REFERENCES

Andlauer, P., and Fourre, L. (1965) Le travail en équipes alternantes. Etude de la nuisance comparée de deux modalités d'alternance. *Rev. franç. Travail*, **19**, 35–51.

Bjerner, B., Holm, A., and Swensson, A. (1955) Diurnal variation in mental performance, a study of three shift-workers, *British Journal of Industrial Medicine*, **12**, 103–10.

Browne, R. C. (1949) The day and night performance of teleprinter switchboard operators. *Occupational Psychology*, **23**, 121–6.

Fitts, P. M., and Jones, R. E. (1947) Analysis of factors contributing to 460 'pilot-error' – Experience in operating aircraft controls. Memorandum Report TSE AA – 694 – 12, Aero Medical Laboratory, Dayton.

Folkard, S. (1981) Shiftwork and performance. In C. L. Johnson, D. I. Tepas, W. P. Colquhoun, and M. J. Colligan (Eds), *Biological Rhythms, Sleep and Shiftwork*. MTP Press, pp. 283–305.

Folkard, S., Monk, T. H., and Lobban, M. C. (1978) Short- and long-term adjustment of circadian rhythms in 'permanent' night nurses. *Ergonomics*, **21**, 785–99.

Gadbois, C., and Queinnec, Y. (1984) Travail de nuit, rythmicités circadiennes et régulation de l'activité. *Le Travail Humain*, **47**(3), 195–225.

Harris, W. (1977) Fatigue, circadian rhythm and truck accidents. In: R. R. Mackie (Ed.), *Vigilance, Operational Performance and Physiological Correlates*. New York: Plenum Press, pp. 133–46.

Hildebrandt, G., Rohmert, W., and Rutenfranz, J. (1974) Twelve- and twenty-four hour rhythm in error frequency of locomotive drivers and the influence of tiredness. *International Journal of Chronobiology*, **2**, 97–110.

Kleitman, N. (1963) *Sleep and Wakefulness*. Chicago: University of Chicago Press.

Kubler, G. (1956) Variations périodiques de la fréquence et de la gravité des accidents du travail dans plusieurs industries à feu continu. *Thèse Med., Strasbourg*.

Leplat, J. (1972) La psychologie du travail en ergonomie. In M. Reuchlin (Ed.), *Traité de psychologie appliquée*, Vol. 3. Paris: PUF, pp. 61–136.

Leplat, J. (1985) *Erreur humaine, fiabilité humaine dans le travail*. Paris: A. Colin.

Leplat, J., and Cuny, X. (1977) *Introduction à la psychologie du travail*. Paris: PUF.

Meers, A. (1977) Signification du rythme nycthemeral pour la performance en situation industrielle. In: P. Andlauer, J. Carpentier, and P. Cazamian (Eds), *Ergonomie du travail de nuit et des horaires alternants*. Paris: Cujas, pp. 81–112.

Monk, T. H., and Embrey, D. E. (1981) A field study of circadian rhythms in actual and interpolated task performance. In: A. Reinberg *et al.* (Eds), *Night and Shiftwork, Biological and Social Aspects*. Oxford: Pergamon Press, pp. 473–80.

Montmollin, M. de (1967) *Les systèmes hommes-machines*. Paris: PUF.

Queinnec, Y., and de Terssac, G. (1981) Variation temporelle du comportement des opérateurs: le cas des processus à feu continu. *Le Travail Humain*, **44**(2), 39–53.

Queinnec, Y., de Terssac, G., and Thon, P. (1981) Field study of the activities of process controllers. *Proc. First Europ. Annual Conf. on Human Decision making and Manual Control*, Delft. Univ. Technol., pp. 195–202.

Queinnec, Y., de Terssac, G., and Dorel, M. (1984) Temporal organization of activities in process control. In: Wederburn and Smith (Eds), *Psychological Approaches of Night and Shift Work*. 20.1-20.7, Edinburgh.

Queinnec Y., and de Terssac, G. (1985) Process control with shift-work and human operator's activity in disturbed situations. *Ergonomics*

Queinnec, Y., Chabaud, C., and de Terssac, G. (1986a) Shiftworker's activity considered as the interaction of 'functionnal capacities and tasks to be carried out'. In: M. Haider, and M. Koller (Eds), *Night and Shiftwork: Longterm Effects and their Prevention*. Peter Lang Verlag, Frankfurt am Main, Bern, New York, pp. 51–8.

Queinnec, Y., Teiger, C., and de Terssac, G. (1985b) *Repères pour négocier le travail posté*. Travaux de l'Université Toulouse-le-Mirail, Toulouse.

Reinberg, A. (1974) Fatigue et rythmes biologiques. In: Bugard (Ed.), *Stress, fatigue et dépression*, Vol. 1. Paris: Doin, pp. 41–55.

Terssac, G. de, and Queinnec, Y. (1982) Human reliability in process control with shift-work. In: Kageyh Noro (Ed.), *The 8th Congress of International Ergonomics Association*. Tokyo, Japan, pp. 214–15.

Terssac, G. de, Queinnec, Y., and Thon, P. (1983) Horaires de travail et organisation de l'activité de surveillance. *Le travail Humain*, **46**(1), 65–79.

Wojtczak-Jaroszowa, J., and Pawlowska-Skyba, K. (1967) Night and shiftwork. I. Circadian variations in work. *Medycyna Pracy*, **18**, 1.

New Technology and Human Error
Edited by J. Rasmussen, K. Duncan and J. Leplat
© 1987 John Wiley & Sons Ltd

Part 6: Industrial Studies of Human Error — II

INTRODUCTION

In Chapter 19 Duncan speculated that the nature of new demands on operators of the future can be anticipated by reference to those industries which have already had resort to advanced technology over the last few years. Extrapolation is usually a chancy business, but it is important to reflect on what automation has already meant in terms of the demands placed on operators. Such a stock-taking is provided in Bainbridge's review (Chapter 24). Without attempting to assess her review, some of her arguments deserve underlining, before turning to the other chapters in Part 6.

If the human is required to intervene only rarely in the control of a process, then errors are more likely for a number of reasons. Skill declines in the absence of intervening practice. Simulation may provide an effective alternative, but specification of simulation facilities calls for careful appraisal of important differences in the conditions for acquisition of different skills. For example, the perceptual-motor skills of tracking plant responses to restore stability require quite different simulation facilities from the cognitive skills of fault diagnosis. So much may be obvious, but it is by no means obvious what will constitute effective simulation facilities for these or other skills in industrial process control. Should simulation support or exercise what Bainbridge calls the 'working store', the context of recent predictions and decisions about the process, on which some skilled performance must rely? And just what sort of simulation would that entail?

These are only some of the error prevention problems produced rather directly by automation which are discussed by Bainbridge. They deserve urgent attention, not least because the consequences of error at the limits of automation, when man has to intervene, will very likely be serious, even catastrophic.

In the earlier discussion of cognitive control (Part 2), it was noted that the chapters by de Keyser and Herry provide important evidence on errors arising from differences between different representations of the process corresponding to differing expertise, both between people and in the same person at different stages of cognitive development.

De Keyser describes how the process operator's knowledge and representation of the process — the 'operational image' — changes during training and experience at work. In particular, the formal knowledge acquired during initial training has only a limited capability to support the operator's interpretation of plant phenomena.

Cognitive development is interpreted as a multi-stage process. The progressive structuring of knowledge depends crucially on interventions during plant incidents, some of which in continuous metal casting can be frightening, to say the least. Understanding of plant time scales and process dynamics is not immediate: it evolves. But the paradox noted by Bainbridge and by Duncan applies here also. The occasions when plant unreliability is manifest are precisely those when human reliability can be improved, when effective cognitive structures can evolve, and when the operator's blocks or fixations can be overcome. To intervene and to guide the operator may, however, conflict with the economy and safety of the system. Simulation is then inevitable.

De Keyser (Chapter 22) emphasizes that operators must both experience and overcome the difficulties presented by plant failures if they are to acquire more efficient cognitive control structures. Moreover, these experiences must be carefully managed. Novel situations which require thought patterns beyond the current stage of cognitive development may predispose the operator to revert to more elementary representations and strategies, especially of a sensori-motor type, before eventually attaining thought-out, conceptualized, and generalized strategies. This is not and seems unlikely ever to be achieved by training before plant operation begins.

De Keyser also points to certain realities of the changing scene in industrial process control that are perhaps too easily ignored, or at least are poorly represented in the research literature. Against the comparative wealth of human factors research on continuous control, she contrasts the reality of modern process plant which, aside from start-up and shut-down, confronts the operator with all-or-none situations. Again, operators rarely take information for granted. Verbal communications with other staff are seen as more reliable than instrument readings. But the social factors in operating modern industrial processes tend to be neglected by research. She goes on to argue that as product quality and optimization of process conditions are automated, the operator's job comes to demand more difficult planning, or regulatory functions: taking account of plant capacity, the work schedule and different team habits; anticipating incidents, and making projections.

There is a very real danger that research programmes may proceed with little regard to the changing scene. De Keyser's point is well taken.

Chapter 21 deals with the observation that process operators will sometimes depart from a clearly specified procedure. It is an observation which is familiar enough but, laziness and other delinquencies aside, we know rather little about this sort of behaviour, and there may be a dangerous tendency to ignore what are seen as gratuitous or imponderable aberrations. Herry's analysis has a simple starting point — the procedure is not specified by the operator. Although the procedure leaves operators in no doubt as to what action is required, its logic invariably escapes them.

Whenever we provide instructions for others to carry out we may, deliberately or unwittingly, omit our rationale. Instructions to the householder for mending or replacing a fuse are often clear enough. But replacing a smaller with a larger capacity fuse is a notoriously common solution for getting lights back on in the home. The reasoning of those instructed, however limited, will probably be applied; we ignore this at our peril, and sometimes at theirs.

In industry, drills and procedures for emergencies and accidents typically concentrate on action sequences at the expense of any kind of explanation. It may be recalled that Rasmussen (Chapter 3) argued that error recovery is often not amenable to prior specification of actions to be taken. In that case the variety of states confronting the operator may only be interpreted by a rather sophisticated representation of the interaction between plant characteristics and human control operations up to each stage. This is an important general issue and we shall return to it in Part 9.

Herry's paper (Chapter 21) clearly shows that it may be far from straightforward to make the reasoning behind procedures explicit or intelligible to the point where operators reliably adhere to instructions. To exemplify the difference between the person specifying the procedure and the operators, she describes how the 'expert' can resolve the conflict when actions entail short-term outcomes contrary to the objective but nevertheless achieve the objective in the long term. Such action sequences are among those prescribed, and her operators are reluctant to carry them out because of their concern about the immediate consequences.

Herry makes the further point that operators' difficulties in functioning at the level of her expert may not merely be a matter of lack of formal knowledge, but rather a still to be achieved capability to produce action with certain 'organizational properties', of which she cites several examples in line with a general extension and application of Piaget's theory. In the above example, the expert is capable of *a priori* anticipation of future changes in physical states of the environment, and of actions exhibiting this 'organizational property'.

Lastly, errors arising from differences between different representations of the process, and corresponding to differing expertise, lead Duncan to describe operators' models of plant functions when discussing the elicitation of heuristics and their gradual refining in critical discussion. Like Brehmer, in Part 3, he draws attention to the difficulties which may flow from differences or discrepancies between the designer's and the user's representations of a system.

New Technology and Human Error
Edited by J. Rasmussen, K. Duncan and J. Leplat
© 1987 John Wiley & Sons Ltd

21. Errors in the Execution of Prescribed Instructions. Design of Process Control Work Aids

N. Herry
École Pratique des Hautes Études, Paris

SUMMARY

Errors in the execution of prescribed instructions are analysed in terms of deviations between the operator's action logic and the action logic of the designer of the instructions. These logics are characterized by the implementation of distinct properties of action organization; that of the operator being unsuitable to understand the bases of the instructions.

INTRODUCTION

The aim of this investigation is to design work aids, i.e., aids to support the execution of prescribed instructions to recover accidents in an automated process. These aids have to be used by operators controlling the process in the control room. The design of these work aids called for prior analysis of the difficulties in using prescribed instructions as well as of the resulting difficulties in accident recovery.

This chapter concentrates on the interpretation of observed deviations between the prescribed work method and the work method actually used.

To this end four types of logic will be distinguished:

1. The operator's logic of process working.
2. The operator's action logic, resulting in the actual work method used.
3. The logic of process working of the expert who designed the prescribed instructions.
4. The action logic of the instructions prescribed and the resulting prescribed work method.

We shall see that the deviations between the actual work method and the prescribed work method can be explained by deviations between the various logics.

239

We shall then go on to present five properties of action organization which were used as a basis for the analysis and comparison of the different logics. These properties will be used to identify the bases of the errors observed in recovering accidents.

What follows is not a complete account of the research. Rather, we have chosen to emphasize the theoretical framework of the analysis and to outline an example which shows its general interest.

The results are obtained from 'paper and pencil' type simulations. These simulations are based on a model of the industrial process which provided a real-time reproduction of the sequence of events, and took into account the actions proposed by the operators. Trends in plant variables (normally available in the control room) were provided as the accident was going on.

ACCIDENT AND PRESCRIBED INSTRUCTIONS CHARACTERISTICS

The accident analysed is the result of a break in a closed water loop, causing drastic changes in process thermodynamics. The operators are fairly well acquainted with normal process working, but have scant knowledge of process working during an accident, since they have never had to deal with it in reality. It should therefore be noted that the operators have to cope with a situation new to them.

The prescribed instructions were designed so that the operators can normally apply them without understanding the process working.

The operator's task consists simply in recovering the accident by following the instructions. The instructions indicate the actions to be performed under well-defined conditions. Also, the conditions of success or failure of the actions are often defined.

The conditions for the performance and success of the actions are expressed in the form of two variables:

1. The difference between actual water temperature and the saturation temperature, above which water converts to steam. This difference is used to evaluate the risk of water vaporization.
2. The total volume of water: process constraints require that a correct volume of water is maintained.

The action logic underlying the prescribed instructions is only partially expressed in their drafting.

The prescribed instructions only refer to successive states of the process by specifying the limits of operating variables. However, they do not refer to relationships between variables which are the basis of the underlying action logic and which might enable an understanding of the transformations between successive states of the process.

The prescribed instructions cover neither the amplitude nor the duration of the physical phenomena resulting from the actions to be performed.

Thus the operator, who does not know the relationships involved between variables, will not see the reasons for performing the actions prescribed and will understand neither the connections between the prescribed instructions nor their objectives. In this sense it can be argued that following the prescribed instructions would not be 'motivated' by an understanding of their basis.

WORK METHODS–ACTION LOGICS–PROCESS WORKING LOGICS

These observations lead us to formulate a hypothesis for interpreting the deviation between the prescribed work method and the actual work method.

This deviation appears to be caused by a lack of coherence between the prescribed instructions and the operator's logic of process working.

Most of the operators refuse to apply the prescribed instructions without a knowledge of their basis. At the same time, and though it is not required, their action logic leads them to take into account their own representation of the process working.

The prescribed instructions themselves result indirectly from a logic of process working which is peculiar to the expert who devised the instructions. But the operator's mental representation of process working does not necessarily match that of the expert who devised the instructions. That is why the operator could not re-establish the links of the chain connecting the prescribed instructions to their underlying action logic since this derives from the process working logic of the expert (see Table 1).

The prescribed instructions would therefore appear to the operator as not fully justified, hence the choice of a work method different from that prescribed.

We have two indications of the deviation between the prescribed instructions and the operator's mental representation of process working:

1. The discrepancies observed between the prescribed work method and the actual work method adopted.
2. The discrepancies between the action logic underlying the prescribed instructions and the operator's action logic. These discrepancies cannot be observed, but can be deduced from the operator's verbal reports during an ongoing accident recovery.

Operators making allowances for their own representation of process working results in two types of strategy:

1. An initial long-term strategy involving attempts, not always successful,

to understand the basis of prescribed instructions and process transformations.

2.   A second short-term strategy adopted to compensate for inability to understand the reasons for prescribed actions and for the process transformations observed. This gives priority to the maintenance of the plant at all times in a state considered to be safe.

Given the difficulties in understanding the working of the process, it seems that operators have generally adopted a short-term strategy. However, at different times in recovering the accident, their interpretations of physical phenomena were:

1.   Either integrated into a longer term strategy, i.e., performance of intermediate actions to reach a long-term goal.
2.   Or not integrated into any action logic, as if there was a dissociation between process working logic and action logic or an inconsistency between the choice of actions performed and the interpretation of ongoing process transformations.

Table 1: *Presentation of logics and work methods*

EXPERT	*OPERATOR*
Expert's process working logic Process working rules taken into account in the bases of the prescribed instructions and proceeding from: Relationships between variables expressing the process transformations	**Operator's process working logic** Process working rules specific to the operator (proceeding from training and experience on the field)
Action logic *Underlying the prescribed instructions* Available controls for acting on relationships between variables to reach the objectives of the prescribed instructions (safety objectives and return to normal plant configuration)	**Operator action logic** Influenced by the prescribed instructions and the process working rules taken into account
Prescribed instructions or prescribed work method Sequences of actions which have to be performed, based on safety variables states which cover successive process states	**Actual instructions or actual work method** Sequences of actions actually performed. (Information monitoring and actions on displays/controls panels)

LOGICS AND PROPERTIES OF ACTION ORGANIZATION

A comparative analysis of the properties of action organization which characterize the various logics makes it possible to go further in the interpretation of the deviations between them. This analysis is based on the assumption that the adult can adopt several types of reasoning characterized by different properties of action organization. These different properties, in turn, originate in structural properties which characterize the various stages in the development of operational intelligence, as described by Piaget.

According to this theory, errors in recovering the accident result from implementing unsuitable properties of action organization (Vermersch, 1976).

We shall distinguish here five properties of action organization.

1. The dynamic or static nature of process working monitoring:
    (a) Dynamic, when monitoring is by means of relationships between variables which refer back to a working mode of the process (to different degrees of accuracy and consistency).
    (b) Static, when monitoring simply involves identifying the state of the variables, without linking them to each other, by reference to a standard or to safety requirements.
2. The ability *a priori* to anticipate physical phenomena and conversely the ability to interpret them *a posteriori*. Anticipation is especially useful for understanding actions which have a long-term effect but no short-term effect, or for understanding 'detour actions' which make it possible to reach a long-term goal with an immediate effect contrary to this goal.
3. The degree of coordination of information to be simultaneously taken into account and of actions to be performed over the same period.
4. The degree of coordination of successive information processing and of resulting successive actions.
5. The use or non-use of the reversibility of certain actions to the process (i.e., allowing or not allowing for the possibility to return to initial status by performing the reverse action).

These properties of action organization underlie the level of complexity in the operator's mental representation of the basis of prescribed instructions. They determine the work method actually employed in recovering the accident.

ERRORS IN RECOVERING THE ACCIDENT AND INADEQUACY OF PROPERTIES OF ACTION ORGANIZATION INVOLVED: ONE EXAMPLE

To illustrate why it is of interest to point out these properties of action organization, let us take the example of a prescribed action involving depressurization by reduction of water inlet flow.

Diagnosis errors during performance of this action can be explained by the inability *a priori* to anticipate physical phenomena (second property of action organization).

Depressurization by reduction of water inlet flow is a detour action. Its long-term goal is to maintain a sufficient water volume by acting on the main possible cause of insufficient water, i.e., by reducing the water flow rate through the break. However, this depressurization action causes a short-term loss of fluid volume which is contrary to the long-term goal. This demonstrates the conflict which can arise between a short-term objective (maintaining a correct volume at all times) and a long-term objective (reducing the water flow rate through the break), even if this means a short-term loss of volume.

This example also illustrates the advantages, described above, of anticipating the physical phenomena resulting from a detour action.

The expert's action logic makes it possible to anticipate the long-term positive result, since the expert knows that the short-term loss of volume can be discounted, whatever its size may be, for the benefit of the long-term reduction in flow rate through the break.

However, the operators never spontaneously anticipate *a priori* the results of process actions. They only carry out interpretations of physical phenomena observed *a posteriori*. Their inability to anticipate long-term results leads them to opt to maintain a correct water volume value at every moment. The operator's action logic does not therefore solve the long-term/short-term conflict. It does not follow the line taken by the action logic underlying the prescribed instructions and may explain why instructions are not applied. Accordingly, the operator may be led to delay the prescribed action and even to perform some other action not prescribed — which may not be accurate and sometimes even ineffective — with the aim of increasing the fluid volume without depressurizing and, therefore, without acting on the main factor.

On the other hand, the strict application of the prescribed instructions does not call for anticipation of physical phenomena. The conditions for the performance and success of this depressurization action are defined in the prescribed instructions.

CONCLUSION

The deviations between prescribed and actual work methods have been interpreted as deviations between logics — those used by the expert who devised the prescribed procedure and those used by the operator.

The operator's action logic would therefore not include the properties of action organization which characterize the expert's action logic. Then the operator would not be in a position to establish a relationship between the knowledge of the process working he may have previously acquired and the prescribed instructions. However, during accident simulation, verbal reports, concerning the process working, show that operators possess all or part of the theoretical knowledge necessary to establish this relationship. Deviations between work methods would therefore result not only from a lack of theoretical knowledge, but also from the implementation of action organization properties unsuited to understanding the bases of prescribed instructions.

The devising of this type of prescribed instructions, describing in detail the successive actions to be performed, is a factor which probably does not motivate the implementation of those action organization properties which enable understanding the bases of the instructions and the working of the process. On the other hand, it is likely that these instructions led to a short-term strategy adopted by the operators. This short-term strategy depends on an action logic or a class of action organization properties different from that underlying a longer term strategy, which aims to understand and thus anticipate process transformations (Weill-Fassina, 1976).

Failures in attempts at long-term strategy could then mean that this type of strategy depends on a class of action organization properties which is psychologically more 'expensive' to implement than the class of properties corresponding to a short-term strategy.

These failures could also mean that passing over a short-term strategy in favour of a longer term strategy, calls for prior inhibition of recourse to the least expensive properties of action organization; inhibition which in itself represents a certain cost.

In this light it would be worth while analysing the relative cost of the implementation of certain action organization properties (e.g., cost of anticipation), as well as the cost of inhibiting the least expensive properties (e.g., immediate action with no attempt at anticipation).

Further investigation of this matter could be of particular interest for the analysis of incidental, unfamiliar situations in automated processes where the operators can implement several classes of properties.

The analysis presented in this paper provides new data for operator training, design of work aids and design of control rooms.

REFERENCES

Vermersch, P. (1976) Analyse de la tâche et fonctionnement cognitif dans la programmation de l'enseignement. *Bulletin de Psychologie*, 33(343), 179–87.
Weill-Fassina, A. (1976) Guidage et planification de l'action par les aides au travail. *Bulletin de Psychologie*, 33(344), 343–9.

New Technology and Human Error
Edited by J. Rasmussen, K. Duncan and J. Leplat
© 1987 John Wiley & Sons Ltd

22. Structuring of Knowledge of Operators in Continuous Processes: Case Study of a Continuous Casting Plant Start-Up

V. de Keyser
University of Liege

SUMMARY

Control room operators' knowledge was investigated:
- by comparing operators from three plants with the same technology but different work organizations;
- by analysing, in a new plant, how novice operators diagnose incidents during the startup.
- by analysing in this plant which information and from which source the operator utilizes, observed three months after the startup.

INTRODUCTION

Man's reliability in continuous processes has given rise to many works and the particular role of control room operator has been well to the fore in the studies. *

Our purpose is not to add a stone to a building which is already impressive, and to envisage instants when temporary situations or human shortcomings are liable to occur: stress, night work, monotonous activity, interferences, etc. Here we concern ourselves with the conditions required for a cognitive development, allowing in general an operator to be reliable — without prejudging the factors which might intervene, at any instant, to lower this reliability transitorily. Accordingly, it is a developmental point of view, attempting to discriminate what can now lead to a lasting modification of his knowledge, influencing the whole of the man–machine system in which he is integrated, in technological development, in the nature of information carriers supplied to the operator in work organization.

Many situations of learning and of building up experience, have been laboratory situations, specially for industrial tasks. Such conditions, which allow the strict verification of some hypotheses, none the less invalidate the interplay of complex interactions, in the reality of work. We shall take, as 'pretext' of the study, the design and start-up of a steelmaking continuous casting plant, imparting within this concept a very special orientation to the acquisition of knowledge of the operators. The commissioning of the continuous casting plant was quite remarkable. It was the result of a multidisciplinary team comprising doctors, architects, safety engineers, ergonomists, and design offices. Management and trade unions worked together. This very tightly knit team met, more than two years before the start-up, to include working conditions at the level of the actual project.

The constraining dynamics of this procedure — deliveries to be maintained, installation to be designed, plans to be revised — nevertheless allowed the ergonomists to question themselves on the future which these installations had in store for the skills of the operators and for the way of increasing them at three points in time:

1. Before the start-up of the continuous casting, at the time of a prior study in European plants with the same technology.
2. During start-up, in incident discussion groups which were held after the first tests.
3. After start-up, in the evaluation of the information carriers of the control room.

These were observations which, even though long and systematic, were taken nearly 'on the run', so as to attempt to capture the instants of preferential knowledge structuring, which habit, routine, and self-assurance which are being established will quickly modify.

BEFORE START-UP: THE CASE OF THREE PLANTS**

The scientific literature on control room operators has modelled the image of a man, a kind of 'natural regulator of the system', capable of monitoring the balance of the process, to diagnose and even foresee incidents. His knowledge of the process and of the installations, acquired by practice, would consist of operating images, varying in their richness, complex, in accordance with his expertise. The observation and work analysis of the three operators, in three different plants with continuous casting, give shades of meaning to this typical picture (see Figure 1).

Continuous casting is a highly automated process and it is sequential, in spite of its name. The steel, from the melting shop, is cast in a tundish, then it is divided into two streams in moulds, whence, solidified as a billet, thanks to a water-cooling mechanism, it goes down through rollers which guide it. This is the billet which, at the end of its run, will be cut, and at the end of the caster, cut-to-length by torch cutters. One of the most feared accidents is the breakout, a tear of the billet: the steel then flows inside the caster. Another is the clogging of the flow at any level of the installation; the risk then is a run-off at the tundish and splashes of molten metal on the floor.

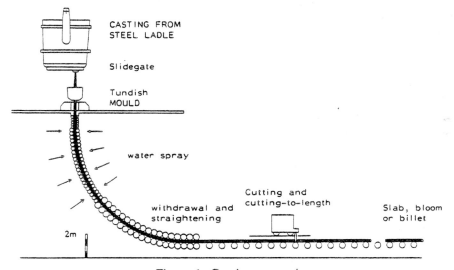

Figure 1. Continuous casting

After casting a few ladles, the tundish and the moulds are changed: they go for relining. The process is then momentarily interrupted. Thus it is a sequential production, characterized by a start-up, then a variable casting time in accordance with the product characteristics and an end of casting. The automation, well developed, concerns the casting. The parameters appear to be controlled by the data processing programs and there is no process adjustment or rebalancing during the work. In contrast, at the start-up, there is a delicate speed control to be undertaken, but this is done on the floor and not from the control room. The maintenance of the installation is fundamental. Parameter stability rests on it, which is a *sine qua non* condition of the automation. Hence there are competent maintenance teams in the plant, well integrated in production. Even though all the process and caster parameters can still be collected in the control room and be displayed on mimic boards and dials, as in the continuous processes studied conventionally, they do not seem to take on the same strategic importance for the operators.

It is clear that, for the process and the installations, there is no longer a real operators' diagnosis. In the event of an incident, at best they make a prediagnosis and warn the appropriate departments. Their task is oriented towards the distribution of information. The control room becomes a dispatching department. Continuous casting operates following a law of all or nothing. Either the automation operates and accordingly the operator has a very small role — or it does not operate and the field is wide open for maintenance, supervision and management, who attempt to solve the problems. Thus here one is dealing with a sufficiently high automation level, so that even the actual reason for the presence of an operator in the control room is subject to questioning. Is it justified? The differential analysis of the three plants, at the level of the installations, work organization and of operators' knowledge, gives interesting information.

It is different in the three cases:

1. In plant A, the operator concentrates nearly exclusively on the tasks of managing the flows of information and of material: planning, team coordination, regulation with other departments and particularly the melting shop. The view which he has is a structural perspective, in terms of the system. The foreman controls the operations on the floor and keeps a direct contact with the installations and the product. The control room is distant from the floor.
2. In plant B, the operator is also the foreman. He does not remain continuously in the booth. The mimic boards of the latter have been designed so that they can be consulted from a distance, from outside.

    Planning of the casting is undertaken in another place, by a regular planning department man.
3. In plant C, the situation is somewhat similar to plant A: the operator manages the flow of information and serves as hub to the team. While he does not actually do some planning, he adjusts the casting programme in accordance with the incidents. The control booth overhangs the installation.

Thus, there appear three functions — control, management of information flow, casting planning — which, in accordance with the case, may or may not be combined.

Work analysis

Work analysis shows a very random monitoring of the process and of the installations from the control room and, in any case, little or no anticipation of incidents from there.

Design of control room and work organization (Figure 2)

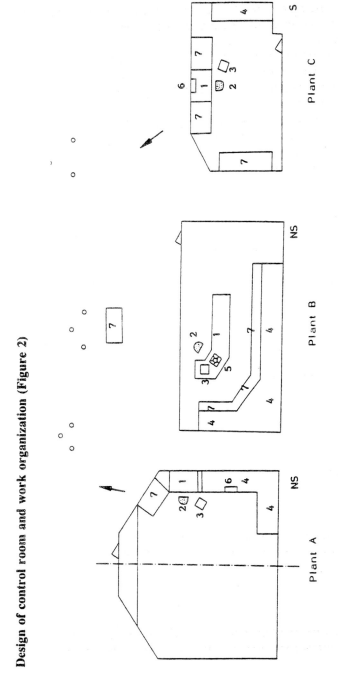

Figure 2. Design of control room in plants A, B, and C

The software does not appear to be disputed. When one explores the knowledge of operators from incident cases, in accordance with a technique developed by Iosif (1968, 1969) and De Keyser and Piette (1970), one perceives that:

1. In plant A, the operator has essentially acquired a structural competence, but that his process and installation operating images are very poor.
2. In plant B, the operator–foreman knows very well, and very thoroughly the caster and the installations, but that he controls the whole of the system less well.
3. In plant C, again, one is faced with a thorough structural knowledge and slight knowledge of process and installations.

So it seems quite clear that it is the operator's role and not the wealth of the coded information which is supplied to him — essentially the same in all cases — which influences the way in which knowledge is structured; where he must no longer intervene, make decisions, actually diagnose causes of incidents, the operating images shrink hard and fast.

In contrast, in the cases where he maintains his control on a set of decisions, his knowledge remains solid. It does not seem possible to impute the observed differences to initial training inequalities, even though one has to be cautious. What appears as remarkable is the appearance in force, in plants A and C, of a structural competence — of coordination, management, planning — which becomes informally the most important for the reliability of the system.

These findings lead to a consideration of the different fields where operator knowledge can be developed and of the relationship between ergonomics and work organization. The 'natural regulator' of the process and of the installation only exists as formed by the requirements of the system and some practice; it is an illusion to believe that, in a highly automated system where his intervention is one of the smallest, man develops, without necessity knowledge which he will not use — and that in the limiting conditions he will not succeed in developing, because of the lack of an adequate feedback from his actions.

Therefore, either the operator can at a given instant prove indispensable – and the situation and the work organization must be thought of in terms of this possibility — or it is not useful that he should still control the process and the installations, and therefore the control room and its information carriers must take this into account. The ergonomic design of the control room would appear therefore fundamentally linked to this organizational philosophy.

Referred to the multidisciplinary ergonomic team, these results of the preliminary survey in plants A, B, and C led the team to the following decision: keep an operator in the control room, but he should be polyvalent. If necessary, he would be asked to replace the foreman and would keep a direct contact with the caster and the product. He would also provide part of the planning. Therefore, the supporting option from the cognitive standpoint was selected.

AT START-UP: VERBAL ANALYSES OF INCIDENT CASES

The training plan envisaged by the plant for the 260 workers of the future caster had been very intensive. It was broken into five phases (from three days to twelve weeks), going from theory to practice. Actually, while the first phase consisted in a series of information on casting, practical courses in the firm were envisaged at the end of the training.

Analysis of this plan by the ergonomists had shown a gap: no preparation for incidents, their analysis, and the means of dealing with them (Duncan, 1981). With this in view, a sixth phase was added during start-up and its objective was to evaluate the theoretical and practical training undergone during the sixth month which had passed, to impart information which had been found useful for the operators, but also to reduce the anxiety and the stress on start-up, which had been seen to be very high. In the initial project for the sixth phase, fictitious incident cases were to be analysed, daily, for two hours, by mixed teams (maintenance/production) on the spot. Guidance was provided by the foreman and one of the ergonomists. The experiment was to last six weeks and the discussions were recorded in full. This plan was followed, apart from one exception: the group never discussed prepared fictitious cases, but they imposed the analysis of actual situations which they had experienced during the day.

The analysis of the contents of the tapes showed some major difficulties, in spite of the training received.

Anxiety of start-up

It is clear, from listening to the recorded tapes, that the workers are frightened. The operating knowledge learnt during training and the knowledge of utilization which they must use to control the system (Richard, 1983) are poles apart. One switches from simple laws or rules, elements of theory, to a complex system, with interacting multiple variables whose behaviour cannot be predicted. Management is absorbed by technical tasks, steel controls and the workers feel left to themselves, at least in what concerns the reliability of the installations. The quirks and simple breakdowns of the plant worry them more than whether the product is up to specification. Straight off, a kind of division of work appears. Production and its quality stem from the management which also participates in the development of the programmes. The hard part is left to the workers and to lower management and this means not only the hard part but also the coordination of the teams, some contacts with associated departments, with the overhead travelling cranes, etc. This coordination, optimizing the information flow in the system, has been called 'structural regulation'. And a theme which forcefully returns in the conversations is the one of having 'just missed a catastrophe', imminent accident, the luck of having missed it.

In the incident analysis, imputation phenomena

Incidents that occurred during the day were analysed daily by the workers following the fault tree method. In some cases, it was not possible to detect the factors at the origin of the incident, because of insufficient information. In other cases, it was possible and the discussion between the participants was an interesting continuation of the teaching process started by the training of the first five phases. Many ergonomic and technical suggestions were made to improve the reliability and effectiveness of the installations, but imputation phenomena, conventional in accident analysis, were already in play, as, for example, was the case when studying a tundish run-off. The stopper end to close occasionally the casting orifice came off and was lodged in the hole: hence a rapid rise of molten steel in the tundish and a run-off which could have caused some casualties.

Various hypotheses were put forward by the participants to explain why tne head had broken — stopper defect, cheap type of stopper but weaker than another available in the market, etc. — which were laid directly at the door of management. But actually, further enquiry found there was no breakage, but most likely, wrong screwing of the head by a worker just before use. This hypothesis had been rejected by the group and never appeared in the discussion.

A delicate space–time identity

The workers have difficulty in grasping the respective relationships and the trajectory over time of the continuous caster, the overhead travelling cranes servicing it and the transport plant which travels in the shop, forming a dynamic whole. While the training has made them familiar with some topography of the site, it has not succeeded in making them apprehend the relationship of the various elements with respect to each other. During the discussions the workers illustrated their speech with gestures, moving pieces of wood, solids, to explain to each other how some parts worked, formed a single piece, how a movement was propagated, etc.

But what appeared most lacking was the notion of duration of the operations, the chronology of actions, intervention times and the speed at which a variation entails an incident or a stoppage.

In the discussions were found many diagnosis errors or the selection of inappropriate operating methods, the result of a wrong estimate of the time available.

How many seconds does it take for a tundish run-off, if the casting hole is clogged — taking into account the height of the molten steel? After how many hours should a tundish be changed? What is the life of a roller?

To give a figure, to propose an estimate from formulae or theoretical laws have hardly any meaning for the workers: it is only the specificity which interests them, the very special case — and it is not a matter of clock time, but rather of an action time: 'how much time have I got for . . .'. Even if these time regulations imply recourse to memory, the experience of past events and a cognitive reconstruction of what happened during these times, one clearly sees the appearance in the discussions of sensori-motor behaviours, feelers, with their failures or success being judged through incidents. If they appear, it is because the estimate was wrong. The dysfunction in the feedback of the action which it provides has a teaching virtue — just like the alarm system in Kortland and Kragt (1980) which was used less to warn the operators of a danger, than to inform them on the significance of their anticipatory intervention.

The non-exploitation of the theoretical acquisitions of training

We have pointed out the difficulty of putting into practice the operating knowledge imparted during training. As an example of this, in an unscrewing incident of the tundish stopper head, a discussion arose among the workers on the force which could have broken the head to pull it towards the hole. They said it was a vortex effect, but what law governed it? Did the orifice section, the depth of the molten steel, or the level where the stopper was, affect the suction force? Trying to settle it, the participants very naturally used a reasoning frame related to daily life: the image of the emptying bath tub was adopted and the sensation of suction force on the hand placed close to the hole was used as reference, this being a sensation and not any mathematical expression whatsoever.

The analysis of these difficulties met by the participants during start-up makes one think that:

1. The training given, even though substantial, neglected:
    (a) preparation for incident analysis;
    (b) comprehension of work in dynamic terms;
    (c) integration of caster in a more complex system, with interacting multiple variables.
2. Behaviour of sensori-motor type, with feelers, search for immediate feedback of the actions are used as support to rough sketches of reasoning. The theory acquired in training remains unused.

3. From start-up, a division of work is established between workers and
    management: the former tend to 'dominate' the installations and the
    latter the product.
4. The learning of the multiple process times seems one of the fundamental
    points — and difficult to attain, even with simulation type training — of
    human reliability: the incident would keep a central role and a 'teaching'
    virtue in it.

AFTER START-UP, THE USE OF INFORMATION CARRIERS IN THE CONTROL ROOM

Three months after start-up of the installation, a first evaluation of the use
of information carriers in the control room was undertaken. One of the
ergonomic criteria imposed on the design office had been the maintaining of
some redundancy of available information and in particular the direct view
of the installation. The wall-mounted mimic boards had been kept to provide
a stable information background and because various observations and
enquiries by the workers stressed their importance. The screen images had
been designed on a participative basis.

Table 1: *Enquiry index of the information carriers during the various sequence phases (estimate on 30 sequences)*

Information source	Enquiry index *	Preparation phase	Start-up phase	Normal operation	End of casting
Mimic boards		4	22	3.3	2
Screens		5.6	23	5.4	4
Installations		1.1	73	5.3	2.9
Intercom communications		33.6	66	27	25
Giant display		0	55	5.5	4.5

*Takes into account the frequency of the enquiries made of the source weighted by the time of the phase concerned.

Table 1 clearly shows the instant where one is during the course of the
process. The use of the information carriers is different: this argues in favour
of a redundancy. But what is obvious is, in this highly automated sector, the
preferential place left for the uncoded intercom information — considered
also as more reliable by the operators. In any case, but especially in the
event of incidents (which are not shown in this table, which refers to normal
sequences), one resorts to a direct, social link.

The direct view of the installations is especially useful on start-up, a time which appears as the most sensitive, with much collecting of information.

The finer analysis of the various sources during the sequences shows clearly the operators' hesitation (they look for exactly the same variable on different information carriers) or even fixation (they return many times to a given information carrier, to keep on checking the same information).

Thus, there would be more doubts on non-verbal rather than verbal information. And, in any case, at start-up, the screens are far from occupying the operators' attention in a big way.

CONCLUSIONS

The observations made on continuous casting operators in different steel-making plants, but especially within the framework of the design of a new installation, have shown some tendencies or characteristics which may be useful to stress if one wishes to understand how human reliability is structured:

1. The operators' cognitive dimension is not an item of data in itself: it appears to be intimately modelled by the level of automation, work organization, the design of the installation, and by the information carriers.
2. The current development of continuous processes, when they are stable and well controlled by the process control computers, tends to strip from the control room operator the regulation of the process, the software, and sometimes even the installations. However, it seems that this same worker has to develop a structural competence — in order to have the opportunity of coordinating and of planning the activity and the production in the sector.
3. Behaviour of the sensori-motor type, feelers, the use of operating images drawn from daily life, mark the start-up of the installation and are the starting point of a cognitive structuring where the acquisition of space–time identities is a difficulty which training does not overcome in a system as complicated as that referred to here.
4. Three months after start-up, it is still the verbal information, not coded through screens or mimic boards — none the less made with worker participation — which is the most used, and appears the surest. The social factor seems to be closely linked to cognitive structuring.
5. Two hypotheses conflict in the light of these results. The first recalls some resistance to change: the operators, skilled workers, would have some difficulty in adjusting to the new technologies. They would give priority to the usual behaviour in the working world, resorting to the senses, to the touch, and to verbal exchanges, etc.

A better thought-out training, the recruitment of higher qualified technicians, would have resulted in avoiding these dangers. Actually, in definite cases, the operators, even though young and qualified, have all had a 'traditional' past in the plant.

The other hypothesis is that, in a complex system, such as continuous casting, no manual and no course will succeed in providing operators with operating knowledge which would miraculously correspond to utilization knowledge. Too many parameters come into play: and in the resulting uncertainty — productive of anxiety for the workers — a structuring of inductive knowledge, which would follow developing thresholds, as described by Vermersch (1978), meets the requirements, not of a special logic of the operator which would conflict with the logic of an expert, but simply with the requirements of the situation.

Lengthy discussions with engineers and design offices before the construction of the project, make us argue in favour of this second hypothesis. Actually, in attempting to sort the pertinent information to present to the control room operator, in organizing the alarms to appear on the screens, in imagining incidents' scenarios for possible simulation, we were able to measure the lack of knowledge of the experts, concerning the actual operating conditions. This is one of the dangers of design ergonomics, when there is no reference situation in the firm to be analysed: it must be extrapolated from other contexts.

From the gap between these models and practice, there arise problems which ergonomists can assist in solving.

REFERENCES

De Keyser, V. (1981) La fiabilité humaine dans les processus continus, les centrales thermo-électriques et nucléaires. Rapport CCE (720-ECI-2651-C-(0), CERI, Bruxelles.

De Keyser, V., and Piette, A. (1970) Analyse de l'activité des opérateurs au tableau synoptique d'une chaîne d'agglomération. *Le Travail Humain*, 33(3–4), 341–52.

Duncan, K. D. (1981) Training for fault diagnosis in industrial process plant. In: J. Rasmussen, and B. Rouse (Eds), *Human Detection and Diagnosis of System Failures*. New York: Plenum Press.

Iosif, G. (1968) La stratégie dans la surveillance des tableaux de commande. I. Quelques facteurs déterminants de caractère objectif. *Revue roumaine des Sciences sociales*, 12(2), 147–63.

Iosif, G. (1969) La stratégie dans la surveillance des tableaux de commande. II. Quelques facteurs déterminants de caractère subjectif. *Revue roumaine des Sciences sociales*, 13(1), 29–41.

Kortland, K., and Kragt, H. (1980) Process alarm systems as a monitoring tool for the operator. *Third Int. Symposium on Loss Prevention and Safety Promotion in the Process Industries*, Basle, 15–19 September.

de Montmollin, M. (1983) L'intelligence de la tâche. Rapport du groupe Communication et Travail, Université de Paris XIII, Villetaneuse.

Richard, J. F. (1983) Logique de fonctionnement et logique d'utilisation. Rapport INRIA 2029–83, Le Chesnay.
Vermersch, P. (1978) Une problématique théorique en psychologie du travail. *Le Travail Humain*, **41**(2), 263–78.

*Abstract of these works in V. de Keyser — 'La fiabilité humaine dans les processus continus, les centrales thermo-électriques et nucléaires'. EEC Report — DG XII, C.E.R.I. Brussels 1981 and M. de Montmollin — 'L'intelligence de la tâche'. Groupe Communication et Travail, University of Paris XIII, Villetaneuse 1983.

** This research has been undertaken under the auspices of ECSC-DG5.

New Technology and Human Error
Edited by J. Rasmussen, K. Duncan and J. Leplat
© 1987 John Wiley & Sons Ltd

23. Reflections on Fault Diagnostic Expertise

K. D. Duncan
University of Wales Institute of Science and Technology

SUMMARY

Verbal reports of fault diagnostic rules in the form of short sequences of heuristics; two criteria: coherence of enquiry when plant information is withheld, and effect on novices' capability to solve novel problems. The issue of acceptable success probability of heuristic strategies; 'design error'; differences between designers' and operators' mental models of process plant.

INTRODUCTION

New technologies increasingly call for powerful ways of training people to solve fault diagnostic problems. Among the crucial issues, three stand out: the status of verbal report; the human proclivity for heuristic strategies; and the sometimes different models of plant and equipment held, on the one hand, by designers and, on the other, by operators and users.

VERBAL REPORT

Since we have for some time relied on verbal report in developing diagnostic rules for fault diagnosis training, it now seems important to describe in more detail the techniques we have employed. We recognized, at the outset, the *potential distortions* inherent in the necessarily *serial production* of protocol (Duncan and Shepherd, 1975). Secondly, in these days of 'expert systems', it is important to be explicit about the point that *much expertise*, and in our experience the most important diagnostic expertise, *almost certainly does not exist in verbal form*. This cannot be overemphasized. We would therefore urge the protagonists of expert systems to give high priority to easing the difficulties which human beings frequently experience when trying to express their expertise, be it in words or in other forms still to be explored. And the less brash 'knowledge engineer' may recognize in our approach the care taken to make the dialogue with the expert a *congenial* one. Earlier experiences in programmed instruction suggested that whether the dialogue was interesting and rewarding for the subject matter expert could make or break the whole enterprise.

Although the primary purpose in this, as in any exercise in applied psychology, was utility, nevertheless, applying two tests which will now be described has arguably captured and represented something of diagnostic skill, *per se*. In any event, the empirical evidence of the transfer of expertise to novices is undeniable (see Chapter 19).

Over several years, our attempts to persuade operators and other people to express how they diagnose faults from control panel arrays show:

1. That they invariably have difficulty in putting what they are doing into words.
2. That they nevertheless can usually comply with what they see as a reasonable request.
3. That such 'diagnostic rules' as they seem to be applying are typically *short sequences of heuristics* — see Figure 1.
4. That they frequently wish to revise their expressions of these heuristics, once they are in verbal form.
5. That further revisions are prompted by further diagnosis and by discussion with other operators in the course of jointly attempting to diagnose a fault.

The information elicited in these verbal reports is subjected to two tests of whether verbal expressions correspond at all well with the diagnostic process.

As a first test or check, we employ a technique of *withholding plant information* until it is requested. We show the operator or other subject a simulated instrument panel, but without any indications on the instruments; the only information provided is that an audible alarm has occurred, signalling a fault somewhere in the plant. From the order in which people request information we are able to check their first attempts at verbalization.

This first test eliminates some rules, combines others, and refines still other rules to make them more precise. This is done with individuals and then with groups so that people may compare and debate what it is they are doing, within the acknowledged limits imposed by words, and also with the explicitly acknowledged distortions which this requirement might impose on expressing what they really do when diagnosing a fault in the operating situation. This procedure helps to turn what could be a rather tedious experience into one which is acceptable and, sometimes, interesting or amusing. Once the set of heuristics or diagnostic rules seems beyond further improvement, i.e., further discussion with plant information withheld, in both individual and group sessions, ceases to yield further changes or refinements, the second test is applied.

The first test relies largely on judgements as to whether the sequence of plant information sought is consistent or coherent with verbally reported rules. Sometimes there is little doubt, for instance, instrument readings are sought in a sequence which is contrary to the rules, however interpreted. Efforts to reduce doubt may be made jointly by the investigator and the informant, or the investigator may resort to judicious choice of faults, and therefore of instrument readings. Nevertheless, at this stage there is no attempt to quantify and, to this extent, the first test is fallible. The second test, on the other hand, is essentially quantitative.

The second and major test incorporates the verbally formulated diagnostic rules into a training programme for novices. This is a test both of how much diagnostic skill has been captured and of how well the verbal expression of this skill in diagnostic rules has been understood and applied by novices. Their understanding, measured in terms of capability to solve novel diagnostic problems, is encouraging. Indeed, of the various options open to training, it is fair to conclude that diagnostic rules developed in this fashion are probably the best bet (see Chapter 19).

This is not to gainsay that nowadays critics of verbal report can marshal arguments which are much more formidable than those levelled at the classical and notoriously unreliable methods of introspection and retrospection. In many situations verbal report produces incomplete, over-elaborated or false representations (Nisbett and Wilson, 1977). Clearly, verbal report can be useless or worse, but whether it is useful, or not, is an empirical question. Verbal coding may produce demonstrably more or less distortion; and any intermediate abstraction or inference entailed by verbal coding may rule out its use (Ericsson and Simon, 1980). Just how useful verbalization may be will ultimately turn on methodological sophistication, and not least on the instructions given to the subject (Leplat and Hoc, 1981).

An important departure from classical introspection, where people attempted to analyse their experiences, sensations and imagery, or lack of them, is a tradition of encouraging individuals to talk, or think aloud, while performing a task. The protocol thus produced is recorded by the investigator who looks for evidence which might indicate intentions, focus of attention, the nature of a strategy, and so forth. Many pitfalls in 'thinking aloud' techniques have been pointed out, notably the constructive *caveats* by Claparede (1934), but the technique of asking subjects to talk while working towards the solution of a problem, for all its faults, was arguably one of the more significant methodological advances in psychology (Miller *et al.*, 1960, pp. 192–4). To obtain useful information, *eliciting verbal reports in the context of problem solution is of the essence*. At least some, if not many, of the problems of interpreting subjective reports in the early days of psychology illustrate all too clearly 'what happens when "thought" is analytically divorced from its context of action' (Humphrey, 1951).

In the case of process control tasks, it has been argued, notably by Bainbridge, that protocols obtained from operators provide insights into how they make decisions. She has used protocol material to model the cognitive processes underlying these decisions, acknowledging that it is 'necessary to assume that there is some non-distorting mapping from the underlying thought processes to the verbal protocols' (Bainbridge, 1974).

This is a strong assumption to which the writer is sympathetic. But strong assumptions must pass strong tests, hence the two suggested in this paper. Just what constitutes a strong test of anything may, in the last resort, be a matter of taste. Our predilections are for *coherence of enquiry* when operators are 'starved' of plant information, and for the *intelligibility* of strategic verbal statements to novice problem-solvers. Any representation of expertise should be *communicable*. In which case its adequacy may be quantified in tasks demanding solutions, in particular, solutions to novel problems.

To summarize briefly, the expert must have a non-trivial task in mind; the investigator must take active steps to facilitate the external representation of expertise; and every device must be employed to test the efficiency of the process. As far as we are aware, the tests we have applied to the case of diagnostic problem solving go beyond the methods so far employed to represent the 'internal' basis of skill or expertise.

Lastly, it is worth mentioning that the requirement to solve problems when plant information is withheld until requested not only reveals to our experienced operators that they can more clearly formulate verbal expressions of their expertise, but also it can lead them to make remarks and to behave in ways which suggest that the underlying expertise itself has undergone a substantial revision.

HEURISTICS

Reason (in Part 1) made the point that one of the well-established findings of modern cognitive psychology is the over-use of heuristics. The uncritical extension of heuristics or guesses, especially after prolonged practice in rather restricted contexts, is a common human failing. That it can be very dangerous during problematic operations in hazardous industries goes without saying. Clearly, the over-hasty use or naïve over-extension of heuristics can lead to more trouble.

But at the end of the day, whether we like it or not, we have to resort to heuristics because in effect we have no alternative; too many fault diagnostic problems are not amenable to algorithmic solution because exhaustive specification of the set of possible faults is not a practical proposition. Also we have discerned, in experienced operators, heuristic strategies for fault diagnosis which are impressive (Chapter 19). *The central problem is how to refine heuristics to the point where their success probability is acceptable.*

At this point, a word or two about the heuristics which were used is in order. Some were deceptively simple and straightforward. The first heuristic, 'Scan the panel . . .' is one such (see Figure 1). I have since asked other operators to comment on this rather simple heuristic. One operator said, 'You scan the panel for as long as you dare!' Another operator who, it seemed, was more able to put into words what 'scanning the panel' involved, said, 'I know that if I wait as long as possible before "chasing that hare" [referring to one of several diagnoses the operator was considering at the time] I shall miss the other signs'. This is an instance, if my interpretation is reasonable, of an operator who has intuitively grasped the well-established human tendency differentially to weight evidence favouring a hypothesis under test and to discount evidence inconsistent with it. These comments during diagnosis illustrate the shorthand nature of the expressions offered when diagnostic rules are sought, and which later exchanges with operators suggest is typical. It underlines how much more a rule may mean than is at first realized, and perhaps how much more it may come to mean to a trainee with increasing practice in fault diagnosis. It is also a salutary warning of how much may be lost if one does not persist beyond the first attempts to construct some verbal representation of a diagnostic heuristic.

(a) Scan the panel to locate the general area of failure, i.e., feed, reactor/heat-exchange complex, Column A or Column B.
(b) Check all control loops in the affected area. Are there any anomalous valve positions?
(c) High level in a vessel and low flow in associated take-off line indicate either a pump failure or valve failed 'closed'. If valves OK (see b), then pump failure is probable diagnosis.
(d) High temperature and pressure in column head associated with low level in reflux drum indicate overhead condenser failure — provided all pumps and valves are working correctly (rules b and c).
(e) If the failure is in the reactor/heat-exchange complex, determine whether it is in the reactor or the heat-exchange system. A failure in the heat-exchange will produce symptoms in Column A but not in B. A failure in the reactor will produce symptoms in both columns.
(f) If the failure is in the feed system, check whether it is in stream X or stream Y. Because of the nature of the control system, a failure in the Y stream will produce associated symptoms in both the X and Y streams. A failure in the X stream will show symptoms in the X stream only.

The diagnostic rules differ in generality. The first four rules (a–d) are rather general in that they might apply to many diagnostic tasks of this kind. The last two rules (e and f) deal with plant-specific difficulties. Both are examples of a general problem in diagnosis, symptom referral, enabling diagnosis despite symptoms referred by a feed-forward loop (rule e) and by a feedback control loop (rule f).

Figure 1. Diagnostic Rules

A related point is that, while it is usually necessary to explain to novices the application of the last two rules which deal with symptom referral, people with experience in the petrochemical industry often spot the fact that we have built into our fictitious plant the rather frequent problem of symptoms referred forward, or symptoms referred back by major loops in the overall process.

However, while it certainly is possible to enable people to solve this kind of problem by the application of heuristics rules, it must be stressed that training in itself is almost certainly not going to be enough, and that we are now reaching diminishing returns. However ingenious the training, the possibility seems remote of improving on first line, control room diagnosis of novel failures beyond the 90% or mid-90% level which we can now achieve. On the strict criterion we have employed of problems not previously encountered, this still leaves a high probability of 'first shot' failure, which in many industries is quite unacceptable. The way ahead may be a radical change in how diagnostic problems are represented in the first place — in plant design, before training begins.

PLANT AND EQUIPMENT DESIGN: REPRESENTATIONS AND MODELS

The powerful influence of capital-intensive economic philosophies combined with ingenious control systems will sometimes lead to plant where the human operator is only retained to solve problems and make decisions when things go wrong, and has rather little experience of interacting with the plant, except on these rare occasions, when there will be little experience to go on. Furthermore, every effort will be made to make capital-intensive or hazardous plant reliable. The more reliable the plant, the less opportunity there will be for the operator to practise direct intervention, and the more difficult will be the demands of the remaining tasks requiring operator intervention.

Against this backdrop a whole series of problems of simulation fidelity inevitably arise since, given the costs and the hazards involved, there is no question that operators will have adequate opportunities to train from scratch with real equipment or plant. The attempt to devise simulators in turn raises the tricky problems of:

1. Events which have never happened but might.
2. Still worse, of events which have not even been foreseen.

Training may succeed in providing operators with generalizable diagnostic skill but, as noted in the previous section, there are limits to what may be achieved, and post-training probabilities of diagnostic error remain uncomfortably high.

An expression frequently used by others in this volume and elsewhere is design error. This may be the most formidable human error of them all — the *fons et origo* of many subsequent 'errors' by operators and maintenance personnel, the original sin. Naturally enough, advanced technologies tempt design engineers to virtuoso performance. However, when industrial developments are driven by production control and economic considerations, with little or no analysis or planning of the overall scheme of things at the work place, the design engineer's role is severely circumscribed. The designer is no more culpable than other human beings trying to cope with galloping technologies, indeed, the designer's role and its difficulties, call for a positive and fundamental reappraisal, and raise issues beyond the scope of this chapter, issues to do with organizational structures, education, traditions in the engineering disciplines, and institutional pressures.

Brehmer makes an important point in his paper (Brehmer, Chapter 10), when he points out that 'technology makes relations between actions and outcomes opaque', which among other things means we have to consider the 'representations . . . models created by the designers . . . for the explicit or implicit purpose of facilitating a foreseeable range of decisions', but decisions, be it noted, which will not be for the designer to make. We must beware of major differences between the decision maker's representation or model and the designer's model of the system.

There are probably many important differences between the designer's model and the operator's model of process plant. One instance may be the model of a loop. I suspect the designer's model of a loop has to do with taking an output signal to some comparator and maintaining 'set point' by feeding signals to an effector device. At a more detailed level, the designer's model may represent the quality of sensor information, the power and other response characteristics of the slave device, and the comparator functions which ensure adequate tracking of the set point, avoid hunting when perturbations occur, and so forth.

The operator's model of a control loop, precisely because, by its very nature, it copes with a difficulty at least for a time, seems to emphasize the *masking* of process problems in the early stages of their development. In this respect novices differ from experienced operators. Novices usually concentrate on how well the set point is matched, on whether, say, a vessel level indication is within limits. The experienced operator is not unconcerned about matching the set point, but is often very concerned about the behaviour of the slave device, say, a slave valve on the feed line to the vessel. If the slave valve, in this example, tended to remain in a wide open position, or alternatively to remain nearly closed, an experienced operator would probably infer feed line problems, e.g., changing feedstock characteristics or 'line chokes'.

Developing process problems such as these may be masked, although not indefinitely, by an acceptable match of the parameter sensed (temperature, pressure, etc.) with the set point — and the novice would be no wiser. However, the experienced operator's model keeps him on the look out for masking such as this and will anticipate impending problems provided, that is, that adequate indications of the behaviour of slave devices is available. That control room instrumentation of slave device behaviour is often non-existent or primitive may be taken as further evidence of rather different models held by designers and experienced operators.

More prosaically, the quality of control room indications of slave device behaviour may merely reflect the financial pressures on designers. For instance there are substantial cost differences between: displaying the signal sent to a slave valve; displaying 'open' and 'shut' signals from limit switches; and displaying the track of the valve position as sensed by an induction device. The instrumentation of Three Mile Island Unit Two may have been the result of an inadequate model of how operators detect developing plant failures, or simply the result of penny-pinching, or both. In any case, the 1979 accident dramatically illustrates what may be at stake when a design takes insufficient account of the operator's model for anticipating and controlling process malfunctions.

Another illustration of differences between the representation of the designer and that of the operator may be seen in petrochemical plant design. A feature of plant design in this industry is a consequence of the design engineer's increasing — and, it should be said, praiseworthy — concern with thermal economy. For example, if a reactor generates heat and requires substantial cooling systems, rather than simply controlling the temperature by cooling towers, the plant designer will often employ heat exchangers and transfer the recovered heat to another plant unit which is driven by heat, e.g., a distillation column.

This makes good sense, but it introduces the diagnostic difficulty which doctors designate as 'referred symptoms' in medical diagnosis. Thus if a reactor developed a fault, the symptoms might not first appear, and would not appear only, in the reactor instrumentation. The first panel symptoms might be loss of 'boil-up' in the distillation column.

Do operators always develop a process model which incorporates the 'referred symptoms' complication? If they do, then their model is again different from the designer's, which I suspect is very much a heat extraction and transport model. So we have another diagnostic problem for the operator which, as it follows from other sensible plant design considerations, was probably not envisaged by anyone: the problem of symptoms referred forward, or referred back by major loops in the overall process.

This is a design error, by definition, since we can be reasonably, sure that the diagnostic complications were not *intended*. Moreover it is a design error resulting rather directly from the designer's model of the plant, which is limited in a way that an experienced operator's model is not.

CONCLUSION

This is not so much a conclusion as an afterthought, prompted by the complexities of some fault diagnostic training. More exactly, it is an uneasy feeling that new technologies will often mean that the tasks which people have to perform, will become more and more elaborated, in the sense that there are more and more components and subroutines. And if training means that people acquire plans and action sequences, which they subordinate, to varying degrees of subroutine status — the very essence of skill some would say — then the demands, on whatever internal monitor or inspector checks whether performance is coping or not, may increase to the point where major slips or lapses become too frequent for comfort, and any further training or experience is counter-productive. So although training may reduce the likelihood of errors due to lack of understanding, it may increase the probability of errors due to slips or lapses. We can be confident only that the consequences of both types of error may be dire.

REFERENCES

Bainbridge, L. (1974) Analysis of verbal protocols from a process control task. In: E. Edwards and F. P. Lees (Eds), *The Human Operator in Process Control*. London: Taylor and Francis.

Claparede, E. (1934) La genese de l'hypothese. *Archives de Psychologie*, 24, 1–154.

Duncan, K. D., and Shepherd, A. (1975) A simulator and training technique for diagnosing plant failures from control panels. *Ergonomics*, 18, 627–41.

Ericsson, K. A., and Simon, H. A. (1980) Verbal reports as data. *Psychological Review*, 87, 215–51.

Humphrey, G. (1951) *Thinking*. London: Methuen.

Leplat, J., and Hoc, J.-M. (1981) Subsequent verbalization in the study of cognitive processes. *Ergonomics*, 24, 743–55.

Miller, G. A., Galanter, E., and Pribram, K. H. (1960) *Plans and the Structure of Behavior*. New York: Holt.

Nisbett, R. E., and Wilson, T. D. (1977) Telling more than we know: verbal reports on mental processes. *Psychological Review*, 84, 231–59.

New Technology and Human Error
Edited by J. Rasmussen, K. Duncan and J. Leplat
© 1987 John Wiley & Sons Ltd

24. Ironies of Automation

Lisanne Bainbridge

Department of Psychology, University College, London

SUMMARY

By taking away the easy parts of his task, automation can make the difficult parts of a human operator's task more difficult. Problems and solutions, including support for cognitive skills and mental workload using man–computer collaboration, are discussed.

'Irony': combination of circumstances, the result of which is the direct opposite of what might be expected. 'Paradox': seemingly absurd though perhaps really well-founded statement.

The classic aim of automation is to replace human manual control, planning and problem solving by automatic devices and computers. However, as Bibby and colleagues (1975) point out: 'even highly automated systems, such as electric power networks, need human beings for supervision, adjustment, maintenance, expansion, and improvement. Therefore one can draw the paradoxical conclusion that automated systems still are man–machine systems, for which both technical and human factors are important.' The present chapter suggests that the increased interest in human factors among engineers reflects the irony that the more advanced a control system is, so the more crucial may be the contribution of the human operator.

This chapter is particularly concerned with control in process industries, although examples will be drawn from flight-deck automation. In process plant the different modes of operation may be automated to different extents, for example normal operation and shut-down may be automatic while start-up and abnormal conditions are manual. The problems of the use of automatic or manual control are a function of the predictability of process behaviour, whatever the mode of operation. The first two sections of this paper discuss automatic on-line control where a human operator is expected to take over in abnormal conditions, the last section introduces some aspects of man–computer collaboration in on-line control.

INTRODUCTION

The important ironies of the classic approach to automation lie in the expectations of the system designers, and in the nature of the tasks left for the human operators to carry out.

The designer's view of the human operator may be that the operator is unreliable and inefficient, so should be eliminated from the system. There are two ironies of this attitude. One is that designer errors can be a major source of operating problems. Unfortunately, people who have collected data on this are reluctant to publish them, as the actual figures are difficult to interpret. (Some types of error may be reported more readily than others, and there may be disagreement about their origin.) The second irony is that the designer who tries to eliminate the operator still leaves the operator to do the tasks which the designer cannot think how to automate. It is this approach which causes the problems to be discussed here, as it means that the operator can be left with an arbitrary collection of tasks, and little thought may have been given to providing support for them.

Tasks after automation

There are two general categories of task left for an operator in an automated system. He may be expected to monitor that the automatic system is operating correctly, and if it is not he may be expected to call a more experienced operator or to take over himself. We will discuss the ironies of manual takeover first, as the points made also have implications for monitoring. To take over and stabilize the process requires manual control skills; to diagnose the fault as a basis for shut-down or recovery requires cognitive skills.

Manual control skills

Several studies (Edwards and Lees, 1974) have shown the difference between inexperienced and experienced process operators making a step change. The experienced operator makes the minimum number of actions, and the process output moves smoothly and quickly to the new level, while with an inexperienced operator it oscillates round the target value. Unfortunately, physical skills deteriorate when they are not used, particularly the refinements of gain and timing. This means that a formerly experienced operator who has been monitoring an automated process may now be an inexperienced one. If he takes over he may set the process into oscillation. He may have to wait for feedback, rather than controlling by open-loop, and it will be difficult for him to interpret whether the feedback shows that there is something wrong with the system or more simply that he has misjudged his control action. He will need to take action to counteract his ineffective control, which will add to his workload. When manual takeover is needed there is likely to be something wrong with the process, so that unusual actions will be needed to control it, and one can argue that the operator needs to be more rather than less skilled, and less rather than more loaded, than average.

Cognitive skills:

Long-term knowledge

An operator who finds out how to control the plant for himself, without explicit training, uses a set of propositions about possible process behaviour, from which he generates strategies to try (e.g., Bainbridge, 1981). Similarly an operator will only be able to generate successful new strategies for unusual situations if he has an adequate knowledge of the process. There are two problems with this for 'machine-minding' operators. One is that efficient retrieval of knowledge from long-term memory depends on frequency of use (consider any subject which you passed an examination in at school and have not thought about since). The other is that this type of knowledge develops only through use and feedback about its effectiveness. People given this knowledge in theoretical classroom instruction without appropriate practical exercises will probably not understand much of it, as it will not be within a framework which makes it meaningful, and they will not remember much of it as it will not be associated with retrieval strategies which are integrated with the rest of the task. There is some concern that the present generation of automated systems, which are monitored by former manual operators, are riding on their skills, which later generations of operators cannot be expected to have.

Working storage

The other important aspect of cognitive skills in on-line decision making is that decisions are made within the context of the operator's knowledge of the current state of the process. This is a more complex form of running memory than the notion of a limited capacity short-term store used for items such as telephone numbers. The operator has in his head (Bainbridge, 1975) not raw data about the process state, but results of making predictions and decisions about the process which will be useful in future situations, including his future actions. This information takes time to build up. Manual operators may come into the control room quarter to half an hour before they are due to take over control, so they can get this feel for what the process is doing. The implication of this for manual takeover from automatically controlled plant is that the operator who has to do something quickly can only do so on the basis of minimum information, he will not be able to make decisions based on wide knowledge of the plant state until he has had time to check and think about it.

Monitoring:

It may seem that the operator who is expected solely to monitor that the automatics are acting correctly, and to call the supervisor if they are not, has a relatively simple task which does not raise the above complexities. One complexity which it does raise of course is that the supervisor too will not be able to take over if he has not been reviewing his relevant knowledge, or practising a crucial manual skill. Another problem arises when one asks whether monitoring can be done by an unskilled operator.

We know from many 'vigilance' studies (Mackworth, 1950) that it is impossible for even a highly motivated human being to maintain effective visual attention towards a source of information on which very little happens, for more than about half an hour. This means that it is humanly impossible to carry out the basic function of monitoring for unlikely abnormalities, which therefore has to be done by an automatic alarm system connected to sound signals. (Manual operators will notice abnormal behaviour of variables which they look at as part of their control task, but may be equally poor at noticing changes on others.) This raises the question of who notices when the alarm system is not working properly. Again, the operator will not monitor the automatics effectively if they have been operating acceptably for a long period. A classic method of enforcing operator attention to a steady-state system is to require him to make a log. Unfortunately, people can write down numbers without noticing what they are.

A more serious irony is that the automatic control system has been put in because it can do the job better than the operator, but yet the operator is being asked to monitor that it is working effectively. There are two types of problem with this. In complex modes of operation the monitor needs to know what the correct behaviour of the process should be, for example in batch processes where the variables have to follow a particular trajectory in time. Such knowledge requires either special training or special displays.

The second problem is that if the decisions can be fully specified then a computer can make them more quickly, taking into account more dimensions and using more accurately specified criteria than a human operator can. There is therefore no way in which the human operator can check in real-time that the computer is following its rules correctly. One can therefore only expect the operator to monitor the computer's decisions at some meta-level, to decide whether the computer's decisions are 'acceptable'. If the computer is being used to make the decisions because human judgement and intuitive reasoning are not adequate in this context, then which of the decisions is to be accepted? The human monitor has been given an impossible task.

Operator attitudes

The writer knows of one automated plant where the management had to be present during the night shift, or the operators switched the process to 'manual'. This raises general issues about the importance of skill to the individual. One result of skill is that the operator knows he can take over adequately if required. Otherwise the job is one of the worst types, it is very boring but very responsible, yet there is no opportunity to acquire or maintain the qualities required to handle the responsibility. The level of skill that a worker has is also a major aspect of his status, both within and outside the working community. If the job is 'deskilled' by being reduced to monitoring, this is difficult for the individuals involved to come to terms with. It also leads to the ironies of incongruous pay differentials, when the deskilled workers insist on a high pay level as the remaining symbol of a status which is no longer justified by the job content.

Ekkers and colleagues (1979) have published a preliminary study of the correlations between control system characteristics and the operators' subjective health and feeling of achievement. To simplify greatly: high coherence of process information, high process complexity, and high process controllability (whether manual or by adequate automatics) were all associated with low levels of stress and workload and good health, and the inverse, while fast process dynamics and a high frequency of actions which cannot be made directly on the interface were associated with high stress and workload and poor health. High process controllability, good interface ergonomics and a rich pattern of activities were all associated with high feeling of achievement. Many studies show that high levels of stress lead to errors, while poor health and low job satisfaction lead to the high indirect costs of absenteeism, etc. (e.g., Mobley et al., 1979).

APPROACHES TO SOLUTIONS

One might state these problems as a paradox, that by automating the process the human operator is given a task which is only possible for someone who is in on-line control. This section will discuss some possible solutions to problems of maintaining the efficiency and skills of the operator if he is expected to monitor and take over control; the next section will introduce recent proposals for keeping the human operator on-line with computer support.

Solving these problems involves very multidimensional decision making: suggestions for discussion will be made here. The recommendations in any particular case will depend on such factors as process size and complexity, the rate of process change, the speed and frequency of process or automatic control failure, the variability of the product and the environment, the simplicity and cost of shut-down, and the qualities of the operator.

Monitoring

In any situation where a low probability event must be noticed quickly then the operator must be given artificial assistance, if necessary even alarms on alarms. In a process with a large number of loops there is no way in which the human operator can get quickly to the correct part of the plant without alarms, preferably also some form of alarm analysis. Unfortunately a proliferation of flashing red lights will confuse rather than help. There are major problems and ironies in the design of large alarm systems for the human operator — see Rasmussen and Rouse (1981).

Displays can help the operator to monitor automatic control performance, by showing the target values. This is simple for single tolerance bands, but becomes more complex if tolerances change throughout batch processing. One possible solution is to show the currently appropriate tolerances on a VDU by software generation. This does not actually get round the problems, but only raises the same ones in a different form. The operator will not watch the VDU if there is a very low probability of the computer control failing. If the computer can generate the required values then it should also be able to do the monitoring and alarms. And how does the operator monitor that the computer is working correctly, or take over if it obviously is not? Major problems may be raised for an operator who is highly practised at using computer generated displays if these are no longer available in an emergency. One ironic but sensible suggestion is that direct wired displays should be used for the main process information, and software displays for quantitative detail (Jervis and Pope, 1977).

'Catastrophic' breaks to failure are relatively easy to identify. Unfortunately automatic control can 'camouflage' system failure by controlling against the variable changes, so that trends do not become apparent until they are beyond control. This implies that the automatics should also monitor unusual variable movement. 'Graceful degradation' of performance is quoted in 'Fitts Lists' of man–computer qualities as an advantage of man over machine. This is not an aspect of human performance to be aimed for in computers, as it can raise problems with monitoring for failure (e.g., Wiener and Curry, 1980); automatic systems should fail obviously.

If the human operator must monitor the details of computer decision making then, ironically, it is necessary for the computer to make these decisions using methods and criteria, and at a rate which the operator can follow, even when this may not be the most efficient method technically. If this is not done then when the operator does not believe or agree with the computer he will be unable to trace back through the system's decision sequence to see how far he does agree.

One method of overcoming vigilance problems which is frequently suggested is to increase the signal rate artificially. It would be a mistake, however, to increase artificially the rate of computer failure as the operator will then not trust the system. Ephrath (1980) has reported a study in which system performance was worse with computer aiding, because the operator made the decisions anyway, and checking the computer added to his workload.

Working storage

If the human operator is not involved in on-line control he will not have detailed knowledge of the current state of the system. One can ask what limitations this places on the possibility for effective manual takeover, whether for stabilization or shut-down of the process, or for fault diagnosis.

The straightforward solution when shut-down is simple and low cost is to shut down automatically. The problems arise with processes which, because of complexity, cost or other factors (e.g., an aircraft in the air) must be stabilized rather than shut down. Should this be done manually or automatically? Manual shut-down is usable if the process dynamics can be left for several minutes while the operator works out what is happening. For very fast failures, within a few seconds (e.g., pressurized water nuclear reactor rather than an aircraft), when there is no warning from prior changes so that on-line working storage would also be useless, then reliable automatic response is necessary, whatever the investment needed, and if this is not possible then the process should not be built if the costs of failure are unacceptable.

With less fast failures it may be possible to 'buy time' with overlearned manual responses. This requires frequent practice on a high fidelity simulator, and a sufficient understanding of system failures to be sure that all categories of failure are covered. If response to failure requires a larger number of separate actions than can be made in the time available, then some must be made automatically and the remainder by a highly practised operator.

Long-term knowledge

Points in the previous section make it clear that it can be important to maintain manual skills. One possibility is to allow the operator to use hands-on control for a short period in each shift. If this suggestion is laughable then simulator practice must be provided. A simulator adequate to teach the basic behaviour of the process can be very primitive. Accurate fast reactions can only be learned on a high fidelity simulator, so if such reactions are necessary then this is a necessary cost.

Similar points can be made about the cognitive skills of scheduling and diagnosis. Simple pictorial representations are adequate for training some types of fault detection (Duncan and Shepherd, 1975), but only if faults can be identified from the steady-state appearance of the control panel, and waiting for the steady-state is acceptable. If fault detection involves identifying changes over time then dynamic simulators are needed for training

(Marshall and Shepherd, 1981). Simple recognition training is also not sufficient to develop skills for dealing with unknown faults or for choosing corrective actions (Duncan, 1981).

There are problems with the use of any simulator to train for extreme situations. Unknown faults cannot be simulated, and system behaviour may not be known for faults which can be predicted but have not been experienced. This means that training must be concerned with general strategies rather than specific responses, for example simulations can be used to give experience with low probability events, which may be known to the trainer but not to the trainee. No one can be taught about unknown properties of the system, but they can be taught to practise solving problems within the known information. It is inadequate to expect the operator to react to unfamiliar events solely by consulting operating procedures. These cannot cover all the possibilities, so the operator is expected to monitor them and fill in the gaps. However, it is ironic to train operators in following instructions and then put them in the system to provide intelligence.

Of course, if there are frequent alarms throughout the day then the operator will have a large amount of experience of controlling and thinking about the process as part of his normal work. Perhaps the final irony is that it is the most successful automated systems, with rare need for manual intervention, which may need the greatest investment in human operator training.

MAN–COMPUTER COLLABORATION

By taking away the easy parts of his task, automation can make the difficult parts of the human operator's task more difficult. Several writers (Wiener and Curry, 1980; Rouse, 1981) point out that the 'Fitts list' approach to automation, assigning to man and machine the tasks they are best at, is no longer sufficient. It does not consider the integration of man and computer, nor how to maintain the effectiveness of the human operator by supporting his skills and motivation. There will always be a substantial human involvement with automated systems, because criteria other than efficiency are involved, e.g., when the cost of automating some modes of operation is not justified by the value of the product, or because the public will not accept high-risk systems with no human component. This suggests that methods of man–computer collaboration need to be more fully developed. Dellner (1981) lists the possible levels of human intervention in automated decision making. This chapter will discuss the possibilities for computer intervention in human decision making. These include instructing or advising the operator, mitigating his errors, providing sophisticated displays, and assisting him when task loads are high. Rouse (1981) calls these 'covert' man–computer interaction.

Instructions and advice

Using the computer to give instructions is inappropriate if the operator is simply acting as a transducer, as the computer could equally well activate a more reliable one. Thompson (1981) lists four types of advice, about: underlying causes, relative importance, alternative actions available, and how to implement actions. When following advice the operator's reactions will be slower, and less integrated than if he can generate the sequence of activity himself; and he is getting no practice in being 'intelligent'. There are also problems with the efficient display of procedural information.

Mitigating human error

Machine possibilities for counteracting human error range from simple hardware interlocks to complex on-line computation. Except where specific sequences of operations must be followed it is more appropriate to place such 'checks' on the effects of actions, as this does not make assumptions about the strategy used to reach this effect. Under manual control human operators often obtain enough feedback about the results of their actions within a few seconds to correct their own errors (Ruffell-Smith, 1979), but Wiener and Curry (1980) give examples of human beings making the same types of errors in setting up and monitoring automatic equipment, when they do not get adequate feedback. This should perhaps be designed in. Kreifeldt and McCarthy (1981) give advice about displays to help operators who have been interrupted in mid-sequence. Rouse (1981) suggests computer monitoring of human eye movements to check that instrument scanning is appropriate, for example to prevent tunnel vision.

Software generated displays

The increasing availability of soft displays on VDUs raises fascinating possibilities for designing displays compatible with the specific knowledge and cognitive processes being used in a task. This has led to such rich veins of creative speculation that it seems rather mean to point out that there are difficulties in practice.

One possibility is to display only data relevant to a particular mode of operation, such as start-up, routine operations, or maintenance. Care is needed, however, as it is possible for an interface which is ideal for normal conditions to camouflage the development of abnormal ones (Edwards, 1981).

Goodstein (1981) has discussed process displays which are compatible with different types of operator skill, using a classification of three levels of behaviour suggested by Rasmussen (1979), i.e., skill based, rule based, and knowledge based. The use of different types of skill is partly a function of the operator's experience though the types probably do not fall on a simple continuum. Chafin (1981) has discussed how interface design recommendations depend on whether the operator is naïve/novice/competent/expert. However, he was concerned with human access to computer data bases when not under time pressure. Man–machine interaction under time pressure raises special problems. The change between knowledge-based thinking and 'reflex' reaction is not solely a function of practice, but also depends on the uncertainty of the environment, so that the same task elements may be done using different types of skill at different times. It could therefore confuse rather than help the operator to give him a display which is solely a function of his overall skill level. Non-time-stressed operators, if they find they have the wrong type of display, might themselves request a different level of information. This would add to the workload of someone making decisions which are paced by a dynamic system. Rouse (1981) has therefore suggested that the computer might identify which type of skill the operator is using, and change the displays (he does not say how this might be done). We do not know how confused operators would be by display changes which were not under their own control. Ephrath and Young (1981) have commented that it takes time for an operator to shift between activity modes, e.g., from monitoring to controlling, even when these are under his control, and one assumes that the same problems would arise with changes in display mode. Certainly a great deal of care would be needed to make sure that the different displays were compatible. Rasmussen and Lind's recent paper (1981) was about the different levels of abstraction at which the operator might be thinking about the process, which would define the knowledge base to be displayed. Again, although operators evidently do think at different levels of complexity and abstraction at different times, it is not clear that they would be able to use, or choose, many different displays under time stress.

Some points were made above about the problems of operators who have learned to work with computer generated displays, when these displays are no longer available in abnormal conditions. Recent research on human memory (e.g. Craik, 1979) suggests that the more processing for meaning that some data have received the more effectively they are remembered. This makes one wonder how much the operator will learn about the structure of the process if information about it is presented so successfully that he does not have to think about it to take it in. It certainly would be ironic if we find that the most compatible display is not the best display to give to the operator after all! (As usual with display choice decisions this would depend on the task to be done. A highly compatible display always supports rapid reactions. These points speculate whether they also support aquisition of the knowledge and thinking skills needed in abnormal conditions.)

A few practical points can be suggested. There should be at least one source of information permanently available for each type of information which cannot be mapped simply on to others, e.g., about layout of plant in space as opposed to its functional topology. Operators should not have to page between displays to obtain information about abnormal states in parts of the process other than the one they are currently thinking about, nor between displays giving information needed within one decision process. Research on sophisticated displays should concentrate on the problems of ensuring compatibility between them, rather than finding which independent display is best for one particular function without considering its relation to information for other functions. To end on a more optimistic note, software displays offer some interesting possibilities for enriching the operator's task by allowing him to design his own interface.

Relieving human workload

A computer can be used to reduce human workload either by simplifying the operator's decisions, as above, or by taking over some of the decision making. The studies which have been done on this show that it is a complex issue. Ephrath and Young (1981) found that overall control performance was better with manual control of a single loop, but was also better with an autopilot in the complex environment of a cockpit simulator. This suggests that aiding is best used at higher workloads. However, the effect of the type of aiding depends on the type of workload. Johannsen and Rouse (1981) found that pilots reported less depth of planning under autopilot in abnormal environmental conditions, presumably because the autopilot was dealing with the conditions, but more planning under emergency aircraft conditions, where they suggest that the autopilot frees the pilot from one-line control so he can think about other things. Chu and Rouse (1979) studied a situation with both computer aiding and autopilot. They arranged for the computer to take over decision making when the operator had a queue of one other task item to be dealt with and he was controlling manually, or after a queue of three items if the autopilot was controlling. The study by Enstrom and Rouse (1977) makes it clear why Rouse (1981) comments that more sophisticated on-line methods of adapting computer aiding to human workload will only be possible if the workload computations can be done in real time. (It would be rash to claim it as an irony that the aim of aiding human limited capacity has pushed computing to the limit of its capacity, as technology has a way of catching up with such remarks.) Enstrom and Rouse also make the important point that the human being must know which tasks the computer is dealing with and how. Otherwise the same problems arise as in human teams in which there is no clear allocation of responsibility. Sinaiko (1972) makes a comment which emphasizes the importance of the human operator's perception of the computer's abilities: 'when loads were light, the men appeared willing to let the computer carry most of the assignment responsibility; when loads were heavy, the men much more often stepped in (and) over-rode the computer'. Evidently, quite apart from technical considerations, the design of computer aiding is a multidimensional problem.

CONCLUSION

The ingenious suggestions reviewed in the last section show that human beings working without time pressure can be impressive problem solvers. The difficulty remains that they are less effective when under time pressure. I hope this chapter has made clear both the irony that one is not by automating necessarily removing the difficulties, and also the possibility that resolving them will require even greater technological ingenuity than does classic automation.

REFERENCES

Bainbridge, L. (1975) The representation of working storage and its use in the organisation of behaviour. In: W. T. Singleton and P. Spurgeon (Eds), *Measurement of Human Resources*. London: Taylor and Francis, pp. 165–83.

Bainbridge, L. (1981) Mathematical equations or processing routines? In: J. Rasmussen and W. B. Rouse (Eds), *Human Detection and Diagnosis of System Failures*. New York: Plenum Press, pp. 259–86.

Bibby, K. F., Margulies, F., Rijnsdorp, J. E., and Withers, R. M. J. (1975) Man's role in control systems. *Proc. 6th. IFAC Congress*, Boston.

Chafin, R. L. (1981) A model for the control mode man–computer interface. *Proc. 17th. Ann. Conf. on Manual Control*, UCLA. JPL Publication 81–95, pp. 669–82.

Chu, Y., and Rouse, W. B. (1979) Adaptive allocation of decision making responsibility between human and computer in multi-task situations. *IEEE Transactions on Systems, Man and Cybernetics*, SMC-9, 769.

Craik, F. M. (1979) Human Memory, *Annual Review of Psychology*, **30**, 63.

Dellner, W. J. (1981) The user's role in automated fault detection and system recovery. In: J. Rasmussen and W. B. Rouse (Eds), *Human Detection and Diagnosis of System Failures*. New York: Plenum Press, pp. 487–99.

Duncan, K. D. (1981) Training for fault diagnosis in industrial process plant. In: J. Rasmussen and W. B. Rouse (Eds), *Human Detection and Diagnosis of System Failures*. New York: Plenum Press, pp. 553–73.

Duncan, K. D., and Shepherd, A. (1975) A simulator and training technique for diagnosing plant failures from control panels. *Ergonomics*, **18**, 627.

Edwards, E. (1981) Current research needs in manual control. *Proc. 1st. European Annual Conference on Human Decision Making and Manual Control*. Holland: Delft University, pp. 228–32.

Edwards, E., and Lees, F. P. (Eds) (1974) *The Human Operator in Process Control*. London: Taylor and Francis.

Ekkers, C. L., Rasmooij, C. K., Brouwers, A. A. F., and Janusch, A. J. (1979) Human control tasks: A comparative study in different man–machine systems. In: J. E. Rijnsdorp (Ed.), *Case Studies in Automation Related to Humanisation of Work*. Oxford: Pergamon Press, pp. 23–29.

Enstrom, K. O., and Rouse, W. B. (1977) Real-time determination of how a human has allocated his attention between control and monitoring tasks. *IEEE Transactions on Systems, Man and Cybernetics*, SMC-7, 153.

Ephrath, A. R. (1980) Verbal presentation. *NATO Symposium on Human Detection and Diagnosis of System Failures*, Roskilde, Denmark.

Ephrath, A. R., and Young, L. R. (1981) Monitoring vs. man-in-the-loop detection of aircraft control failures. In: J. Rasmussen and W. B. Rouse (Eds), *Human Detection and Diagnosis of System Failures*. New York: Plenum Press, pp. 143–54.

Goodstein, L. P. (1981) Discriminative display support for process operators. In: J. Rasmussen and W. B. Rouse (Eds), *Human Detection and Diagnosis of System Failures*. New York: Plenum Press, pp. 433–49.

Jervis, K. W., and Pope, R. H. (1977) Trends in operator–process communication development. Central Electricity Generating Board, E/REP/054/77.

Johannsen, G., and Rouse, W. B. (1981) Problem solving behaviour of pilots in abnormal and emergency situations. *Proc. 1st European Annual Conference on Human Decision Making and Manual Control*. Holland: Delft University, pp. 142–50.

Kreifeldt, J. G., and McCarthy, M. E. (1981) Interruption as a test of the user–computer interface. *Proc. 17th. Annual Conference on Manual Control*, UCLA, JPL Publication 81–95, pp. 655–67.

Mackworth, N. H. (1950) Researches on the measurement of human performance. Reprinted in: H. W. Sinaiko (Ed.), *Selected Papers on Human Factors in the Design and Use of Control Systems*. New York: Dover Publications, pp. 174–331.

Marshall, E. C., and Shepherd, A. (1981) A fault-finding training programme for continuous plant operators. In: J. Rasmussen and W. B. Rouse (Eds), *Human Detection and Diagnosis of System Failures*. New York: Plenum Press, pp. 575–88.

Mobley, W. H., Griffeth, R. W., Hand, H. H., and Meglino, B. M. (1979) Review and conceptual analysis of the employee turnover process. *Psychological Bulletin*, **86**, 493.

Rasmussen, J. (1979) On the structure of knowledge — a morphology of mental models in a man–machine system context. Riso National Laboratory, RISO-M-2192, Denmark.

Rasmussen, J., and Lind, M. (1981) Coping with complexity. *Proc. 1st European Annual Conference on Human Decision Making and Manual Control*. Holland: Delft University, pp. 70–91.

Rasmussen, J., and Rouse, W. B. (Eds) (1981) *Human Detection and Diagnosis of System Failures*. New York: Plenum Press.

Rouse, W. B. (1981) Human–computer interaction in the control of dynamic systems. *Computing Surveys*, **13**, 71.

Ruffell-Smith, P. (1979) A simulator study of the interaction of pilot workload with errors, vigilance, and decisions. NASA TM-78482.

Sinaiko, H. W. (1972) Human intervention and full automation in control systems. *Applied Ergonomics*, **3**, 3.

Thompson, D. A. (1981) Commercial air crew detection of system failures: state of the art and future trends. In: J. Rasmussen and W. B. Rouse (Eds), *Human Detection and Diagnosis of System Failures*, New York: Plenum Press, pp. 37–48.

Wiener, E. L., and Curry, R. E. (1980) Flight-deck automation: promises and problems. *Ergonomics*, **23**, 995.

New Technology and Human Error
Edited by J. Rasmussen, K. Duncan and J. Leplat
© 1987 John Wiley & Sons Ltd

Part 7: Error Sources, Reasons or Causes

INTRODUCTION

Characteristic of the workshop was the interaction between approaches to human error which are normally considered by separate groups or schools, such as reliability engineering, social judgement studies, and work and traffic safety. The discussions served to reveal that related problems were the focus of the different approaches, even though they were considered from different points of view. The consequences of the common trend towards more cognitively oriented studies made it possible to interrelate research and to formulate problems in terms of more general concepts related to the cognitive control of human behaviour. As will be seen from the review of discussions in Part 8, this was a general experience.

One topic was, however, subject to particular discussion by exchange of notes before as well as after the meeting. This topic was related to the question whether human errors are *caused* by external events or features of the work design and therefore can be controlled by proper design — which is the traditional human reliability point of view — or whether errors are reflections of a subjective risk perception and homoeostasis and therefore difficult to control beyond a certain measure — which is the point of view of the social science approach to safety.

The contributions to the first two parts of this volume, on the definition of error and the relationship to cognitive control, seemed to indicate that the points of view of the different quarters were not incompatible, and that they were developing in a way creating common ground for exchange and cross-fertilization. Consequently, a discussion emerged, which is the topic of Part 7.

New Technology and Human Error
Edited by J. Rasmussen, K. Duncan and J. Leplat
© 1987 John Wiley & Sons Ltd

25. The Role of Human Action in Man–Machine System Errors

Donald H. Taylor

The University, Southampton

Now: Donald Taylor & Associates Ltd

SUMMARY

The *theory of human action* is compared with the *theory of behaviour* as they both apply to *accidents* and *risk taking*. *Reason-giving explanations* are shown to be different from those in terms of causes. It is argued that both are necessary to understand *human errors*.

TWO DOMAINS OF EXPLANATION

The study of human error has progressed from analytical modelling in terms of component failure, to consideration of man–machine systems as a whole, and the parts played by various processes within them. This has resulted in schemes for tracing, classifying and predicting errors that are much more useful and sophisticated than the older methods (Rasmussen, 1982). However, including humans as not-quite-mechanical parts of the overall system brings in terms, used familiarly to describe and explain what people do, which are not quite the usual ones for mechanical systems. Failure to realize this, and failure to understand the crucial difference between similar-sounding terms, tends to confound and limit our thinking about man–machine systems, and at worst reduces it to little more than the old mechanical analogy. It is mainly with the terminology of human affairs, and the nature of its difference from that of mechanical systems, that this paper is concerned.

There are two pairs of similar-sounding terms which are often used loosely and interchangeably. They are:

	BEHAVIOUR	ACTION
and		
	CAUSE	REASON

The terms on the left are properly used to describe either human or non-human activities; those on the right properly describe only human activities.

For example, a machine malfunction may be described in terms of its behaviour, and explained in terms of what caused it. It is also possible to say this about a person. However, in the case of a person's inappropriate action, we could perhaps get an explanation by asking him his reason, in a way that we cannot do with a machine. To speak of the 'action' of a machine can only refer to its behaviour, but this is not true of a person. A person's actions are his own responsibility; they are what he does, usually of his own volition. His behaviour could well be caused (made to happen) by factors beyond his control, and volition does not enter into it. We can thus use two description/ explanation systems for what people do, but properly only one for what machines do. This is a major source of confusion when studying a man–machine system. One set of terms can be used anywhere in the system, the other in only a part of it.

ACTIONS AND ERRORS

Since reasons relate to actions, which generally are intended, it is very difficult for a person to explain errors and accidents by giving reasons. Part of the difficulty is that accidents by definition cannot be intended. Since the outcomes were unintended, the person can give no explanations of them other than by appealing to causal factors beyond his control. If none can be found, accidents and errors are truly meaningless events (Taylor, 1981). There is no doubt that accidents and harmful unintended outcomes can arise from actions, and also no doubt that actions can be later judged as errors (as in the saying: marry in haste, repent at leisure). However, there is a sense in which, at the time, any voluntary action had a reason which was valid to the actor, and on this basis it can be argued that 'all actions are correct'. The difficulty of accepting this statement is related to the difficulty of accepting people's reasons for what they do.

It is of course quite easy to judge other people's actions as erroneous. To tell another person that he is making an error (by acting as he does) is either to say that his beliefs about the state of the world are erroneous, or that we do not agree with his system of values. We might add that this is not only our own view but that any reasonable person would agree with us. There is usually available a 'reference set' of actions considered to be proper or reasonable at the time by some (perhaps notional) set of persons, and the explanation of erroneous actions has to do with whether they can be fitted into this reference set.

In behaviouristic terms, the 'reference set' for consideration of the desirability or correctness of alternative behaviours is the empirical value of the outcome: this is what underlies the principle of reinforcement. It also underlies a whole theory of 'social action': ethnomethodology, which is seen by some of its critics (e.g., Ions, 1978) as having no point of contact with a 'moral universe'. It seems appropriate that some part of a discussion about human error should be held in this universe, and this seems to imply that a single set of 'desirable' actions is not enough.

Separating the notions of propriety of actions and the value of their outcomes, with regard to safety, leads to a conceptual situation such as shown in Figure 1.

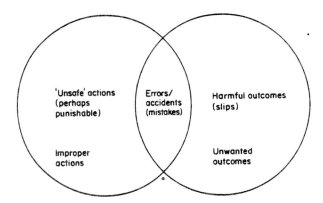

Figure 1. Two 'reference sets' describing undesirable occurrences. The left-hand circle is in the action domain, and would be explored through reason-giving explanations; the right-hand circle is in the domain of behaviour, and would be explored by causal explanations

The reference sets of improper actions and of harmful outcomes will generally be much alike, but need not be isomorphous. The degree of overlap will be determined by how 'realistic' the system is. Typically, the set of unsafe actions will be embodied in a set of rules, customs, or procedures, and the link between improper actions and harmful outcomes will be probabilistic and empirically studied. It could well be, however, that some actions are considered to be improper (unsafe) on *a priori* grounds. It is even possible for the rules governing improper actions to take the form of taboos or superstitions, and for the 'harmful outcomes' to be myths or self-fulfilling prophecies. Whatever they are, there is no escaping from the fact that the left-hand set in the diagram is subjectively decided by each and every individual, who will use it to guide and explain much of what he does.

Much ingenuity may go into designing systems that are safe against caused errors of all kinds, but to design a system that is proof against any kind of improper action, however perverse, would probably rob it of all its functions. If this is true, human actions and the reasons for them must be considered even on the 'hardware' side of the man–machine system.

THE PROBLEM OF INACTION

In a man–machine system, it is highly unlikely that the man will pay attention to (and be in full control of) the system 100% of the time. Modern tasks such as process control and various kinds of watchkeeping perhaps demand too little attention from the operator rather than too much. In addition, we seem to be psychologically programmed to reduce the need for detailed attention to tasks, through spontaneous development of autonomous skills and behaviour sequences. If a task is not entirely what a person chooses to be doing, any 'spare capacity' gained by not having to pay attention to it may give him opportunities to do other things instead; this is after all what our 'labour-saving' world seems to be about. Also, not paying attention to a task for a while brings about a temporary loss of control; this may provide uncertainty, novelty, and excitement, and may relieve boredom. Again, there seems to be cultural support: without willingness temporarily to lose control there would be no adventure, no heroics, no innovation, and no risk. Nothing ventured, nothing gained.

To lose control of a system is to exit from the 'normal' action sequence, and to be subject to events determined by causes rather than by reasons. If this happens involuntarily, it may be easily understood as a situation in which errors or accidents could occur (a 'risky' situation); it is not so easy to understand if the loss of control was voluntary or deliberate. The reason for this is that absence of control is a totally familiar situation to all of us (who has never been rained upon?), it is only of interest if there is a harmful outcome, and in the present context only if control could have been had, but was not. However, arguing backwards from a harmful outcome to the quality of a decision that preceded it does not make sense unless one considers what could reasonably have been expected at the time: the decisions that a 'reasonable man' would have taken. The only way to determine 'reasonableness' is to enquire into reasons.

RISK TAKING

Taking a risk is an action (or an inaction) involving a temporary loss of control (Taylor, 1976). Not paying continuous attention is a risk in this sense; it is also a familiar feature of life, a biological necessity, and can have instrumental advantages. Voluntarily taking a risk may be justified or not, as any other action may be, but is subject to the same paradox of necessarily appearing justified to the actor at the time. Risk taking is a unique aspect of human affairs in which the domains of action/reason and behaviour/cause come into probably their closest and most important contact.

THE ANALYSIS OF ACTION

Having to rely upon analysis of human action in the study of man–machine systems seems at first to have some bizarre consequences. One of the most basic differences between reason and causes as explanations is that *reasons cannot be completely analysed objectively*. Any data that are collected in this area will have a variable degree of credibility. The skilled investigator of such data will need qualities of tact, trustworthiness and sensitivity not currently a part of normal training in the social sciences, but perhaps not impossible to find. There are considerable implications for organizational climates which could facilitate or frustrate such enquiries.

Faced with the necessity for subjective data, the investigator of errors and accidents may find the following tactical guidelines helpful:

1. The principal threat from subjective data is that they could represent the opinions of only one person, and are unverifiable. Much can be done to ameliorate this through the doctrine of intersubjectivity, introduced into formal psychological research by Shotter. It invokes: 'the shared frameworks of meaning within which we interpret the significance of what we do and what we experience' (Shotter, 1975).

    Society could not exist without such frameworks; the task of the intersubjective scientist is to clarify and formulate frameworks for use in identifying what needs explaining and deciding on what counts as intelligible explanation.

2. The prospects of intersubjective agreement are improved if what is being considered is structured and detailed rather than monolithic. There is thus considerable scope for taxonomies of error, such as Rasmussen's, which analyse the explanatory factors involved in errors. Such taxonomies may need to include the possibility that reasons and causes are different and independently useful forms of explanation. Structured group discussions of taxonomies and parameter influences may also help to improve the quality of data obtained by subjective means.

CONCLUSION

The present argument is forcible: it is designed to show that there is no escaping from the limitations of completely objective enquiry in matters concerning accidents and errors. By so doing, it attempts to bring about an expansion of paradigms in scientific methodology. In so doing, it is hoped that new progress will be gained, and the dignity of rational enquiry will not be lost.

REFERENCES

Ions, E. (1978) *Against Behaviourism*. Oxford: Blackwell.

Rasmussen, J. (1982) Human errors. A taxonomy for describing human malfunction in industrial installations. *Journal of Occupational Accidents*, **4**, 311–33.

Rasmussen, J. (1983) Skills, rules and knowledge; signals, signs, and symbols, and other distinctions in human performance models. *IEEE Transactions on Systems, Man and Cybernetics*, **13**(3), 257–66.

Shotter, J. (1975) *Images of Man in Psychological Research*. London: Methuen.

Taylor, D. H. (1976) Accidents, risks and models of explanation. *Human Factors*, **18**, 371–80.

Taylor, D. H. (1981) The hermeneutics of accidents and safety. *Ergonomics*, **24**(6), 487–95.

New Technology and Human Error
Edited by J. Rasmussen, K. Duncan and J. Leplat
© 1987 John Wiley & Sons Ltd

26. Reasons, Causes, and Human Error

Jens Rasmussen
Risø National Laboratory

SUMMARY

The relationship between human adaptation and learning and errors is discussed, and it is argued that the errors neither can nor should be avoided. This leads to a discussion of the distinction between causes and reasons in explanations of human behaviour with reference to cognitive control mechanisms. The relationship with the 'risk-taking behaviour' of social psychologists is considered and the need for consideration of error recovery for design of error-tolerant systems is discussed.

INTRODUCTION

The circumstances to be considered in discussions of 'human errors' during interaction with complex technical systems are so complicated and varied that each case is unique in many respects. Any attempt to generalize and to describe models useful for a particular purpose, therefore, will look less acceptable if considered from another point of view. This is particularly so, because differences in emphasis in generalizations will lead to different choices of those conditions which are left implicit in formulation of concepts, and of those which are properly explained. It is thus to be expected that a treatise on the nature of human error derived from the point of view of a social psychologist as in the present case Don Taylor, and of a systems engineer as myself will lead to discussions about basic issues. Don Taylor and I have been involved in such discussions before, during, and after the meeting at Bad Homburg — discussions which have shown a need for a more careful and explicit concept analysis for the models to be understood and accepted in cross-disciplinary exchange. This has been the aim in the following sections, which also, hopefully, will show that I do not find any great difference in the underlying basic conceptions.

HUMAN ERROR AND LEARNING

The more one studies human errors, the more difficult it becomes to view them in the same way as faults in technical components, and the more they appear to be closely related to the very reason for the presence of human beings in technical systems: their ability to adapt to the peculiarities of the systems including those not foreseen by the designer. In the following, these adaptive mechanisms will be discussed with reference to the framework used to describe the cognitive control, as shown in my Figure 1 of Chapter 6.

Skill-, rule- and knowledge-based behaviour are not alternative human processes; they are categories of behavioural control which are probably all active at all times. During familiar work situations, when immediate activity is controlled by know-how and automated subroutines, the conscious mind has time left for other business, which may be to plan the future, to monitor the effects of past activities, or to speculate on private troubles. The degree to which people tend to use knowledge-based functional reasoning to monitor their activities during familiar work situations probably depends very much on their individual disposition, but the opportunity to do so certainly also depends on the design of the man–task interface.

The variation in human behaviour when control moves downwards during training and adaptation probably has important implications for man–task mismatches, which may ultimately be judged human error if not corrected in due time. In general, the only information available to the person to judge the proper limits of adaption will be occasional mismatches of behaviour and environment. In this way conscious as well as subconscious experiments are part of the adaptation mechanisms at all levels of cognitive control.

The efficiency of human interaction with the environment at the *skill-based level* is due to a high degree of fine-tuning of the sensori-motor schemata to the time–space features in the environment. Changes in the environment will often be met by an updating of the current schema by a subconscious reaction to cues or a consciously expressed intention: 'Now look, be careful, the road is icy'.

However, frequently the updating of the current schema will not take place until a mismatch has occurred, for instance when walking on to more uneven ground, adaptation of the current motor schema to the actual features of the environment may first happen after the feet have detected the mismatch by stumbling. The point here is that adaptation and fine-tuning of sensori-motor schemata basically depend upon mismatch occurrences for optimal adjustments. The proper limits for fine-tuning can only be found if surpassed once in a while.

If the optimization criteria for manual skill development are speed and smoothness of movements, optimization can only be constrained by the experience of the precision tolerance limits. This means that the distribution curve representing variability in time–space coordination is not a characteristic of the person, but reflects tolerance limits of the environment, and the 'risk sensitivity' of the individual. This feature of human behaviour has also been identified and discussed by researchers in traffic safety which is related to a high skill manual control task. It appears (Chapter 4) that beyond a certain limit, efforts to decrease accident frequency may influence the accident patterns, but not the general risk level.

Also the development of efficient rules-of-thumb and know-how at the *rule-based level* of Figure 1 Chapter 6, depends on a basic variability and experimentation to develop and adjust the proper rules and to identify the information patterns which are suitable signs to control the rule application. The initial conditions for this adaptation by a novice are either knowledge-based rational planning or a set of simplified stereotype procedures supplied by an instructor. In both cases the process of adaptation will lead to experiments, some of which are bound to end up as human errors in unfriendly work environments.

The rational process of analysis, evaluation, and planning of an informed novice will not be maintained during a familiar work situation. The use of symbolic information for rational inference will gradually be replaced by use of convenient signs which are empirically correlated with the conditions necessary for the steps in a work procedure. This information may very well be informal information, like relay clicks and mechanical noise. Such signs are, however, not reliable guides if the internal structure of the task environment changes, as it may in the case of component faults. In that situation the convenient signs may lead the person into a trap in terms of acts on wrong premises. Again, occasional experience of unacceptable adaptation may serve basic control functions in the learning mechanism.

Formal work procedures will normally be based on signs and readings which are functionally defining the required initial states, and the planning of the steps and their mutual relationships in the work sequence will be made under consideration of likely variations in the work context. During adaptation, not only the formal sign will be replaced by more convenient, informal signs, but the sequence of work elements may — consciously or subconsciously — be rearranged to have a more natural and smooth sequence, judged from the immediate, normal experience with the task. This deviation from 'working according to rules' is the hallmark of experienced people, but is bound to give experiences which, depending on the consequences, give rise to human error and the related blame after the fact.

It should be considered here that the adaptation to informal signs and rules-of-thumb is not generally the result of conscious decisions, but found as a result of the general variability of human behaviour. Adaptation can be an evolutionary process, where effective variations survive and are integrated in behaviour, whereas the unsuccessful are experienced as lapses and later avoided.

At the *knowledge-based level*, where people are trying to cope with unfamiliar situations and therefore have to base behaviour on functional analysis, evaluation, and planning, we will consider two major groups of man–task mismatches.

One group includes those cases when people have proper intentions, but fail to implement them. In such cases people may commit errors during reasoning due for instance to slips of memory, lack of knowledge, or to high workload — it may be difficult by unsupported, linear reasoning to deal with the complex causal net of the real world. It is not, however, possible to establish a complete set of preconditions to consider in practical work situations, and logically to make sure your considerations are reliable. The only reliable test will be to judge the response from the environment — and to correct yourself when unsuccessful. With the risk that you commit what later may be judged an error. Not even scientists are reliable — measurement of the atomic weights did first converge on whole numbers when theoretical considerations asked for that — and supplied the stop rule for the necessary efforts (Kuhn, 1962).

The other major category includes cases when man's acts are in good correspondence with his intention, which, however, serves a subgoal not acceptable from an ultimate task or system performance point of view. An illustrating example may be the situation when an operator in a disturbed process plant has several alternative hypotheses on the failed state which he has to test. Theoretically, the test of hypotheses could be done conceptually, but faced with the system itself, test by means of manipulations on the system will be a tempting solution. In case the hypothesis is incorrect, this act may add another disturbance to a system in an unknown state, and the result after the fact may be accusation of serious decision error.

The conclusion of this discussion is that 'errors' are basically the effect of human variability in an unfriendly environment, and that this variability is an inherent element in human adaptation. In consequence, there are no such things as 'human error' data, characterized only with reference to human functions or mechanisms. Human errors are man–task mismatch situations. Categories and frequencies found in data collection systems therefore depend on the characteristics of both human beings and task environment. These considerations relate nicely to Don Taylor's 'risk-taking' behaviour. Basically, human performance seems to be a balance between a desire to optimize skills and a willingness to accept the risk implied in exploratory acts.

REASONS AND CAUSES

The question of reasons and causes in explanation of human behaviour which Don Taylor very appropriately raises can, I think, be discussed with reference to the framework of Chapter 6.

Reasons

A *reason* can be stated as an explanation of the choice by an agent which has alternative possible responses to the state of affairs in its environment. A human being may have reasons for an act, but there may also be reasons for the actions of a machine albeit then with reference to the designer's choice — stored in the machine. I have elsewhere (Rasmussen, 1983) discussed reasons and causes in relation to proper functions and faulty performance of machines. In that context, reasons relate to explanations of a designer's choice of a particular design and its intended function, while causes represent the origin of disturbed functions. Similar use of the words may apply to the behaviour of a system user. Reasons relate to the pattern of a particular, intended behaviour chosen by a user. Conscious intentions may not be present for the individual actions, but only related to the entire activity. In very familiar situations, the entire behaviour may be data-driven, determined by the behaviour of the environment, and neither intentions nor reasons may be realized by the person — but still be used as explanations.

Reasons may refer teleologically to the intended target or goal (behaviour product) but also to process characteristics: the reason for the choice of a particular strategy among other possible ones may be to minimize cognitive load, time spent, to maximize pleasure, excitement, etc. Thus reason may refer to other levels of intent or spans of time than that related to the individual actions. A person may have a goal together with a performance criterion related to the way he likes to perform; he may have one reason for pursuing a certain end and another for chosing certain means. The resulting decision leads to an intention which will condition the organism for subconscious performance. In this case, the behaviour will be determined by the dynamic environment, i.e., be 'data-driven' so that changes of states in the environment release or 'cause' the human 'actions'. In other words, you may have reasons for an activity, and intend to follow a general plan, but the individual actions are caused by events or states in the environment.

Causes

Typically any event in a sequence can be considered the cause of a subsequent event, if they are related by virtue of a physical law, cf., causal systems, causality in common-sense explanations. A problem with causal explanations is that the physical reality is a complex network of relationships. Causal explanations are, therefore, typically related to the propagation of occasional changes through the network, in the present context, when occasional disturbances of a system lead to an unacceptable state of affairs. The cause is then pragmatically one or more abnormal events which can be controlled in the future in order to avoid repetitions or which are accepted as explanations.

Human errors are then related to an action which is a link in the causal net — or a non-action, a failure to break a link.

It is, however, difficult to define 'causes' for highly integrated interaction with a dynamic environment for both human beings and machines. We should rather talk about 'deterministic' descriptions, following Russell (1913): the normal function, even of a grandfather clock, is not 'caused' by gravity. Gravity is a determining condition. In the same way, highly coordinated human interaction with an environment, i.e., skilled patterns of movements, is not caused by the environment, but determined by it, since behaviour has the nature of a continuous flow, not a sequence of separated acts. The concept of 'cause' is rather related to common-sense characteristics of behaviour fragments and events which are rather well separated in time. In more continuous forms of behaviour, this description is typically possible for propagation of changes or aberrations from usual behaviour, i.e., when a grandfather clock stops. The 'cause' can then be found to be that the weights reached the floor, that the owner did not wind it, that he was interrupted by an urgent call, etc., depending upon the stop rule for analysis. On the other hand, the reason for the normal function is the need for a uniform movement to measure time. A reason of the owner not to wind the clock might be a wish to avoid its chiming that keeps her awake.

To sum up, 'reasons' in my vocabulary are typically used to explain human

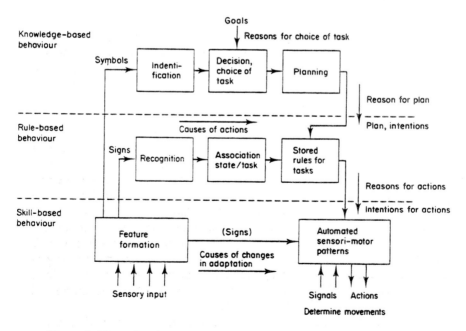

Figure 1. The role of reasons and causes in control of human behaviour

choices among alternatives during system design or, in general, choices among alternative activities in the interaction with the environment. 'Causes' explain release of events in temporal sequences related by general laws. As I understand Don Taylor, I agree with his basic position, but I do not find the distinction behaviour — cause/action — reason particularly useful. In his 'plea for reasons', he modifies his statement 'All actions are correct' by the qualification 'at least for the person at the time', which to me indicates that our divergences are at least partly of semantic nature. Furthermore, his distinction is not necessarily related to the distinction human being/machine, only to the degree of autonomy in choices among alternatives in responses. In our time of artificial intelligence, even a machine can be designed to choose among unforeseen alternatives guided by its own evaluation and general performance criteria (reasons). Hopefully, this debate will continue and serve to bridge interdisciplinary differences in concept formulations. Figure 1 shows the role of reasons and causes in control of human behaviour.

ERROR RECOVERY

If variation of human behaviour is an important ingredient of the development of smooth skills and professional know-how, and experiments on the environment are necessary for problem solving, definition of error should be related to a lack of recovery from unacceptable effects of exploratory behaviour.

Error recovery depends on observability and reversibility of the emerging unacceptable effects. Reversibility depends largely on dynamics and linearity of system properties, whereas observability depends on the properties of the man–environment interface which will be greatly influenced by the use of advanced information technology.

Error observability depends on a mismatch between the expected and the actual system response to human actions. At the level of skilled patterns of behaviour there is an adaptive man–system interaction, where the patterns of behaviour are continuously adapted to absorb variations in coordination. Only when variations exceed the limits of adaptability in the current regime and cues call for modification, is it usually referred to as an error (for instance by stumbling). Error corrections then depend on the availability of alternative control patterns, and whether the cues for activating these patterns are received before control is lost irreversibly. This means that error recovery is tightly related to specific dynamic properties of the actual interface configuration. This kind of error recovery comes into play typically only in direct 'hands-on' interaction. The behavioural consequences of this mechanism will be close to Don Taylor's 'risk-taking' behaviour.

Related to the control and coordination of a sequence of skilled routines, error recovery may be influenced by various features. The information needed for control of actions and for observation of errors may be related to different time spans and to different levels of abstraction. The information used *en route* to control activity in pursuit of an intention or goal may be totally unrelated to the intention itself. In an habitual sequence of skilled action complexes, the individual complexes are released by stereotype cues. Judgement of system responses in terms of intended outcome may require identification of functional states and predictive judgement. A model of the simultaneous control of actions and movements, and of the higher level comparison of system responses to the intended outcome is required. This problem is also discussed by James Reason referring to the hierarchical complex of plans between the basic goal or intention and the elementary control of actions.

In the present context, a major problem is the introduction of modern information technology as a communication medium between humans and machines, for instance in the form of computer controlled display systems. It goes without saying that information for control of actions will be included. It is, however, also important that information about future effects upon system performance and information about reasons necessary as reference for judgements is available for the human user to serve as basis for performance evaluation and error correction.

The basic rule for system design appears to be not to avoid human errors, but to make system response to errors reversible and observable for the users. Only when the effects of possible errors are unacceptable to the system or its environment (an example may be nuclear power), and the risk involved in the probability for lack of correction is too high, should removal of the possibility of erroneous acts be considered, as for instance by interlocks or physical barriers.

Therefore, I do *not* argue, as Don Taylor seems to understand me ('A plea for reasons', page 303), that 'we cannot live with operator variability, without being able to understand it' and 'therefore have to design physically error-proof systems'.

On the contrary, designers have to live with user variability and to aim at error-tolerant system designs, which means systems which responds in an observable and reversible way to human actions. The requirement for 'physically error-proof designs is only related to circumstances when the effects of human acts (due to, for instance, system dynamics) cannot be made reliably reversible. In such cases, the requirement for physical barriers or interlocks in order to avoid traps is both functionally and ethically feasible. Nobody would accept the design of a fifth floor balcony without a hand-rail.

REFERENCES

Kuhn, T. (1962) *The Structure of Scientific Revolution.* University of Chicago Press.

Rasmussen, J. (1983) *Skills, Rules, and Knowledge; Signals, Signs, and Symbols; and Other Distinctions in Human Performance Models.* IEEE Transactions on Systems, Man, and Cybernetics, Vol. SMC-13, No. 3.

Russel, B. (1913) On the notion of cause. *Proc. Aristotelian Society*, Vol. 13, pp. 1–25.

New Technology and Human Error
Edited by J. Rasmussen, K. Duncan and J. Leplat
© 1987 John Wiley & Sons Ltd

27. A Plea for Reasons — A Reply to Rasmussen

Donald H. Taylor
The University, Southampton
Now: Donald Taylor & Associates Ltd.

SUMMARY

A review of *philosophical types of explanation* is related to analysis of *faults* and *errors*. The contribution of *human variability* to system error is analysed into three components: executive, adaptive, and purposive. *Reason giving* is assessed as a form of *explanation* of *human errors*.

THE CONTEXT OF THIS CHAPTER

At the workshop at Bad Homburg, I argued two main theses:

1. That there are two domains of explanation concerning human affairs: behaviour/cause and action/reason. Since only the first of these can apply to machines, this could lead to confusion in explaining man–machine system functioning, especially at the interface.
2. That in considering mistakes, since it is impossible intentionally to make a mistake without subscribing to some other purpose, all voluntary actions are by definition correct, at least to the actor at the time of the action.

There are difficulties with both of these arguments: with the first because it borders on a rather complicated area of philosophy, the detailed study of which is hard to justify on technological grounds alone; and with the second because it is untrue! (at least, using the word action in a familiar sense).

The departure point for this paper is Rasmussen's workshop presentation, in which he found the first point above not particularly useful, and disagreed fundamentally with the second. The first point needs further explaining, and the second leads towards a fundamental re-examination of the role of the human operator in high-technology systems, which also needs closer scrutiny.

303

THE USES OF EXPLANATION

Of the many that there may be, I will focus on the use of explanation or understanding of human errors in *the design of safe man–machine systems*. I take this to mean that prevention of errors, (or at least of their unacceptable consequences) is the main consideration, and that explanation of past errors is of interest only in preventing future accidents by improvements in man–machine system design.

TYPES OF EXPLANATION

It is necessary to distinguish clearly between several different kinds of explanation. Clarity is most important here; quite different kinds of explanation can look much alike, and I think that confusion between them is the major source of difficulty in the field of human errors. I have found a book by a namesake (Taylor, 1970) most helpful in explaining the different types of explanation.

In brief, Taylor (op. cit.) sets out four kinds of explanation:

1. *Scientific explanation*. This is such as to show why events have to happen in particular ways, by appealing to laws of nature. We probably regard this as the most powerful form of explanation, but I have argued that we need to go beyond it in the study of errors and accidents (Taylor, 1976).

2. *'What explanations'*. These are such as to explain what some thing or event is: a redescription in some other terms. The redescription may be in scientific terms (e.g., to describe some state transitions as part of a Markov process), or may concern practical decisions (e.g., we have an unacceptable plant state, and the operators are trying to correct it), or may be somewhere in between.

3. *Mental-state explanations*. If mental means non-physical, there cannot be mental causes of physical events. Nor are there any bits of behaviour that invariably accompany a mental state, which would enable it to be identified with certainty. Taylor concludes that mental states often refer to patterns of behaviour, and thus by redescribing the patterns are forms of 'what explanation'. It seems to me that much of cognitive psychology employs explanation of this type, using scientifically compatible terms as much as possible.

4. *Reason-giving explanations*. There are two basic components in a reason-giving explanation:
   (a)   a belief about facts;
   (b)   a value system containing wants, purposes, obligations, or moral principles.

A person may give 'his reason' for his action, which if given sincerely cannot be challenged as inaccurate, however false his beliefs or bizarre his values. However, for 'his reason' to constitute 'a reason' in anyone else's estimation, his value system must to some extent overlap with one's own. Reasons cannot be used as explanations unless there is sincerity, for which of course there is no absolute test. It is also worth noting that when we use the phrase '*the* reason (why x happened)' we are often suggesting a scientific explanation, and not a reason-giving one at all.

Thus prepared, and using Rasmussen's analyses of error as a base, I would now want to address the same points of view as expressed in my 'pre-workshop' paper, namely that skill in bringing about trustworthy (sincere) communication between people is essential if we are to understand and be able to control errors in man–machine systems, and that the need to rely on other models of explanation than the familiar scientific one will grow, rather than fade away, as technology advances.

FAULTS AND ERRORS

Rasmussen defines faults and errors as 'causes of unfulfilled system purposes'. Although this definition could be taken in a purely mechanistic sense (e.g., the purpose of this rocket is to shoot red flares into the sky, but an ingredient was omitted, and it failed to ignite), I think that he means not that the *system* has purposes, but that its designers and users do. He links faults and errors not only to purposes, but to judgements made about them, normal or accept-able standards, requirements, etc., making up a value-system to which people can debate and subscribe to. However, I think I detect an assumption that there is one superior purpose (system output perhaps) against which all others (subgoals, etc.) should be judged. If this were logically true, then the system purpose may as well be taken in a mechanistic sense, because there can ultimately be no debate about what is correct and what is not.

The process of fault explanation therefore begins with a mismatch to a value-system, and proceeds backwards along a causal chain until conditions for stopping are met: usually that a 'familiar and therefore reasonable' expla-nation can be given for conditions at that point in the chain, and that something can be done to alter them. Restating this to conform with the above models of explanation, one is trying to assert that given the conditions at that point in the chain, and the relevant natural laws, the faulty output is (scientifically) explained, and that if a particular change could be made to certain of the conditions, a correct output would occur, and this also (given the relevant natural laws) would be scientifically explained. If the stop point happens to be a human operator, it is very unlikely that any relevant natural laws are known, and the assertion therefore fails (the path disappears).

Assuming that further back in the chain conditions appear to be normal, this leaves us with a very unpalatable conclusion: that the operator is the 'cause' of the error, but that no causal explanation can be given! The classical method of fault diagnosis therefore cannot be relied upon in man–machine systems.

HUMAN VARIABILITY

Assuming next that all of the non-human parts of a man–machine system can be 'cleaned up' by classical fault diagnosis, leaving only human errors, Rasmussen considers the latter as man–task misfits. Given from the preceding argument that errors are misfits between output and a value-system, is this a change in the definition of error? I think not, *given that we can regard the 'task' as the implementation of a value-system*. I believe that this is implicit in the meaning of the word task. It follows that there are *three* ways in which human variability can contribute to system error:

1. System behaviour and the operator's value-system remaining constant, operator behaviour, despite his best efforts, is too variable to avoid mismatch.
2. The operator's value-system and his ability to implement it remaining constant, his adaptability is insufficient to match changes in system behaviour.
3. System behaviour and the operator's abilities remaining within acceptable limits, the operator adopts a value-system which conflicts with system purposes, and he causes a mismatch with the latter.

These three aspects of variability can now be mapped on to the types of explanation detailed above. We cannot as yet rely too much on formal scientific explanation of human variability, because we do not know of relevant universal laws governing it. Type 1 variability (above) is associated mainly with the skill-based level of operation, for which we usually adopt mental-state explanations. Thus we find discussions of schemata, blobs-and-boards, etc., along with less well-modelled concepts of mental load, fatigue, and stress. All of these, according to Taylor's argument, are 'what explanations', primarily based on observed patterns of behaviour.

Type 2 variability (system change) of course stems from deterministic causes; the variability itself can therefore in principle be explained scientifically. However, from the point of view of the operator in real time, what is needed is a 'what explanation': simply 'what is happening'. Knowing this may help the operator to make appropriate choices for action. A 'what explanation' will afford a powerful model for beliefs about facts, therefore the operator will later be able to give his reasons for acting as he did. Because under these Type 2 assumptions we are not questioning the operator's value-system, his reasons will be a report of his beliefs about the system state, and his deliberations on them.

Type 3 variability (variability of purpose) does not formally enter Rasmussen's account, but is implied in several parts of his discussion. By pointing out the need for 'operator experiments' to optimize performance, he refers to a 'system sub-purpose' which may result in failure to meet the main system purpose, which is nevertheless justifiable. An overall system purpose may consist of a particular mix of mutually incompatible subsystem purposes, the optimality of which is viewed differently by different people in the system. Finally, individuals may use the system for their own private purposes (this does not have to mean heinous misuse of plant; it could simply be for example that an operator wants to demonstrate his mastery of the control system in order to gain recognition or promotion). Only reason-giving explanations will serve here, because the variables are value-systems.

Rasmussen's overall responses to problems of Type 1 and Type 2 variability are the classical ones of feedback, observability, and reversibility. If these are successful, they remove the need for explanatory models of error (and for this discussion!) by widening the definitions of acceptable system behaviour within which 'errors' will not have harmful consequences. (The implications of risk will not have harmful consequences. (The implications of risk homoeostasis theory may well need to be considered here.) Type 3 variability, however, could be so wide and intangible that the only solution seems to be to design systems that will accommodate an indefinite number of purposes without inconsistency. Even if this were possible, it would leave unanswered the questions of optimization of function, and of the notorious instrumentality of man in finding new purposes for multipurpose systems. The study of purposes (i.e., human value-systems), and hence of reason-giving explanations, is in my view inescapable.

SKILLS, RULES, AND KNOWLEDGE

Rasmussen explained at Bad Homburg that his skill–rule–knowledge diagram could be analysed two-dimensionally, with causal chains proceeding from left to right along the x-axis, and choices (implying reasons) needing to be made in the vertical direction. I would like to expand on this interpretation in terms of the types of explanation listed above.

The horizontal movement, or unfolding of temporal sequences, is explainable causally (scientifically) where physical interactions are involved. The three levels are themselves classic examples of 'what explanations' (and Reason's slips, where they fit in at the bottom right, seem to be another). The question of movement between levels (discrimination or feature formation) is more complex. It seems to depend upon whether or not the operator makes a deliberate choice. If he does, he will be in a position to give reasons by way of explanation. However, he may not know why he made a particular choice, or perhaps even that he made one, or further still that any possibility for choice existed, in which cases he will be unable to give his reasons. If he does not, we have to regard discrimination as a rather obscure mental process, and seek a 'what explanation' for it. At the knowledge level, reason giving would be the expected form of explanation: it would be hard to believe in a consistently good problem-solver who could not analyse his reasons for what he did when solving problems.

It is perhaps this latter thought that leads Rasmussen to divide reasons and causes by saying that reasons explain the structure of a system and its normal function, and that causes represent the origin of disturbances. It seems necessary to add that reasons also may explain what operators do to an abnormally-functioning system in order to correct it. Thus, to put the argument rather bluntly, it is not only designers who have reasons: operators do as well, and ultimately it is a question of whether we can allow the 'system liveware' this degree of autonomy.

I conclude, rather harshly perhaps, that Rasmussen feels that we cannot, or at least that if we have to live with this much 'operator variability' without being able to understand it, then we must design systems that are physically error-proof. In that case it will not matter what the operators' reasons are, or whether or not they have them, or even whether they are beings who are able to have them. This (if true) is a poor future for man in man–machine systems, and one which I find difficult personally to support or believe in. I might be forced to admit that where the potential harm from system malfunction includes major disasters, it is no place to argue about fundamental freedoms and the quality of operators' working lives, but not all new-technology developments are catastrophically risky, and my own preference would be for a broader approach where smaller risks are concerned. It seems possible that error research will take its cue mainly from the industries in which the costs of potential errors are highest, and yield strategies which will not be appropriate in all circumstances. We should perhaps not allow the technical difficulties in dealing with reason-giving explanation to avoid designing industrial environments where they are likely to be important; much could be lost by such an approach.

THE TECHNOLOGY OF REASON GIVING

For a person to be able to give a reason for some choice (3) that he makes, he must have two things:

1. A set of beliefs about the state of the system (about data or facts).
2. A value-system containing purposes, obligations, goals, wants, or moral principles.

He must be able to reason that, given his beliefs (1) his choice (3) will help to implement his value-system (2). If he reports *sincerely* on both (1) and (2), he is giving an explanation of why he did (3).

The practical difficulties involved in (1) are those of information processing and presentation. The technical goal is to collect and present relevant information such that any skilled and reasonable person would arrive at the same set of (correct) beliefs about the system as any other; a difficult goal perhaps, but attainable in principle. However, the value-system (2) is more difficult to fathom: it will consist in practice of a complex mixture of organizational goals (often very unclearly stated), obligations to obey instructions, seldom-observed rules, social obligations to fellow-workers, personal wants and ambitions, etc. In traditional work culture, what distinguished a 'worker' from a 'manager' was that the latter was used to making choices and giving explanations of them in terms of reasons, while the former was not expected to. As Bainbridge pointed out, the high-technology worker in automated systems is *there* to take over, diagnose, problem-solve, etc., in other words to have reasons for making choices, and a very ambiguous situation develops if these are systematically ignored or disallowed. Reason giving, as a way of communicating to others what is happening, is a skill in itself. Sincerity, humility, and objectivity (the main components of the skill) do not burst forth easily from all of us; some practice and encouragement may be needed!

There are also difficulties in accepting reasons as explanations: in agreeing that a person giving 'his reason' for what he did has in our opinion 'a reason' for having done it. We may suspect deception, either that the person knowing 'his reason' is falsely giving another in the hope that it will be accepted, or that he does not know why he acted and is trying to persuade us that he does. We may not understand (let alone agree with) the value-system on which the reason is based. We may not know how to judge sincerity, how to create conditions under which it is likely to be present, nor how to convince other people that we have recognized it. However, we must all possess these skills informally, otherwise we could not be friends or form trusting relationships with anybody. Perhaps it is more a matter of professionalizing these skills and learning to create organizational climates in which they are some use, rather than starting a whole new technology.

The uses of reason-giving explanations are quite easy to list, and quite relevant to man–machine systems. Since reason giving requires a person to reveal his beliefs and evaluative views:

1. If we agree about evaluative views (e.g., about plant purposes and priorities), a person may be giving reasons for actions (e.g., by citing facts) seek to convince us of action priorities, or that a particular *design strategy* is correct.
2. A person may seek to justify his actions (i.e., explain his choices) among

those who hold similar beliefs/values. If the actions were wrong, he may hope to do this by persuading others that his aims were reasonable, or that his *intentions* were good.

3. If there are differences about what is right (which cannot be settled empirically), by explaining his actions a person may hope to show that his *action priorities* are right, (e.g., in conflicts between safety and productive efficiency, safety and personal convenience).
4. Giving reasons may reveal something of a person, perhaps the level on which he thinks it right to function (e.g., Rasmussen's levels), perhaps to show others how to perform a task well, what to look out for, how to make choices based on sound beliefs, what his own value-system is, i.e., what his *operating strategy* is.

If we were able to understand these things about plant operators, and communicate our understanding to and from them, industrial life might become much safer. Wilpert and Kjellén both referred to studies where seemingly much had been achieved in that direction, and some features of organization development (such as quality circles) seem to offer further opportunities. Verbal protocol techniques may offer a way into this area, if attention is paid to issues of sincerity and trust, but the conceptual and practical difficulties may still be quite large, as Brehmer and Dörner have both indicated.

However, none of the above uses of reason-giving explanations is particularly bizarre or unbelievable; they are all in everyone's experience. What does seem strange and unfamiliar is to assemble them into a *technology*, to develop systematic skills out of what we know about how to be human, and to take these skills out into the work place among strangers, to some common purpose. Technology is 'the science of the industrial arts': perhaps there is an art in being human . . .

REFERENCES

Taylor, D. H. (1976) Accidents, risks, and models of explanation. *Human Factors*, **18**, 371–80.

Taylor, D. M. (1970) *Explanation and Meaning*. Cambridge: Cambridge University Press.

New Technology and Human Error
Edited by J. Rasmussen, K. Duncan and J. Leplat
© 1987 John Wiley & Sons Ltd

28. Some Observations on Error Analysis

Jacques Leplat
École Pratique des Hautes Études — Paris

SUMMARY

Nature of the genesis of diagram: the designation of chaining link; the normal chain and the goal; goal and motive of the action. The explanation of errors: two types of errors, what is a redefined or actual task? Causes, errors, and types of tasks.

INTRODUCTION

Analysis of the genesis of error, as of accidents, raises difficult theoretical problems. It leads us to ask especially about the nature of the links between the events preceding the error or accident and about the justification of these links. It also poses the problem of the type of explanation: by reasons, by causes. It is to both these types of questions that the following brief observations will be addressed.

NATURE OF THE GENESIS DIAGRAM

A method has been described (see above) for organizing and presenting the events which enter into error or accident genesis. The application of this method, as the interpretation of the diagram to which it is a guide, raises problems which make apparent the role of the mental representations of the analyst and the nature of the justifications which permit the establishment of links between the events in question.

The designation of the chaining link (coded by '→')

The relations represented in the diagram are based on knowledge of the work; consequently for the same accident, the diagrams can be different if the knowledge of the analysts who draw them differ, if these analysts have different mental representation of the system's functioning.

It will first be noted that links are justified by knowledge or rules of different types: physical (example 'rain → wet ground'), electrical (example

311

'no current → no light'), organizational (example 'worn tool → presence at the tool store'). It will then be observed that the same event (not peculiar to new technology!) can give rise to different types of links according to the mental representation the analyst has of the production of this event. Several types of rules being sometimes possible, the analyst will remember those which agree with his mental model of the situation. Here are three rules which can be invoked to explain the event 'X sweeps'. According to the rule with which the analyst agrees, different events will appear in the diagram.

1. Rule 1: 'If floor dusty, the operator must sweep it' (dusty floor → X sweeps).
2. Rule 2: 'When the supervisor is present, X is always occupied' (supervisor present → X sweeps).
3. Rule 3: 'When driving machine breaks down, find other work' (breakdown of machine → X sweeps).

It can happen that the terminal event is overdetermined, i.e., explained conjointly by two or more rules. To find the relevant rule(s) obliges one to analyse the work situation precisely.

The 'normal chain' and the goal

From any point of the accident chaining it is possible to represent the chain of events leading to a successful result. This 'normal' chain of events can be more or less long, and represents the events which lead to the goal of the operator, those which have not been achieved. Deviation from desired goals represent a *loss of control*: the subject was not able to reach his goal (Figure 1).

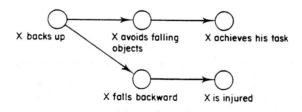

Figure 1. Accidental and normal chain with the same origin

Goal and motive of the action

When the action is a human one, expressions with the words 'want', 'must' are often (wrongly, as only facts must appear on the diagram) placed on the diagram. For example, e.g., 'X wants to get away', 'X must repair the damage'.

We can identify two ways in which these words are used (Figure 2):

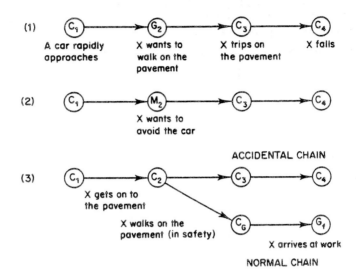

Figure 2. Chain of events expressing goal (1), motive (2), and normal chain of events (3).
C_1: event; G_2: representation of the goal; M_2: motive; C_G: realized goal; G_f: final goal

1. The formulation refers to the goal of the action, here, to walk on the pavement. We could represent the successful outcome of the action with the goal to be reached (C_G) and the deviation from this with the resulting outcome (C_4: X falls). There exists a sequence of more and more distant goals (to walk on the pavement, to go to work, etc.).
2. The formulation indicates the *motive* of the action, what stimulates the activity: to avoid the car, which may conceivably be achieved through different goals (go towards the other pavement, walk beside the pavement, etc.). It is this motive that gives meaning to the subject's action: it urges him to react and to achieve his goals.

To express the goal or the motive may be explained by the desire to justify the relation '→'. If they are not expressed, the relations '→' (here $C_1 \rightarrow C_3$) could be ambiguous (one can imagine various goals, various motives). That is, different mechanisms may underline the same relation when there is no clarifying information.

Explanation by *motive* and explanation by *goal* may operate together.

They should not appear in the diagram, however, since that should include only observable facts, but *they must be taken into consideration in the interpretation*.

Regrouping makes the diagram more explicit

The diagram can be condensed or developed to accord with more or less fine-grained 'event units'. So, by developing it, it is possible to make an event more explicit. To introduce intermediate events is a means of revealing the mechanism of accident and error production. A similar problem is discussed by Clancy (1983) with the definition of rules in an expert system.

THE EXPLANATIONS OF ERRORS

One could throw a little light on this debate about causes and reasons by introducing the distinction between 'prescribed task' or 'task for experts', and 'actual task' or 'operator's task'. 'Expert' refers here to the person who knows perfectly the task to be carried out. The expert can be the designer or the supervisor. This distinction has often been used under various different names (on this point see Leplat and Hoc, 1983). Hackman (1969) used the term (redefined task for actual task), implying that the operator modifies the task when he internalizes its goal and conditions of performance. He does not, for example, work at the same tolerance level as prescribed, nor does he control all that is asked of him.

Two types of errors

With reference to Figure 3, two types of error are defined.

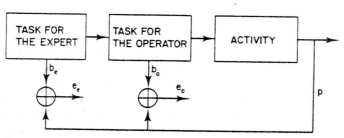

Figure 3. The two types of error; b_e and e_e: goal and error for the expert; b_o and e_o: goal and error for the operator; p: performance

1. Error for the expert: the difference between goal set by the expert, the prescribed goal, and the actual performance, $b_e - p = e_e$

2. Error for the operator: the difference between the goal set by the operator, the redefined goal, and the performance, $b_o - p = e_o$

The following cases may occur if the prescribed goal and the 'redefined' goal do not coincide.

1. $p = b_o$, b_o/b_e: error for the expert but correct response for the subject (corresponds to a mistake: the operator did not do what the expert would have done).
2. p/b_o: the operator has not achieved the goal that he was aiming for. This error is also generally an error for the expert (corresponds to a slip: the operator does not do what he wanted to do).

The operator may not achieve his desired goal for various reasons. Reason has explained some of these using the notion of schema. However, the operator may not achieve the desired goal also because he lacks the necessary skills (the driver could not control the skid because he had never learnt to drive on certain roads). It seems that in this case, contrary to what Taylor has said, the driver can give reasons for his error.

What is a redefined or actual task?

The problem posed by such a distinction is to know how to determine the real or redefined task, in other words the task really carried out by the operator. This task is composed of the goal plus the conditions that the operator has really taken into consideration. These may be identified through an analysis of the activity. Just like the prescribed task, or task for the expert, the actual or real task, or task for the operator, can be described in more or less detail, with the implicit part varying in proportion. We have examined in greater detail elsewhere the problems confronted in the characterization of this 'real task' (Leplat and Hoc, 1983). In as much as the goals and the conditions taken into consideration by the operator may be made explicit, the actual task lies in the domain of objective analysis and its description is of the same order as that of the prescribed task. However, the actual task also represents the goal and the conditions of performance internalized by the subject and thus, in this sense it lies in the domain of subjective analysis. The actual task may also be considered as the model — internalized and externalized — of the activity. This model can be checked by setting what it predicts against what is observed during the activity. We have shown (Leplat and Hoc, 1983) how this actual or real task could be elaborated by the analyst by a progressive adjusting of a model of the activity (in the case of fault finding).

Causes, reasons, and types of tasks

In a conceptualization such as this what happens to explanation by causes and explanation by reasons? We would suggest that in as much as the actual task is considered from an objective point of view (in other words, by its externalization), the conditions of execution may be considered as so many causes, since they are by definition taken into consideration by the operator and therefore causally affect his activity. When we consider the mechanism whereby the task is internalized and becomes the actual subjective task, it is reasons that we are mainly interested in. The question is then asked as to why it is such a goal or such conditions that have been internalized and what is the origin of the possible differences between the prescribed task and the actual or redefined task. Looking for an answer to this question leads inevitably to a consideration of the operator's more general goals and motives.

With the process of internalization of the task put forward here, we have a means of conceiving the direct relations existing between explanations by causes and explanations by reasons. These two types of explanation of human activity would be mutually complementary.

This brief look at the problem does not reply directly to all the questions raised by Taylor and Rasmussen, but rather suggests a perspective which could be used to examine them.

REFERENCES

Clancey, W. J. (1983) The espitemology of rule-based expert system — a framework for explanation. *Artificial Intelligence*, **20**(3), 215–52.

Hackman, J. R. (1969) Towards understanding the role of tasks in behavioral research. *Acta Psychologica*, **31**, 97–128.

Leplat, J., and Hoc, J. M. (1983) Tâche et activité dans l'analyse psychologique des situations. *Cahiers de Psychologie Cognitive*, **3**(1), 35–48.

New Technology and Human Error
Edited by J. Rasmussen, K. Duncan and J. Leplat
© 1987 John Wiley & Sons Ltd

Part 8: Review of Discussions

INTRODUCTION

In this part we begin to take stock. Here, Lucas and Patrick take up and collate arguments about new technology and human error which arose in the discussion sessions. Their accounts are personal and lay no claim to be definitive. Rather, their reports are selective — in the nature of things they could not be exhaustive — and attempt to convey the flavour of the debate by quoting from the transcripts. Not surprisingly they often deal with related arguments and occasionally overlap.

Links between the reports are notable when touching on issues which the participants found significant or problematic. There were instances, as Lucas reports, on incompatible mental models of the same process held by different people, as well as inconsistent mental models of a system apparently held by the same individual. Some, but not all of these accounts by participants must be qualified to the extent that they depend on verbal report. As will be seen in the report by Patrick, there was a wide ranging discussion of both the reliability and value of verbal report, especially of how protocol may be subjected to scrutiny and independent check. The discussion raised fundamental issues of access, of the status of the data, and about the inference of a mental model.

The feasibility of checking mental models and their importance to an understanding of human error were reported by participants, for example, noting control panel instruments consulted by operators, and social interactions with other members of the working team. The evidence presented for major differences in the way a system may be represented, leads to both theoretical and methodological problems. Representation of the task is of the essence in adequate simulation, a technique which is necessarily widely used for studying human error. But when the prescribed procedures for coping with emergencies clearly differ from the procedures adopted by operators, as was reported, which if either of these should be the basis of simulation?

The same observation of discrepancies between that which is stipulated and that which is practised, led to a theoretical debate on differing representational logics. Of particular interest, not least to the English delegates, was an extension of the Piagetian notion of successive stages of understanding or expertise, attributed to the influential work of Vermersch (e.g., Vermersch, 1979).

It would be wrong to overemphasize the distinction between theory and method, indeed there was no clear-cut separation between the two in the discussions which took place, and many of the contributions would be inappropriately classified as one or the other. For example, the careful observation of changes in performance and report over time which case studies make possible, may more readily capture a dynamic feature of human error genesis which other approaches might miss. There were many pleas to combine methods, in particular to combine clinical and data analysis methods to disentangle the various factors contributing to human error. Classical experimental design was seen as inappropriate, especially the 'laboratory task' which several participants would abandon in favour of more realistic problems and situations. Both Lucas and Patrick report this debate. So for the future, we need developments in task analysis rather than in experimental design. Certainly, an old problem remains: the necessity to design tasks which are amenable to experimental study in laboratory conditions and, at the same time, capture crucial demands of industrial operations. It is the problem of simulation, writ large.

The sessions devoted to the difficult questions of taxonomy and the theoretical underpinnings of classifications, saw some of the more lively and sustained arguments. These are among the more difficult questions, precisely because to classify data in any non-trivial way is to subscribe to a theoretical argument, if only implicitly. That adequate taxonomies of human error will necessarily be multifaceted eventually emerged as common ground. The workability of the distinction between intention and understanding was debated at length and with some scepticism, although it accords quite well with everyday experience and observation, as well as with more systematic investigations. In the course of this discussion, the important point was made that a social theory, if it were to make sense, would probably avoid the thorny question of individual intention. The point is important because it raises the question of different levels of theory which may be appropriate when considering human error. Whether such higher order theories would eventually yield to the scalpel of reductionism is another matter.

There may have been more agreement about ideas and theoretical notions than was immediately apparent. In any event it would have been surprising, not to say disturbing, if a group of scientists had concentrated on their points of agreement. As Lucas points out earlier distinctions between knowledge-based and rule-based behaviour maps quite well on to the idea of the different levels of representation of the same system or different representational logics.

Finally (Chapter 32) Patrick makes three points which were made by many participants in different ways: the rapid pace of technological change; the lack of study of errors *in situ*, typically because of costs and hazard; and the problems of comparing rare, possibly catastrophic errors, quite apart from their sheer infrequency. It is a daunting prospect. On the positive side it may be possible to communicate state of the art technique to designers, managers and others, but human factors specialists have not excelled in this respect in the past — in many cases through no fault of their own, at least as several participants saw the current situation. If this problem is not solved then human factors specialists will continue to function, with decreasing effectiveness after the fact, that is to say tinkering with human factors' problems built into systems at the design stage.

REFERENCE

Vermersch, P. (1979) Peut-on utiliser les données de la psychologie génétique pour analyser le fonctionnement cognitif des adultes? *Cahiers de Psychologie*, 22, 59–74.

New Technology and Human Error
Edited by J. Rasmussen, K. Duncan and J. Leplat
© 1987 John Wiley & Sons Ltd

29. Mental Models and New Technology

Deborah A. Lucas
University of Lancaster
Now: Human Reliability Associates Ltd.

SUMMARY

This chapter reviews discussions concerning the relevance of 'mental models' to the study of human error in relation to new technology. The problems of studying such models are noted. The use of Piaget's notion of 'stages' and Rasmussen's (1982) model of human performance is discussed.

'In interacting with the environment, with others and with the artifacts of technology, people form internal, mental models of themselves and of the things with which they are interacting. These models provide predictive and explanatory power for understanding the interaction' (Norman, 1983, p. 7).

The issue of the effect of mental models on the work situation was raised on a number of occasions during the workship. The aim of this section is to present those practical and conceptual ideas which were highlighted during these discussions.

The study of mental models is novel for both the areas of traditional human factors and academic cognitive psychology. Cognitive psychology has generally focused on highly controlled laboratory tasks and has avoided, for the most part, the problem of describing real-task domains. Traditionally, human factors research has focused on behaviour and has steered away from attempting to conceptualize the causes and effects of this behaviour. However, with the introduction of new technology (in particular the digital computer) into process control systems, the study of the operators' model of the system he is controlling has become important (see Rasmussen, 1980). Carroll (1984) points out that the development of mental model theories is a major area of research in current software human factors' research and is also likely to be an important factor in future software design.

Some observations on mental models have been made by Norman (1983). In particular he has distinguished between four different ideas: the target system, the conceptual model of the target system, the user's mental model of the system, and the scientist's conceptualization of that system. The target

321

system is that which is being used or learnt by the user. The conceptual model is that invented to provide an accurate, consistent, and complete model of the target system. The user's mental model is a functional but not necessarily (or usually) a technically accurate representation of the target system. At the workshop the discussion of mental models centred around the representations of the user or operator of the system in contrast with the model of the 'expert' who designed the system.

Herry reported an investigation into the operator's use of prescribed instructions when process failures occurred in an automated industrial process. Her results highlighted the differences between the mental representations of the industrial process by the 'expert' who devised the prescriptions and the operator who had to apply them. In the ensuing discussion it was emphasized that different cognitive models of a system may be ideally suited to different tasks, or even to the same task. It is not possible to maintain that one type of representation of the target system is, in some respect, 'better' than another. The operator's model derives from his familiarity with the usual operation of the process and is ideally suited to allow diagnoses of the situations he might encounter to be made easily, and often very quickly. The expert's knowledge, on the other hand, is more suited for circumstances where the knowledge of first principles is needed and where important decisions need not be made very quickly. This is an important point since it is usually implicitly assumed that the goal of the operator is to achieve a completely consistent and accurate model of the target system (i.e., he or she should eventually have the same model as the designer of the system). In relation to this point, Carroll (1984) notes that multiple mental models may coexist within the same person. For instance, a person who both designed and later uses a system may develop two different representations of the system.

A rather different point was made by de Keyser who noted that it was possible for operators to hold two *contradictory* models of the process. This did not seem to constitute a problem for the person. 'In the past year we have been looking at the mental representation of the operator . . . One thing we find in our research is that, in the mental images of the operator, it is possible to have many contradictions and it doesn't matter for the operator.'

Norman (1983) mentioned this feature of mental models. He concluded, from his observations of the mental models of people using a variety of technological devices, that such representations are 'surprisingly meager, imprecisely specified, and full of inconsistencies, gaps and idiosyncratic quirks' (p. 8). For Herry and de Keyser, there was a notable similarity between this aspect of the user's mental models in industrial situations and Piaget's observations on children's knowledge. Piaget's theoretical ideas are used as a basic conceptual framework by both Herry and de Keyser in their own research.

One advantage of using developmental notions of 'stage' in the study of a user's mental models is that it is possible to capture the idea that models differ in sophistication as people learn to use a system. Such an approach is in contrast to the mechanistic analytical frameworks which have generally been used. Here researchers have tried to define a conceptual device whose simulated function is imputed to the user (see, for example, DuBoulay *et al.*, 1981; Carroll and Thomas, 1982; Young, 1983). The notion of using developmental theory as a framework for studying man–computer interaction is also discussed by Whiteside and Wixon (1984).

The use of developmental theory in this context raised a number of issues during the discussion at the workshop. In particular, questions were put concerning how it is possible for users to move between different types of representation of a target system and how different mental models are acquired. One idea proposed was that the pressure of time may prevent an operator moving towards an expert's representation of the system. However, there was a general agreement that this time factor was too limited an explanation for such a shift.

Much of the discussion centred on whether it was possible to train a person to operate at a given cognitive level. Is there an invariance of stages of mental representation of a target system such that, for instance, a person only becomes an expert when he/she has passed through various operator representations of the target system? If this were the case then there would be obvious implications for the training of personnel in industrial situations. In particular, such a view would imply that experts in industrial systems could not be taught through university courses but would have to start as apprentices and gradually progress to being design engineers. Duncan took up this point:

> There is an assumption that somewhere in the universities or technical schools we know how to start at the top level without bothering about the lower order stages. . . . From a Piagetian position, the necessity of an invariance, or an almost invariant sequence, of stages through which it is necessary to pass makes it implausible to suggest that you can start to produce an expert from a university course in chemical engineering.

Reason suggested that the theoretical ideas of Karmiloff-Smith (see for example Karmiloff-Smith, 1979, 1984) would be very relevant to the theoretical notions of Herry and de Keyser. This model might also shed light on how switching between different models might occur. Karmiloff-Smith has been trying to develop a theory of the processes by which children grapple with new problems. Her research focuses on the general issue of the representational systems which mediate children's problem solving. In her view the change in children's development in solving problems comes from a constant motivation for *control* over both the external world and one's own internal model of the problem. Her model shows how such control is gradually gained and how children who have been successful on a task go on to try to understand why certain procedures are successful.

The discussion at the workshop also highlighted another potentially very relevant theoretical model. Rasmussen (this volume) differentiates between knowledge-based, rule-based, and skill-based behaviour. This classification appears to map well on to the different types of mental representations of the target system which were noted. Using this scheme, the 'expert' would be employing knowledge-based behaviour while the 'operator' would be using rule-based behaviour. One question raised was whether the work situation should be designed so that an operator can make the mental shift to knowledge-based behaviour in order to understand situations he or she is not familiar with or whether there should be two types of user. Rasmussen put the point clearly:

> The discussion is should you do what you can to make it possible for the data operator to go into the knowledge base to apply general rules? Thus it would be possible for the same person to switch between very effective rule-based behaviour and thinking on basic laws and first principles. Or should you accept that there are two different ways of thinking and devise or have one equipment operator with one kind of presentation and another system manager with his kind of presentation matching these two different kinds of work?

Duncan pointed out that if the latter were the case then the whole question of who is the 'expert' would be open to debate. If a graduate engineer cannot actually operate a plant then who is the 'expert'?

One practical question concerns how it is possible to ascertain the nature of a particular mental model. It has been pointed out (Norman, 1983) that different representations of a system may give rise to the same functional outcome. This implies that the observation of the operator's behaviour is not an adequate technique to establish the nature of mental models. One commonly used method is to obtain a verbal protocol from operators. There are, however, a number of problems with such a method (see Chapter 30).

Rasmussen pointed out that the different ways of representing the information held by the expert and the operator may be compared to the distinction between 'procedural' and 'declarative' knowledge. This distinction between 'knowing that' (or declarative knowledge) and 'knowing how' (or procedural knowledge) is widely used in modern cognitive psychology. In particular, while the distinction is not absolute, most declarative knowledge can be expressed verbally while much procedural knowledge cannot. One might expect that the expert would be able to verbalize his model while the operator might only be consciously aware of fragments of his model of the target system. It is clear that the data from verbal protocols need to be validated from other information sources. De Keyser pointed out some such additional sources including making observations of the operator's use of information presented in displays and the use of social communication. In her outline of the directions for future research she also suggested that the influence of the work organization on mental models of the operators should be investigated.

REFERENCES

Carroll, J. M., and Thomas, J. C. (1982) Metaphor and the cognitive representation of computing systems. *IEEE Transactions on Systems, Man and Cybernetics*, SMC-12, 107–16.

Carroll, J. M. (1984) Mental models and software human factors: An overview. IBM Research Report.

DuBoulay, B., O'Shea, T., and Monk, J. (1981) The black box inside the glass box: Presenting computing concepts to novices. *International Journal of Man–Machine Studies*, 14, 237–49.

Karmiloff-Smith, A. (1979) Micro- and macrodevelopmental changes in language acquisition and other representational systems. *Cognitive Science*, 3, 91–118.

Karmiloff-Smith, A. (1984) Children's problem solving. In: Lamb and Brown (Eds), *Advances in Developmental Psychology*, Vol. III. Hillsdale, NJ: Erlbaum.

Norman, D. A. (1983) Some observations on mental models. In: D. Gentner and A. Stevens (Eds), *Mental Models*. Hillsdale, NJ: Erlbaum.

Rasmussen, J. (1980) The human as a systems component. In: H. T. Smith and T. R. G. Green (Eds), *Human Interaction With Computers*. London: Academic Press.

Whiteside, J., and Wixon, D. (1984) Developmental theory as a framework for studying human–computer interaction. In: H. R. Hartson (Ed.), *Advances in Human–Computer Interaction*. Norwood, NJ: Ablex.

Young, R. M. (1983) Surrogates and mappings: Two kinds of conceptual models for interactive devices. In: D. Gentner and A. Stevens (Eds), *Mental Models*. Hillsdale, NJ: Erlbaum.

New Technology and Human Error
Edited by J. Rasmussen, K. Duncan and J. Leplat
© 1987 John Wiley & Sons Ltd

30. Methodological Issues

J. Patrick
University of Wales Institute of Science and Technology

SUMMARY

This chapter discusses methodological issues in the study of human error including those concerning definition, verbal report, case study, experimental methodology, simulation, and accident analysis.

INTRODUCTION

There are at least three general aspects of human error and new technology which increase methodological difficulties for research in this area. Firstly the rate of change of technology, in for example man–machine interfaces, makes it difficult for the necessary scientific interventions, including analysis of the problem, collecting evidence and implementing solutions, to be completed in time. Solutions which do emerge from research may be rapidly outdated or inappropriate as further technological advances occur. The problem is exacerbated by the fact that much human factors' expertise is a reaction to a problem state, rather than a planned research programme at the design stage of a new system.

A second difficulty is intrinsic to this field of study. The primary aim of any system is to minimize error. How then is the phenomenon of human error to be studied, especially in real situations? Furthermore, the study of human error is particularly important in those potentially hazardous industrial or military contexts where the costs of human error are likely to be high and the consequences unacceptable. In the search for data, researchers have used various types of simulation to investigate human error tendencies under various conditions. This research strategy is, however, more difficult to implement than may at first appear. A simulation (or simulator) provides a *representation* of the *task* found in the real situation and, therefore, the investigator has to decide which features of the real situation should be represented in the simulation and which ones can be omitted. To make such a decision it is necessary to know when the human error phenomenon under investigation is changed by features omitted in the simulation. In the area of flight simulation, one solution has been to evaluate different simulation designs using a comprehensive full-scale simulator (Simon, 1979). Generally, however, the reason for employing simulations is that the real situation is often inaccessible and the costs or consequences of any error may be severe. Comparison between the real and the simulated situations will then be out of the question.

Thirdly the nomothetic approach typically adopted by research may be ill-suited to the investigation of rare human errors associated with operation or maintenance of complex systems. Human error events may infrequently occur at different stages of a complex process, making them difficult to compare and there may only be a small number of operators to observe or interrogate after such incidents.

Faced with these difficulties it may be necessary to train designers, managers, operators or technicians in techniques for analysing a task, identifying the more difficult error-prone sub-tasks or problems and formulating solutions in terms of redesign or new training regimes. Such a course, if feasible, would mean that psychological and other human factors methods would be utilized more directly by those required to maintain or improve performance. The role of the human factors specialist then changes to one of identifying *when* technologies change sufficiently to require a different set of tools or methodologies to solve any new problems they present.

HUMAN ERROR: METHODOLOGICAL ISSUES

Not surprisingly, the issues of definition and classification of human error were extensively debated. A range of different methods of investigation was also discussed. Indeed it might be a sounder strategy to investigate such an elusive phenomenon as human error with a range of methods rather than with just one which might be blinkered in important respects. At least five different methods were discussed at the workshop: verbal reports, case histories, experiments, simulations, accident and error analyses. These are not mutually exclusive as, for example, all experiments in this area utilize some form of simulation although not all simulations utilize experimental methodology.

Definition and classification of human error

It is often useful to make a distinction between *operational/empirical* and *theoretically based* definitions. Typically there is little disagreement about the former as they relate to observable events (e.g., ability X is what ability test X measures). On the other hand theoretical definitions may vary considerably as to the mechanisms underlying or contributing to the phenomena. Corresponding differences in the types of causal factors and their relative contribution may therefore be expected in theoretically oriented definitions.

Rasmussen made the important point that whether or not an event is *labelled* 'human error' is largely arbitrary and will depend upon what he terms 'the stopping-rule' employed by the investigator. An accident or fault occurs when there is some deviation from normal system functioning and it is usually possible for an investigator to trace back through a causal net to identify various preceding system failures. Rasmussen points out that whether this analysis stops at the human operator and allocates the failure to human error, or identifies a technical failure as the cause (even though the operator might have been expected to cope with it), or traces the cause back to an error on the part of the designer, is problematic. Even to reach agreement on an operational or empirical definition of human error may be difficult. However, the labelling or definition issue is not so disturbing if one remembers that the primary objective of any analysis of error is to minimize and prevent future accidents or system failures. Therefore, analysis should concentrate on revealing the interrelations between system components (man or machine) with the *objective* of identifying a design, training or organizational solution which will prevent such future system failures. Such a view is proposed by Leplat in his description of the INRS method of accident analysis which is well suited to identifying future *preventive* measures.

Theoretically oriented definitions of human error will vary with the different types and levels of explanation used to construct taxonomies or models of human error. Again the appropriateness of the categories in a taxonomy of human error will be determined by the purpose for which the taxonomy is constructed and its associated explanatory and predictive power. It was evident from the workshop that it is premature to attempt to formulate a theory of human error at our present state of knowledge. It was agreed that any tentative taxonomy of human error should at least encompass behavioural, contextual, and conceptual factors as Reason proposed. Rasmussen suggested that a multifaceted taxonomy should be constructed to describe and analyse events involving human malfunction and this would include such factors as both internal and external descriptions of human malfunction together with performance shaping factors in the wider environment. It will be a challenging task not only to disentangle the relative contribution of these factors in the classification of system failures but also to gather sufficient data in various contexts to be able to test and validate such a model.

Reason makes an important distinction between two types of human error: slips (or lapses) and mistakes. The former are actions which are not planned or intended while mistakes are the consequence of incorrect plans which are nevertheless intended. A number of participants (Taylor, Brehmer) stressed that if one is to speak of error at the level of an individual's action, then it is necessary to impute the person's intention together with a description of the technical system. It is difficult if not impossible systematically to infer human intention from action. Brehmer commented that since only action is observable and both a person's intention and understanding are unobservable, it is logically impossible to solve such an equation with two unknowns. The alternative strategy of utilizing verbal reports will be discussed below.

Just as the cognitive psychologist tends to focus at the level of the individual so the social organizational psychologist examines error in terms of group situations or organizational structures. Wilpert observed that it may not be necessary to include the notion of intention in, for example, a social theory of human error. However, while the cognitive psychologist may have difficulties in attributing intention to action, the organizational psychologist may also have difficulties in discovering the salient factors contributing to systems failures at an organizational level either because of blatant dishonesty or the tendency for people to fail to acknowledge their own faulty actions. The important methodological point is that even within psychology different types of explanation may be used to describe human error and different taxonomic systems will result. However, translating between different taxonomies based on different types of data and structuring procedures would be difficult without empirical or statistical evidence.

Verbal reports

One potentially important means of collecting information concerning both normal and abnormal system operation and control is through verbal reports. These may come from operators, technicians or experts. They may be collected in real or simulated situations and they may be provided at the time of system functioning or retrospectively. A special session of the workshop was devoted to consideration of the utility of such verbal reports in the study of human error.

The topic of verbal report and verbalization is an old one in psychology although the debate has recently been revived, as Brehmer pointed out, in articles by Nisbett and Wilson (1977) and Ericsson and Simon (1980). Nisbett and Wilson suggest that retrospective verbal reports are likely to be unreliable and biased indicators of a person's own behaviour. They remark that there is a tendency for subjects to theorize about their own previous cognitive processes and to produce accounts which depart from reality. On the other hand Ericsson and Simon not only criticize the methodology used in many of the experiments cited by Nisbett and Wilson but argue that the reliability of verbal data depends upon various task parameters. They argue that there is a need to produce a theory concerning the generation of verbal data. During the workshop a similar view was expressed by Brehmer who also suggested that we need to develop various methods of using verbal reports as data:

> We should remember that verbal reports are only data and that they are subject to the same sorts of checks and controls that other data require.

There may also be other fundamental problems in using verbal protocols to analyse cognitive processes of operators in complex systems. Duncan made two important points:

> In a verbal protocol you will necessarily acquire a serial account. Secondly it is dangerous to assume, especially in view of the difficulty which subjects have, that expertise exists in verbal form until the moment of recording the protocol. My conclusion therefore would be that you may have transformed things to the point where they may be useless indications of expertise and therefore, since I believe protocols are useful, you are dutybound to regard a protocol as a hypothesis to be tested. I regard it as relatively rich in hypothesis generation.

A similar view is expressed by Ericsson and Simon who distinguish situations in which verbalization is of information already verbally encoded from those which may require verbal recoding or those which require the subject to perform various intermediate information processing activities (e.g., filtering, inference) in order to generate a verbal response. Verbalization may produce various distortions if information has not been directly verbally encoded and also if information is not readily available in short-term memory. Leplat and Hoc (1981) discuss these issues in the context of work situations and differentiate between verbalizations in terms of the types of cognitive processes to which they refer and the type of instructions given to the subject. They conclude that retrospective verbal reports can be useful particularly in the study of new or complex tasks involving control at a representational level over a period of time.

Rasmussen also stressed that in various situations a verbal protocol may be unreliable. He remarked that one important requirement in the analysis of protocols derived from operators is to have an analyst with sufficient specialist knowledge of the domain in question.

It is evident that investigators agree that while verbal reports may not be valid indicators in some circumstances, further research is needed to determine the range of situations in which they are valid. Research should also consider their utility in the context of complex industrial scenarios in which they may provide either design or training solutions.

Case studies and critical incidents

It is necessary to study the evolution of the man–machine system in investigating the development of an operator's knowledge of a complex process and the conditions under which this might be inadequate or inappropriately applied. This point is made by de Keyser in Chapter 22. The case study method has the advantage of being able to encompass the *temporal* aspects of cognitive development within the demands of a specific work situation. (Application of Rasmussen's multifaceted taxonomy of human error may be more feasible through the case study method in which the investigator has access to all aspects of the work situation. It will nevertheless be difficult unambiguously to disentangle the effect of various factors and their relative contribution to a systems failure.) De Keyser describes a case study of a new continuous casting process in the steel industry in which the researchers were able to study aspects of job organization, control room design and the operator's knowledge both *before* and *after* start-up of the new plant. Analyses of technical incidents relating to the plant were used to provide training for malfunctions. Analyses of these incidents with the operators revealed to the researchers some of the operator's cognitive difficulties. Two general sources of error were identified: the problem of both temporal and spatial orientation with respect to the casting process; and the interrelationships between system components. Such information could then be used in devising training solutions to overcome such difficulties.

Other participants at the workshop stressed the importance of using critical incidents to gather information concerning human error. Such incidents may be real or simulated. Griffon-Fouco discussed the role of a retrospective analysis of real incidents in the collection of data concerned with nuclear power plants (Chapter 18). In-depth analysis of the chronology, causes, and preventive actions associated with such incidents was a useful source of information for improving control room design, operating procedures, and also training.

Experiments

Experimental methodology might be used for two general purposes. It can be used firstly to validate improvements in system design and secondly to investigate human error tendencies in simulated situations. Various problems associated with the former application of this experimental method were elaborated by Rasmussen who commented:

> We need to develop an experimental method or methodology using verbal data and using complex scenarios to verify or validate design concepts.

Rasmussen emphasized that it is difficult to perform simple experiments in the classic tradition to validate improvements in system design for various reasons. Firstly, there is the problem of the validity of isolating a part of a system for experimental investigation. Secondly, as discussed above, it is difficult by definition to perform experiments on rare events possibly occurring under abnormal conditions. Thirdly, there is the problem of the availability and selection of subjects for such experiments. Not only is there a limited supply of operators of complex systems but the use of existing operators to investigate the efficacy of changes in design may be invalid since their existing habits and knowledge could interfere with testing the 'new' system design. On the other hand it is not possible to use naïve subjects since considerable technical knowledge is usually a prerequisite for operation of the system. Rasmussen cited as an example the need to validate safety parameter display systems which have been required subsequent to the Three Mile Island incident.

Simulation research may provide the key to unravelling some of these issues. Simulations may also provide a vehicle for developing and testing a new form of experimental methodology for validating system changes.

The problem of using laboratory tasks to investigate human error tendencies was emphasized during the workshop by both Brehmer and Dörner. It is difficult to include all the critical real-world task parameters in a laboratory study. This may qualitatively change the cognitive demands of a task and make it an invalid means of investigating human error tendencies. The temporal dimension of complex tasks is often missing in laboratory studies which led both Brehmer and Dörner to utilize complex dynamic simulations to investigate decision making in organizational systems. Brehmer pointed out that even within what he termed 'static' problems, people do not learn normative rules from experience and are unable to develop statistical hypotheses. However, in 'dynamic' problems (such as a fire control situation) the relationships over time between the decision making and the manifestations of the problem are complex for the person to master. Leplat pointed out that with such problems the representation of the problem might be changing together with the referent or criterion for evaluating performance.

Investigators of human error have to achieve a difficult compromise between the use of realistic problems which are difficult to analyse, except in a qualitative or idiosyncratic manner, and the use of trivial problems with which traditional experimental methodology can cope but which may not generalize solutions to the real situation.

Simulations

Some of the general aspects concerning the use of simulations have already been discussed. Simulation in its widest sense refers to some *representation* of a real work situation. This may take the form of for example a realistic equipment simulator, a symbolic display of a process plant on a VDU or a photograph or some simulated social or management behaviours appropriate for specific situations. The reason for simulation in the context of human error is similar to that of experimental methodology.

Simulation may be used in the attempt to expose the cognitive deficiencies of an operator, technician or manager. The problem of attempting to externalize covert cognitive processes is an old one in psychology but is particularly acute in training people to operate complex (and possibly hazardous) systems. Dörner in Chapter 9 discussed the use of what he termed 'simulated realities' to study cognitive processes. He was able to use a simulated situation to identify various cognitive deficiencies occurring at the various stages of goal analysis, accumulating and restructuring information, planning and implementation of action. For example, people may use inappropriate analogical reasoning in coping with and reducing the uncertainty associated with new systems or typically the 'planning stage' may neglect various side-effects or long-range effects of a person's proposed actions.

Simulation may also be coupled to training. There is a need to reduce the cost of complex full-scale simulators which are often used for training. The availability of low cost microcomputers has provoked researchers to consider which tasks or parts of task can be effectively trained with devices which may have low physical 'fidelity' to the real task. The literature indicates that if any simulation used in training is going to produce high positive transfer, it is necessary faithfully to represent the psychological demands of the real task. This is a relatively straightforward matter in, for example, procedural or decision-making tasks for which it is possible to train with simulations involving low physical fidelity. It may of course be desirable to manipulate a variety of features of the simulation in order to improve the learning situation (such as the provision of feedback). Duncan discussed an interesting application of simulation for training faultfinding of a process control plant. In the simulation, unlike the real situation in which a lot of information was readily available, various indicators of the state of the plant were 'withheld' from the trainee who requested information. It was possible not only to observe typical mistakes but also to intervene and provide the trainee with an heuristic for faultfinding and subsequently to monitor the trainee's use of it.

Simulations are also necessary in validating training or design changes and the argument is often made that for this purpose high physical fidelity simulators are required. This may be true when the costs or consequences of error in the real situation are high.

Accident and error analysis

Research concerned with accidents, safety, and reliability has been a traditional area of human factors. Retrospective analyses of accidents or near misses can provide information concerning potential areas of risk and possible preventive measures. Such information may be aimed at the level of an industrial sector, industry, company, department or the individual. Analyses of accidents or incidents may adopt a clinical or statistical approach or indeed both. Even within the clinical or statistical approaches, methods vary in terms of the data sources used, the manner in which the data are structured, and also the manner in which data are aggregated if indeed this is attempted.

Leplat (1982) points to the problems of applying reliability methods to assess the probability of error associated with different activities of the human operator. Many work procedures are not strictly standardized. Assessing the probability of human error is exceedingly difficult and potentially unreliable irrespective of the data sources used. Leplat described the INRS method of analysing accidents which initially maps out the relationships between various conditions and other factors which may precede an accident. In this sense the method adopts a clinical perspective and depends partly upon the skills of the analyst, together with the analyst's knowledge of normal system functioning in which the accident occurred. Analyses may differ between analysts.

As soon as one attempts to move away from the analysis of an individual accident to collate and aggregate data on a wider basis, other methodological issues are raised. One problem is deciding what categories to use in classifying or coding factors relating to accidents (and also differentiating different types of error). Any attempt to subsequently recode or reclassify incidents may prove difficult in practice. Leplat discussed how data from the INRS method can be coded into various categories (such as the individual, task, equipment and environment) and how data can be aggregated between different accidents. A similar approach was adopted by Griffon-Fouco in the collection of human error data associated with nuclear reactor trips. By using questionnaire and statistical techniques it was possible to identify the conditions under which different types of error tended to occur.

The categories of classification schemes will obviously vary between human error studies depending on the context and purpose of the investigation. As accident analyses move from company level to encompass different companies in the same industry, or even different industries, it will become increasingly difficult to interpret the data. Kjellén argued the importance of the concept of deviation from a system's norm in such accident analyses. Leplat pointed out that not only will norms vary *between* organizations but also *within* organizations.

CONCLUSION

Some of the methodological issues raised at the workshop were intrinsic to the study of human error while others related to specific methods adopted by investigators in the area. Most research on human error is empirically based and much of it is not driven by strong theoretical notions. Rasmussen and Reason presented models which could be developed to support more theoretically driven research in the area. These developments are desirable although whether and how such theoretical models can be interdisciplinary and applicable to the range of contexts encompassed by human error studies are questions for the future.

One issue raised during the workshop which cannot be solved by scientific development is the level of human error which is acceptable to society. It is a political judgement of how much should be invested in research and development, and one which depends upon a political judgement of what levels of human error society finds acceptable in different systems contexts.

REFERENCES

Ericsson, K. A., and Simon, H. A. (1980) Verbal reports as data. *Psychological Review*, **87**(3), 215–51.

Leplat, J. (1982) Accidents and incidents production: methods of analysis. *Journal of Occupational Accidents*, **4**, 299–310.

Leplat, J., and Hoc, J. M. (1981) Subsequent verbalization in the study of cognitive processes. *Ergonomics*, **24**(10), 743–55.

Nisbett, R. E., and Wilson, T. D. (1977) Telling more than we know: verbal reports on mental processes. *Psychological Review*, **84**, 231–59.

Simon, C. W. (1979) Applications of advanced experimental methodologies to AWAVS training research. *NAVTRAEQUIPCEN 77-C-0065-1*, Orlando.

New Technology and Human Error
Edited by J. Rasmussen, K. Duncan, and J. Leplat
© 1987 John Wiley & Sons Ltd

31. New Technology and Decision Making

Deborah A. Lucas
University of Lancaster
Now: Human Reliability Associates Ltd.

SUMMARY

This chapter reviews discussions concerning the effects of new technology on the decision making of the human operator. It covers the following areas: the altered nature of decision making; the use of informal verbal information by operators; how to provide prescriptive solutions for emergencies; and, certain aspects of training.

INTRODUCTION

Many human errors in industrial contexts take the form of operators' diagnostic failures of a system malfunction. It is therefore clear that the need to prevent errors of diagnosis is of prime importance with large-scale automated processes. This concern was reflected throughout the papers and discussions at the workshop. The purpose of this review is to present briefly a number of points which were raised concerning the effects of new technology on the decision making of the human operator.

THE CHANGING NATURE OF THE DECISION

There are perhaps two outstanding design implications of automated processes which make decision making particularly difficult. The first of these is that automated processes often do not need the intervention of an operator except in the case of a malfunction. This means that making a diagnosis will be a rare and unusual event and probably also a stressful one. The tendency for a person who is under stress to perseverate between a few alternatives and to revert to habitual modes of thought has been widely reported. It is therefore clear that the training of operators is very important. However, it is difficult to simulate a real-life emergency for training purposes. Thompson (1983) points out that the motivational effects of a real emergency cannot be achieved in a simulation. At the workshop Kjellén noted that the outcome of a decision in terms of failure or success is different in a simulated task. Kjellén also questioned the use of simulated tasks involving the withholding of information. It was pointed out that this training technique may be misinterpreted by designers to indicate that human operators need less information about the process than they currently receive.

The second difficulty with automated processes is that, as Duncan pointed out, there is an impoverishment of the 'cognitive coupling' between an operator and the process. Before the introduction of computer-mediated supervision of industrial processes there was usually a direct sensory feedback between the operator and the task (for example, in the use of manually operated valves). However, with automated processes, a computer often acts as an intervening mediator and, as was noted by many participants at the workshop, this has serious implications for the nature of the information available to the operator and for any diagnostic judgements the operator must make. Brehmer described how new technology changes the decision making of operators from a dynamic process to a static one. Whereas, in dynamic decision making, the environment changes as a function of a series of decisions (as in a steering task), in a static decision the operator has to make one judgement and then hope for the best. Rasmussen also emphasized that with automated processes any decisions must be made as if the process was static and not reversible. Psychological research into static decision making has shown that human beings do not make judgments according to normative models. Instead we employ intuitive rules of thumb (see Simon, 1983). As Kahneman et al. (1982) have clearly illustrated these intuitions are susceptible to a number of biases. In particular, two potentially erroneous cognitive heuristics which have been well documented are: the limitations on the availability of instances which can be retrieved from memory; and the representativeness of such examples.

As well as making control more remote Duncan noted that the use of computer-mediated supervision may mask the start of a malfunction in the process. This would serve to make the operator's diagnostic judgement more difficult. Particular emphasis was given by Bainbridge to the inherent difficulty of any situation where a diagnosis is made partly by the human operator and partly by the controlling computer. In such cases it is vitally important to provide the operator with alternative sources of information in case the computerized system fails.

PROVIDING RELEVANT INFORMATION FOR OPERATORS

The questions of how to provide a human operator with the relevant information to make a diagnosis and how to present such knowledge in the most easily accessible form were raised on a number of occasions during the workshop. One major problem highlighted was how to find out the information that operators actually use to make decisions. De Keyser pointed out that workers may be biased in the types of information they are prepared to select as being relevant. However Brehmer maintained that people cannot accurately say which cues they are using to make a judgement. It is not that incomplete statements are made, as in the case of a person saying he reached a decision using only a few of the set of cues which were actually employed, instead people tend to give false information. Brehmer also noted that his subjects generally tended to describe their judgemental strategies as being more complex than they actually were. Rasmussen pointed out that operators probably alter their pattern of monitoring information when they know they are being supervised. The Hawthorne effect will also apply to such situations. All these factors emphasize the difficulty of ascertaining what is the relevant information for making a decision in a complex environment.

One type of information that human operators appear to use frequently is informal verbal information. The use of verbal communication may stem from a lack of trust in computerized displays or in a sense of the operator being in competition with the computer. De Keyser pointed out that verbal communication may be used either to check a diagnostic judgement or as an alternative source of information. Kjellén noted the importance of social communication between workers as a probable reason behind the widespread use of verbal information. However, there is one major drawback with this source of knowledge, it is exceedingly subject to error. Two main biases have been reported. Firstly, there is a tendency to distort a verbal message in the direction of the expected inputs (Campbell, 1958). Secondly, a general bias exists to abbreviate and simplify verbally transmitted information and to omit certain details (Bartlett, 1932). Thus the reliance placed by operators on such informal sources of information has obvious implications for the decision-making process.

Patrick has reviewed the discussion on the presentation of information via automated displays (this volume). However, of particular relevance to the issue of decision making was the comment by de Keyser that design engineers were tending to use the same displays in all parts of an industrial plant. This is potentially a problem because different diagnoses may require different types of information. In addition, the decision-making processes of individual operators might be optimized if they were presented with information relevant to their 'mental model' or representation of the process.

One final point here was made by Rasmussen who mentioned that researchers are beginning to tackle the considerable problems involved in the study of information retrieval in computerized systems. One fruitful line of investigation concerns the use of an alarm system to guide such retrieval.

PROVIDING SUPPORT FOR THE OPERATOR

At the workshop the issue of how best to support a human operator during a system malfunction was discussed. It was agreed that this was an area of considerable importance. Both Leplat and Herry noted the significance of the way in which prescriptive solutions were explained to the operators. Herry outlined a number of reasons why an operator may not be prepared to follow these prescriptions (Chapter 21).

It was pointed out that there was a potential danger with providing operators with prescriptive solutions in the form of algorithms and heuristics. Reason noted that these constitute a finite set and therefore run the risk of placing limitations on the operator's skills. He stressed the importance of establishing what happens in a situation which falls outside the range of such solutions. Brehmer emphasized the need to understand the nature of any interaction between an operator's general knowledge of the process and the heuristics he was provided with. The ensuing general discussion concerning the differing representations of the process by operators and designers is reported elsewhere (Chapter 29).

One final discussion topic concerned the implications for training operators in industries where changes in technology can occur very quickly. Rasmussen pointed out that it is possible to buy and install a new computer system in a matter of weeks. However, to alter the training of operators may take perhaps a year and the alteration of the organization to work teams will take even longer. This is obviously a considerable problem. Reason noted the need for further research in the time constraints required to accommodate for such changes. A practical example of changing training and reorganizing work crews was outlined by Griffon-Fouco. However, it was recognized that the retraining of operators is still a cause for concern. Griffon-Fouco pointed out that in an emergency situation the operator may respond on the basis of his initial training. Reason noted that on other occasions the most recently learnt information may be used by the operator in making a diagnosis. In conclusion Brehmer noted that there was a long history of learning studies in psychology which were relevant to this issue.

REFERENCES

Bartlett, F. C. (1932) *Remembering*. Cambridge: Cambridge University Press.

Campbell, D. T. (1958) Systematic error on the part of human links in communication systems. *Information and Control*, **1**, 334–69.

Kahneman, D., Slovic, P., and Tversky, A. (1982) *Judgement under Uncertainty: Heuristics and Biases*. Cambridge, Mass.: Cambridge University Press.

Simon, H. (1983) *Reason in Human Affairs*. Oxford: Blackwell.

Thompson, J. A. (1983) Non-cognitive factors in performance under stress. Medical Research Council, PS 3/83.

New Technology and Human Error
Edited by J. Rasmussen, K. Duncan, and J. Leplat
© 1987 John Wiley & Sons Ltd

32. Information at the Human–Machine Interface

J. Patrick
University of Wales Institute of Science and Technology

SUMMARY

This chapter discusses information requirements at the human–machine interface. Factors which determine these requirements for both performance and training situations are considered.

INTRODUCTION

New technology typically involves changes in the human–machine interface which unfortunately are rarely of benefit to the user. The need to inculcate human factors expertise at the design stage is a well-known problem which was inevitably raised at the workshop. The extent to which new technology impoverishes or enriches the human–machine interface depends upon the expertise of the designer. Brehmer pointed out that new technology interferes with information which is input to and output from the human operator via the interface. Even slight changes in both the *nature* of the information available and the manner in which it is *represented* might have serious effects on performance. Lucas (Chapter 29) has discussed this issue in terms of the development of appropriate mental models for operators. The workshop discussed on various occasions the changes in information available at the human–machine interface as a consequence of new technology and the factors which should be considered to improve design.

Bainbridge illustrated some of these issues in the context of the process control industry in which traditional control rooms are being replaced by new computer management and information systems. Typically information displays have to be requested and accessed sequentially by the user. This will make greater memory demands upon the operator which may be especially problematic during difficult decision-making tasks. Shepherd (1985) comments on a similar problem which led to redesign of the manner in which plant information mapped on to the computer 'pages' which were available to the operator. In the workshop Herry also commented on the potential

341

danger of replacing traditional control panels in which a range of presented information is available and may help the operator to update his or her mental model of the state of the plant. Bainbridge made some further points. The codes and formats are usually changed by the new computer interfaces which will create problems for existing operators. (Such systems are of course also vulnerable to breakdown.) Bainbridge commented that there is also an implicit assumption that the operator is able to process and react to absolute values of stimuli. Evidence from psychology suggests that the human operator is more likely to react to change and will tend to process *patterns* of events whether visual, conceptual, temporal, or strategic. Reaction will also be influenced by expectations and assumptions. This has been demonstrated to be true in diverse research areas in psychology — for example, Rabbitt (1981) who discussed the importance of speed–error trade-offs in reaction time studies; the role of set in problem solving (Duncker, 1945; Luchins, 1942); the potency of advance information in determining allocation of attention and processing of information (Goetz et al., 1983). Consequently, designers need to be persuaded that contrary to their belief that the human information processor is robust and error-free, in reality even slight changes to the type or manner in which information is presented at the interface may produce dramatic performance changes. Duncan mentioned that new information displays may well lead to changes in both perception and weighting of the evidence by the operators.

The question arises of how we begin to prescribe the nature of the information which should be available. Which factors need to be considered in the provision of such information? To what extent is it possible to prescribe different interface designs for different tasks? These issues will be discussed with respect to aiding performance and training of the operator.

AIDING PERFORMANCE

The workshop generally agreed that there was a need for more intelligent aiding of the operator's performance, e.g., in problem-solving situations. Interfaces need to be tailored to provide the appropriate type and amount of information to support performance.

Rasmussen stressed the need for 'error-tolerant' and 'observable' systems. The effect of actions and the development of error may not be readily available information to the operator. Time lags often occur although for either error recovery or system control there is a need for rapid feedback information together with displays of action courses for the operator. The increased use of automated subsystems leads not only to the lack of involvement of the operator but also to the difficulty of accessing the necessary information when human intervention, possibly in an emergency, is required. In this context, de Keyser emphasized the potential importance of providing temporal information concerning the development of a plant or process. A recent development in computer management systems is the possibility of providing the operator with predictive information concerned with his control strategy (in the form of 'what if' statements). This form of aiding is likely to be powerful if it is directly related to the demands of the task. Despite the infrequency of human interventions, when they do occur the costs of hazards which may be associated with error suggest that optimal interface design is an important consideration.

One important factor which will determine the optimal interface design is the nature of the task. Tasks can impose different psychological demands upon the human operator. Task performance needs to be sustained by appropriate information at the interface and this will, for example, range from the more cognitive, decision-making tasks to, say, procedural or motor tasks. Analysis of the psychological demands and skill bases for such tasks will provide the first step in prescribing the information required by the operator at the interface. Rouse (1984) has considered the design of computer-based decision support systems which he concludes will depend upon various characteristics of the task. These include how frequently the task occurs and whether it can be solved by a familiar action sequence or whether it requires search and identification of possibly a novel solution to a problem. In the past, in the process control industry, information at the operator's interface has included support for failure identification and detection and the use of on-line procedural guides for start-ups and shut-downs (Morris, 1982).

Even the *same* task can make different demands which have implications for its information requirements at the interface. This could occur in two ways. Firstly, the same task performance can be supported by different skills. For example it is possible that a problem may be solved on the basis of memory of its perceptual characteristics or by application of some heuristics. Secondly, as Rasmussen has argued in various publications, even within the same control task the operator has to move between different levels and types of information which he terms an 'abstraction hierarchy'. For example, when the process is not in a steady state the operator has to assess the overall consequence of the disturbance for the system function and safety. This involves systems information at a high level of abstraction. Subsequently the possibility of counteracting the disturbance by reconfiguration of the system has to be explored before finally the cause of the disturbance is established at the lowest level of the hierarchy — that of physical parts and processes. Consequently even performance of the *same* task needs to be supported by different types of information at the interface.

Finally the level of expertise of the operator is also a factor which needs to be accommodated by interface design. There is a tendency with new technology to reduce the redundancy of information available. This is likely to be problematic for the novice user. Also, as Reason pointed out, an inherent problem of 'cognitive ergonomics' is that as operators inevitably learn and proceed to more 'automatic' levels of performance, slips and lapses will tend to occur. Eventually it may be possible to provide even the experienced operator with aiding procedures which would mitigate against the occurrence of such 'skilled' errors.

Such differing information requirements suggest the need for flexibility in interface design. There is no reason why this cannot be provided by the new generation of computer management and information systems currently being introduced into the process control industry.

AIDING TRAINING

The information required to facilitate learning of a task will differ from that required for aiding performance. Some of the *generalizable* features of instructional support include: the provision of advance information; practice accompanied by feedback; different amounts and levels of remedial help; breaking down the task into smaller sub-tasks to achieve mastery; the development of appropriate learning strategies. Other features of instructional support are *specific* to the type of task being learned. This argument has been put forward by Gagné in his well-known description of a learning hierarchy of intellectual skills and more recently by Merrill (1983) in his component display theory. These approaches suggest that different types of learning require different training conditions and methods. For example, learning to remember a 'fact' would be achieved in a different manner to learning a new 'concept' or 'procedure' or 'problem-solving behaviour'.

Consequently the information available at the interface has to be carefully designed to optimize the learning process. During the workshop Duncan discussed training techniques for faultfinding. Training has to ensure that appropriate faultfinding strategies are learned and applied to novel fault situations. In order to accomplish this the 'rules of thumb' used by experienced operators were identified and then used in what Duncan terms a 'withheld' training technique. This involved the trainees requesting symptom information during training. This allowed their faultfinding strategies to be monitored and corrected where necessary. Considerable improvements in subsequent performance were observed (Duncan, 1981; Marshall and Shepherd, 1981).

Another important factor which needs to be accommodated by interface design is related to the hypothesized 'stages' of skill acquisition. Such stages were originally proposed by Fitts (1962) in the context of perceptual motor skills and more recently by Anderson (1982) for more cognitive skills or knowledge. Such theories suggest that qualitative changes take place in the information required during learning as the trainee becomes more skilled at the task.

CONCLUSIONS

There are various factors which need to be considered in designing more effective interfaces for either performance or training situations. At the present time the availability and representation of information at the interface is largely unsystematic. Rasmussen noted that gradually more intelligent and economic information retrieval systems are becoming available, some of which are general purpose. Nevertheless, as de Keyser observed, there is an urgent need for research to explore the effect of different types of information display on operator performance. From a training perspective it is beneficial to link training solutions directly to the human–machine interface by 'embedding' the appropriate computer-based training facilities. Such interface designs are likely to be cost-effective and become more widespread in the future.

REFERENCES

Anderson, J. R. (1982) Acquisition of cognitive skill. *Psychological Review*, **89**(4), 369–406.

Duncan, K. D. (1981) Training for fault diagnosis in industrial process plant. In: J. Rasmussen and W. B. Rouse (Eds), *Human Detection and Diagnosis of System Failures*. Plenum.

Duncker, K. (1945) On problem solving. *Psychological Monographs*, **58**, 5.

Fitts, P. M. (1962) Factors in complex skill training. In: R. Glaser (Ed.), *Training Research and Evaluation*. University of Pittsburgh. (Reprinted 1965 – New York: Wiley.)

Goetz, T. E., Schallert, D. L., Reynolds, R. E., and Rodin, D. I. (1983) Reading in perspective: what real cops and pretend burglars look for in a story. *Journal of Educational Psychology*, **75**, 500–10.

Luchins, A. S. (1942) Mechanization in problem solving: the effect of Einstellung. *Psychological Monographs*, **56**, 248.

Marshall, E. C., and Shepherd, A. (1981) A fault-finding training programme for continuous plant operators. In: J. Rasmussen and W. B. Rouse (Eds), *Human Detection and Diagnosis of Systems Failures*. Plenum.

Merrill, M. D. (1983) Component display theory. In: C. M. Reigeluth (Ed.), *Instructional Design Models: An Overview of their Current Status*. Lawrence Erlbaum.

Morris, N. M. (1982) The human operator in process control: a review and evaluation of the literature. Report No. 82-1. Center for Man–Machine Systems, Research University of Georgia.

Rabbitt, P. M. A. (1981) Sequential reactions. In: D. H. Holding (Ed.), *Human Skills*. Wiley.

Rouse, W. B. (1984) Design and evaluation of computer-based decision support systems. In: G. Salvendy (Ed.), *Human Computer Interaction*. Elsevier.

Shepherd, A. (1985) Hierarchical task analysis and training decisions. *Programmed Learning and Educational Technology*, **22**(2), 162–76.

New Technology and Human Error
Edited by J. Rasmussen, K. Duncan, and J. Leplat
© 1987 John Wiley & Sons Ltd

Part 9: Epilogue

The papers and discussions in the book indicate important trends in human reliability studies stemming from rapid technological development and supported by a shifting emphasis in psychological research.

The requirements for systematic analysis and prediction of the effect of human variability as it interacts with technical systems are becoming increasingly pronounced. This has been most evident in industries such as nuclear power and the chemical process industry. In other areas, such as large computer databases and consumer goods outlet chains, the potential effects of human error can also be so serious that risk analysis will be required during systems design.

Another prominent change is the widespread introduction of complex 'interfaces' between human beings and their work content, made possible by modern information technology. This change in the content and form of communication between human beings and their work context makes it increasingly difficult to base design on empirical evidence from previous applications. A fundamental change in data collection and analysis is needed which will generate and transfer empirical findings across a *variety* of technological implementations.

This will only be possible if models and empirical findings can be formulated in terms referring to functions and traits, which go beyond overtly observable task 'elements' — a change in approach to human errors that is reflected throughout the contents of this book. In effect, this leads to models in terms of human information needs and processing capabilities, a development which, fortunately, runs concurrently with a move in psychological research away from exclusively behaviourist methods towards more cognitively oriented approaches.

Behaviourist approaches have influenced human error and reliability studies since the earliest days. The first methods of analysis were closely related to the tradition of Taylorist work study, were concordant with behaviourist psychology, and were adequate for many routine manual production processes. In consequence, analysis was performed only in achievement terms, the method of analysis became dependent on the context, and different approaches evolved in industrial risk analysis, work safety research, and traffic safety. The swing towards cognitive studies appears to lead to the possibility of more coordinated research in the traditionally different reliability and safety research areas.

Another consequence of the work reported in this book is that human error cannot, *in itself*, be a topic of research. Errors are so intimately related to human adaptation and to normally effective patterns of behaviour, as to be only adequately described when considered in the complete context of goal directed human activities. In effect, this means that the object of study becomes human learning and adaptation and the consequences of long-term interaction with a task environment presenting varied requirements embedded in otherwise stable conditions.

The approach to the topic, then, is that put forward by Brunswick (1957), namely that the modelling of the task environment is as important as the modelling of the human being. This in turn has several implications.

One will be that the interest of psychologists should include studies of the internal processes demanded by the structure of work. Students of human work behaviour in modern industry should be intimately familiar with technology, not only to consider the social effects on the quality of working life, but also to be able, during systems design, to participate in the matching of the functions of plant and equipment to human capabilities and preferences.

Another consequence will be the need for a change in empirical research. The focus must be on analysis of cognitive performance during the work situation, and on laboratory experiments involving more realistic task contexts. The traditional experimental task tends to be well structured, has a well-defined goal, and task requirements are stable. In addition, the subjects, who are very often psychology students, are relatively untrained. The pay-offs and penalties of performance are rarely drastic and often trivial.

In contrast, industrial tasks may depend on a vaguely defined overall performance criterion, and the detailed goal structure must often be inferred by the worker or operator. The task will vary as the demands of the technical system vary with time. The working conditions as well as the system itself are both liable to change. To cope with advances in technology, workers must be highly trained and allowed to use what strategies they will. They have to recognize that costs and benefits from their work may have very large values.

To conclude, studies of human errors will require new techniques. Some of the developments which will be necessary are indicated in the contributions to this book. But a good deal of careful consideration and application will be necessary before it is possible to verify, correlate or integrate the models and findings of research on work safety, on traffic safety, and in the fast developing process industries.

REFERENCE

Brunswick, E. (1957) Scope and aspects of the cognitive problem. In: H. E. Gruber *et al.* (Eds), *Contemporary Approaches to Cognition*. Cambridge: Harvard University Press.

Subject Index